PHILO

THE EARLIEST PORTRAIT TYPE

From a IX. century Ms. in the Bibliothèque Nationale.

See Bibliography, no. 56, and page v.

THE
POLITICS OF
PHILO JUDAEUS

PRACTICE AND THEORY

BY

ERWIN R. GOODENOUGH

PROFESSOR OF THE HISTORY OF RELIGION
FELLOW OF JONATHAN EDWARDS COLLEGE
YALE UNIVERSITY

WITH A

GENERAL BIBLIOGRAPHY
OF PHILO

BY

HOWARD L. GOODHART
AND
ERWIN R. GOODENOUGH

NEW HAVEN
YALE UNIVERSITY PRESS
LONDON · HUMPHREY MILFORD · OXFORD UNIVERSITY PRESS
1938

TO

MR. AND MRS. PHILIP J. GOODHART

AS A TOKEN OF OUR GRATITUDE
FOR THEIR INSPIRING INTEREST

PORTRAITS OF PHILO

THE illustrations in this volume are self-explanatory except for the portraits of Philo.

Four of them are taken from the magnificent Greek Codex of John Damascenus (Bibliothèque Nationale, Ms. gr. 923, see no. 56 in the Bibliography), dating from the ninth century. The manuscript contains the famous Catena of the Damascene, with hundreds of marginal portraits of the authors quoted put in alongside the quotations. Philo appears in this manuscript more than forty times as a bust in a round medallion, always the same distinctive figure with black hair and beard, and wearing a stole with crosses. An example of this type is reproduced on the plate (A) facing page 142. Obviously the legend of his conversion by St. Mark had been so accepted that he was regarded in the period as a Christian saint; it is probably to this legend that we owe the preservation of his writings. In one case his bust is crowded with a bust of Josephus into a single medallion (see the plate (B) facing page 142). In another he stands a full length figure in the Greek white chiton and himation which were conventional for Christian saints; here again he wears a stole marked with Christian crosses (see the plate facing page 125). But the origin of this figure is fortunately preserved to us in the portrait reproduced as our frontispiece, where he stands exactly in the position and garb of the other full-length portrait, but with no stole or crosses. Since the plain figure is clearly the prototype of the Christianized one, it is natural to assume that the former is a type which goes back to an original in which Philo was not thought of as a Christian, back very likely to some manuscript of Philo which came from Hellenistic Jewish hands. That it is an actual portrait of Philo, we do not, of course, suggest: but it is certainly the earliest Philo-type in art, and, since this copy itself comes from a ninth century manuscript, the original must have been very old indeed.

The plate facing page 178 shows Philo wearing the dress and typical hat of a medieval Jew. In the plate facing page 314, he is in the bloom of the Renaissance (the *Nuremberg Chronicle,* 1492). It is interesting that a century later Rembrandt was so impressed with Philo's personality that he painted "My Father as Philo the Jew," now at the Ferdinandeum, Innsbrück; see Wilhelm Bode, *The Complete Work of Rembrandt,* Paris, 1897, I, 74, Pl. 20.

H. L. G.
E. R. G.

PHILO'S POLITICS:

PRACTICE AND THEORY

ERWIN R. GOODENOUGH

CONTENTS

(The Table of Contents of the Bibliography will be found on pages 129–130.)

FOREWORD

NEARLY ten years ago I began an investigation of Philo's political and legal thought which has led me in a great number of unexpected directions. The book I was trying to write was repeatedly begun, and yet each time I found that a fragment had grown into an independent study which I published separately. What was planned for my original book is now all scattered: the background is largely in "Hellenistic Kingship,"[1] though interesting points in the Jewish tradition are discussed in "Kingship in Ancient Israel";[2] the practical adaptation of Jewish law is in *Jurisprudence*;[3] the natural law, God as king, the Jewish law, law in the subjective realm, and the use of legal and political imagery in Philo's "Mystery" are in *By Light, Light*.[4] So there is left to be discussed here only that part which deals with Philo's relations with the Roman government, his personal attitude toward society, and his political theory. To present these in isolation from the rest is difficult, since the new material and ideas are intelligible only in terms of those already described,

1. "The Political Philosophy of Hellenistic Kingship," *Yale Classical Studies*, I (1928), 53–102. Hereafter cited as "Hellenistic Kingship."

2. *Journal of Biblical Literature*, XLVIII (1929), 169–205.

3. *The Jurisprudence of the Jewish Courts in Egypt: Legal Administration by the Jews under the Early Roman Empire as Described by Philo Judaeus*, New Haven (Yale University Press), 1929. Hereafter cited as *Jurisprudence*. The thesis of this work is that the treatises *De Specialibus Legibus*, i–iv, are based upon the adaptations made in Jewish courts in Alexandria to the laws of Greeks and Romans. That thesis has been strongly opposed by some scholars, notably by Heinemann: see his *Philons griechische und jüdische Bildung*, Breslau, 1932, 180 ff. But it has been so widely accepted, that I may hope, to quote de Zulueta from his review of the reviews in the *Journal of Egyptian Archeology*, XVIII (1932), 94, that I have "proved my point."

4. *By Light, Light: the Mystic Gospel of Hellenistic Judaism*, New Haven (Yale University Press), 1935. Hereafter cited as *By Light, Light*.

while to repeat what is otherwise available seems pointless. At
the risk of confusing the reader I have been obliged to adopt the
compromise of explaining some matters over again and of giving
only references for others. Still, although this study is really the
concluding section of a larger work, it is my hope that what follows will be intelligible by itself.

E. R. G.

*New Haven, Connecticut,
  1 April 1938.*

PHILO'S POLITICS

CHAPTER I

POLITICS DIRECT

A SINGLE incident is known to us from the life of Philo. It comes from a time when the terrors of a Jewish pogrom raged in Alexandria. Conscious of the mad Caligula's desire for divine honors, the Alexandrian mob had insisted that Jews put up cult statues of him in their synagogues. The Jewish refusal gave the mob an opportunity to plunder and murder at its pleasure; rapine was sanctified by ostensible horror at the Jewish *lèse majesté*. Jews of the city, herded by the thousands from their homes, in hourly danger of death, had only the hope that the insane emperor himself would exempt them from his demand for worship. In their extremity they selected a commission, certainly from their most gifted political leaders, to take the perilous journey to Rome in late autumn, there to try to win the respite which only the emperor could give them. Philo was chosen as head of this group, and upon him and his associates fell the almost hopeless task. For in Rome the embassy had to trail the mad emperor month after month, stomaching his jibes, holding their peace and keeping their dignity in the face of unceasing abuse and insult. Philo it was who had to present the case and give the proper answers to the emperor's persiflage. He also had to hold his group steady throughout the months when upon any or all of them might fall a flippant sentence of death, and their families and race perish with them. Eventually he accomplished the impossible. He won from Gaius a niggardly toleration for the Jews. The most remarkable part of the story is the sequel: the man who led this commission is now universally represented as one so wrapt up in metaphysics that he had no practical sense or interest.

This extraordinary verdict upon Philo, in spite of the character he showed in the one incident we have from his life, has been built up from the impression of his writings. For his treatises have relatively little to do with social matters, and the passages where he does remark upon law and politics as aspects of society are couched always in idealistic language. So, apparently without extended examination of this particular point, his closest students, M. Émile Bréhier[1] and Dr. I.

1. *Les Idées philosophiques et religieuses de Philon d'Alexandrie* (hereafter abbreviated as *Les Idées*), Paris, 1925, 14–34.

Heinemann,[2] have alike despaired of attaching any importance to his political statements. Yet the fact remains that Philo, who could have executed his commission at Rome, must have known men and Romans in a masterful way. The *a priori* assumption must be that he was a man who might mean a good deal when he refers to the state and to politicians.

From the point of view of political philosophy three attempts have been made to determine Philo's ideas. Pantasopulos[3] attacked the problem of the two laws, natural and positive, to explain the nature of each and the interrelation of the two. His last chapter opens up the problem of the state. But the study is quite inadequate for the subject. The author has isolated a number of interesting passages, identified them as Stoic or Pythagorean with tolerable correctness, but since he did not himself go on with the subject he can be said to have done little more than open it.

Geiger's[4] work is likewise that of a beginner, and similarly is useful chiefly as a collection of passages. In spite of Bréhier's brilliant correlation of Philo's remarks on kingship with the Neo-Pythagorean fragments, Geiger is so convinced that all of Philo's philosophy is drawn from Stoicism that he thinks Philo can be taken as a text for doctrines of the middle-Stoa.[5] The task to which he set himself still remains to be done.

Tracy[6] has been much less ambitious as a beginner. Starting out from my own previous suggestions[7] he has been the first to study the two po-

2. See especially his *Philons griechische und jüdische Bildung* (hereafter abbreviated as *Philons Bildung*), Breslau, 1932. An interesting example of Heinemann's general approach is the section in this work on the King (pp. 184–202), where he gives an instructive analysis of the Greek as contrasted with the Hebraic elements in Philo. Heinemann treats Philo from the point of view of his "sources," on the implicit assumption that Philo's direct source for one notion was Plato, for another was the Neo-Pythagoreans, etc., treating these always as literary sources. He therefore concludes (p. 202): "Schon dies erste Bild aus seiner Darstellung des Profanrechts veranschaulicht lehrreich, wie vorsichtig man mit dem Versuche sein muss, aus seinen Angaben auf die praktische Durchführbarkeit, geschweige auf die tatsächliche Durchführung seiner Ideale zu schliessen." Philo is still for Heinemann only "the first theologian" and "evidence of the religious tendencies" of the day (p. 5).

3. *Die Lehre vom natürlichen und positiven Rechte bei Philo Judaeus* (Diss.), München, 1893.

4. *Philon von Alexandreia als sozialer Denker*, Stuttgart, 1932 (*Tübinger Beiträge zur Altertumswissenschaft*, XIV).

5. A single example: Geiger (p. 5) quotes the Platonic–Neo-Pythagorean account of creation in *Opif.*, 146, and *Spec.*, iii, 207, in which the human νοῦς is πρὸς ἀρχέτυπον ἰδέαν, τὸν ἀνωτάτω λόγον, τυπωθείς, and comments that Philo, in telling of creation, "sich in der Terminologie ganz an die Stoa anlehnt."

6. *Philo Judaeus and the Roman Principate* (Diss.), Williamsport, Penna., 1933.

7. In "Philo and Public Life," *Journal of Egyptian Archeology*, XII (1926), 77–79, and in *Jurisprudence*.

litical treatises of Philo, *In Flaccum* and *Legatio ad Gaium,* on the assumption that Philo was a man with important political interests and experience, and hence of significance for his ideas. Tracy's limitation in the fields of philosophy and religion made the handling of other works by Philo quite beyond his scope, and prevented any adequate appraisal of the two treatises he did discuss from the point of view of political theory.

The excellent first chapter of Tracy's work presents very well "The Political Status of Philo," so that I shall only summarize that matter as he has outlined it. Philo had political standing from the point of view of four groups, the Jewish organized community (πολίτευμα) in Alexandria, the Jewish race as a whole, Alexandria as a corporate city, and the Roman Empire or emperor.

The Jewish πολίτευμα in Alexandria has often been discussed.[8] It seems to have been a Jewish state within the Alexandrian city-state. Jews had their own courts and officials, and seem to have been independent of the Greeks in Alexandria except in their obligation to conform to the general government of the city, represented, in Philo's day, by the Roman prefect who took the place, locally, of the Ptolemies of old. In this Jewish corporation it would appear that Philo played an intelligent part, at least, if he did not have an important administrative post of some sort through the greater part of his life.

The Jewish sense of solidarity as a race, though scattered throughout the world, often appears in Philo's writings, with such emphasis that it clearly represents an additional political loyalty for him. Philo called this racial group ἡ καθολικωτέρα πολιτεία 'Ιουδαίων,[9] and for it he was ready to give his life.

Within Alexandria Philo was at once a citizen and an alien. He was a citizen in so far as he was subject to the general rule of the prefect, paid taxes, and had definite recognized rights. He was an alien in so far as he had no share in the Greek organization of the city which the Romans had largely continued. But the relation of the Jewish community of Alexandria with its ruler, the Roman prefect, and, in a sense, with its parallel, the Greek commonwealth of the city, were highly important for him.

8. See my *Jurisprudence,* 15 ff.; also Tracy, 9–13. Further bibliography will be found in those places.

9. *Legat.,* 194. See Tracy, 9; Geiger, 95–118; L. Finkelstein, *Akiba,* New York, 1936, 67 and 324, n. 93.

The Roman emperor, since Egypt was a proprietary colony of the emperor himself, had immediate and ultimate control of Egyptian affairs. For Alexandrian citizens in ordinary times he was but a shadow behind the prefect, one of whom the Alexandrians were frequently reminded, but with whom normally they would have had nothing to do. Yet it was Philo's lot to live in a stormy period when both Jews and gentiles of the city rushed to Rome to appeal a local matter to the emperor in person. Philo's being a subject of the great Roman Empire, in a province of the emperor himself, was then a highly important part of this political setting.

The Romans on the whole scorned the Jews personally, but recognized them as good and profitable citizens, and encouraged them with such great political privileges as that of living in Alexandria with a distinct Jewish polity. Yet the Jews were a subject people, a tribute paying race, and as such, in comparison with the Romans, immeasurably inferior. So long as a Jew minded his business and paid his taxes he was ordinarily let alone; but he had any political rights at all only by Roman condescension. They could be revoked instantly, and a pogrom begun, if it suited Roman, especially imperial, pleasure to do so.

These were the four political units which Tracy has rightly described as defining Philo's political status. It is clear that any serious crisis in Jewish life at Alexandria would have been complicated by involving all four of them. The local Jewish political unit would clash with the local Alexandrian one of the gentiles, while the larger racial feeling of the Jews, like the larger gentile empire, universalized the local issue. Everything in the situation made for uncertainty from the Jewish point of view. It is obvious that, in a day when even Roman senators had to guard every reference they made to imperial administration, a Jew in Alexandria, especially a wealthy Jew and as such one worth crushing, would have had to be extremely careful in what he said about his Roman governors. If he mentioned them at all, it must have been cryptically or rhetorically. The statement of James I of England was equally true of a Jew in Philo's day: "It is atheism and blasphemy to dispute what God can do; . . . so it is presumption and high contempt in a subject to dispute what a king can do, or say that a king cannot do this or that." In such a case people must express themselves largely in speeches of flattery and idealism, turn matters as best they can now and then to the advantage of themselves or of their people, and resist openly only as a last and most desperate measure. This is not nebulosity in politics but the shrewdest practicality. Plato and Aristotle had no successors as political theorists in the Hellenistic Age largely because the hellenistic rulers wanted to hear, if anything, only flattering descriptions of ideal kingship, so that politicians had to put their criticisms or suggestions in the form of almost imperceptible innuendoes within idealistic rhetoric.

Philo was keenly aware that it was suicide for one in his position to speak his mind frankly,[10] and thereby at once shows his political realism. In the midst of his allegories Philo has concealed a statement which is so much the epitome of his whole attitude toward the politics of his day that it must be quoted at length:

As the good man is an observer not only of human life but also of things in the universe, he is well aware how much has on occasion been blown in by necessity, chance, opportunity, force, and lordly power (δυναστεία), as well as what plans and achievements, though mounting to heaven, these same forces have scattered and destroyed by merely holding their breath. Consequently he will feel obliged to shield himself with caution (εὐλάβεια), for caution is the proper protection against one's suffering sudden calamity, since it seems to me that caution is for an individual what its wall is for a city. So then are those people not out of their wits, completely mad, who are rash enough to display inopportune frankness, and dare at times to speak and act in defiance of kings and tyrants? They do not seem to perceive that they are not only like animals putting their necks under the yoke, but that they are betraying their whole bodies and souls, as well as their wives and children and that especially kindred crowd and community of companions and relations. Now it is possible for the charioteer and driver with all freedom to goad his horses and urge them on, or to check them and hold them back just as he wishes. So they are branded and beaten and mutilated and suffer before they die every savage and pitiless torture, and then are led away to execution and killed.

These are the rewards of untimely frankness, not of frankness as used by people of discriminating judgment, but the rewards allotted to silliness, madness, and incurable insanity. What do you mean? When a person sees a winter storm raging, and a heavy adverse gale, and a hurricane rushing down and piling up the sea with waves, a time when one ought to lie in a harbour, does he set sail and put out to sea? What pilot or skipper was ever so drunk

10. Although παρρησία was in general an ideal of Philo which he frequently praised (*Spec.*, iv, 74; *Prob.*, 99 ff.; *Heres*, 5 ff.). See Geiger, 76 f.; E. Peterson, "Zur Bedeutungsgeschichte von παρρησία" (in the *Reinhold Seeberg Festschrift*, 1929).

or maddened by wine that while such storms as I have described were raging he would want to cast off, when his ship would be swamped by the seas rushing over it and be swallowed up with its crew? The man who wants to sail in safety must wait for a favorable wind, one that is propitious and gentle. And what? When a person sees a bear or a wild boar or a lion sweeping down upon him, the hope being to pacify and mollify the beast, does he inflame it and tantalize it, until he actually offers himself as a banquet and feast to the pitiless carnivores? Is it true that one gets nothing by trying to oppose serpents and Egyptian asps and other creatures which bear destructive poison, and inflict sure death upon those they attack? Surely it is far better to use incantations and make them manageable and so to escape suffering calamity from them.

Are there not certain men who are more savage and treacherous than boars, snakes, and asps, men whose treachery and hostility can be escaped only by mollifying and propitiating them? So for example Abraham the wise man did obeisance (προσκυνήσει) to the sons of Chet (whose name means those who "disperse"), because the emergency convinced him he must do so. He did not consent to this act of obeisance because he honored those who by race and habit were the natural enemies of reason, and who "disperse," fritter away, and piteously squander education, the coin of the soul; but he feared their present power and irresistible strength and took care not to provoke them. In this way he could preserve that great and powerful treasure and achievement of virtue, that best dwelling place of wise souls, the double cave, which he could not occupy when fighting and warring, but only when he was cultivating and serving reason (or the Logos).[11]

What? Are not we also, as we loiter in the market place, often "dispersed" by the rulers, and "dispersed" by the beasts of burden? But we "disperse" for each from a quite different motive; for we give way to the rulers out of honor, but to the beasts out of fear lest we be injured by them. Now when occasion offers it is a good thing to oppose our enemies and to destroy their power of attack (βία), but lacking such opportunity it is safe to keep quiet, while if one wishes to get any benefit from them it is advantageous to propitiate them.[12]

This seems to be plain enough. The Jews could hardly have mistaken Philo's meaning, and Macchiavelli himself, had he written from the point of view of the Prince's subjects, could have given no more realistic advice. Beasts and asps the Jew may well consider the Romans in his

11. Philo explained the double cave shortly before in *Som.*, ii, 26, as a retreat into a life of consideration of the two-fold problem of philosophy, the problems of God and of the created world, including man.

12. *Som.*, ii, 81-92.

heart, but they must be handled softly and propitiated by any man who does not want to ruin himself and his race together. The sarcasm at the end is obvious. Philo has compared harsh rulers to savage and deadly animals throughout. When he mentions how in the market place the Jews have to make place for their rulers and the pack animals alike, it is part of the very caution he is counselling that he should distinguish between the two, once the rulers in Alexandria have been distinctly referred to, and say that one gives way out of honor to the rulers, but out of fear to the beasts. If the passage were called into question, he could insist that the first part was perfectly general and had no reference to the Romans, while he had properly indicated that one gives way to Romans out of honor. But his Jewish readers would quite well have understood that the reason Philo gave way to each was the same, because he knew that if he did not he would be crushed. And the Jews would also have understood by the last sentence that if Philo had it in his power to destroy the Roman power he would gladly have done so. The propitiating attitude he was advising was the only one a sensible Jew or other non-Roman subject in the Empire could take under existing circumstances. But he loved the Romans no more than the skipper of a tiny boat loves a hurricane.

Obviously a man who could write such a passage may have had more that was important to say of politics. Philo's political writings are of two types, those which are avowedly discussions of Jewish relations with the Romans, and those of the sort just quoted, fleeting passages in writings not generally political in subject matter, where references are made to society and its problems. The second type, to be considered in the next chapter, clearly, by the fact that the passages are concealed, follows Philo's principle of caution. But the openly political treatises, which at first sight appear much more simple and direct, present curious problems by the very fact that they seem to throw this caution to the winds. These treatises deal with the crisis of the Jews in Alexandria under Flaccus the prefect and Gaius Caligula the emperor.

In Flaccum, the first of these open political writings, tells us that Flaccus had been appointed prefect of Egypt by Tiberius, and that, in Philo's opinion, he had been an ideal ruler until the death of Tiberius and the succession of Gaius had made him uncertain of his own position at Rome. For Flaccus' friends were precisely those whom Gaius saw fit to execute as being dangerous or uncongenial, and Flaccus had justifiable fears that he might be equally suspect. Three Alexandrians persuaded him that his only recourse was to play into their hands and so gain the support of the city of Alexandria.[13] Their price, according to Philo, was that he give Alexandrians a free hand with the Jews. Flaccus capitulated, and had begun by turning against the Jews every lawsuit in which a Jew was involved, when a crisis was brought on by the unfortunate coming of Agrippa to Alexandria. Agrippa had just been confirmed at Rome by Gaius as king in his Palestinian principality, and called at Alexandria on his return to the east instead of sailing directly to Palestine. At Alexandria he conducted himself with all modesty, says Philo, but Flaccus was forced to recognize his presence, even though Agrippa's higher title, "king," seemed to reflect upon the dignity of the prefect. Agrippa was of course reckoned as being a Jew. The situation was at once capitalized by the Jew baiters of the city as a pretext for insults to Agrippa and the Jews in general, and at last culminated in a great "rag" in which a harmless madman was taken to the gymnasium, set up in mock royal splendor before the multitude, and hailed as king by the Syriac word for king so that no one would mistake the person being caricatured.

After this the crowd naturally went farther. Under pretence of loyalty to Gaius, using that loyalty "as a screen," the mob decided to set up images of the emperor in the synagogues. Tracy suggests that the "screen" was intended deliberately to shield from punishment those who had insulted Agrippa, and he may be right, though it seems just as likely that the mob was simply running away with itself. Certainly Flaccus made no attempt to stop the rioters: instead he soon outlawed the Jews as a body and turned them over to the mob without reservation. Perhaps, as Tracy thinks, Flaccus justified this last step by the fact that some Jews had forcibly resisted the Alexandrians who had set up images of Gaius in the synagogue. In any case, the dam was now completely down. Murder, public humiliation of prominent Jews, plunder, and rape, the usual business of a pogrom, went on unchecked.

The story now becomes slightly confused, since Philo does not indicate periods of time with any accuracy. It would appear that on the accession of Gaius, certainly some time before the rioting, the Jews of Alexandria had drawn up an honorific decree for the new emperor in

13. *Flac.*, 20–24. On these men see Stein in Pauly-Wissowa, *Real-Encyclopädie*, IX, 2061 f.; XII, 581.

which they had gone to limits allowed by their law in recognizing his sovereignty. They had taken this decree to Flaccus and asked him to forward it to Gaius. Flaccus had promised to do so, and then had suppressed the document, making it appear, says Philo, that the Jews were the only disloyal and ungracious subjects of the new emperor. When Agrippa came to Alexandria the Jews showed him a copy of the decree, and Agrippa himself sent it on to Gaius with a statement of how Flaccus had withheld it. The story of the honorific decree breaks off in Philo's narrative with no especial connection with what follows. As the text now is the reader might assume that it was the arrival of this decree to Gaius which prompted him to come to the rescue of the Jews in Alexandria. For when matters were at their worst Gaius suddenly sent from Rome a centurion with his guard to arrest Flaccus. In the trial which followed the two men who had led him to turn against the Jews were his chief accusers. Flaccus was condemned, humiliated, exiled, and soon afterwards executed.

With this *In Flaccum* closes. Why did Philo write it, and for whom? At first sight it appears far indeed from being a "cautious" treatment of politics or of politicians, but its purpose and audience are concealed by the fact that its beginning is lost. This loss of the first part of the work, together with the problem of fitting what we have of it into Eusebius' report of Philo's writings,[14] has made considerable controversy. It seems useless to go over the ground in detail again. In spite of the fact that Lewy[15] still oddly seems to follow Schürer,[16] on this point Massebieau[17] and Cohn[18] seem certainly to have been right. Their conclusion is that Philo originally wrote a work in five books describing the misfortunes of the Jews under Gaius, of which we have an abridgment in *Legatio*. But, says Eusebius, Philo wrote a "second treatise" (δεύτερον σύγγραμμα, which could not possibly mean the second book of the first treatise, as Schürer understood it) describing in greater detail the sufferings of

14. *HE*, II, v, vi.

15. Hans Lewy, *Philon von Alexandrien VON DEN MACHTERWEISEN GOTTES*, Berlin, 1935.

16. *History of the Jewish People*, II, iii, 349–354. This represents the point of view of the second German edition. In later editions he slightly modified his judgment, but not essentially, because of the arguments of Massebieau in the study cited in the following note. His modifications are available in English in the Index Volume, 97–99.

17. "Le Classement des oeuvres de Philon," *Bibliothèque de l'École des Hautes Études, Sciences Religieuses*, I (1889), 65–78.

18. *Einteilung und Chronologie der Schriften Philos*, Leipzig, 1899, 421–424: reprint from *Philologus*, Supplementband VII.

Jews in Alexandria. This "second treatise" must be identified with *In Flaccum,* a distinct writing whose purpose and audience might well have been different from the other. We are thus thrown back upon internal evidence for its purport.

The document shows clearly that it was written for a gentile reader, and for one not familiar with Alexandria. With details quite superfluous for a Jew of Alexandria Philo explains the way in which certain quarters of the city were assigned to Jews;[19] how an attack against Jews in Alexandria would be felt by Jews throughout the Empire;[20] the organization of Jews under a council as set up by Augustus;[21] how the method of punishment was varied in the city for offenders of different social ranks;[22] the Jewish custom of keeping their women, especially their virgins, in close confinement;[23] Jewish simplicity of living;[24] the feast of the tabernacles.[25] The way in which each of these matters is explained makes it extremely likely that Philo was writing for a gentile, and probably for a Roman, audience.

Further, *In Flaccum* tells us that it was written after the death of Gaius. In two passages[26] Gaius is denounced sharply, while in the second of the two Philo speaks of him definitely in the past tense. Yet Tracy[27] has noticed that elsewhere in the treatise Philo speaks of Gaius with profound respect. Whereas in *Legatio* it will appear that Philo's invective is directed against Gaius himself, here it is directed against Flaccus, while the imperial office, even with a Gaius in power, is shown to be an instrument, however unwitting, of the will of God. The thesis of the document is perfectly plain: it is a bold warning that any prefect will bring himself to the gutter if he deals unfavorably with God's chosen people. "Flaccus is an unmistakable witness," wrote Philo in his last sentence, "that the race of Jews does not lack the protection (ἐπι-κουρία) which comes from God." Philo's tone is completely respectful. He will join the Jews in honorific decrees to the emperors, and support an equitable prefect to the end. There is no hint of a buried hatred of Roman rule as such. But the treatise is the expression of a Jew with an intense conviction of racial superiority, and in this it harmonizes perfectly with the more concealed utterances to which we shall come in the next chapter. With great dignity it points out the traditional rights of

19. *Flac.,* 55.   20. Ibid., 45.   21. Ibid., 74.
22. Ibid., 78 ff.   23. Ibid., 89.   24. Ibid., 91.
25. Ibid., 116.   26. Ibid., 13, 180.   27. *Op. cit.,* 30.

Jews, and the fatality of a prefect's abusing them. With it went another and similar section which demonstrated that the fall of Sejanus had been due to his having persecuted the Jews.[28]

If the treatise was thus written for a gentile audience after the death of Gaius, for whom could it have been devised if not for the new prefect himself? Its thesis, which Schürer rightly called "de mortibus persecutorum," might well have been acceptable to Jewish readers, but in that case the treatise would have been written for Jewish readers as this is not. But under what circumstances would Philo, with his boasted "caution," have dared write and publish such a document? Under few circumstances, it must be admitted, except those of the few months succeeding the fall of Gaius, when Jewish chauvinism for once rose to the surface in Alexandria. For when the Jews heard of Gaius' death they actually took up arms against their former persecutors, and Claudius had to instruct the new prefect to quiet the fighting. Then both Greeks and Jews again sent an embassy to Rome, and this time Claudius upheld the Jews in their claims of exemption from the imperial cult, and in their traditional privileges. The Alexandrians, still not content, tried to involve Agrippa, but Claudius vindicated him and instead condemned the arch conspirators in Alexandria, Isadore and Lampo, to death. A final letter from the emperor to both Greeks and Jews in Alexandria warned both parties to keep the peace, and so the trouble was ended.[29] That is, following the tragedies of the pogroms came a period in which the Jews were entirely vindicated, given imperial protection, and their chief enemies killed. At such a time it would not be at all impossible that Philo wrote *In Flaccum* and published it. He may even have taken it, at the head of a Jewish committee, and presented it to the new prefect as the Jews' account and explanation of the earlier stages of the controversy, an account in which a new confidence was but thinly concealed.

The original title of *In Flaccum* was probably the title given the "second treatise" by Eusebius, *De Virtutibus,* "On the Virtues," which now appears as the alternate title of *Legatio.* It is very unlikely that Philo would have published this writing with a title, "Against Flaccus," which simply made it a denunciation of Flaccus. The earlier part of the

28. *Flac.,* 1.
29. See H. J. Bell, *Juden und Griechen in römische Alexandrien,* Leipzig, 1926. (*Alte Orient, Beiheft ix.*)

treatise, the part which is lost, had nothing to do with Flaccus, and the traditional title is too harsh. "On the Virtues" is exactly what a politician like Philo would have called this scathing contrast between Jewish virtues and the vices of those Romans who, by failing to respect the Jews, had brought themselves to destruction. For if I have rightly interpreted the spirit and purpose of *In Flaccum,* or *De Virtutibus,* we must see at once that it was the product of a politician who combined boldness with cleverness to an amazing degree. Its author might indeed have been selected by the Jews of Alexandria to represent them before Gaius![30]

Philo's *Legatio ad Gaium* shows the same vigorous political mind as *In Flaccum.* Massebieau and Cohn seem to have established that, as we have it, *Legatio* is an abridgment of the work on the subject mentioned by Eusebius as being in five books.[31] So again we are presented with a long fragment, and the purpose and audience of the original must be judged entirely from the treatise itself.

The first chapter of *Legatio* (§§1–7) is itself a fragment. In it Philo begins a general and philosophic discussion of politics whose loss is much to be deplored. He opens with a rhetorical reproof: men look with their senses to fortune, τύχη, which is admittedly very fluctuating and unstable, instead of trying to get with their reasons to the only stability, the things of nature. The great fact of nature, Philo then abruptly suggests, is God's providential care of mankind, and especially of the "race of suppliants" (τὸ ἱκετικὸν γένος). This race is, of course, the Jews, and Philo begins, strangely, to plunge the reader into the Mystery.[32] The Jews are Israel, which means, he says, "seeing God." The mystic vision given to Jews, vision of that Deity which is beyond all categories, even the categories of virtue, is hidden from other men, since they have no higher gift than reason, and reason can rise not even to the Powers of God, the Creative and Ruling Powers.

How far Philo went on into the Mystery we do not know, since the continuity suddenly breaks off; but enough has been given for us to suspect his immediate objective. Philo was clearly going on to present

---

30. Siegfried Ritter, "'Αρετή und der Titel von Philos 'Legatio,'" Ἐπιτυμβιον *Heinrich Swoboda dargebracht,* Reichenberg, 1927, 228–237, suggests that the word here is an abbreviation for ἀρετὴ θεοῦ, and so an indication that the virtue being celebrated is that of God in vindicating the Jews. Any solution is conjectural.

31. See notes 17 and 18 above.

32. The Jewish "Mystery" is used as a *terminus technicus* in accordance with the meaning given the word in my *By Light, Light.*

the Jewish race in terms similar to those used later by the Christian apologists, who claimed that all mankind was safe from divine wrath only because of the presence of the Christians.[33] Philo must have continued with the claim that the great rule of God was the first fact of nature, and that, a second fact of nature, humanity was joined to God by the Jews, who were the link between man and God because of their mystic powers of vision, and hence were the "race of suppliants" who alone could bring to men God's favor. The care of God for all men was in a sense secondary and derivative, for the care for the Jews came first. Philo is clearly making only a more philosophic approach to the thesis of *In Flaccum,* the thesis that since God and the Jews have this peculiar relationship the Jews are under his protection, and their abuse or mistreatment will bring upon the miscreants the terrible vengeance of the God of the universe.

With no warning the next sentence[34] begins with the career of Gaius. The perfect condition of the Empire effected by Gaius' predecessors, its wealth, peace, and happiness, came to its highest expression, says Philo, in the universal burst of joy at Gaius' accession. But the joy was short lived. In his eighth month Gaius became ill, and not only were his subjects distressed for his life, they began to be alarmed at a change in his character which the illness seemed to have brought about. Still when he began to improve men hailed the event as the recovery of the savior and benefactor (σωτὴρ καὶ εὐεργέτης) who was to bring the salvation (σωτηρία) of peace and prosperity to all men individually and collectively.[35] But the recovery of Gaius was a curse rather than a blessing, for now his real character became manifest. He not only continued to live his new life of debauchery, but he became definitely malicious. First he treacherously murdered the young co-emperor,[36] then turned upon Macro, the man who had done most to get Tiberius to make Gaius his successor.[37] Macro was killed, and afterwards Gaius' father-in-law, Silanus,[38] both of them, according to Philo, because they gave him too good advice, tried to keep him from excesses, and true to the ideal royal character. To the advice itself we shall return. Faced with these murders, the public did their best to find excuses for Gaius, since they could hardly believe they had been so deceived in one whom they had at first made their idol;[39] but still they were becoming restless, especially the

33. See, for example, Justin Martyr, *Apology,* II, vii.
34. *Legat.,* 8.   35. Ibid., 19–22.   36. Ibid., 22–31.
37. Ibid., 32–61.   38. Ibid., 62–65.   39. Ibid., 66–73.

senators for the death of their colleague Silanus, the knights for their most conspicuous member, Macro, and the royal family because they did not know who of them might not follow Tiberius' grandson.[40]

It was because he saw himself becoming shut out from his human associations, Philo says, that Gaius began to associate himself with divinity.[41] He first compared himself to the demigods (Oh that he had imitated their benefactions to mankind)[42] then to Hermes, Apollo, and Ares.[43] By the time Philo has reached this stage in the narrative, his invective knows no restraint. He heaps upon Gaius every appalling name for villain and public enemy he can muster. He a god indeed who was not only a human being, but in his humanity was one who flouted every virtue manifested by a deity!

While Gaius' character was thus decaying, the rest of the world deplored the change, but met the mad man with flattery and acquiescence in his raving pretensions. Only the Jews, because of their strict monotheism, refused to concede an inch beyond what was lawful for them.[44] Accordingly they were left helpless. For Gaius had declared himself the Law of the Empire, which meant, in his interpretation, that all previous legal guarantees were done away, and royal favor become the only protection. The old guarantees of rights given the Jews went with all the others, and no royal favor took its place.[45] The Alexandrians were quick to seize the opportunity to begin a pogrom. The preliminaries, as reported in *In Flaccum,* are omitted, but the sufferings themselves vividly described. The culminating horror was not murder, pillage, rape, burning alive, mutilation of corpses, but the setting up of images of Gaius as deity in the synagogues, especially a great bronze statue of him in a four-horse chariot, apparently as Apollo.[46]

Such horrors, arising from the mad claims of Gaius, Philo goes on elaborately to contrast with the characters and regimes of Augustus and Tiberius. None of the hatred of the Roman rule as such, which has appeared and will appear more fully from the Allegorical Writings, is here suggested. Instead, with rhetorical fulsomeness, Philo describes the ideal Roman ruler as an instrument in God's hands to bring men all the

40. *Legat.,* 74–75.   41. Ibid., 75.   42. Ibid., 78–92.
43. Ibid., 93–113.   44. Ibid., 114–118.
45. Ibid., 119. On these Jewish rights at Alexandria see the stele of Julius Caesar as reported by Josephus, *C. Ap.,* II, 37 (iv); *Antiq.,* XIV, 188 (x, 1).
46. *Legat.,* 120–137. Philo's horror at the representation of this sun god in a chariot within a synagogue contrasts strangely with the mosaics in synagogues of Galilee a few centuries later where the sun god in a four-horse chariot was depicted by Jews themselves on the floors!

benefits promised by the hellenistic philosophy of kingship.[47] Presented with this ideal of rulership in Augustus and Tiberius, says Philo, the Jews never once broke their legal restrictions and deified them; nor did these rulers expect or desire the Jews to do so, as witness their unbroken patronage of the race and recognition that Jews must always give their first loyalty to Jewish law.[48] Gaius not only showed himself to be of another temper in desiring divine honors at all, but he was vicious in his hatred of the Jews for refusing him such recognition. In his hatred he was stirred up by legations from the Alexandrians, but especially by one Helicon, a witty favorite of Gaius, an Alexandrian slave who knew the laws of the Jews very well,[49] and so could make the most painful home-thrusts at them.[50]

At Alexandria the Jews did not know about this favorite and his malicious influence with Gaius, and so they decided to send an embassy to Gaius to renew the protestations of loyalty already forwarded to the emperor by Agrippa in the honorific decree, and, we understand, on the basis of those protestations to ask Gaius' intervention in the pogroms. But there seems to be another hiatus here, for the actual sending of the embassy and its exact mission are most inadequately described. We suddenly find ourselves in Philo's personal company on the banks of the Tiber, rather confused at the precise reason for our coming.

It is at this point that it is hardest to fit the narrative of the incidents of *In Flaccum* with that of *Legatio*. In the former it appears that the pogrom was largely instigated, or, perhaps, patronized, by Flaccus: his madness was interrupted only by the centurion sent by Gaius to arrest him and, presumably, to put a stop to the pogrom. Philo gives no reason for Gaius' sending the centurion, but implies that he was prompted to do so by the Jewish decree sent by Agrippa. In *Legatio,* however, that decree seems to have done no good: Flaccus is not mentioned at all, nor any such incident as the mission of the centurion to give the Jews relief. It would appear that the only hope the Jews had lay in the success of that embassy of Jews under Philo which sought the intervention of Gaius himself.

When the two accounts are put together it would seem that Flaccus himself played an insignificant part in the pogrom. It was instigated largely by the Greeks in the city, and Flaccus offended only by not re-

47. *Legat.*, 138–151. See Bréhier, *Les Idées,* 18–23, and below, pp. 102 f.
48. *Legat.*, 152–161.   49. Ibid., 170.   50. Ibid., 166–177.

sisting their proposals. His downfall, as Philo himself makes clear, was inevitable as soon as Gaius murdered the young co-emperor and took complete rulership. Philo in *In Flaccum* has connected Flaccus' humiliation with the persecution of the Jews only as a threat for his successor. Further, it would appear that the fall of Flaccus did not help the Jews particularly, so that Philo had to lead his embassy to Gaius, with its great danger and little hope.

As *Legatio* now stands, then, it suddenly presents Philo beside the Tiber at the head of his legation. At his first meeting with Gaius the emperor showed himself surprisingly friendly, and thereby, Philo modestly says, deceived everyone but Philo himself, who suspected a sinister duplicity.[51] While, in anticipation of their next summons to Gaius, the others were congratulating themselves and Philo was worrying, they were suddenly told that Gaius had gone to the worst possible extreme by ordering that his statue as Zeus be set up in the holy of holies of the temple at Jerusalem. The trouble was instigated by Capito, revenue collector in Judaea, a native of Ascalon (Philo points out that Capito was later repeatedly tortured on the rack), who stirred up some foreigners in Jamnia to erect an altar to Gaius. This the Jews at once tore down, and when news of their disrespect came to Gaius, the emperor was inspired by Helicon (who later was killed by Claudius) to order the great gilded statue of himself for the temple.[52] Petronius, governor of Syria, was instructed to provide a powerful military escort for the statue to guarantee its protection. But he understood how lightly Jews would throw away their lives in an attempt to stop such an outrage, and so called a council meeting to consider. What Petronius really dreaded, says Philo, was a great war in Judaea, with the probability that Jews in Palestine would be helped by Jews from all over the world. (I cannot help thinking that Philo's putting this into Petronius' motivation was again a covert way of introducing the notion that an attack upon Jews in Palestine would mean a simultaneous rising of Jews everywhere in the Empire.) The council sympathized with Petronius, and decided to delay the event by taking as much time as possible for making the statue. Meanwhile Petronius tried to frighten the Jews into giving him permission to erect the statue. In this he completely failed.[53] For a great army of the Jews, men, women, and children, came unarmed to beg Petronius to kill them or let them kill each other as willing sacrifices in

51. *Legat.*, 178–183.   52. Ibid., 184–206.   53. Ibid., 206–224.

the temple rather than carry through the project. They asked that he delay until they could send an embassy to Rome. Such an embassy, Petronius knew, would be fatal for himself, so instead of allowing the Jews to send it he again slowed up the sculptors while he wrote to Gaius that the delay was occasioned by the desire to make the statue unusually fine, and by the fear that a war just at harvest time,[54] in case the Jews revolted, would curtail the supplies for the army.[55]

Gaius was furious at the delay, but answered only that Petronius should proceed at once now that the harvest was gathered.[56] Shortly afterwards Agrippa, who knew nothing of the whole affair, arrived at Rome. When Gaius told him the situation he fainted dead away (or pretended to do so) and was carried to his house. As soon as he recovered he wrote a long letter (or Philo writes one for him) protesting against putting up the statue. In the letter Agrippa recalls the favor and honor shown the Jews by former emperors, the tested loyalty of the Jews, the danger of inciting them because of their great numbers throughout the Empire, and their sensitiveness as shown by their attitude toward Pilate's dedicatory shields. He ends with a personal appeal that Gaius will not carry out what he, Agrippa, must consider an indignity to him personally.[57] Gaius was, or feigned to be, moved by this letter. He restored Herod Agrippa to favor and dispatched a letter to Petronius telling him not to disturb the temple, but unfortunately adding that any people who wanted to erect statues or altars to him anywhere except in Jerusalem itself might do so, and Petronius was to protect them from Jewish interference. Sane and generous a compromise as this must have appeared to Romans, it only threw the whole matter back to the riot of Jamnia and promised endless fighting in Palestine. Actually fresh trouble so soon occurred that Gaius quickly lost patience and again ordered that his statue, this time one to be made in Rome, be set up in the Jewish temple. He planned to have this done while he was on a journey to Egypt.[58]

Here there appears to be another hiatus, for §§339–348 are a general summary of Gaius' fickle character which has little to do with the foregoing. Indeed this section has likewise no immediate connection with what follows. The story of Philo's own embassy was lost from sight

54. Josephus makes it the time of planting: *Antiq.*, XVIII, 272 (viii, 3); *BJ*, II, 200 (x, 5).
55. *Legat.*, 224–253.   56. Ibid., 254–260.   57. Ibid., 276–329.
58. Ibid., 330–338.

during the extended account of the difficulties in Palestine. A long time must have elapsed for all these events and the tedious correspondence to have been carried through. Philo had crossed to Rome in the winter, but it was well past the harvest time when Gaius wrote his second order to Petronius, and still later, apparently, when he countermanded it at Agrippa's request, and then renewed it because of fresh riots in Palestine. If Philo's order of events is correct, the first order was issued after their arrival at Rome, following the first royal audience, and the second audience came subsequent to the last order. This would mean that the group must have waited nearly a year for the second interview, with the implication that the Jews of Alexandria were helpless derelicts on the coast and in the cemeteries all that time.

Whenever it took place, the second hearing before Gaius as described at the end of *Legatio,* is quite the most amazing part of the work. The legation of Jews was finally called before Gaius along with the legation of Greeks from Alexandria. The Jews were again greeted with a fair kindliness from the emperor which this time made them all despair of their lives as well as their cause. While the crowd cheered, Gaius rebuked them for not recognizing his divine nature; he said that in sacrificing *for* him they had still not sacrificed *to* him. Then, while they followed as best they could, he walked rapidly through gardens and buildings, giving instructions to the builders for alterations. Suddenly he stopped and asked them why they did not eat pork, and again walked rapidly away. As he walked he told them, apparently over his shoulder, to speak on the Jewish ideas of justice. It is conceivable that Philo rather spread himself at such an opportunity, but his oration had to be delivered on the run to the constantly retreating back of the emperor, who talked most of the time to the builders. Meanwhile the crowd were having great sport with the Jews, even striking them openly, so that they did not know when they should be murdered. Suddenly Gaius stopped and gave his famous judgment: "These men appear not so much wicked as unfortunates and fools for not believing that I have been endowed with the nature of deity."[59] With that he dismissed the gathering.

Philo closes the treatise by saying that the terror of the legates had been not for themselves but because they knew that if they failed in

---

59. *Legat.,* 367: οὐ πονηροὶ μᾶλλον ἢ δυστυχεῖς εἶναί μοι δοκοῦσιν ἄνθρωποι καὶ ἀνόητοι μὴ πιστεύοντες, ὅτι θεοῦ κεκλήρωμαι φύσιν.

their seemingly impossible mission they would be a symbol of the fall of the Jewish race before the mobs of any city who wanted to repeat the plunder and violence of the Alexandrians. His last statement is that he is now ready to go on to the "palinode," a word whose possible meaning here has raised many interpretations. It is likely that it was some sort of conclusion which told of the fall of Gaius, and which went back to the theme of the introduction, the protecting providence of God for the mystic suppliants and intercessors of humanity, the Jewish race.

What is most interesting for our purpose is to ask of *Legatio* as of *In Flaccum* what Philo's purpose was in writing it, and for what audience he intended it.

Philo wrote *Legatio* after the accession of Claudius,[60] and, it seems to me, for presentation to that emperor, just as *In Flaccum* seems to be designed for some new prefect in Alexandria. The latter is full of suggestions for the proper conduct of the prefect's office, as well as of warning to one who would abuse his privileges. The same is true of *Legatio* for the emperor. It has the most elaborate formulation of what was the function of a proper ruler, and what effect he should have upon his subjects and realm, though such formulation Philo himself never expresses in his own name, but always puts into the mouth of another, such as Macro. All that he will say in his own person about rulers appears in the quite unexceptionable praise of the *almost* divine rules of Augustus and Tiberius,[61] a passage which, I am sure, represents the Jewish compromise with the divinity of kingship as officially pronounced in the honorific decree from Alexandria. The point is that Philo has so constructed the treatise, just as he did *In Flaccum,* that without writing a passage in which he presumes to play the part of Macro and advise the ruler, or speak out unsolicited on matters beyond his province, he has written what in the end is a treatise almost directly concerned with the province of rulership, and certainly one which leaves the clearest impression of his ideas.

In both documents, too, the official function, for its success or failure, is represented as hinging directly upon the attitude the ruler takes toward the Jews. Philo's hatred of the Empire is veiled in his flattery of a Roman who would respect Jewish "rights," but there is recurrent in-

60. *Legat.*, 206.
61. Ibid., 136–161. On the way in which this passage harmonizes with Philo's political philosophy see below, pp. 110 ff.

dication that not only will God strike a man who lacks proper respect for Jewish ways and people: the Jews themselves, he brings out clearly, scattered as they are in large numbers throughout the world, constitute a great menace to the whole Empire in case they should be provoked to rise in a body. Unquestionably this expectation gave the Jews courage to attack the Romans a few years later, only to prove a delusion. The Jews at Alexandria were easily put down during the great war, and were so hopelessly outnumbered elsewhere that Palestine found itself isolated against the Roman armies. So Jews were to write with this suppressed but confident defiance for only twenty-five years more; thereafter such a note, except for the brief days of Bar Cochba, was never to sound in their writings or speeches again, or, if it did, was to rumble only in the futile dreams of Messianic retribution. Yet it is interesting that Philo did not put his threats of Jewish solidarity into personal statements of his own. They are cleverly worked into quotations purporting to come from Petronius and from Claudius' friend, Herod Agrippa. But their effect is no less telling in the general impression Philo makes by the treatise.

It seems to me very clear that the author of these two political documents was himself a fearless and experienced politician, whose ideas for the practice and theory of statecraft are of great importance. We shall expect little that is outspoken about the Romans, for Philo's "caution" had to be the better part of his valor. Even here, where he is trying to make direct suggestions to his rulers he must do so by indirection, point out faults only in those whose faults had brought them to universal discredit, and flay, if he must flay at all, only dead horses. He must always, as he does, distinguish between the sanctity of political office and the (dead) villains who have abused their office. It is the fact that Philo makes exactly these distinctions which marks him as a vivid realist in politics.

Before reviewing the political theory which Philo has put into these treatises it will be well to read some of his remarks about the actual situation from his other writings.

CHAPTER II

POLITICS IN CODE

IN the early part of the preceding chapter an extraordinary statement of Philo was quoted in which he urged caution upon any Jew who had dealings with Roman governors.[1] The passage is itself only a part of an extended allegorization of the character of Joseph, who typified to Philo the politician. It is my conviction that the entire allegory of Joseph is a clever piece of *double entendre,* a fierce denunciation of the Roman character and oppression, done in a way, and in a document, which would give it fairly wide currency among Jews, but would seem quite innocuous if, as was unlikely, it fell into Roman hands.

For Philo wrote several sorts of treatises, some of which were designed exclusively for a circle of educated Jews, to all appearances for Jews who lived by the "Mystery." The greatest series of treatises of this sort was the *Allegory of the Sacred Laws,* a series of discussions which would have been intelligible only to people thoroughly conversant with the text of the Old Testament, and of interest only to Jews who understood the method and objective of mystic allegory. While this series is Philo's greatest work, philosophically, for the general reader it has always proved so dull that Philo could have been confident that Roman officials would not sit up nights to read it. He could then speak in it about as he pleased so long as he veiled his attack in allegory, and, when he brought his remarks near to Alexandria, appear to "give way to the Romans in honor."

De Somniis is that treatise of the great *Allegory* in which Philo discusses the nature of dreams on the basis of the dreams recorded in Genesis. There were originally three books, each devoted to a particular kind of dream, but of these we now have only the second and third. Joseph appears in the second book only briefly, in a connection that will be discussed later.[2]

In the third book (our second book) Joseph is at the outset contrasted with Isaac. There are two types of men, Philo says, those who apply the nature of the good to many things, and those who ascribe it only to the Best; or those who regard the good as a mixed thing in contrast with

1. See above, pp. 5 f.   2. See below, p. 32.

those who regard it as unmixed. The people who speak of the good in the restricted sense associate it exclusively with reason, so far as man is concerned; the others speak of the good as though it applied also to the soul, the body, and to external circumstances. The latter is clearly the point of view of both Plato[3] and Aristotle,[4] and while it will appear later that Philo vacillated between the two conceptions of the good, in this present connection he insists that it ought to be restricted to its idealistic meaning. For in contrasting Isaac and Joseph he is anxious to contrast the man engaged in political affairs, the *politicus,* with the spiritually minded person, and for this the distinction between those who live only for metaphysical realities, and those who, confusing values, live also for material things, is an excellent one for his purpose. Isaac is the ideal man of single purpose, and Joseph is the type of "much mixed and mingled opinion" (πολυμιγὴς καὶ κεκραμένη δόξα),[5] for though Joseph is not totally devoid of higher interests he places value upon "unreasoning sensation" (τὸ ἄλογον αἰσθήσεως) as well as upon metaphysical perfection. He also has a love of bodily pleasure and "empty opinion" (ἡ κενὴ δόξα), by asserting which he destroys "equality."[6] This is the sort of man, the *politicus,* the meaning of whose dream Philo goes on to expound.

Joseph's first dream had to do with the sheaves. Joseph had a sheaf, likewise each of his brothers. These are explained as representing the affairs of life by which a man supports his household.[7] But while all the ten brothers represent various virtuous traits of character, Benjamin represents mere pretense,[8] and Joseph himself represents again "empty opinion," a phrase which by its frequent repetition will gradually gain significance. To make clear the person to whom he is referring by his treatment of Joseph Philo suddenly leaps ahead of his story, temporarily forgets the sheaves, and says that this is the man who is appointed ἐπίτροπος "or governor of all Egypt," the place second in honor to the king (βασιλεύς).[9] No such title is given Joseph in Genesis, and the use

3. *Laws,* 728d ff.; Philebus, 66c f. The idea is already apparent in the Gorgias, 477a ff., and Taylor (*Plato,* 115, n.) seems right in inferring that it is pre-Academic.

4. Health and a measure of material prosperity are of course included with virtue of the soul as goods, though on a lower plane, in the Aristotelian βίος τέλειος; *Eth. Nic.,* 1098b 12 ff.

5. *Som.,* ii, 15. This passage seems to me to go back to some standard Jewish allegory, familiar to Philo's readers, where the ποικίλος χιτών of Joseph was explained in terms of the specious attraction of ποικιλία in the democratic state as described in Plato, *Repub.,* 557c: ἱμάτιον ποικίλον; cf. 561e. The coat of Joseph is not mentioned here, but is throughout being taken as the symbol of Joseph's character.

6. Ibid., 16.   7. Ibid., 31.   8. Ibid., 42.   9. Ibid., 43.

especially of the word ἐπίτροπος must have told any person in Alexandria what Philo meant. For ἐπίτροπος was in Philo's day one of the official translations of the title of the *Praefectus Aegypti*. Flaccus is so called by Philo,[10] and the title appears elsewhere.[11] To make his reference clear Philo also brings out the Scriptural description of Joseph as having honor in Egypt second only to that of the king or emperor. Joseph, in short, typifies that ἐπίτροπος of all Egypt whose honor was second only to the emperor's. Philo is using Joseph as a type to vent his secret hatred of not just the politician, but specifically of that Roman ruler who was immediately over Philo and his own circle. That Jew would have been dull indeed who did not understand the reference.

So he treats other details in the same spirit. Joseph's badges of office, the ring and the necklace, are vaguely but disparagingly explained to make them marks of dishonor rather than honor.[12] Joseph climbs into the second chariot, a symbol of how his mind is filled with "arrogance" (τῦφος) and empty snorting.[13] He devotes himself to laying up grain, which represent one who cares for the body but not for the soul.

Indeed Joseph's very name means "addition," and this is elaborately explained:

Empty opinion is always adding the spurious to the genuine, the alien to the indigenous, truth to falsehood, the superfluous to what is sufficient in itself, luxury to living, and arrogance (τῦφος) to life.[14]

Philo goes on to illustrate at length. Such a man is not satisfied with plain and adequate fare, but must go to all lengths to secure delicacies. Simple clothing is rejected for costly *purple* garments, or summer clothes of exquisite fineness "like a spider's web," or costumes elaborately ornamented with embroidery and dyed designs.[15] "Empty opinion" also demands for its houses pillars, capitals, and archetraves im-

10. *Flac.*, 2.
11. Dio, *Epit.* LXXVII, xxi, 3, 4; cf. Stein in *Archiv für Papyr.*, IV, 151. The word apparently has that meaning in a papyrus printed in Mitteis-Wilcken, *Chrestomat.*, II, 372, V, 21, from the Second Century, and certainly has it in the papyrus recounting an embassy to Augustus, published most recently in the *Papiri della Società Italiana*, X, 99 (no. 1160, line 9).
12. The necklace is the κύκλος καὶ τροχὸς ἀνάγκης ἀτελευτήτου in contrast to the ἀκολουθία καὶ τὸ ἑξῆς ἐν βίῳ καὶ ὁ εἱρμὸς τῶν τῆς φύσεως πραγμάτων. This would appear to be the Stoic cycle of necessity which the Jewish community seems to have rejected for the Platonic-Pythagorean theistic order of nature. The ring is a sign of faithlessness, a gift from a royal human being in contrast with the spiritual gifts of God.
13. *Som.*, ii, 46: ὑποτυφούμενος ὑπ' αἰώρας φρενῶν καὶ κενοῦ φυσήματος.
14. Ibid., 47.   15. Ibid., 52.

ported from Asia, Africa, and all Europe, and in furnishing it has a collector's eye for Doric, Ionic, and Corinthian sculpture,[16] as well as for every other type of extravagant display. People of this type scorn olive oil as an ointment, and bring the most costly unguents from Syria, Babylonia, India, and Scythia.[17] A simple cup is not enough: there must be a great assortment of gold and silver goblets.[18] That Philo had the Romans in mind throughout this description is not only inherently probable, but is made certain by a parallel description of Trimalchian festivities in his *De Vita Contemplativa,* 48 ff., where the banquets he is describing are called, when given by Greeks, imitations of Italian extravagance and luxury. So engrossed does he become in his scornful account of Romans' debauchery in *De Somniis* that he finally bursts into the following:

What is the use of providing an unstinted number of silver and gold goblets, except for the gratification of great arrogance (τῦφος) and empty opinion which is always swinging to and fro? And when some people are crowned they are not satisfied with a fragrant garland of laurel, or ivy, or violets, or lilies, or roses, or of any sort of green bough or flower, for they pass by the gifts which God has given them in the seasons of the year, and shamelessly put golden wreaths on their heads, the heaviest sort of burden, in the middle of the crowded market place.[19] Can we think that they are anything else than slaves of empty opinion, although they say that they are not only free men but are even the rulers over many other people? . . . Who has not heard of such men or seen them? Who has not constant experience of them, is not used to them? So that the Holy Word very aptly calls "addition" the man who is an enemy of humility (ἀτυφία), and comrade of arrogance (τῦφος). For just as, to the great detriment of proper growth, there come out on trees superfluous growths, which farmers take down and prune away in their care for what is necessary, so the false man full of arrogance grows out as a sucker (παρανέβλαστεν) upon the true life that is characterized by humility, and no husbandman has been found to this day to cut off this injurious growth at the very roots.[20]

Philo has gone out of his way to make his reference clear. The arrogant ones he is describing are those people who call themselves rulers of many peoples, and whom all his audience will have seen daily vaunting themselves in the marketplace. Philo's hatred of them glows at

---

16. *Som.,* ii, 54 f. 17. Ibid., 59. 18. Ibid., 60 ff.
19. See the note by Colson, *ad loc.* 20. *Som.,* ii, 61–64.

white heat. In comparison with the divine course of nature in social matters, as represented by the Jewish life, the Romans are suckers, drawing the very life from the true tree. Let them spread themselves before their captives, and call themselves, as they sport their crowns, rulers of men; far from being rulers they are really only slaves as compared with the virtuous Jew. The great Husbandman has not yet appeared to prune the vine of society by hacking them off at the very roots, but, it is clear, Philo was looking for him to come. His language is strikingly suggestive not only of the pruning of the vine in the Fourth Gospel, but also of Q's account of John the Baptist's Messianic announcement that now that the Messiah was about to come, the axe would at last be laid at the very roots of the unfruitful trees.[21] If it is now recalled that much as he felt obliged for the present to propitiate the Romans, he was ready to attack and destroy their power when the opportunity came, it would appear that Philo was not only awaiting the Husbandman, but would swing an axe with him when he came.

Philo is usually represented as the complete antitype of the Apocalyptic writers, a man who found his life in metaphysics and mysticism, and who was a total stranger to the hysterical hatred of Rome that looked for a militant Messiah. If the interpretation of these passages is correct that description of Philo is totally unjustified. He would seem to have had too much political sagacity to sign his name to books in which the Romans were specifically denounced. He was too large minded not to see the value of much in Greek and Roman thought. He was no fanatic, and knew that so long as the Messiah had not yet come, one must get on with the Romans in the most conciliating spirit possible. So Philo kept his Messianism to himself. But one could secretly think, hope, and hate. And Philo seems to me to be assuring his Jewish friends that he was passionately doing all three.

People, Philo goes on, who did not fully understand, mourned for Joseph because he had been devoured by a wild beast. But it is Joseph, as the type of "arrogance," who is himself the wild beast and devours everyone who comes near him.[22] Nay those who have suffered from such a "hurt," though we mourn them as dead, are truly alive, for they

21. Mat. iii, 10; Luke iii, 9. On Philo's remarks about the Messianic king see further, pp. 115 ff. It is generally supposed that there was little interest in the Messianic hope in Hellenistic Judaism, but probably the hope was less discussed only because of the danger of doing so: see Sibyll., iii, 46–50, and G. F. Moore, *Judaism,* ii, 329 f.

22. *Som.,* ii, 66.

have not been carried away by a wild beast but have been translated to heaven like Elijah in a rush of unquenchable and immortal light. They were forbidden by law to fulfill their religious duties as they should, so they were taken to heaven to become whole burnt offerings as they themselves were dissolved in the ethereal beams.[23] Here another important aspect of contemporary Judaism, what amounted almost to the deification of the political martyrs, and the notion that they became sacrifices to God for Israel, seems clearly present also in Alexandria.[24]

The picture leads Philo to a brief digression on the insecurity of material things and the safety of retreat in contemplation. But he soon returns to his subject, and goes back to interpreting the sheaves of Joseph's dream. The point of the dream is that Joseph's sheaf arose and stood upright, while the sheaves of the others turned toward his sheaf and made obeisance to it.[25] So does a man who is filled with "empty opinion" put himself above all things, above cities, laws, and ancestral customs (Jewish Law), and the affairs of each of these. From leadership of the people (δημαγωγία) they go on to become "officials of the people" (δημαρχία);[26] they overturn the affairs of their neighbours to establish their own, and in every way put under the yoke all minds, even those which are free and unslavish.[27] Why then did the sheaves of the virtuous brothers bow to the sheaf of such a person? Because they could not for the moment help themselves. When a ruthless man gets into the ascendancy, one who is modest and pious is helpless, and a man who is cautious bows his neck. The right minded man knows that as chance blows up such eruptions, it also in time wilts them, and he is willing to submit to the temporarily inevitable and wait. It is at this point that Philo goes on to give the advice against resistance and frankness, and for subtle propitiation of savage rulers, quoted above.

But though the sheaves bowed, when Joseph's "arrogance" reached a certain height his brothers had to protest at whatever risk. For the brethren said, "Shall you be a king and rule over us?" The word

---

23. *Som.*, ii, 67.

24. Philo may well have had in mind, as he wrote, the dying prayer of Eleazor according to IV Mac. vi, 28 f.: ἵλεως γενοῦ τῷ ἔθνει σου, ἀρκεσθεὶς τῇ ἡμετέρᾳ περὶ αὐτῶν δίκῃ. καθάρσιον αὐτῶν ποίησον τὸ ἐμὸν αἷμα, καὶ ἀντίψυχον αὐτῶν λάβε τὴν ἐμὴν ψυχήν. Cf. ibid., 17, 21 f.

25. *Som.*, ii, 78.

26. Δημαρχία means the office of the δήμαρχος; it is no accident that δήμαρχος was the regular Greek word for *tribunus plebis*. The Roman tribune had of course no administration in Alexandria, but the word gives color to the passage.

27. Ibid., 79.

"king" meant to any son of the East in Philo's day a claim to divine rank. This is the point at which the brethren protested. While they would bow to the mere assertion of force, they could not call Joseph "king," in the full sense. For, says Philo, the strong man in whom is "right opinion" (ὀρθὸς λόγος) will, for all his cautious behavior, hate the "love of arrogance,"[28] and will always hold that the only true king in the full sense is God. To God should be given the real prostrating (προσκύνησις) and honor (τιμή), and if any ruler takes to himself the "honor" of God and calls upon his subjects to a cult of himself personally (πρὸς τὴν ἰδίαν θεραπείαν), a proper man will be violently enraged.[29] In such a case the only thing to do is to speak out boldly, and refuse to recognize any man as Lord. The obligation is clear, for as slaves or servants of God the Jews (such Philo has in mind here throughout) are not free to acknowledge another Lord. In their servitude to God are rewards greater than in any liberty.

In this passage Joseph has served consistently to represent the Roman, or Roman rule, and Philo has expressed a very succinct view of his attitude. Roman extravagance and arrogance are described with loathing, and the necessity of caution in dealing with them clearly indicated. But the attitude of flattery and compliance is not to be carried to the point of admitting the deity of any Roman ruler: rather than that, martyrdom is freely to be welcomed, for the reward of martyrdom is translation into supernal light. The Roman regime, however, will continue only until the Messiah lays it low.

Having said what he wishes to say about the Romans as governors, Philo is led by the word *politicus* to raise another question. Apparently the reader was quite aware that Philo was himself a *politicus,* and if so, and if his denunciation of the *politicus* was valid, where then did he himself stand? It is for this reason, it seems to me, that Philo suddenly shifts to the first person, and begins confessing that he himself has not lived in proper detachment from the political affairs of Alexandria.

I would pray that I myself might be able to remain steadfastly in those things which have been recognized [as the real values] by those men [i.e. Joseph's brothers]. For they are the scouts, the watches, the overseers of matters immaterial, strict in censorship, and sober through all their lives, so that they are deceived by none of the usual cheats. But hitherto I have been drunk

28. *Som.*, ii, 95 ff.   29. Ibid., 99.

and beset by great uncertainty, and like the blind I need a staff and guide; for perhaps if I had support I should not stumble or slip.[30]

The passage that follows is too long to quote.[31] Philo points out that these people who know the ideal way of life are the only guides through its complexities, but he admits that when he does temporarily come out of his habitual intoxication with political concerns he is torn between regarding the best guides who counsel detachment as friends or enemies. His own life is of course not the ideal. But now for the moment (καὶ νῦν), while he is temporarily writing in quiet he will renounce the dreaming Joseph of politics no less sharply than the true counsellors do.[32]

To this struggle between Philo the philosopher and Philo the man of public affairs we shall return in the next chapter. Here Philo's hope of not being utterly condemned for his political activities lies in the change of Joseph's own later life. In his old age Joseph turned to better things. Beginning with his rejection of bodily pleasure as represented in Potiphar's wife he, an exile in Egypt from his brethren who typified the nobler counsellors, asserted

his desire for continence and zeal for piety; he claimed the goods of his kinsmen and father from which he seemed disinherited, and deemed it right that he should again possess that portion of virtue which was properly his own. So gradually going on to better things, as though he were seated upon the pinnacle and ultimate goal of his own life, he announced what he had accurately learned from his own experience, namely that he belonged to God.[33]

Once he had reached this condition his brothers could return to him and be reconciled. So Philo, who also follows these men, at whatever a distance, finds comfort in Joseph's change of mind. At the end Joseph's ultimate alienation from material things was victoriously symbolized by the fact that his bones were carried off and buried with his fathers, not left in fleshly Egypt. Such, we understand, is Philo's ultimate hope. He must carry on his present mode of life still for a time. Yet he knows that the life of detachment is far superior, and hopes at the end to be able to return to it. When one reflects that Philo as an old man has to become involved in the most perilous political undertaking of his career, one

30. *Som.*, ii, 101 f.
32. Ibid., 104.
31. Ibid., 103–109.
33. Ibid., 106 f. Cf. Gen. l, 19.

wonders whether he ever did succeed in separating himself, and whether he really would have been happy had he actually done so.

Joseph's second dream starts Philo on another important allegory.[34] The sun and moon and eleven stars suggest a bit of astrology not to our purpose, but then lead to the conception of the man of strife and "empty opinion," again our Roman, who thinks that the forces of nature were designed to do him service. Xerxes' overturning the laws of nature to bridge the Hellespont and put a canal through Athos, and the Germans' taking up arms against the sea, are other examples. But his chief example is given in plain terms. He tells the story of a certain man whom he knew personally in very recent years, one of these "rulers" (ἡγεμονικοί), indeed "he had Egypt in his charge and under his authority" (τὴν προστασίαν καὶ ἐπιμέλειαν εἶχεν Αἰγύπτου), that is he was the Roman prefect of Egypt. This person tried to break the Jews' allegiance to their laws, and directed his attack especially against the Sabbath, thinking that the other Jewish laws would go with the laws guarding this one institution. At first he forced the Jews to break the Sabbath, but could not deflect their allegiance to it. So he tried to persuade them by pointing out that in time of pestilence, terrible fire, or similar natural catastrophes the Jews could not thus keep their right hands closed, their left hands under their shawls, or sit unmoved in their synagogues. In such an emergency they would have to do the best they could to protect and save themselves and their belongings. So far as the Jews were concerned the prefect insisted that he was himself a great natural calamity, for he was "fate and necessity not only in name but its very power revealed standing near you." Such a man, Philo concludes, was an extraordinary phenomenon, a new type of evil brought from over seas or from some strange universe, for he dared, wretch as he was, to compare himself to God.[35]

The prefect to whom Philo is referring may have been Flaccus, but I doubt it. It seems inherently improbable that Philo could have written the great bulk of his corpus after the reign of Gaius, since he was at that time an old man, and to see Flaccus in this prefect would be to throw a very large part of Philo's writing into those late years. It will appear that Philo knew prefects and Roman officers of various kinds. Once an official had been recalled in disfavor Philo could express himself quite openly about him, since no one would have risked coming to the fallen

34. *Som.*, ii, 110 ff.   35. *Ibid.*, 123–130.

man's defence. So in *In Flaccum,* after Flaccus had been disgraced, we saw that Philo could write freely about his character and administration, as in Claudius' reign he could vilify Gaius in the most direct way. Here Philo calls no names, but to the readers of his work as it first appeared he made his reference clear by saying that he had known this particular prefect "yesterday or the day before," which seems to indicate the prefect immediately preceding the incumbent at the time of writing. Philo is throughout making himself as specific as he dares. It should be noted that the sudden reference to Roman conduct of Egypt, superficially so abrupt a departure from the general allegorical mazes of the section, is no break at all since Philo has been talking about the Romans all along. It is just that here is the first incident about which he dared to speak directly. Its connection with the preceding is veiled in the code language of the context.

Philo now goes on to an allegorical discussion of "empty opinion" (κενὴ δόξα) and "arrogance" (τῦφος) as contrasted with "truth" (ἀλήθεια), "right reason" (ὁ ὀρθὸς λόγος), and "modesty" (ἀτυφία). The discussion is general, and only its connection with the preceding, and the fact that it is these code words which he is discussing, would suggest that Philo is still speaking of the Romans. But he begins by saying that such men are the chorus leaders (οἱ κορυφαῖοι) of empty opinion, and the chorus that follow them do all in their power by treachery and violence, when they see people who are trying to make their lives shine with virtue and truth, to drag them into the land of darkness and phantasms.[36] The virtuous ones are the followers of "right reason," in whose service they are free, but these followers of "empty opinion" want to take them and "right reason" itself and enslave them, though "empty opinion" ought to be slaves to them.[37] I am not talking about dreams, Philo warns the reader, but about things that are like dreams. For what seem to be great things to unpurified minds are small indeed to minds with truth as their standard.[38] Philo does not tell the reader what it is he is talking about, what these apparently great things are that are really trifling. Instead he goes on to ask whether right reason in general, and in its specific applications, can be prostituted by admitting the superiority of "empty reason." Shall it lay aside its own ancient "arrogance" to prostitute itself before sham and counterfeit "arrogance"?[39]

36. *Som.,* ii, 133 f.   37. Ibid., 135 ff.   38. Ibid., 138.
39. Ibid., 139 f.

No, one must trust in God.[40] There is always Miriam to be thought of, the symbol of hope. For, he points out elaborately, the fact is that however prosperous and safe some people may appear for a time, they often perish at the least expected moment.[41] So we must pray God to be ever merciful to the race in protecting it from the lure of false appeals.[42] And this in turn God can do only as we keep reason steadily dominant over the passions.[43] With this Philo concludes the allegory of Joseph.

Vague as is the closing section, when it is recalled that "empty opinion" has throughout represented Roman domination, and "arrogance" the spirit of Rome and Roman rulers, while "truth" has represented Judaism and "right opinion" (ὀρθὸς λόγος) the true Law,[44] the meaning seems clear. Philo is urging the Jews not to give up their Jewish faith and hope and surrender to the blandishments and prosperity open to them by renouncing their Judaistic isolation and making one with the Roman cause; not to give up allegiance to their true Law to accept the "empty opinion" of the Roman system. The Jew has a true pride and sense of superiority before which the Roman "arrogance" is dross. And Philo is adjuring them to hope for the destruction of the foes of Judaism, who are bound to fall through their own sins. Jews must pray for the peace of Israel, that is its ultimate freedom, for which Jews can hope only as they themselves keep free from the temptations of the flesh about them. Like the martyrs of IV Maccabees, the Jews could keep the Law only as they kept reason as the king and pilot in complete mastery over the passions. Truly Philo was not talking about dreams, but about what seemed great things to the tempted Jew. Philo's own nephew, Tiberius Alexander, it will be recalled, succumbed to the temptation, and found a brilliant career by going over to the Romans, had probably already apostatized when Philo wrote this paragraph, since by 46 A.D. he had gone so far in Roman circles that he was made procurator of Palestine. Such an exhortation could only have been given thus in allegory. Philo might openly criticize a fallen prefect, but not the Roman rule as such and its constant attraction to influential Jews. Veiled as it is, the Alexandrian Jew would have recognized the symbols, and understood this really passionate appeal. This allegory of the dreams of Joseph is the call, necessarily almost in code, for Jews to

40. *Som.*, ii, 141.
41. Ibid., 142–148.
42. Ibid., 149.
43. Ibid., 150–154.
44. On ὀρθὸς λόγος as true law, and hence here as the Jewish Law, see *By Light, Light*, 54–58.

remain Jews, to conciliate the Romans when necessary, but to live confident within themselves of their own unmeasured superiority, and assured that the God of justice would some day overturn these Roman up-
starts and give to Jews their proper place at the head of the world.

Joseph appears in other parts of the great *Allegory* with the same sig-
nification. In the first book of *De Somniis,* Joseph is explained as
belonging not to the pure ascetic, not to the utterly base. His coat of
many colors represents the fact that he is a mixture of the two.

He wore the extremely variegated web of the politeia, in which a very tiny
portion of truth is mingled with many and large portions of lies, probabilities,
plausibilities, and conjectures, the sort of things from which all the sophists of
Egypt sprang up, as well as the augurs, ventriloquists, soothsayers, and those
skilled decoyers, enchanters, and spell-binders from whose insidious arts it is
very difficult to escape. Wherefore Moses showed the insight of a philosopher
in introducing this cloak as being defiled with blood, since the whole life of a
man engaged in political affairs is defiled, for he makes war and others make
war on him, and he is the target for missiles and weapons thrown by unreckoned chance contigencies. Just scrutinize the too imbroiled leader of the
people upon whom the affairs of the state depend, without being alarmed by
those who hold him in admiration. You will find that many diseases lurk in
him, that he is entangled in many disasters, which try violently to throttle
his soul and imperceptibly wrestle with it and seek to overthrow it and to
cast it down, either because the multitude are dissatisfied with his leadership,
or because a more powerful rival is attacking him. For Envy (φθόνος) is a
harsh enemy, hard to be rid of, who always fastens himself to reputed prosperity, and whom one cannot easily escape.[45]

This is the politician. Philo is again aware that, himself a politician,
he is impugning his own character. So his reaction is similar to those
we have already seen, when he cries out in the next sentence:

Why should *we* vaunt ourselves in the fact that the florid politeia is draped
about *us* like a costly garment, deceived by its manifest comeliness, but not
perceiving its invisible and dangerous ugliness, its covert insidiousness? Let
us then put off this flowery robe and put on the sacred one woven with the
brocade of the virtues.[46]

But there is no reason to think that Philo ever did so.

In another treatise of the *Allegory, De Mutatione Nominum,* Philo
speaks of Joseph (and oddly with him of Benjamin) as similarly typify-

45. *Som.,* i, 220–223.   46. Ibid., 224 f.

ing the politician from this unfavorable point of view. He is "executor of the concerns of the body." His name is again translated as "addition," and the word is explained as the elaboration of the things of nature with superfluous additions. Most people think that a man of fortune is at the same time a man of prudence, to represent which mistake Joseph took the name Psouthonphanech (as the Septuagint reproduced it), which Philo explains as meaning "a mouth pronouncing judgement." His younger brother was by his father given the name Benjamin, meaning "Son of days";

and as day is illuminated by the sunlight visible to our senses, so we compare "empty opinion" to it. For "empty opinion"[47] has a certain brilliance to the outward sense in the acclamations of the mass and herd, in the decrees which are enacted, in the dedications of statues and images, in the purple robes and golden crowns, in chariots and four-horse cars, and in processions of the multitude. He who is ambitious of such things is naturally called "Son of days," that is of visible light and the brilliance of "empty opinion."[48]

Joseph's mother was aware of the other side of the picture. The happiness of such men she knew to be only apparent, for they are actually made wretched by being constantly exposed to malice, envy, strifes, enmities irreconcilable until death, and the like. The birth of such a manner of living is death to the soul. Again the reference to the Roman rulers is hardly veiled at all, and again Philo shows his implacable hatred. The peculiar image of the unworthy ruler as being illumined by a "sensible" light, brilliance, or beam (φῶς αἰσθητόν, λαμπρότης αἰσθητή, φέγγος αἰσθητόν), will be considered later.[49] It is notable that the inevitable flail of such men, as in the passage just quoted, is Envy.[50]

The word "arrogance" (τῦφος) has frequently appeared as a standing epithet to represent the Roman civilization and government. Philo uses

---

47. Philo is using the *terminus technicus* κενὴ δόξα now with the other meaning of δόξα, "glory." I have kept the other meaning in translation since for the English reader the continued use of the term is the most essential feature.

48. *Mut.*, 92 f.   49. See below, p. 57.

50. See below, p. 47. Philo frequently refers to Joseph. Apparently Joseph is a passing reference to the Romans in *Mut.*, 171–174, cf. 89 ff.; it may be a veiled reference to them at *Det.*, 5 ff., 28; *Sobr.*, 12–15. In *Mig.*, 158 ff. Joseph would appear to be the Jewish politician like Philo who tries to keep both true wisdom and a hand in public affairs, by being a mean between the man who lives exclusively for Jewish piety on the one hand, and the Roman, here Pharaoh, whose life is entirely in political affairs as he rules Egypt, on the other. See also *Deus*, 191–121; *Mig.*, 203 f.; *LA*, iii, 179; *Mut.*, 89 f., 215. Joseph is referred to with general disapproval in *LA*, iii, 26; *Cher.*, 128; *Det.*, 17. He appears to meet approval in *Post.*, 80 ff.; *Mig.*, 17; and to be even a symbol of continence in *LA*, iii, 237 ff.

the word freely throughout his writings, usually with the Cynic connotation, that is as a word of contempt especially applied to the life of those involved in material complications, as contrasted with the life of those who withdraw from society and matter.[51] Proselytes coming into Judaism leave "arrogance" for "humility."[52] In the relations of men with God their "arrogance" results in idolatry.[53] In the political realm it appears in general as the source of all social difficulties.[54] It is from this general point of view that "arrogance" is made specifically to represent the Romans, not only in the passages discussed but also in the allegorization of Jethro, Moses' father-in-law. Jethro, as "arrogance," is the soul attached to the mother, civil law, rather than to the father, natural (or Jewish) law,[55] and so Jethro legislates without regard to the higher law. As such he represents a city and constitution made up of mixed inhabitants who vacillate between empty opinions.[56] The specific application to the Romans appears clearly when Jethro is the civil ruler in contrast with Moses, who here represents Judaism. In such a relation Jethro is called "superfluous arrogance" (ὁ περισσὸς τῦφος). For Jethro's is the spirit which, even in times of peace (it will be recalled that Philo lived at the beginning of the *pax Romana*), arouses conflict without ceasing between races, regions, and cities, and even in private houses, setting every man against every other, so that affairs of life are kept in constant turmoil. It is truly marvelous, Philo says, when a man can keep his soul tranquil in such an environment, and no one marvels at the "wise man" who succeeds in doing so more than Jethro himself.[57] If I am right in my interpretation, a Jewish reader would have understood Philo as saying: The Romans have thrust themselves upon the world as an impertinent superimposition; they introduce war everywhere and their presence has even disrupted the peaceful coördination of family life. The Jews of Alexandria have shown themselves "wise

51. Before the Cynics the word, when applied to people, meant simply pride or madness. The Cynic use is illustrated by Monimus, *ap. Diogenes Laert.*, vi, 83: τὸ γὰρ ὑποληφθὲν τῦφον εἶναι πᾶν ἔφη; and Crates (*ap.* ibid., §86): τὰ δὲ πολλὰ καὶ ὄλβια τῦφος ἔμαρψεν. See also ibid., §26. In Plutarch τῦφος is the proverbial quality of the unphilosophic man; see his *Quomodo quis suos in virtute*, 81c f.; *De recta ratione audiendi*, 39d. See Philo, *Cont.*, 39; *Spec.*, ii, 259; *Virt.*, 195; *Mig.*, 160; *Cher.*, 42; *Mos.*, i, 88.

52. *Spec.*, i, 309. Abraham, in coming from τῦφος into ἀτυφία leaves death for life. *Dec.*, 80; *Ebr.*, 124 (cf., 95); *Virt.*, 17.

53. *Post.*, 165; *Spec.*, i, 21, 27–30, 53, 79; iii, 125; *Cher.*, 91; *Dec.*, 80; *Ebr.*, 124; *Mos.*, ii, 169, 270; *Fug.*, 90.

54. *Praem.*, 24, 25, 27.

55. See below, p. 74.

56. *Ebr.*, 36–40.

57. *Gig.*, 50, 51, 53.

men" in keeping free of the general confusion; they have refused to mingle with the parties concerned, and go on living in their traditional way. This ability to live undisturbed has caused favorable comment on all sides, and has particularly been recognized by the Roman rulers themselves.

The claim that Romans had recognized the value of the Jewish stand is not at all surprising. For while many Romans express themselves most scornfully when describing the Jews,[58] and Roman policy was by no means consistent in dealing with them, the Romans did on the whole allow the Jews remarkable special privileges not only of religion but of law, and could never have done so, in the face of popular dislike of the Jews, if they had not recognized the value of the Jewish bloc.

Jethro and the "superfluous arrogance" seem even more clearly to refer to the Romans in the following passage: Jethro symbolizes "arrogance," Philo says, for the name Jethro

when translated means "superfluous" (περισσός), and "arrogance" is a superfluous addition to the true (ἀψευδής) life, an addition which ridicules the principles of equality and the essentials of life (τὰ ἴσα καὶ ἀναγκαῖα τῷ βίῳ), and does honor to the inequalities of greed.[59] And it honors human things above divine things, custom above laws, profane things above the sacred, mortal above immortal, and, in general, appearance above reality. It even dares to intrude itself into the rank of the legate (σύμβουλος), and to instruct the "wise man" not to teach those things which are alone worthy of being learned, namely the "commandments of God and the law" (Exod. xviii, 20), but to teach instead the contractual arrangements (συμβόλαια) of men with each other, those very things, that is, which as a rule produce associations of men without any real common ground between them (τῆς ἀκοινωνήτου σχεδὸν αἴτια κοινωνίας).[60]

Here the meaning of "arrogance," and the relation of "the arrogant man" with the "wise man," are the same as in the preceding passage, but that the "arrogant man" is here the Roman is made even more probable by the reference to the office of the σύμβουλος. For σύμβουλος

---

58. See Schürer, *A History of the Jewish People in the Time of Jesus Christ*, II, ii, 291 ff., and Hausrath, *Neutestamentliche Zeitgeschichte*, III, 71–81.

59. πλεονεξία is a *terminus technicus* in political philosophy for the King's claim to the "lion's share": see "Hellenistic Kingship," 76. For a figurative use see *Mos.*, i, 153: *By Light, Light*, 185 n.

60. *Mut.*, 103 f. Like Colson (note *ad loc.*) I can see no reason for reversing the meaning as Wendland does following Mangey, by omitting the μή of line 29 in his edition, and adding μή in line 30. See Colson's excellent note.

is Polybius' regular translation of the Latin *legatus*. It is known from Livy that a group of ten men were sent out *more maiorum* to adjust the legal problems of new provinces, men whose usual title was *legati iuridici*,[61] and it was to do the same work in Egypt that the *iuridicus Alexandreae* accompanied the Egyptian prefect. To this officer, it seems, Philo is referring. For while the usual Greek title of the official was δικαιοδότης,[62] Philo preferred to use the more general term σύμβουλος as being sufficiently intelligible without being quite so direct. All through these passages the indirectness of approach is obviously studied, and with reason. Now it is notable that Philo represents such an officer as trying to get the Jew, the "wise man," to give up his insistence upon his own legal tradition, and to accept as an adequate substitute the Roman official legal adjustments for the realm. This attack on Judaism seems to have been much more general, and more dangerous, than the direct attempt of the prefect to make the Jews abandon their Sabbath. Philo calls these legal adjustments men's contractual relations (συμβόλαια), to bring out by the pun that they are the creation of the σύμβουλος, and at the same time to belittle them in contrast with the divine laws of his own race, which are "the principles of equality and the essentials of life." Philo seems to be telling his readers that the judgments and legal arrangements made by the *iuridicus* are, in comparison with the law of Moses, conventions as contrasted with valid law, the profane as contrasted with the sacred, the effect of which is to pervert any social relationships between men. It is this type of general criticism of the Roman system which Philo has been seen to bury deepest in allegory during his discussion of Joseph's dream, for it would have estranged the most liberal governors from the Jews.

The *iuridici* do not seem to have been always so anti-Jewish. Since Jethro, Moses' father-in-law, is also called in the Bible by the name Reu-el[63] which Philo translates "pastoral care of God," Philo can distinguish the *iuridicus* who, full of "arrogance," tried to dissuade the Jews from insisting upon legal distinctiveness, from the *iuridicus* who upheld the Jews in their loyalty. For there is a story of Jethro in Exodus xviii that on one occasion he came to Moses and found him overbur-

---

61. xxxi, 11, 18 (202 B.C.); xxxvii, 55, 4 (190 A.D.): see von Premerstein in Paully-Wissowa, XII, 1149.

62. See s.v. *"Iuridicus in Aegypten"* in Paully-Wissowa, X, 1151 ff. (Rosenberg), and Mommsen, *Provinces of the Roman Empire*, II, 268.

63. Exod. ii, 18.

dened with every sort of legal decision. He urged Moses to appoint deputy justices who would relieve him of most of the cases while he reserved the more important decisions for himself. Two parts of this story stand out as Philo here interprets it, the actual advice Jethro gave, and the fact that he left his own flocks to come to see Moses. Philo makes the following deductions:

The great man [Moses] accepts all he advises, and enacts that it is suitable that smaller legal claims be assigned to smaller [officials], the great claims to greater officials.[64] And frequently the wiseacre [Jethro] changes and goes over from the flock of which, blind as he was, he had received the leadership: he seeks out the divine herd and becomes no contemptible part of it, for he is amazed at nature for her skill as a shepherd, and admires the authority which she exercises in the care of her herd.[65]

Jethro, still the Roman *iuridicus,* is thus the prototype of those men who made the legal adjustment which recognized Jewish law in Alexandria. For by making Jethro's distinction, Romans could reserve for themselves the more important matters and let Jews decide among themselves the rest. The Roman officials who made this concession were to Philo not "arrogant men," but men who represented the "pastoral care of God." The coming of Jethro to Moses led Philo to add that some, at least, of these officials were so impressed with the value of Jewish law that they became "God-fearers." Such an attitude on the part of Romans would not be anomalous, for there is mention in Acts x, 1, 2 of Cornelius, a Roman centurion at Caesarea, who was "a devout man, and one that feared God with all his house, who gave much alms to the poor and prayed always." Philo himself says of Petronius, the Roman governor of Syria:

He had, as it appears, some sparks of the Jewish philosophy and piety: he may have learned it long since, by reason of his zeal for education, or only from the time when he assumed control of those regions of Asia and Syria where Jews are populous in every city; or his soul may have been thus disposed toward those things naturally worthy of attention by some spontaneous and self-prompting and self-teaching inclination.[66]

64. καὶ ὁ μέγας πάντα πειθαρχεῖ, νομίσας ἁρμόττον εἶναι μικροῖς μὲν τὰ μικρά, μεγάλοις δὲ τὰ μεγάλα δίκαια τίθεσθαι.

65. *Mut.,* 104 f. In the last sentence Philo is identifying Moses' rule, and with it the Jewish administration of society, with the rule of nature. This passage, which bothered Colson (see his notes *ad loc.*), seems to me one of the very few in Philo's writings which he has misunderstood.

66. *Legat.,* 245.

Philo is uncertain about the history of Petronius' interest in Judaism, but seems sure that Petronius knew the Jewish law and piety, and respected them. Vitellius is also represented by Josephus as doing what he could to give the Jews freedom in observing their law.[67] In view of the fact that the Jews did keep their legal privileges, it is not surprising that there were a few influential Romans who were friendly with the Jews, though Philo implies that they were on the whole quite exceptional.

The passages thus far discussed have all been from the great *Allegory* designed especially for an inner circle of Jewish readers. But "arrogance" takes us into another passage, one in the *Exposition* which seems to me to have been written with gentile, and even Roman, readers in mind,[68] and which is again a denunciation of their domination and mode of living. Moses, says Philo in the passage, could not give pure law in any existing city because every city is full of untold evils, evils both social and religious. He continues:

In cities arrogance flourishes, the most subversive of all things, and some people admire and venerate it, and dignify "empty opinions" with golden crowns and purple robes, and with a multitude of servants and chariots, in which the so-called "blessed and happy ones" (οἱ λεγόμενοι μακάριοι καὶ εὐδαίμονες) are carried on high. Sometimes mules and horses are harnessed to the chariots, sometimes human beings, who bear the burden on their necks and are crushed down in soul even more than in body by such an excess of insolence (ὕβρις). Arrogance makes also many other evils, pretentiousness, pride, and inequality. These are the causes of foreign and civil wars, and they leave nothing whatever at rest, whether public or private, on land or sea. What need is there of recalling the sins of these people to each other? For by "arrogance" even divine things are belittled, though they are esteemed as worthy of the highest honor. And what sort of honor would there be in the absence of truth, which is honorable both in name and fact, just as falsehood is on the contrary dishonorable in nature? And the belittling of divine things is obvious to those who have keen perception. For they hold sacred a myriad painted and sculptured forms; they erect temples for them and provide altars with images and statues, and to images of such a sort, though they are all inanimate, they vouchsafe honors on a par with the Olympians and the gods. Such people the sacred Scripture aptly compares to children begotten of a harlot. For just as such children are registered as having for their fathers all

67. *Antiq.*, XVIII, 90 f.
68. See my "Philo's Exposition of the Law and his De Vita Mosis," *Harvard Theological Review*, XXVII (1933), 109–125.

the men whom the mother has had as lovers, since no one knows the man who is their actual father, so the people who live in cities do not know the truly existing God, and deify an innumerable host of things falsely so called. Then, since different gods were in honor among different people, the disagreement which prevailed about the Supreme Being begat as well the divergences in all other matters. Moses, who first perceived this, wished to do his legislating outside of cities.[69]

Here are people who have recently, in great civil wars, overturned land and sea in their great and sinful expeditions against each other; people who now vaunt themselves in crowns and purple garments, and humiliate their subjects by treating them like beasts. It seems incredible that anyone in Alexandria in Philo's day would not have recognized the Romans. Yet how would Philo have dared circulate such a passage among the Romans themselves? The only possible answer is that none of these passages is definite enough to arouse suspicion by itself, and that Philo thought he might safely risk a single one in a treatise for gentiles. Under cover of a criticism of their religious vagaries he is even bold enough to call the Romans a harlot's litter of bastards!

We may conclude this section, in which Philo's covert remarks about Romans for Jews have been considered, with a passage buried in still another treatise for the inner circle. He is commenting upon the verse which we read: "It destroyed every living substance which was on the face of the earth."[70] The Septuagint reading which Philo is following has for "living substance" ἀνάστεμα, a strange translation of the Hebrew, but one behind which Philo did not look. For ἀνάστεμα means any protuberance or erection. How Philo could take it as a political reference is made clear from a phrase in Diodorus Siculus, xix, 92, ἀνάστημα βασιλικόν, where it means royal majesty or pomp. The text then meant to Philo that God would destroy all royal pomp, and he accordingly explains it:

It is not without reason that [Moses] has used the word ἀνάστεμα. For this is the name of ambition and pride, as a result of which men come to despise not only divine but even human laws. But ambition and arrogance are apt to

69. *Decal.*, 4–9. There is a fragment from the lost fourth book of Philo's *LA*, which reads: "If you take away the material resources from politicians you will find only empty τῦφος, without any intelligence. For so long as there is no lack of external goods, politicians seem attended by insight and sagacity; but when they lose their abundance of possessions they seem simultaneously to lose their power to think." Harris, *Fragments*, p. 7.

70. Gen. vii, 23.

appear upon the surface of our earthly and corporeal nature, when the face is held loftily and the eyebrows are contracted. For there are some men who come near to one with their feet, but with their chests and head and neck lean back, and are actually borne backwards and bend away like a balance. The result is that with one half of their body, in consequence of the position of their feet, they project forward; but they project backwards with the upper portion of their chests, drawing themselves back like people the muscles and tendons of whose necks are in pain so that they cannot bend in a natural manner. But men of this kind it was determined to put an end to, as one may see from the records of the Lord and the divine history of the Scriptures.[71]

Certainly in the lost Greek original one of these words for pride was τῦφος, and the caricature Philo is drawing is likewise again recognizable. It is the Roman "arrogance" (τῦφος), the thing which through its hateful representatives is destroying both divine and human laws, against which Philo is raging. Every detail of this description of their absurd stiffness is familiar from other descriptions of rulers, who studied such rigidity in order to appear the superhuman king. Similar descriptions have come to us from a wide range of writers and periods.[72] The Jews who read this passage must have known what rulers Philo had in mind, and have gloated with him at their eventual destruction by the God of the Jews. Philo is saying to the Jews that their Scriptures promise them that the hated Roman "arrogance" is to be laid low.

These passages of Philo have told us what we might have expected, but had no record of. The Jews of Alexandria, for whom Philo was spokesman, hated and despised their Roman masters. To the Jew a Roman ruler was normally a wild beast with power, and often with inclination, to devour or crush him. As such the Roman had to be conciliated in every way possible, since there was no hope of successfully opposing him. And yet the Jew had not the first thought of surrendering his heritage to become merely a Roman subject. He would go on unobtrusively observing his peculiar traditions, and defend them as best he could. He would make himself appear to the Roman as so exemplary a citizen in every other way that he was worth protecting in what would have seemed to the Roman an unaccountably passionate allegiance to the harmless but silly customs of a race. When the Roman attacked Judaism directly, then the Jew was willing to suffer to the

71. *QG*, ii, 24.
72. Xenophon, *Cyropaedia*, VIII, i, 40–42; Lucian, *Cataplus*, 16; *Gallus*, 12; *Adv. Indoctum*, 21; *Hercules*, 3; Ammianus, XVI, x, 9, 10.

death, if need be, to keep his religious identity. While the racial leaders, like Philo, would try every expedient to avoid a direct challenge, they would play the political game even to bearding Gaius in his den rather than let Israel or its ideals perish. Martyrdom had no terrors, since the political martyr was translated to heaven and became a saving force for the people. Yet martyrdom was not sought. If the Jewish race could, by clever manipulation, get the Roman to let him alone until such time as God would send the great Husbandman to pull down the Roman for his sins, that was by all means the policy to follow. The destruction of Roman "arrogance" may be described as the work of "Envy," or of the Good Husbandman, or of fate or necessity. Of one thing the Jew was sure, that he need only be patient for a different social order to come into existence, one in which those worthy of power, that is, themselves, would have it. Meanwhile if individual Romans took a more friendly attitude to the Jews, they would be gladly received and flattered, though such individuals by no means blinded the Jews to the significance of Roman power as such.

CHAPTER III

POLITICS BY INNUENDO

P HILO'S political life is beginning to appear to have had many layers and facets. In spite of the fact that we know of only a single political appointment given to him, his remarks about the political situation show an amazingly realistic combination of insight, caution, and boldness. In the first chapter we saw him writing treatises for gentiles, if not for the prefect and emperor in person, masterfully insinuating what should be the attitude of a ruler toward his subjects, and especially toward the Jews. In the second chapter we were eavesdropping while to his intimate friends he whispered the bitterest hatred of the Romans, and hope for a day when the Jews would no longer have to endure their arrogance.

There is one more extended approach to politics and the ruler in a treatise which Philo wrote under still different circumstances. Beside Philo's *Allegorical Interpretation of the Jewish Law,* and the *Questions and Answers on Genesis and Exodus,* stands a third great series of commentaries on the Pentateuch, usually referred to as the *Exposition of the Jewish Law.* The distinctive points of this *Exposition* as contrasted with the other two series, particularly the former, the *Allegory,* I have discussed elsewhere,[1] and shown that the differences indicate that the *Exposition* was intended for gentiles as clearly as the *Allegory* and *Questions* were designed for Jews. It appeared that the *Exposition* did not look to ordinary gentiles, but was especially adapted to be given to those seriously interested in learning about the Jewish religion. The *Exposition* therefore reads quite differently from the *Allegory* written for Jews who knew the Old Testament in elaborate detail, and who were ready for a commentary which would, largely by allusion, expound the truths of the Mystery. For in the *Exposition* Philo had always first to tell the scriptural narrative in a form which those who had never heard it would comprehend. In this spirit he began the *Exposition* with the creation, that is, with the demonstration of Jewish (Platonic-Pythagorean) metaphysics. Next he told of the revelation of God to the Jews,

1. "Philo's Exposition of the Law and his De Vita Mosis," *Harvard Theological Review,* XXVII (1933), 109–125.

beginning with the revelation to Abraham (really, in an introduction to the *Life of Abraham,* with the revelation to some of the earlier patriarchs), then going on to the revelation to, or through, Isaac and Jacob. To each of these three a biographical book was dedicated, though unfortunately only the *Life of Abraham* is preserved. Each of the patriarchs was a type of mystical perfection, and in the stories of their lives (as well as in a separate *Life of Moses* which was a still more elementary introduction for gentiles) the higher aspirations of Judaism as a Mystery were indicated.[2]

But Judaism was notorious for being a law and a way of life as well as a mystic metaphysic, even at Alexandria, so that Philo went on in the *Exposition,* still obviously for uninformed outsiders, to tell his ideals of rulership in the *Life of Joseph,* and then to present the wonders of the Jewish Law in the treatises *On the Decalogue* and *On the Special Laws.*[3] Sundry ethical details of importance were discussed in *On the Virtues,* and then the whole series was brought together in a book of conclusions entitled *On Rewards and Punishments.*

It is *De Josepho* from the *Exposition* which is important for Philo's politics.[4] Now if this treatise was, like the rest of the series, designed for gentiles, it is obvious that, however interested they might have been in Judaism, Philo could not use the career of Joseph as a screen for vituperation of Roman rulership and domineering arrogance as he did in isolated passages of the *Allegory.* Actually the interpretation of Joseph, who still represents the *politicus,* is so much the contradiction of everything which Philo says about Joseph in the other series that I wonder someone has not insisted that the two could not have been written by the same author.

For Joseph is here still not only the *politicus,* but, as the treatise goes on, obviously again the Roman prefect in Egypt. Yet since he was writing for gentiles Philo could hardly make him the embodiment of "arrogance." Rather, in this new picture, Joseph is an exalted type of person, second only to his three mystic forebears who knew how to direct their lives toward the ideal goal (τὸ ἄριστον τέλος).[5]

Jacob recognized in his son Joseph from the outset a "well born

2. This is much expanded in my *By Light, Light.*
3. See my *Jurisprudence.*
4. See above, p. 38. It may be noted in passing that Heinemann (*Philons Bildung,* 449–451) has treated *De Josepho* as an academic reflection of Cynic sources.
5. *Jos.,* 1.

mind, one greater than is associated with a private citizen" (φρόνημα εὐγενὲς καὶ μεῖζον ἢ κατ' ἰδιώτην); he devoted great care to the training of Joseph so that his natural gifts might not smoulder, but might shine forth.[6] That is, the ideal man, Jacob, here recognizes in a true *politicus* a very high type of individual.

The imagery at once suggests the hellenistic idealism of the kingly office and person, which I have treated more fully elsewhere.[7] The conception is so important for Philo, and in general so little understood, that a brief summary must be inserted here. The collapse of the Greek democracy turned men's eyes everywhere to monarchy as a solution of state problems. In local government the tyrant was often given advice as to how his rule might become truly royal, and so the state be secure (get σωτηρία) and the ruler himself be stable and the savior (σωτήρ) of the state. In general the ruler was to do this by becoming lawful (νόμιμος) or just (δίκαιος), words largely synonymous to the Greek. This conception was developed in accordance with each of the current theories of law. So far as possible the king was to leave unmolested the traditional law of the state, and so guarantee the liberties and win the coöperation of his subjects. But the law of the state was itself of divine origin, at least ideally, to any Greek, or rested on divine sanction, whether from originally having been formulated by a divinely inspired lawgiver, or from the fact that any new legislation was subject to appeal to divine oracles. In accordance with this notion of law the king as legislator was to be in conformity with divine or natural law. In explaining how the king might be, or become, so, the old traditions of Homeric kingship, where the king had and gave the precepts (θέμιστες) and

6. *Jos.*, 4; on the ἔκλαμψις of βασιλεία see Dio Chrys., I, 70 f.

7. See my "Hellenistic Kingship." To the material there used should be added: a fragment of Ecphantus in Stob., *Anthol.*, IV, vi, 22 (Wachsmuth et Hense, IV, p. 244 f.), quoted below, p. 98; *Schol. in Homer. Il.*, A, 340, b; Iamblichus, *Vit. Pythag.*, 31; Clem. Alex., *Stromata*, II, p. 122 (Stählin); Suetonius, *Julius*, 77; Cicero, *Rep.*, I, 52; *De Legg.*, III, 2; Themistius, *Orat.*, I, 15 b. In the *Studien zur Geschichte der griechischen Lehre vom Staat*, by Hermann Henkel (Leipz., 1872), 2–37, there is a large collection of interesting material. See also Kenneth Scott, "The Deification of Demetrius Poliorcetes," *American Journal of Philology*, XLIX (1928), 137–166, 217–239; "Plutarch and the Ruler Cult," *Transactions of the American Philological Association*, LX (1929), 117–135; W. W. Tarn, "Alexander the Great and the Unity of Mankind," *Proceedings of the British Academy*, XIX (1933), 123–166. The idea as it appears in Seneca (see especially *De Clementia*, I, i, 2–4, iv, 1) lacks a "clearly defined conception" of the divinity of the king, as A. J. Carlyle has seen (*History of Medieval Political Theory*, I, 31), just as do Stoic references to the king in general. It is in the Pythagorean material that the notion is most clearly at home. This I still hold in spite of the arguments of H. M. Fisch, "Alexander and the Stoics," *American Journal of Philology*, LVIII (1937), 59–82.

judgments (δίκαι) of Zeus, were elaborated in the light of oriental, especially Persian, conceptions. By this, the king was an incarnation of the divine spirit of law, a unique individual with a human body but a superhuman personality. His pronouncements became the code of the realm because he was the vehicle through whom the divine law could become explicit. So while he gave law to men, the king's quality of being lawful was attained by virtue of his being personally a representation of the higher law. In this sense the term "animate law" (νόμος ἔμψυχος) was applied to him. It seems that it was in this sense too that he was described as God revealed (ἐπιφανής). The last modern illustration of this type of ruler is the Roman Pontiff, who is a man, yet by virtue of his office is believed to be filled with the Spirit in so unique a way that his official pronouncements are the immediate formulation of divine truth, the only infallible vehicle of that truth to men. The theory seems first to have been elaborated for Greeks by Pythagoreans in South Italy, was admitted as the theoretical ideal by both Plato and Aristotle, and was apparently accepted throughout the hellenistic world in application to the hellenistic kings.[8] The notion was elaborated to include many other Persian and oriental elements, particularly the comparison of the king to the eagle, as being able to gaze at the sun (the divine source of the spirit-rays which were the spirit-law);[9] the notion that the king is to be a person of majestic appearance, looking the part of one filled with divinity, and thus resplendent, and aloof from human frailty; in consequence the belief that he was a dynamic influence in society for its moral and spiritual elevation, so that to look upon him would bring spiritual catharsis to the individual. He was the shepherd of his people, as in Homer and all the orient and Egypt. In view of this belief, worship of the king was the natural and desirable corollary for a people ever eager to deify any hero who stood out from his fellows by peculiar gifts or powers. By recognizing Demetrius as a god, for example, the Athenians could keep the illusion of their continued independence, for the Athenian state had always been subservient to the gods.

Bréhier recognized the kinship between many of Philo's remarks and the chief extant sources for this theory of kingship, a series of Pythago-

8. Heinemann has suggested that Panaetius or Poseidonius invented the doctrine of the νόμος ἔμψυχος, and that both the Neo-Pythagorean fragments and Philo got the notion thence. See his *Poseidonius*, II, 274 ff. He is unable to bring the slightest evidence for such a statement.

9. It is notable that βασιλεία is gazing at the sun in Dio Chrys., I, 71.

rean (probably on the whole Neo-Pythagorean) fragments.[10] His treatment of Philo's political theory is easily the best that has been done. His defect lies chiefly, as it seems to me, in treating too literally Philo's relations with the extant literature, without recognizing the possibility of that literature's being but an expression of what was in Philo's day a political axiom in Egypt and the Levant, if not, judging from Cicero and later writers, in the Empire in general.[11] But I should not like to go on without expressing my great obligation to M. Bréhier's remarks on the subject, which seem to me for the first time to have made possible an understanding of much of Philo's thought.

It is not strange that Philo should have applied this theory to the representative of Rome in Egypt, for we know that that was commonly done in the East in the cases of Pompey and Caesar, as well as of less famous Roman generals and representatives.[12] That Philo was actually doing so will appear in the course of the analysis of *De Josepho*.

The first detail of the conception has already appeared from this treatise. Joseph was a person with gifts for rulership which his father recognized from the outset as consisting in a "well born mind, one greater than is associated with a private citizen," and accordingly the father took care to cultivate Joseph in such a way that this nature would shine out brilliantly.[13] In his early years what he was taught was the art of the shepherd, the significance of which Philo makes explicit. Taking from what he calls the "poetic genus" (Homer) the title "shepherds of peoples" (ποιμένες λαῶν) for kings, he points out that as hunting is an important part of the training of a warrior, so the man who is a skillful shepherd will make the best king.[14] Of course Joseph never became king, but Philo is thinking so closely in terms of the theory of kingship that the word has come in unawares. Joseph, however, like all great

---

10. *Les Idées*, 18 ff. The Neo-Pythagorean fragments are those ascribed to Archytas, Sthenidas, Diotogenes, and Ecphantus, and discussed in my "Hellenistic Kingship."

11. So, as already stated, I cannot agree with his suggestion (p. 20) that the fragments present a theory which is "une utopie politique, qui néglige fort toutes conditions pratiques." He recognizes a connection with Plato though not the full extent of that connection, and concludes, erroneously, I think, "Ce que Platon considère comme un mythe a été pris au sérieux par les néopythagoriciens qui en déduisent la nature divine du roi." He assumes, on what ground I cannot see, that the Neo-Pythagorean fragments are of Egyptian origin. It has already been indicated that apparently utopian talk about the ideal ruler was the only vehicle by which the private citizen under hellenistic or Roman rulership could express himself on political matters.

12. Wendland, "Σωτήρ," in *Zeitschrift f. d. neutest. Wissensch.*, V (1904), 340–342.

13. See Diotogenes' paragraph on kingly majesty of appearance as quoted in my "Hellenistic Kingship," 72.

14. *Jos.*, 2, 3.

men, has as his most implacable enemy Envy (φθόνος).[15] To Joseph Envy comes from his brothers' attitude toward him. For whereas in the Allegory the difficulty between Joseph and his brothers is represented as the just resistance of upright men against the "arrogance" and "empty opinion" of a ruler, in complete contrast here it is Joseph the ruler who is upright, and the brothers opposed to him are filled with the evil of Envy. Joseph, the *politicus,* we are now assured to make the contrast sharp, was flawless in his way of life (χρώμενος ἀκάκοις τοῖς ἤθεσι).[16]

So his dreams are described as having been conceived and told in perfectly good faith, though his brothers hated him the more for them, and even Jacob, while much impressed, felt called upon to reprove him for such thoughts as are repugnant to people with a flair for equality and the just relations of kinsfolk.[17]

But Jacob seemed to attach no blame to Joseph for the dreams. He sent off the brothers to allow their rancor time to cool, and only sent Joseph out to them when he thought a safe time had elapsed. That is, the treatment of the episode for the gentile audience is as different as possible from the interpretation which Philo made for the Jews themselves. There Joseph was utterly in the wrong as over against his righteous brothers: here he is inferior only to Jacob; to his wicked brothers he is immeasurably superior. In the same spirit Philo goes on to tell with considerable flourish the story of the wickedness of the brothers in selling Joseph, and the lamentation of the aged Jacob.

At §28, as is his custom in this treatise, Philo breaks into the direct

---

15. See above, p. 33. Philo uses φθόνος almost as an evil spirit. It is essentially μισάρετος καὶ μισόκαλος (*Migr.*, 183; cf. *Abr.*, 191; *Spec.*, iii, 3), and as such is in contrast with God (*Migr.*, 183; *Abr.*, 203). He twice quotes Plato, *Phaedrus*, 247a: φθόνος ἔξω θείου χοροῦ ἵσταται (*Spec.*, ii, 249; *Prob.*, 13), whereby φθόνος is sharply personalized. In connection with bad rulers the word appears as a synonym of their πλεονεξία (*Legat.*, 80), and Macro points out that only by making each part of an empire free from φθόνος so that there will be open and ungrudging flow of trade and good will between its various parts, can a great empire exist at all (*Legat.*, 47 f.). But, as in these passages, every ruler must count on φθόνος as the normal attitude of subjects toward preëminence, although so long as the ruler's demands are moderate (προστάττειν τὰ μέτρια) their φθόνος will not assert itself (*Spec.*, ii, 91). Still it is a general rule that the lesser prizes of life are more desirable than the greater, since the lower avoid τὸν ἐμφυόμενον ἀεὶ τοῖς ὑπερέχουσιν φθόνον (*Agr.*, 121). The man who is overconfident of a continuance of prosperity must watch out for a fall from βασκανία καὶ φθόνος (*Cher.*, 33). Philo's own happiness in the desert was ruined by it (*Spec.*, iii, 3). φθόνος is an age-old attitude of the Egyptians toward the Jews (*Flac.*, 29). It is something that dwells in men's souls (*Virt.*, 223; *Praem.*, 87). In the Messianic Age God will give wealth both public and private φθόνου κρείττονα (*Exs.*, 168).

16. *Jos.*, 6.   17. Ibid., 9.

narrative to give interpretation. "Joseph" is again translated as meaning "the addition of the Lord," but the invidious connotation of "addition" has gone altogether. Instead of the name's signifying that the ruler is personally a man devoted to the lower material excrescences, rather than to the eternal verities, it is the inadequacy of the political state itself that Philo here finds expressed in the term. There is only one true sovereign authority, he says, and to this the "state as seen among peoples" (ἡ κατὰ δήμους πολιτεία) is always an addition.[18] Only in passing at the end does he conclude that the *politicus* is an addition to the man who lives "according to nature."[19] But there is no hint of bitterness. Similarly the multi-colored coat symbolizes primarily adaptability.[20] States take many different forms, vary widely in their laws, and the *politicus* must take on the character of warrior or peaceful man, or what else, and use force or persuasion, as circumstances demand.[21] As to the selling into slavery,[22] the old interpretation still holds: the *politicus* is the slave of the populace. But the fact is pointed out in sorrow, not in scorn. That is, Philo is here gently holding out the idea, familiar enough from the Stoics alone,[23] that earthly government is essentially inferior to the great government of nature in the universe, or as he put it, contrary to the Stoics, the great government of God. The *politicus,* dealing with earthly politics, is concerned with excrescences, "additions," to what is real. He is therefore of course inferior to the man concerned with God more directly. Yet he is a great blessing to man, and his virtue is quite beyond, if he is a proper ruler, the virtue of ordinary men (μεῖζον ἢ κατ' ἰδιώτην).

The narrative is then resumed. Once Joseph was in Egypt, his master, like Jacob, quickly recognized his true character, namely that in whatever he did or said he acted "not without divine wisdom" (οὐκ ἄνευ θείας ἐπιφροσύνης).[24] That is, in all his actions and pronouncements he

18. The passage is more fully discussed below, p. 80.

19. *Jos.*, 31.

20. Ibid., 32 ff. The association of the variegated coat with tyranny was probably a proverbial part of the current king philosophy. See Dio Chrys., *Orat.*, I, 70 where βασιλεία is clothed in white; §81 where τυραννίς has clothing παντοδαπή.

21. Bréhier compares this section with Plato, *Politicus*, 294a, b.

22. *Jos.*, 35 f.

23. Colson has gathered some of the familiar passages in his translation, VI, 600, note to §28.

24. *Jos.*, 37. The ἐπιφροσύνη θεῖα or θεοῦ appears frequently in Philo (Leisegang lists twenty instances in his *Index*) as the provident activity of God toward men or in human affairs. It seems quite interchangeable with one of Philo's most important usages for the λόγος θεοῦ or θεῖος.

followed divine guidance and inspiration, or, in other words, he had the disposition of the ideal hellenistic king. By virtue of the fact that his Egyptian owner recognized this character in Joseph, Joseph was assigned to the superintendence of the household,

but in fact and reality the assignment was made by nature, who was taking steps to give him the rulership of whole cities and a nation, and a great country. For the future *politicus* needed first to be trained and practised in house management. For a household is a city compressed into small dimensions, and household management is a sort of epitome of government, just as a city too is a great house, and state government is a sort of public household management. All this shows clearly that the household manager is identical with the *politicus,* however much what is under the purview of the two may differ in number and size.[25]

For the *politicus* is like a painter or sculptor, Philo continues, who having the art can produce larger or smaller pieces indifferently.[26]

Philo's connecting household management with the work of a *politicus* was no remote *tour de force.* Plato had spoken of the proper management of a city as being impossible if the households within it were not properly regulated, for both were ultimately founded upon the same legal principles.[27] In the *Statesman,* where Plato talks most of kingship, the household manager, the *politicus,* and the King are fully equated.[28] There is a single science used by all alike. Aristotle was also impressed with the similarity, especially in the case of kingship, though after his way he made distinctions.[29] Yet to Aristotle the words house-

---

25. *Jos.*, 38 f.   26. Ibid., 39.   27. *Laws, 790b.*

28. 258e ff. Some of Philo's remarks are very close to Plato's. Cf. 259b: μεγάλης σχῆμα οἰκήσεως ἢ σμικρᾶς αὖ πόλεως ὄγκος μῶν τι πρὸς ἀρχὴν διοίσετον; Xenophon ascribes the same notion to Socrates, *Memorab.,* III, iv, 12. Aristotle, as usual, wants to seem to differ from Plato on this point, though he ascribes the notion to "some," not to Plato in particular: *Polit.,* 1252a 6 ff., 1253b 18 ff., 1255b 16 ff. But he is willing to admit that μοναρχεῖται πᾶς οἶκος (1255b 19). His objection to Plato's statement seems to be based upon the fact that the distinction between the rule of free men and slaves is so great that he cannot include all types of rule under the same ἐπιστήμη. Yet it would appear from 1278b 32 ff. that he classes the rule of a master of slaves with tyranny, and that of οἰκονομία, the proper rule of one's wife and household, with the true forms of government, while in 1259a 37 ff. the rule of a father over his children is so truly royal that father and king, as in the case of Zeus, are interchangeable terms. When he finally admits: ὥσπερ γὰρ ἡ οἰκονομικὴ βασιλεία τις οἰκίας ἐστίν, οὕτως ἡ βασιλεία πόλεως καὶ ἔθνους ἑνὸς ἢ πλειόνων οἰκονομία (1285b 31 ff.) he has come back entirely to Plato's position. I should guess that the comparison was a Greek commonplace.

29. See the preceding note. The rule of a householder over his slaves is δεσποτική, that over his children is πατρική, administered βασιλικῶς, that over his wife is γαμική, done πολιτικῶς. See also *Politics,* Book I passim, especially 1259a 37 ff., and Colson's note to the Philo translation, VI, 600, §38.

hold management (economy) and government (polity) are quite inter-changeable, so much so that he could say of the "best government" that it was "one administered like a household by the best man."[30] Such usage continued on into hellenistic speech, as appears for example in Dinarchus and Polybius.[31]

In having experience as a household manager then, as in making himself a shepherd, Joseph was being trained ideally for the duties of the *politicus*. And it should be emphasized that Philo makes clear that Joseph was appointed to rulership not by man but by nature. Like every true hellenistic ruler, Joseph was conceived as having his office because of the character nature had given him, and because nature or God ideally sees to it that the man with the natural gift for rulership is given the political power.

Philo now goes on to discuss the third great characteristic possessed by Joseph, his continence (ἐγκράτεια) or chastity (καρτερία).[32] He tells with verve the story of the infatuation of Potiphar's wife, and puts a long speech into Joseph's mouth praising the unique chastity of the He-brews, a section obviously inserted as propaganda for the gentile reader. So, he concludes, the *politicus* must be controlled in his relations with women. Wars have frequently been brought about by lust for women, while chastity brings peace and stability. What Philo is doing is to find in the story of Joseph another familiar ideal virtue of the hellenistic king, continence, self-mastery (αὐτάρκεια), or self-control (σωφροσύνη), virtues which were almost always included in a description of the true kingly nature.[33] It is probable that he gives the limited interpretation of the term as implying preëminently sexual control, because that is the problem suggested by the story of Potiphar's wife. But Philo could easily have generalized from this single aspect had he not himself been in that deplorable but historically important line of ethical development which came ultimately to associate the word moral in a unique sense with sexual repression.

Philo next proceeds to develop the injustice and blind impetuosity of Joseph's master in imprisoning him without a hearing, and uses the in-

---

30. *Politics,* 1288a 33 ff.

31. Dinarchus 102, 29; Polybius IV, xxvi, 6, and IV, lxvii, 9.

32. *Jos.,* 40–57. Philo, in contrast to Aristotle, *Eth. Nic.,* 1145a 33 ff., uses the two words synonymously.

33. See my "Hellenistic Kingship," 86 ff. See also Dio Chrys., *Orat.,* I, 14 f. Dio also points out that the king is never a pleasure seeker: ibid., §21.

cident to introduce a new note. The Septuagint calls Potiphar a cook, and Philo makes much of this fact as well as his being a eunuch (Gen. xxxix, 1). As a cook his intelligence is obscured by the smoke of the kitchen, and so he typifies the unintelligent mob. As a eunuch he is also like the crowd, for they have eyes that see not, appear intelligent but have no intelligence, have what appear to be the organs of generation, but no power to generate.[34] So the multitude talks well about virtue, but really knows and practises nothing of it. In spite of his impotence Joseph's master has a wife, for lust (ἐπιθυμία) is really the wife of the mob. Also as a cook he is devoted to pleasure (ἡδονή).[35] This is the type of man to whom Joseph was subject, for Joseph apparently managed all Potiphar's affairs, but was still his slave. Here an aspect of rulership is introduced which Philo did not get at all from current hellenistic praise of royalty, namely that the ruler, however much power he may seem to have, is still the slave of the mob, and must perish if he does not pander to its lust for pleasure. How is the statesman to hold himself in such a situation? Philo has praised the *politicus* enough: he begins at last to talk straight out. There is no point in the *politicus'* trying to fool himself that he is not ultimately the slave of the mob; this fact he must frankly admit. But he is to take the Stoic attitude which insisted that slavery can go no deeper than the body. The master can never own the soul. The statesman is to be aware of his citizenship in the great cosmopolis, and treat the mob as his wards and children.[36] Freed thus from spiritual domination, he will make the following commitment toward his work:

If then I must give judgment, I will do so without favoring the rich man because of his great property, or the poor man from pity of his misfortunes; rather, blinding myself to the ranks and standing of the litigants, I will declare fairly what shall seem to be just. If I am to act as councillor, I will introduce measures for the common good, even though they may not be pleasant. If I am to be an assemblyman I will leave flattering words to others and speak in a salutary and helpful way, reproving, warning, and restraining, and indulging in no raving or insane audacity, but only in sober frankness.[37]

In exercising the powers of his office the *politicus* may have to admonish like a parent, give disagreeable medicine like a physician. For

34. *Jos.*, 58.   35. *Ibid.*, 59–62. Cf. Plato, *Gorgias*, 464*d*, 500*b*.
36. *Jos.*, 67: ὡς ἀγαθὸς ἐπίτροπος ἢ πατὴρ εὔνους.
37. *Ibid.*, 72 f.

even though the physician be a slave, there are times when he must cut and burn his wealthy master. The people do not like such a governor, and will frequently put him into prison, but in doing so they injure only themselves. The governor must fearlessly disregard danger in opposing the mob, and do what is best for the state without heeding popular prejudice or passion. A Roman who knew anything of the problems of imperial rulership would at once have felt the force of Philo's argument, and been impressed with the value as a subject of people who took this point of view toward their governor. For, in spite of his great arbitrary power, every Roman official in Alexandria had to be extremely sensitive to the attitude taken toward him by his subjects. If the subjects suddenly began to send complaints to Rome, or broke out in revolt, his office and his life itself were at once gravely threatened. The sensitiveness of Pilate as recorded in the Gospels to the demands of the influential Jews of Palestine was quite typical. The subject people could hope, if they got rid of one ruler, only to have another sent them. Yet they had great power over the fate of any individual ruler.

Philo's reference to this very delicate subject is masterfully tactful. A Roman reader would not usually like to be reminded that the Egyptian mob had it in its power to destroy the prefect, and that so he was their slave. As Philo alludes to it, the man of great natural endowments and ruling genius is tragically made the slave of a despicable master. The implication is that it is a terrible thing that the *politicus* should have to consult the mob in any way, and Philo's sympathy seems to be entirely with him. So he assures the *politicus* that though he may be thus in the power of the mob, he must fearlessly cut and burn whenever social surgery is necessary. That is, far from taunting the ruler with the mob's power over him, the ruler is exorted to free himself of the mob as far as possible. The passage is the subtlest kind of flattery. When it is recalled that the Alexandrian mob tended perennially to turn against the Jews, and that the only hope of the Jews lay in a strong, fearless, and impartial prefect, the objective of Philo is obvious. He wants the prefect to know, if, as is not unlikely, the substance of this document was reported to him, that the Jews will stand by him in asserting his power over the Alexandrian mob. And nothing would be more apt to dispose the prefect to protect the Jews than precisely this assurance.

The next incident from the life of Joseph brings out another of the characteristics of the ideal king or governor. As soon as Joseph went in among the malefactors he exerted a most extraordinary influence upon them. He appeared to them as a solace for their misfortunes, a human ἀλεξίκακος.[38] This term is unusual, and I suspect it was applied to the ideal king in literature now lost to us. It means a warding off of evil, and was used of apotropaic charms, and as an epithet of Zeus, Heracles, and Hermes. It is known that the king was thought to have properly such an influence upon his subjects. He not only must ward off external evil from them, but by the goodness of his character he must purify the souls of his subjects. Diotogenes said of the good king that he is able to put those that look at him into order: "For to look at the good king ought to affect the souls of those who see him no less than a flute or harmony."[39]

In just this sense Joseph was an "averter of evils" (ἀλεξίκακος). Jailors, Philo says, are about the most hardened people imaginable. But this jailor was at once made gentle by Joseph's supreme virtue (καλοκάγα-θία), so that he made Joseph acting jailor with full charge over the prisoners. This incident is only a bit changed from Genesis, where God is said to have acted upon the jailor's heart to make him friendly to Joseph. Philo changes the story to make Joseph's own character the medium of a great transformation in the jailor's soul. With the same purpose, that of making Joseph into a person who transformed the people and environment about him, Philo gives with fine freedom the next details. Under Joseph's rule, says Philo, the prison was transformed. The prisoners

no longer thought it right to call the place a prison but called it instead a reformatory.[40] For in place of the tortures and punishments which they had been enduring night and day as they were beaten and kept in chains and suffered every conceivable affliction, now they were admonished with the formulae (λόγοι) and teachings of philosophy, and with the conduct of the teacher which was more effectual than any speech. For into their midst, like a

---

38. *Jos.*, 80: παρηγόρημα τῶν συμφορῶν ὑπολαμβάνειν ἀλεξίκακον εὑρηκέναι τὸν ἄνθρωπον.

39. See my "Hellenistic Kingship," 72. I should have noted there that music was regarded by the Pythagoreans as the medicine of the soul. Aristoxenus (Diels, *Frag. Vorsok.*, I, 362, line 25) is reported as saying: οἱ Πυθαγορικοὶ καθάρσει ἐχρῶντο τοῦ μὲν σώματος διὰ τῆς ἰατρικῆς, τῆς δὲ ψυχῆς διὰ τῆς μουσικῆς. Cf. Iamblichus, *Vit. Pythag.*, 163. They took the idea probably originally from the use of music, especially of flute music, to cure the soul attacked by Corybantic excitements. See Rohde, *Psyche* (Engl. Transl.), 307, n. 19, and Ecphantus at my *op. cit.*, 89. On this whole subject see now Pierre Boyancé, *Le culte des muses chez les philosophes grecs*, Paris, 1937.

40. Σωφρονιστήριον. The word probably comes from Plato's *Laws*, 908a.

beautifully executed picture, he put his own life of temperance and every virtue, and so converted even those who seemed utterly incorrigible. These, as
the long-standing diseases of their souls abated, upbraided themselves for
what they had done and repented, while they said to themselves: "Where all
this time has this great good been which at first we failed to find? For lo,
when he shines forth, we see as in a mirror our lack of order, and are
ashamed."[41]

The saving power of the king as expressed by the Pythagorean fragments is certainly what Philo is here again working into his story. The
reformation the king effects is that of putting the soul that is full of
disorder (ἀκοσμία) into order, just the point of view of Diotogenes who
uses the term κατακοσμαθῆμεν for the process. In both Philo and Diotogenes the acts (πράξεις) of the king are stressed as important parts of
the king's making this reforming impression, while Philo couples with
this his utterances (λόγοι), like Plutarch and Ecphantus. The offering
of the life (βίος) of the ruler as essentially the saving force does not
appear in Diotogenes, though he is obviously trying to get at this by
enumerating the aspects of the king's life, his reasonings, plans, way of
soul, activities, and the movements and poses of his body. Cicero, drawing upon the same tradition, does speak of the king's life as being of
peculiar significance, for he says of the ideal ruler:

He embraces in himself all those qualities to which he incites and summons
the citizens, and imposes no law on the people which he does not himself ob-
serve; rather, he presents his life as law to the citizens (*suam vitam, ut legem,
praefert suis civibus*).[42]

That is, in representing Joseph, the ideal *politicus,* as a reforming force
in the personal lives of his subjects, Philo is again following conventional hellenistic notions of the ideal king.

Philo continues his vigorous narrative of the dreams and their interpretation. In §106 an interesting detail appears, that when Joseph came
before the king, Pharaoh recognized in him a "token of wisdom"
(δεῖγμα σοφίας), so that "he will be able with his knowledge to dissipate
the ignorance of the sophists of my court as darkness is dissipated by

41. *Jos.,* 86 f.
42. *De Republica,* I, 52. The vision of God has quite the same effect, according to Philo.
Abraham saw God, now as one, now as three, and was impelled thereby to the twin virtues of
piety and humanity: *QG,* iv, 2. The words in Aucher's translation sound strikingly like
Cicero's: "Ista enim politica suam vitam pro exemplo exhibuit nationi dux atque origo eius
compertus," etc.

light." The image of the ideal ruler as a light of knowledge is not by any means a chance one here, but is an integral part of the conception.

The culmination of Joseph's appearing before Pharaoh was his appointment to be ruler of all Egypt under the king. This incident was what Philo had in mind throughout in representing Joseph as the ideal *politicus*. Now we see that he is more than that, he is really the ideal prefect of Egypt, who, like Joseph, was the supreme ruler of Egypt subject only to the emperor, for the emperor was usually called by Eastern Greek speaking peoples the βασιλεύς, the king. No intelligent person in Alexandria could have mistaken Philo's analogy. The Septuagint says of the appointment only "Lo I establish thee this day over all the land of Egypt."[43] Philo represents Pharaoh as saying:

"Come, then, and receive the supervision (ἐπιμέλεια) of my household and the superintendence (ἐπιτροπή) of all Egypt" . . . Then Pharaoh installed him as viceroy of the kingdom (τῆς βασιλείας διάδοχος), or rather, to tell the truth, as king: for while he reserved the nominal sovereignty (ὄνομα τῆς ἀρχῆς) for himself, he dedicated to Joseph the actual rulership (ἡγεμονία).[44]

It is difficult to see how Philo could have made it more clear that in Joseph he saw the type of the Roman prefect. As has already been indicated,[45] in his day the prefect was called ἐπίτροπος. Philo has also included the fact that the appointment of a prefect implied the reservation of sovereignty, though the incumbent is practically the king since he has been assigned the use of the *imperium* (ἐν τοῖς ἔργοις ἡγεμονία). A more accurate definition of the office of the *praefectus Aegypti* could not be drawn up. For the ἐπίτροπος in Egypt was distinguished from the other ἐπίτροποι by the fact that he had been given by Augustus *imperium* on a par with the *proconsul*.[46] So he came to be known as the governor with the *imperium*, the ἡγεμών, very possibly an abbreviation of ἐπίτροπος σὺν ἡγεμονίᾳ, or some such title. When Philo adds the detail that Joseph's commission included also the supervision of the household of Pharaoh he has completed the essential characterization of the prefect. For that officer functioned not only as the procurator with *imperium*, but he was also the steward of Egypt, since Egypt was a part of the personal estate of the emperor.[47]

43. Gen. xli, 41.   44. *Jos.*, 117 ff.   45. See above, p. 23.
46. Ulpian, ap. Justinian, *Digest.*, I, xvii, 1.
47. On the ἐπιμελητής as a steward appointed by the emperor to look after his special interests see Dittenberger, *Syl. Insc. Graec.*, 872.

Philo has inserted all this into the Old Testament account in order to make the gentile reader understand that when he speaks about Joseph he is really describing the ideal prefect. But it would be indelicate to say so outright. Far from that, Philo would have it appear only that he had found in the Old Testament a splendid character who resembled a prefect by his very virtues. The most loyal gentile could not take offence at such delicate flattery. Philo has waited until the respect and restraint of his handling the subject had been impressed upon the reader before indicating the parallel at all, but when he does indicate it, no citizen of Alexandria could have missed the point. Philo has now told the story of Joseph through the great scene of his coming from prison to interpret Pharaoh's dream, and his being appointed viceroy or prefect. But what of Pharaoh's dreams, and the prefect as an interpreter of dreams? This is a point he must stop to clarify. As usual Philo's reaction to a difficulty is to allegorize it. Neither the hellenistic king nor the prefect was considered, ideally or practically, to be an interpreter of dreams. So in a labored allegory Philo explains that the business of a king or ruler is to lead his subjects from their dreams, that is from their false assumptions and valuations into a true understanding of life.[48] He ends with a few words about the chariot, ring, and necklace, which were explained in *De Somniis* as such shameful tokens.[49] These are explained now as only partially degrading. For Philo here temporarily allegorizes Pharaoh as representing not the emperor but the populace of Egypt, by whom, as he has explained before, the freedom of the prefect is limited. These tokens of royalty, which are really obligations to please the masses, are put upon him by the mob. But although they have ultimate power over him, so long as everything is going well the chain and ring are marks of distinction.[50]

After a further digression in which Philo relates the highly artificial allegorization given this part of the story by some of his contemporaries, he goes on with the narrative.

The first detail of the continued story is a striking addition to the account as it appears in Genesis:

But when Joseph had been appointed viceroy (ὕπαρχος)[51] of the king, and had received the superintendence and headship of Egypt, he took a journey

---

48. *Jos.*, 125 ff.   49. See above, p. 23.   50. *Jos.*, 148–150.
51. ὕπαρχος is found in later inscriptions for *praefectus provinciae; CIG*, I, 373*b* (add.); cf. 1080.

to make himself known to all the people of the country. He visited the districts, the so-called nomes, city by city, and implanted a great love for himself in those who saw him, not only because of the benefits which he conferred upon everyone, but because of the remarkable and exceptional graces which were connected with his appearance and general relations with others.[52]

Here is practical advice indeed. The prefect will be the reforming influence idealized by current political theory if he will bestir himself to get out and acquaint himself with his various types of subjects (including, of course, the Jews). We are strikingly reminded of Philo's description of the first years of Flaccus' rule, when that prefect was entirely exemplary. Flaccus began, Philo tells us, by becoming in a short time master of all the involutions of custom in Egypt, which are so complicated and diverse as to be difficult fully to understand even after a lifelong study.[53] Incidentally, that Philo expected the prefect to live up to the standards of the hellenistic royal nature is made very clear in this passage of *In Flaccum*. For Flaccus did not stop with demonstrating this power of mastering the details of his country: such power in itself, important as it is, is not proof of a "soul made for ruling" ($\psi\upsilon\chi\grave{\eta}$ $\dot{\eta}\gamma\varepsilon\mu o$-$\nu\iota\kappa\acute{\eta}$); instead Flaccus went on to show with abundant clarity the tokens of the more brilliant, the royal, nature ($\lambda\alpha\mu\pi\rho\sigma\tau\acute{\varepsilon}\rho\alpha\nu$ $\kappa\alpha\grave{\iota}$ $\beta\alpha\sigma\iota\lambda\iota\kappa\grave{\eta}\nu$ $\phi\acute{\upsilon}\sigma\iota\nu$).[54] He showed majesty ($\sigma\varepsilon\mu\nu\acute{\sigma}\tau\eta\varsigma$)[55] (with which Philo couples "arrogance," used for once in a good sense); he consulted those in office about important decisions (which probably means that he followed local customs and laws, including the Jewish, whenever possible); he pulled down the haughty, and checked suspicious assemblies. Thus he filled the state with good laws. He also organized the army so as to keep the soldiers from disturbing the public peace. Philo's notion of what constituted a good prefect did not change between the two documents.[56]

Another royal trait, that of a more general self-restraint than the sexual control already indicated, appears as Philo goes on to describe Joseph's meeting his brothers when they came up to buy grain.[57] With

52. *Jos.*, 157. I have followed Colson in a conservative translation here. The Greek of the last phrase is ἀλλὰ καὶ ταῖς περὶ τὴν ὄψιν τε καὶ τὴν ἄλλην ὁμιλίαν ἀλέκτοις καὶ ἐξαρέτοις χάρισιν. In this there may be another reference to the catharsis worked upon his subjects by the very looking at a proper ruler.

53. *Flac.*, 3.   54. Ibid., 4 f.

55. On this attribute of kingship see Diotogenes as quoted in my "Hellenistic Kingship," 72. In *Jos.*, 165 Philo speaks of God as altering the face of Joseph εἰς σεμνότερον εἶδος so that his brothers would not recognize him. See above, p. 33.

56. Flaccus is further discussed from this point of view below, p. 101.

57. *Jos.*, 166 ff.

the great power at his disposal it would have been very easy for Joseph
to have taken revenge.[58] Rather than do this, or rashly trust himself
again to their treachery, Joseph simply held himself in restraint until he
could know what sort of men they now were. Philo does not general-
ize, but the notion of restraint (ἐγκράτεια) was too familiar a part of the
ideal royal nature not to have been worked into the narrative some-
where.[59]

The brothers were at first frightened, but saw in their difficulties the
work of "Right, the ephor of human affairs." When Joseph required
that they leave one of their number as hostage of their good faith before
departing, they recognized that the judgment was one made not by "a
human being, but by divinity, or logos, or divine law" (ἄνθρωπος, ἀλλ'
ἢ θεὸς ἢ λόγος ἢ νόμος θεῖος).[60] That is, Joseph was recognized by the
brothers as being only the vehicle through whom logos or divine law
operated. In his official capacity he was divinity, not humanity. This
statement seems of great importance to me as marking Philo's ultimate
concession to the current theory of kingship. Bitterly as he opposes any
assumption of divinity on the part of the ruler himself, or any cult of
the ruler, Philo is quite ready to admit that the good ruler is the media-
tor of divine rulership to men, and although the ruler must be regarded
as a human being in nature, his royal, official, voice is the voice not only
of logos and divine law, but of God.

Shortly afterwards, as Philo goes on to tell the details of the tests of
the brothers, a statement of Genesis is again misrepresented to bring out
the importance of a ruler's respecting Jewish dietary customs. The occasion is the banquet served by Joseph when the brothers came to Egypt
for the second time. The Hebrew (Gen. xliii, 32) says that Joseph set
separate tables for the Hebrews and Egyptians since it was an abomination for an Egyptian if he must eat with a Hebrew. The Septuagint
softened this by saying that it was an abomination for an Egyptian to
eat with a shepherd. Philo turns the whole to the advantage of the Jew
by saying that Joseph feasted each party

58. Philo says that Joseph did not act like a young man suddenly unbalanced by receiving, as
τοσαύτης ἡγεμονίας διάδοχος, an ἀρχὴν μετὰ βασιλέα πρώτην, a man εἰς ὃν ἀνατολαὶ
καὶ δύσεις ἀπέβλεπον: §166.
59. §166: ἐγκρατῶς τὸ πάθος ἐνεγκών. By translating this "konnte er nur mit Mühe sein
brüderliches Gefühl beherrschen," L. Cohn (Philos Werke [see the Bibliography no. 492], I,
191) has altered the sense by inserting the quite unwarranted "brüderliches."
60. Jos., 174.

according to its ancestral practice (κατὰ τὰ πάτρια), for he strongly disapproved of neglecting ancient laws (παλαιοὺς νόμους), especially at a banquet where pleasures should exceed unpleasantness.[61]

That is, from what Philo says a gentile reader would suppose that Joseph's concern was for the Jewish feeling and law, not for Egyptian prejudice. The notion that Egyptians, despised by all non-Egyptian inhabitants of Alexandria, should have been too good to eat with the Jewish patriarchs was something which Philo had no intention of circulating.

The tables at this great feast, Philo reminds the luxury-loving gentile reader, were set with due modesty, quite without vulgar display (ἀπειροκαλία),[62] a thing which after all only reflects small-mindedness.

The gentile reader is again illumined when Philo paraphrases Joseph's judgment by condemning Benjamin to slavery for stealing the royal cup. In Genesis Judah, as spokesman, declares that all the brothers are the slaves of Joseph, to which Joseph replies that only Benjamin shall be a slave. The rest may go. Philo cannot let it stand as simply as this. He must first bring out clearly the fact that, unlike the frequent harshness of Romans in the colonies, Joseph refused to punish the innocent with the guilty.[63] Second, the reader, though he obviously does not know the narrative which Philo is telling for his benefit, seems to have been thought of as able to recognize that this penalty of slavery for theft is not at all in accordance with Jewish procedure, which assigned the death penalty for robbery, and a fine for petty theft.[64] That is, the reader is a person who knows Jewish legal customs, but not Jewish religious teaching or history, which would probably have described very well the Roman rulers of Egypt who had had practical experience with Jewish legal processes, while they were indifferent to other aspects of Jewish life. Particularly would any Roman official have known that the Jews wanted the death penalty for robbery, since such a Jewish penalty must have secured in each case his open or tacit consent, and indeed was worked into Jewish law at just those points where Roman law would itself have required capital punishment. The next time the Jews desired to enforce such a death penalty for robbery Philo did not want the pre-

---

61. *Jos.*, 202. 62. *Ibid.*, 205.

63. On the importance of this issue in Roman Egypt in general, and especially Philo's eyes see my *Jurisprudence*, 134 f.

64. See my *Jurisprudence*, 145 ff., 230 ff.

fect or the *iuridicus* to quote to them this Jewish precedent which gave slavery as the penalty. So the judgment of Joseph, as Philo paraphrases it, reads:

May I never do such a thing as to condemn so many for the sin of one. For how can it be right to make those men share in a penalty who have not abetted the crimes? Let that man alone be punished, since he alone did the deed. Now I am aware that you have assigned death before the city as the penalty of theft. But I conduct such affairs by equity; I therefore lighten the penalty, and sentence him to slavery instead of death.[65]

In the ultimate reconciliation between Joseph and his brothers Philo again makes Joseph speak in terms of the ideal ruler when he has him refer to "the natural kindliness" (ἡ φυσικὴ φιλανθρωπία) which is his general characteristic, though especially manifest in his dealings with his blood-relations.[66] Among the qualities sung in the panegyric by the brothers, when he reveals his identity, they praise Joseph's readiness to forgive (ἀμνησίκακον), his family affection (φιλοίκειον), sagacity (σύνεσις), restraint (καρτερία), fairness (ἰσότης), and kind behavior (δεξιότης), as well as his total lack of the haughtiness and crudity of other rulers.[67] Far from trying to impress his subjects with his personal superiority, he had made no effort, though of the noblest birth, to dispel the general impression that he was really anything better than the slave of Potiphar.

In complete contrast with the grasping Joseph of *De Somniis,* Philo now goes out of his way to expand a simple statement of Genesis (xlvii, 14) that Joseph brought the purchase money of the grain into Pharaoh's house. Philo changes this statement into a brief warning to people, of a type only too common in Roman provinces, who took advantage of a position of authority to build up their private fortunes. Philo says:

The young man was so exceedingly faithful that, although the circumstances and conditions offered very many opportunities for getting money, and he could soon have become the richest man of his day, he yet preferred the genuine and true wealth to the spurious, and the wealth that "sees" to that

65. *Jos.,* §§220 f. The sentence reads in Genesis: "Far be it from me that I should do so (i.e. keep all the brothers as slaves): the man in whose hand the cup is found, he shall be my bondman; but as for you, get you up in peace unto your father."

66. The φιλανθρωπία of the ideal monarch is so familiar as to need little comment. See, e.g., Archytas in my "Hellenistic Kingship," 60.

67. *Jos.,* 246–249.

which is "blind,"[68] and so he stored up in the king's treasury all the silver and gold which he collected as the price of the grain. He took not a single drachma for himself, but was content simply with the gifts which the king graciously gave him for his services.[69]

Philo does not labor this matter. He dares only drop a broad hint.

In view of the great elaboration with which Philo has expanded the story of Joseph from Genesis, it is highly significant that he omits altogether the circumstantial account[70] of how Joseph used the desperate poverty of the populace during the last years of the famine to destroy all freedom in the lower classes, and to make all Egyptians except the priests the personal slaves of Pharaoh, tilling land to which not they but Pharaoh held the title. Philo did not wish the Romans to know that for such highhandedness one of the great heroes of Jewish history offered an example and precedent.

With this omitted, Philo tells how, after the death of Jacob, Joseph continued his magnanimity toward the brothers (the Jews) who had settled in Egypt. At the end Joseph's character as the ideal monarch is summarized.[71] The main emphasis is this time laid upon the three royal virtues of physical beauty, wisdom, and power of speech. Joseph's beauty of body was witnessed, Philo points out, by the love he excited in Potiphar's wife. Physical beauty was one of the most familiar attributes of the ideal ruler.[72] Joseph's intelligence (φρόνησις or σύνεσις) was witnessed throughout the various vicissitudes of his career in the constant power he manifested to introduce attunement into what was dissonant (εὐαρμοστίαν τοῖς ἀναρμόστοις) and concord into discord (συμφωνίαν τοῖς ἐξ αὐτῶν ἀσυμφώνοις). These Pythagorean terms for the ideal rulership are strikingly reminiscent of the Pythagorean king philosophy.[73] Since this royal intelligence was by the thought of the time a divine thing, Philo has said enough to suggest at once to his readers that externally and internally Joseph fully conformed to the standards of the ideal ruler. But one more thing was necessary for the true king or ruler. He must not only look the part, and have the proper gifts and

68. L. Cohn has pointed out that this expression is paralleled in *Abr.*, 25, where J. Cohn (*Philos Werke* [Bibliography no. 492] *ad loc.*) notes that the notion came from Plato's *Laws*, 631c. *Wealth* which can see is virtue in the soul. Cf., *Cont.*, 13; *Agr.*, 54.

69. *Jos.*, 258.   70. In Gen. xlvii, 13–26.   71. *Jos.*, 268 f.

72. On the king's looking the part see Diotogenes in my "Hellenistic Kingship," 72, and above, p. 45.

73. Ibid., 67 ff.

disposition; he must actually have the ruling power, the active gift. Many a man might look like a ruler, and be extremely intelligent, and yet lack the power of leadership which lifted his words into commands. This, Philo means, was Joseph's ultimate gift in the δύναμις λόγων. The true ruler must be endowed with such a power of speech that he needs no compulsion with it: the people are so captivated at his very words that they rush forward spontaneously to obey.[74]

By virtue of his possessing such a character, and having lived such a life, Philo concludes, Joseph showed himself to be the ideal ἡγεμών, or prefect of Egypt.[75]

De Josepho seems to me, then, to have been written from first to last with a single purpose, namely to insinuate to its gentile readers the political philosophy which Jews wished gentiles to believe was theirs. It took the opportunity to suggest that the real source for the highest political ideal of the East, the ideal of a divinely appointed and guided ruler, had had its truest presentation in Jewish literature, and highest exemplification at a time when a Jew was, in contemporary language, prefect of Egypt. In a sense the treatise presents at the same time another aspect of the familiar and fantastic claim of hellenistic Jews, that the Greeks had some great ideas in philosophy because they had had the sense to borrow them from their source, the Jewish scriptures. Here, in political philosophy, Philo is accepting the kingly ideal of the age: he even goes within a hair's breadth of admitting the current corollary of the ideal, namely that the exalted king was really a divine person; but he traces the notion back to the Torah of the Jews. Philo apparently felt that it was very important that gentiles scrutinizing Judaism should break down in their own minds the general prejudice that Jews were a misfit in contemporary society: quite the reverse, he represents, the gentiles might well find the basic principles of politics clarified in Jewish presentation as in no other.

The treatise is written with a finish of rhetorical form, a vividness, which make it one of the most readable tracts from the period. It will be recalled that Philo has himself given the receipt for this sort of political indirectness:

The *politicus* must not just talk, but must have a two-fold manner of speech,

---

74. On the significance of spontaneous obedience and of the king's logos see my "Hellenistic Kingship," 88 ff. Cf., Cicero, *De Legibus*, III, 2: "magistratum legem esse loquentem."

75. *Jos.*, 270.

the one concerned with the truth and genuine advantage, the other based upon opinion and the giving of pleasure. For the *politicus* can not say right out whatever he thinks it would be advantageous for the people to understand, but must conceal some things for the reason that the hearer is often aroused to opposition by hearing what is not flattering, and flatly refuses to obey the truth, so that no improvement is accomplished.[76]

The *politicus,* Philo continues, must often, like doctors, lie to the patient he is about to cauterize. Philo has of course "lied" in this treatise throughout. Joseph, as a symbol of Roman rule, if not as a symbol of the *politicus* in general, he actually despised. But nothing was to be gained by saying as much outright to Romans. Himself a good *politicus,* Philo thinks it better to insinuate, to flatter, and so perhaps to guide into patronage, these Roman rulers whom he hated in his heart. It was also worth while to remind the gentiles that Egypt had at least once been *ideally* governed—by a Jew.

76. A fragment from the fourth book of the *LA;* Harris, *Fragments of Philo*, 8.

CHAPTER IV

STATESMAN AND PHILOSOPHER

UP to this point Philo's writings seem to have shown him talking about the state under three different auspices. Before the Roman rulers he has defended the Jews openly from pagan attacks, and indicated to those rulers his notion of what official policy should be in regard to the Jews. He has also been caught whispering his scorn and hatred of the Romans to his intimate friends in the Mystery, and again giving political advice to, or over the heads of, gentile proselytes. If the inferences from his writings have been correct Philo was an extremely able judge of political matters, and in all probability he became so as a result of much practical experience. In spite of the fact that the great bulk of Philo's writings are so abstractly mystical as to seem to come from a man of quite a different type, I am convinced that Philo spent a considerable part of his life in active and successful political administration of some kind.

Philo is known to have come from a family which made political activity almost inevitable as society was then organized. For it can never be forgotten that Philo's brother, Alexander,[1] was one of the wealthiest Jews of the world, so much so that when Herod Agrippa was at the lowest point in his apparently hopeless vagabondage Alexander lent to him, because he admired the spirit of Agrippa's wife Cypros, the king's ransom of two hundred thousand drachmae.[2] Large a sum as this was, it must have been only a small portion of Alexander's fortune, since Alexander was under no compulsion to advance the money, could have had no real hope of its ever being returned, and so could not have risked a large part of his capital. It is no wonder that in another passage[3] Josephus says that Alexander was "foremost among his contemporaries at Alexandria both for his family and his wealth." In the Roman world great wealth involved great public obligation: hence it is

1. The references to Alexander (some mss. read Alexander Lysimachus) are collected by Wilcken in Pauly-Wissowa, *Real-Encyclopädie*, I, 1441 (no. 26).
2. Josephus, *Antiq.*, XVIII, 159 f. (vi, 3). Alexander did not even trust him not to spend it all before he had left Alexandria, for he would give Agrippa only five talents outright, along with an order for the rest when he reached Dicaearchia in Italy.
3. Ibid., XX, 100 (v, 2).

not surprising that Alexander had an official title, "Alabarch,"[4] which meant that he was the person responsible to the Romans for the collection of taxes, though whether for the taxes of all Alexandria or only for those of the Jews does not appear.[5] He was also the steward (ἐπίτροπος) of Claudius' mother Antonia, and the personal friend (φίλος ἀρχαῖος) of Claudius. During the riots Gaius had imprisoned him, but Claudius on coming to the throne released him. He married one son, Marcus, to Berenice, daughter of Herod.[6]

Another son of Alexander, Tiberius Alexander,[7] deserted his religion, and had a political career even more brilliant than his father's. We first hear of him when he is appointed Roman procurator in Palestine at about 46 A.D., where he seems to have been a severe but acceptable ruler.[8] He was later made prefect of Egypt by Nero,[9] and there played the part of Flaccus himself in turning the legions of Rome upon the Jews during one of the riots, with the result, says Josephus, that fifty thousand Jews were killed.[10] His appointment as prefect had carried with it the rank of a Roman knight, if he had not received it before.[11] He assisted Corbulo in the expedition into Armenia, in the course of which, as *inlustris eques Romanus,* along with a nephew of Corbulo of minor age, he was considered adequate hostage for the safety of King Tiridates himself.[12] Roman historians especially stress Alexander's part in supporting Vespasian's candidacy for the throne. It appears that the eastern army had declared for Vespasian, but that Tiberius Alexander in Egypt was the first Roman governor to recognize him and formally to swear the legions and populace of a province to his support, so that Vespasian's accession was subsequently dated from this recognition rather than from the day of the army's acclamation.[13] In our last glimpse of Tiberius Alexander he is again in Palestine, this time during the great

---

4. He is given this title in the two passages just cited, and in *Antiq.,* XVIII, 259 (viii, 1).

5. On this title see Pauly-Wissowa, *Real-Encyclopädie, s.v.,* I, 1271. See also M. I. Rostovtzeff and C. B. Welles, "A Parchment Contract of Loan from Dura-Europus," *Yale Classical Studies,* II (1931), 50, with bibliography there listed.

6. *Antiq.,* XIX, 276 (v, 1). Marcus seems to have died soon after the marriage.

7. An interesting sketch of the career of Tiberius Alexander is by A. Lepape, "Tiberius Julius Alexander, Préfet d'Alexandrie et d'Égypte," *Bulletin de la Société royale d'Archéologie d'Alexandrie,* N.S. VIII (1934), 331–341. Beside the bibliography given there see William Smith in his *Dictionary of Greek and Roman Biography and Mythology,* I, 126b.

8. *Antiq.,* XX, 100 (v, 2); *BJ,* II, 220 (xi, 6).

9. *BJ,* II, 309 (xv, 1); IV, 616 (x, 6); V, 45 (i, 6); Tacitus, *Hist.,* I, 11; II, 74.

10. *BJ,* II, 487–498 (xviii, 7, 8).   11. Tacitus, *Hist.,* I, 11; *Annales,* XV, 28.

12. *Annales,* XV, 28.

13. *BJ,* IV, 616 f. (x, 6); Tacitus, *Hist.,* II, 74, 79; Suetonius, *Vespas.,* vi, 3.

war against Jerusalem. Tiberius Alexander is under Titus, of course, but is apparently second in command to Titus alone, a position for which Josephus says he "was well qualified both by age and experience."[14] It is possible that Juvenal refers to a statue of him at Rome.[15]

Clearly the wealth and prestige of Philo's family led its members into public service. I cannot believe that Philo himself broke the tradition. Not only does the single incident known from his life show him bearing the heaviest public responsibility of any man in Alexandria, and that at a time when only the most tested members of the group could have been entrusted with his mission: in addition in most of the very few passages with a personal reference he speaks of himself as a *politicus*. Some of these passages we have already met;[16] others are collected in the Introduction to my *Jurisprudence*.[17] The most important passage I published and briefly discussed some years ago.[18] The passage comes at the beginning of that book of *De Specialibus Legibus* which Philo devotes to Jewish criminal law, and may have been inserted here because at this point Philo approaches the subject matter of his life's routine. As it stands, the passage is a cry against his having had to abandon a life of contemplation in order to devote himself to political matters. The passage is so important I shall quote it again in full:

There was once a time when by devoting myself to philosophy and to contemplation of the world and its parts I achieved the enjoyment of that Mind which is truly beautiful, desirable, and blessed; for I lived in constant communion with sacred words and teachings, in which I greedily and insatiably rejoiced.[19] No base or worldly thoughts occurred to me, nor did I crawl for glory, wealth, or bodily comfort, but I seemed ever to be borne aloft in the heights in a rapture of soul, and to accompany sun, moon, and all heaven and the universe in their revolutions. Then, ah, then peeping downwards from the ethereal heights and directing the eye of my intelligence as from a watchtower, I regarded the untold spectacle of all earthly things, and reckoned myself happy at having forcibly escaped the calamities of mortal life.

14. Josephus gives him two titles: πάντων τῶν στρατευμάτων ἐπάρχων, BJ, VI, 237 (iv, 3); and σύμβουλος ταῖς τοῦ πολέμου χρείαις, BJ, V, 46 (i, 6).

15. So Satire I, 130, was interpreted by B. Holyday, in a note to his translation of Juvenal and Persius, Oxf., 1673, 16, and this most probable conjecture has usually been repeated by subsequent editors.

16. See above, pp. 27, 32.   17. See especially pp. 2 f., 9.

18. "Philo and Public Life," *The Journal of Egyptian Archeology*, XII (1926), 77–79.

19. Ἐνευφραινόμην, a word clearly reminiscent of Prov. viii, 30, where Wisdom in her rapture before the Father says: καθ' ἡμέραν δὲ εὐφραινόμην ἐν προσώπῳ αὐτοῦ ἐν παντὶ καιρῷ, ὅτε ἐνευφραίνετο τὴν οἰκουμένην συντελέσας.

And yet there lurked near me that most grievous of evils, Envy, with its hatred of all that is fair (ὁ μισόκαλος φθόνος), which suddenly fell upon me, and did not cease forcibly dragging upon me until it had hurled me down into the vast sea of political cares (μέγα πέλαγος τῶν ἐν πολιτείᾳ φροντίδων), where I am still tossed about and unable even so much as to rise to the surface. But though I groan at my fate, I still struggle on, for I have, implanted in my soul from early youth, a desire for education which ever has pity and compassion upon me, and lifts me up and elevates me. This it is by which I can sometimes raise my head, and by which, though their penetration is dimmed by the mists of alien concerns, I can yet cast about in some measure with the eyes of my soul upon my surroundings, while I long to suck in life pure and unmixed with evils. And if unexpectedly there is quiet and calm in the political tumults, I emerge from the waves winged though unable to fly, but am blown along by the breezes of understanding (ἐπιστήμη), which often persuades me to run away as it were for a holiday with her from my pitiless masters, who are not only men but also the great variety of practical affairs which are deluged upon me from without like a torrent.[20] Still, even in such a condition, I ought to thank God that while I am inundated I am not sucked down into the depths. Rather, though in despair of any good hope I had considered the eyes of my soul to be incapacitated, now I open them and am flooded with the light of wisdom, so that I am not abandoned for the whole of my life to darkness. And so, behold, I dare not only read the sacred expositions of Moses, but even, with a passion for understanding, I venture to examine each detail, and to disclose and publish what is not known to the multitude.[21]

This passage had traditionally been taken as a reference to Philo's election to lead the embassy to Gaius, but that identification had only to be challenged to be abandoned. As a protest against a life of concern with legal matters the passage has point, while as a reference to the embassy it has no place whatever in its context. Further the passage shows that Philo's literary career as an interpreter of the Bible was a function of his life *after* he had gone into political affairs, carried on as a hobby or escape from politics. If the political life itself began only after Philo

20. The passage is clearly to be understood in the light of Plato, *Rep.*, VI, 509 seq. There διάνοια leads men to τὰ μαθηματικά, etc., a type of knowledge far superior to πίστις and εἰκασία, but much inferior to νοῦς. Deprived now of νοῦς, Philo has left only the eyes of διάνοια, with which ἐπιστήμη seems here synonymous, for though he has wings he cannot fly in his own strength, but must be blown along from without. That is, it is impossible for him, during merely temporary interruptions in his work, to rise into a consummation of perfect mystical apprehension, though he is superior to the mass in still having his powers of διάνοια or ἐπιστήμη.

21. *Spec.*, iii, 1–6.

had become an old man, as he was when he went to Gaius, this would mean, presumably, that his great corpus was composed in the off moments of a generally harassed old age, a supposition which its bulk makes impossible. What the passage tells us is that Philo spent a time in his youth as a recluse (probably with the Therapeutae), but felt that his people needed him so much that he returned to them, and thereafter consoled himself during his leisure hours with writing about the mystic message of the Scriptures, while be devoted his main career to public service.

The question is how much Philo really repented the necessity of living a busy life with men. Our most important single passage for answering it is the following:

For many a time have I myself forsaken friends and kinsfolk and country and come into a wilderness, to give my attention to some subject demanding contemplation, and derived no advantage from doing so, but my mind scattered or bitten by passion has gone off to matters of the contrary kind. Sometimes, on the other hand, amid a vast throng I have a collected mind. God has dispersed the crowd that besets the soul and taught me that a favorable and unfavorable condition are not brought about by differences of place, but by God who moves and leads the car of the soul in whatever way he pleases.[22]

That is, in one of the few passages where Philo speaks of himself he represents his life in the crowd as the supreme tragedy of his life, while in another he says that place makes no difference whatever, and that he is more apt to find his mystical abstraction in the midst of the crowd than in the solitude of the desert. The conflict in Philo's mind was deeper than mere indecision about the value of solitude: it went on until at one time he would think of man as a rounded being, whose full career could not be achieved without a fructification of the spiritual in the physical and social realms, and at another that man could be perfect only as he renounced the material side of human nature, and centered himself as abstractedly as possible in God. It was because of this conflict that in one mood Philo praised the state, in another denounced it, while his political theory seems at first as unstable as his emotions. This chapter will be concerned with Philo's different statements about society.

A definite part of man's nature is its social side. Man is, says Philo, a

22. *LA*, ii, 85.

gregarious and herding animal (ἀγελαστικὸν καὶ σύννομον ζῷον), and is thus commanded by nature to agreement (ὁμόνοια) and social intercourse (κοινωνία); for Nature has given man "reason which brings men together in an attunement and mixture of customs" (λόγος συναγωγὸς εἰς ἁρμονίαν καὶ κρᾶσιν ἠθῶν).[23] This statement, while reminiscent of Plato,[24] is still closer to Aristotle.[25] As men come into their better nature, develop in virtue, the effect is that they become devoted to problems of the household, state, and society (οἰκονομικοί, πολιτικοί, κοινωνικοί), since the result of virtue is the introduction of the best laws and the universal scattering of the seeds of peace.[26] What marks the mind of a man who is running away from God is that he thinks that the "human mind by itself (μόνος ὁ ἀνθρώπινος νοῦς) set up the arts, professions, laws, and customs, and the standards of political, private, and public rights": God is their ultimate author, Philo plainly implies.[27] In this it is recognizable that Philo is true to the best political tradition of Greek civilization. But he alternates bewilderingly between this attitude toward the state and another one, the ascetic and individualistic attitude, which seems to have originated with the Cynics and to have run through much of Stoic and Sceptic teaching, an attitude in which the ideal man is thought to be so exclusively a citizen of the universe that he scorns the corporate life of his environment. There were of course Stoics who, after the manner of Cicero, regarded the world-state as the foundation and background of the civic law and relations of men, and who accordingly thought it the business of the philosopher to devote himself to making the earthly state as near the ideal as possible. The interesting thing is that Philo strongly upholds both solutions of this problem, insisting that the philosopher's concern with the true state, the world, cut him off from obligation or concern with society, and then insisting just as heartily that this contact with the world-state put the philosopher under special obligation to serve the human organization. His remarks on both sides must be examined.

In advocating the participation of the philosopher in politics Philo says that the full development of virtue leads to the political virtues, and

23. *Decal.*, 132.   24. *Politicus*, 311b f.

25. *Polit.*, I, 1253a 8 ff.: διότι δὲ πολιτικὸν ὁ ἄνθρωπος ζῷον πάσης μελίττης καὶ παντὸς ἀγελαίου ζῴου μᾶλλον, δῆλον. οὐθὲν γὰρ, ὡς φαμέν, μάτην ἡ φύσις ποιεῖ, λόγον δὲ μόνον ἄνθρωπος ἔχει τῶν ζῴων. Treitel (*Philos Werke* [Bibliography no. 492], *ad loc.*) suggests that the φύσις in the above quotation from Philo is a Stoic locution for God, not recognizing that it came from Aristotle with the rest of the statement.

26. *Mut.*, 149 f.; cf. *Fug.*, 209.   27. *LA*, iii, 30.

hence that no one should abandon public life for ascetic individualism. Or Philo may reverse it and represent applied virtue as the best introduction to the more metaphysical virtue of the ascetic. From the latter point of view he insists:

Truth would properly blame those who without examination abandon the transactions and business activity of civic life and profess to despise fame and pleasure. For they are pretending, and do not really despise these things; they are only putting forward their filthiness, their somberness, and their austere and squalid way of living as a bait, on the pretext that they are lovers of propriety and self-control and patient endurance.[28]

Any person of acumen, he continues, can readily see through their pretense, and will challenge their hypocrisy, which is revealed in their secretly lending money, taking opportunities for indulgence, and currying favor with men in authority. So he goes on:

You have ridiculed civic life (πολιτεία), perhaps because you have not recognized how serviceable it is. You should first exercise and train yourself in the private and public affairs of life, and become yourselves politicians and household managers by means of the kindred virtues, the household managing and the political virtues; then, when you have in great abundance equipped yourself, go on to the departure into another and better life. For it is good to fight through the practical life before the contemplative life, as a sort of preliminary combat before the more advanced struggle.[29] . . . And in general it is necessary that those who think fit to lay claim to the divine δίκαια should first fulfill the human δίκαια. First it is great folly for those who are unable to compass the less to suppose that they can achieve the greater. Accordingly seek first the virtue which exists among men, that you may be established in the virtue which looks to God.[30] . . . "Flee into Mesopotamia," that is into the middle of the swollen river of life, and take heed lest you be swept away and drowned; rather stand absolutely rigid, and repel with might the torrent of concerns as it pours in upon you from above, from either side, and from everywhere.[31]

Philo speaks[32] with sharp disapproval of the men who

live alone by themselves as though they were in a desert or were disembodied souls; men who recognize neither city nor village nor household nor any or-

---

28. *Fug.*, 33. Colson and Whitaker translate the phrase τὰς ἐν τῷ πολιτικῷ βίῳ πραγματείας καὶ πορισμούς, "the business and financial side of a citizen's life." The context seems to me to imply a wider range of meaning in the πραγματείας.

29. Ibid., 35 f.   30. Ibid., 38.
31. Ibid., 49.   32. *Mig.*, 90; cf. *Immut.*, 16–19.

ganization of men whatever, and despise, in their quest of naked and abstract truth, the things prized by the mob.

Such people, he explains, go against the plain teaching of Scripture not to despise customs and laws founded by excellent men of old. He quotes the Peripatetic doctrine, the same doctrine as was used by Pythagoreans in their legislation, that the goods of life are of three kinds, spiritual, bodily, and external, and apparently approves these as necessary to a man's living a full life.[33] He points out that the Jewish Law is divided like the Decalogue into two tables, one concerned with piety and holiness to God, the other with justice to men and brotherly love. The one is the task of the soul, the other of the body, so that the true life combines both the theoretical and practical. In doing each alike, then, man is following the highest Law.[34]

This attitude seems a reflection of a common one in Philo's day; for Dio Chrysostom develops the same position at length in his oration περὶ ἀναχωρήσεως,[35] where, although Dio recognizes that the philosopher must have quiet for his meditations (§11), yet he sees the fruit of philosophy in an ability to face practical life (§14), and sums up his argument by saying that his purpose has been to show that the soul must be accustomed to perform its duties and carry on its cogitations everywhere, both in complete confusion and in total quiet. Otherwise loneliness and quiet have nothing especial to offer men to protect them from thinking or erring in every sort of anomalous way (§26).

In the passages quoted Philo is quite as specific as Dio in asserting the value, indeed the necessity, of attention to society and public affairs. But in other passages Philo takes diametrically the opposite point of view. The contrast comes out most clearly when Philo, speaking from his heart to Jews in the *Allegory,* compares the philosophy of Joseph with that of his brothers.

It is to counteract the false elements in Joseph's thinking and nature, says Philo, that Jacob sends him to find his brothers. For Joseph's character up to this point, it will be recalled, had been revealed in his many-colored cloak, which signified that he was "an exponent of a doctrine full of mazes and hard to disentangle." It is with an eye to statecraft rather than to truth that Joseph moulds his theories of the three sorts of goods, the external, the bodily, and the psychic.

33. *QG*, iii, 16; on this see Bréhier, *Les Idées,* 18, 260.   34. *Spec.*, ii, 63 f.
35. *Orat.*, xx, ed. de Budé, II, 324–334. See Bréhier, *Les Idées,* 268.

For though these are distinguished from each other by all their natural properties, the politician brings them together and combines them into one, and claims that he can demonstrate that each is in need of each, all in need of all, and that the perfect and complete good is made up of the aggregate resulting from getting them all together, while the individual constituents of this sum, although they are parts and elements of goods, are not themselves fully goods. The politician's argument is that just as neither fire, nor earth, nor any of the four elements from which the universe has been created is the cosmos, which is made up of a collection and mixture of these elements into a single entity, so in the same way happiness is not to be found in external goods, nor in bodily states, nor in the psychic realm, separately and taken apart each by itself. Each of them has the character of being a part or element of the good, but the good itself is an aggregate of them all together.[36]

In contrast to Joseph who holds this erroneous opinion are the brothers who are aware of the real nature of the good, namely that "only that which is noble is good" (μόνον τὸ καλὸν ἀγαθόν), which is the peculiar property of the soul as soul. They recognize that the so-called bodily goods are goods only in name.[37] The mind which enters into the holies of the divine mind is in contrast to the ordinary human mind, which, even when occupied with the noblest human concerns (including specifically statutory laws, τὰ θέσει νόμιμα), is moving always on the level of "opinion."[38]

That is, for practical purposes and from the social point of view, it is true that the good life involves health, wealth, and external peace, as well as spiritual maturity. On this level moves the politician. In contrast Philo esteems the man of the higher level, for whom the good is "peculiar to the soul qua soul" (ἴδιον ψυχῆς ὡς ψυχῆς).[39] He speaks with approval of a person who can flee from household, fatherland, kinsmen, and friends,[40] and says that the most undeniable proof of perfection is for a man to be a fugitive to God, having abandoned all concern for the things of creation.[41] For love of God and love of the world cannot coexist within a single person any more than light and darkness can mingle.[42] The passage has the absoluteness of the "house divided against

---

36. Det., 7, 8.   37. Ibid., 9.   38. LA, iii, 126.

39. The man concerned with political affairs is in Mig., 160 μέσος between Pharaoh, who typifies the realm of the body, and Jacob, who typifies τὰ κατὰ ψυχήν. The same contrast appears in QG, iv, 47, where the vita operativa is described as partaking of both good and evil, the good of the vita contemplativa, and the bad of the vita condecens.

40. Praem., 17; cf. Agr., 65.   41. Sacr., 120.

42. Fragment from John Damasc., Sacr. Parall., p. 370 b (ap. Mang. II, 651).

itself." His remarks about the "politician" are here consistently disparaging, though not all equally bitter. One who is concerned with public affairs would seem to be of a definitely inferior order to one whose concerns are other-worldly; the former is, as we have seen, an "addition" to the man who lives according to nature, with the plain implication that the "addition" spoils the purity of the original.[43] One can become worthy of inheriting God only by fleeing from all handmade and voluntary laws.[44] It was from this point of view that he made his impassioned protest against the degradation and confusion of having to leave a life of contemplation for political duties.[45]

To go into the background of Philo's views of the value of social life would drive us afield into the problem of the nature of the good for man as it was discussed by the various philosophers. Plato and Aristotle could easily be shown to have the same vacillation between praise of the contemplative life and active interest in a philosopher's making practical application of his most abstract thought in public affairs. Cicero speaks of the conflict in Stoicism between a doctrine that the good is only a matter of inner adjustment to nature, to which the Stoics were never consistently loyal in practice,[46] and a teaching which made room for external goods as inferior, but real, goods.[47] It is true that a solution had been offered by the older Stoics, for Diogenes Laertius represents them as teaching that of the three types of life, the contemplative, the practical, and the rational, the third is preferable, since the "rational animal" is expressly designed by nature for both contemplation and action.[48] Such quotations could be multiplied, but Zeller[49] has long ago shown that these statements and their frequent application by Stoics were in real conflict with an ascetic tendency which inclined many Stoics toward the life of a recluse. The point is that Philo's vacillation between the two cannot be taken as indication that he was treating the subject loosely because it had no personal interest for him. His very inconsistency is a reflection of the spirit of the age. In many moods he sin-

---

43. *Jos.*, 31.   44. *Mut.*, 26.

45. *Spec.*, iii, 1 ff.; see above, pp. 66 f.

46. *De Finibus*, IV, ix, 22: Quae est igitur ista philosophia, quae communi more in foro loquitur, in libello suo?

47. *Ibid.*, IV, vi, 15.

48. VII, 130. βίων δὲ τριῶν ὄντων, θεωρητικοῦ καὶ πρακτικοῦ καὶ λογικοῦ, τὸν τρίτον φασὶν αἱρετέον· γεγονέναι γὰρ ὑπὸ τῆς φύσεως ἐπίτηδες τὸ λογικὸν ζῷον πρὸς θεωρίαν καὶ πρᾶξιν.

49. *Philosophie der Griechen*, III, i (1909), 292 ff., 300 ff.

cerely sympathized with the incipient eremitic urge which was already
driving men of his day to the desert; yet, more usually, he agreed with
the attitude later expressed in the letter of James, for he felt that philosophy, or contemplation, must fructify in social manifestation and
benefit. I say that the latter was his more usual feeling since he himself
tells us that he had often tried the ascetic life but had not what the
Church came later to call the "gift" which would enable him to practice the life with success.[50] His own ideal had to be the living of his life
in the crowd, in the course of which he must keep his inner citadel de-
tached from men and filled with divine thoughts, but always with the
end in view that only so could he be ready to direct the private and
public affairs of his fellows.[51] Indeed Philo is to be distinguished from
the other writers of his period in that he has personally and passionately
tried both sorts of life: his vacillation about the value of social life is not
merely an echo of current literary forms, but comes out of the experiences of his own soul.

And Philo is further to be distinguished from other writers of his age
in his sincere attempt to account for the value of the two types of life,
and to offer a picture of their ideal reconciliation. He does so in one of
his most elaborate allegories. By clever manipulation of scriptural texts,
into which we need not go, he justifies the statement that men are the
children of two parents. The father is the "right reason" (ὀρθὸς λόγος)
of nature, or natural law;[52] the mother is the encyclical course of
studies, those based upon human observation and inference. The father
commands us to follow and obey nature, and to pursue naked and bare
truth; the mother demands obedience to "the things made just by stat-
ute" (τὰ θέσει δίκαια), "which the ancients who preferred appearance
to truth established in cities, races, and regions."[53] The children of
these parents, that is mankind, are of four kinds. The first class are
obedient to both parents, the second are obedient to neither, while the
other two sorts are half-perfect (ἡμιτελής), for they obey the commands
only of one or the other of the parents. Of these four the first class, the
one which obeys both parents, is incomparably the best; the second,
obeying neither, is utterly depraved, while those who obey the father
exclusively are superior to those who obey the mother exclusively.[54]

50. *LA*, ii, 85.   51. *Virt.*, 3.
52. See my *By Light, Light*, 388 f.   53. *Ebr.*, 34.
54. Ibid., 35.

Those who follow the statutory law alone, he goes on to explain, are apt to be led into idolatry and superficial philosophy, and thereby lose the finer qualities of the soul. Here is the *politicus* of Philo's other passages. Those who follow the law of nature alone do indeed qualify themselves as priests among men by slaying the brother, the body, and their neighbors, human society; they slay as well their immediate families, that is their tendency to form opinions on the basis of probability.[55] Such action will be thought by God to be worthy of unreckoned praise and reward.[56] Here are the people of ascetic life whom we have been meeting; they are highly praised, but are none the less inferior to those who are obedient to both parents as Philo himself was trying to be. For it would seem that those who obey both laws are no less pleasing to God than those who obey the father only, while there is advantage in obeying the mother also, since one who does so is bound to be an object of love not only to God but also to men, because such a person is motivated by social-mindedness (κοινωνία) as well as by piety.[57] For the ideal man, the sage, is one who can function fully and freely in the realms of piety, natural science, and moral philosophy, both in theory and practice, which latter implies politics and legislation.[58] And yet this same sage is but an alien resident (μέτοικος) in mortal affairs, and he properly contemns, *inwardly* flees from, the life and city of the passions.[59] In another passage[60] the figure of the father and mother is developed more briefly, but with the same conclusion that those who attend to either practical or divine affairs exclusively are half perfect in virtue (ἡμιτελεῖς τὴν ἀρετήν) while only those are complete (ὁλόκληροι) who are distinguished in both.[61]

This I take to be Philo's real attitude. For the *politicus* in its usual sense, the man who centers his life in social problems, Philo had little respect. True, he was better than a man with no spiritual or social sense

55. *Ebr.*, 70.   56. Ibid., 74.   57. Ibid., 84.
58. Ibid., 91 f.   59. Ibid., 100 ff.   60. *Decal.*, 107–110.
61. Heinemann, *Philos Werke* (Bibliography no. 492), V, 35, n. 4, has shown that this passage is quite akin to rabbinic interpretation of Prov. viii, 1: "My son, hear the instructions of thy father and forsake not the laws of thy mother." In the rabbinic explanation (*T. Sanh.* 102a) the father is God, the mother the community of Israel, and so the whole means loyalty to both religion and popular customs. Heinemann thinks that the rabbinic tradition was the source of Philo's interpretation, though he thinks that Philo did not have it from Palestinian teachers directly. The framework of the figure, the laws of the father and of the mother, must go back to this verse, with or without Palestinian suggestion; but the content of Philo's distinction is definitely Greek, very much in harmony with two fragments ascribed to Archytas (Fragments 14 and 15 in Mullach, *Fragmenta Philosophorum Graecorum*, I, 559). It would seem to be a Pythagorean distinction set forth in terms of the scriptural metaphor.

at all, one completely lost in self interest: but none the less a man en-grossed in practical problems to the exclusion of higher interests was essentially inferior to the man who lived for higher things. So com-mitted was Philo to those "higher" things, the mystic quest, that he at times begrudged all contact with material and social existence. But the fully rounded man, as it has appeared frequently in the exposition of the Mystery,[62] returns from the Mystery to be a guide to his fellows. Society, never to be an end in itself for any man, called the mystic with all the compulsion of *noblesse oblige* to dedicate the fruit of his spir-itual experience to the beneficent regulation of the lives of others.[63]

Philo has little to say on the nature and value of the organized state as such. Cities or states are not entirely human creations. At least they are subject in their rise and fall to "what the common multitude of men call Fortune." Τύχη, however, did not belong in Philo's philosophy; she was much too uncontrolled a deity to be adjusted to his monotheism. Instead, in a very significant passage, he calls the majestic roll of the world's dominant powers, Greece, Macedonia, Persia, Parthia, Egypt, Ethiopia, Carthage, Libya, and Pontus, each of which, except the then powerful Parthia, has had to decline. This is not chance, he says, but a manifestation of a great cyclic movement in the Logos (χορεύει γὰρ ἐν κύκλῳ λόγος ὁ θεῖος). The Logos

which is in constant flux (ἀεὶ ῥέων) makes distribution city by city, nation by nation, country by country. What these had once, those have now. What all had, all have. Only from time to time are the possessions of each ex-changed back and forth, to the end that the inhabited world might as a whole be like a single state and enjoy the best of constitutions, a democracy.[64]

This is a purely Heraclitean formulation, combined with the idea in the puzzling fragment of Anaximander[65] that the things which come into existence and pass away "make reparation and satisfaction to one an-

---

62. See, *e.g., By Light, Light,* 230 ff. For example Philo says of Abraham: "For the nature which is pious is also kindly, and the same person will exhibit both qualities, holiness to God and justice to man": *Abr.,* 208. Cf. *QG,* iii, 42, and Geiger, 7–17, who, as usual, is looking so earnestly for Stoic parallels that he misses the meaning of much of his material.

63. It is interesting that in one passage (*Sacr.,* 78 f.) Philo seems to foreshadow the Matthean form of the logion to the rich young man. The contrast is between the good on the level of ordinary life, and on that of the "perfect," or of one aspiring for perfection. Philo's whole vacil-lation, like that of his age, shows how much the medieval attitude was predetermined by the problems of life in the tempestuous hellenistic world, before Christianity and long before the declining days of Rome.

64. *Immut.,* 173–176.   65. Diels, *Frag. Vorsok.,* Anaximandros, 9.

other for their injustice according the ordering of time." It is utterly incompatible with the Stoic cycle of the Logos as the "great year." For in Philo's statement the Logos flux involves a single and eternal phenomenon in which individual foci of predominance emerge and disappear while the Logos keeps everything as a whole in a democracy, that is, in a state of balance. The Stoic notion, on the contrary, saw the Logos develop into a great manifestation of phenomena, and then dissolve into the original oneness in the course of stated epochs. The movement was one of transition of the Logos as a whole with the Stoics: here it is the temporary emergence of parts, and their levelling again as the flux throws out new wave crests. The sea of Logos remains fundamentally unchanged by the temporary rise of a wave. We know that Heraclitus tied up his theory with politics,[66] though the fragments are too scanty for us to have any notion as to how far he developed his thought. Since Philo has in other points betrayed a knowledge of Heraclitean tradition quite beyond our ordinary sources of information about that tradition,[67] it is entirely possible that this highly important passage should be regarded as a reliable bit of Heraclitean teaching. So I regard it myself, though, in the absence of reference to Heraclitus, proof is not to be attempted.

To Philo, then, whether the notion came to him from Heraclitus or not, an individual state was a temporary phenomenon in the great flux of Logos. Since Philo was not, we know well, a materialist in his conceptions of Logos, though he followed the original association of Logos with Law to be found in the Heraclitean fragments, he seems to have considered that the divine Logos, which was in itself a great immaterial formative force and law, was subject to temporary concentrations out of which grew great empires. None of these concentrations had either cosmic or permanent significance. From the point of view of the world of phenomena, the emergence of a particular empire was comparable to the election of an individual citizen to office. Translated into the language of Roman statecraft, the cosmic imperium could be entrusted to an individual nation for a term, as that nation dominated all men for a time, although the cosmic imperium was itself the prerogative of the Logos, the body politic. But I am sure that this conception did not affect Philo's more usual thought that from the point of view of the universe

---

66. See especially his Fragment 91 (Bywater).
67. See my "Neo-Pythagorean Source," *Yale Classical Studies*, III (1932), 155 ff.

as a whole, including God, the rule was a monarchy. God's rule expressed itself in giving off the great Stream of Logos-Law, whose effect upon the material substrata was to produce the phenomenal world. In relation to God the phenomena were subject to a monarchy: in relation to each other there existed a great democracy in which no individual was so important as the body politic of Logos and matter as a whole, and no individual had any more permanent importance than the others. It is unfortunate that Philo has not developed the notion at greater length, but the reason for his failure to do so seems to me not far to seek. It has already appeared that Philo is very cautious indeed in his references to politics. In view of that general wariness, the absence of Rome from the roll of powers takes on significance. If Philo had developed his theory, he must inevitably have concluded that Roman rule would suffer sooner or later the same decline as the others. The only way in which the eternal flux of Logos would or could cease representing itself in the rise and fall of empires would be by the assertion of the monarchy of God in a more direct way, the erection of a Kingdom of God to rule the world in place of the succession of human kingdoms. That is, the logical outcome of Philo's remarks leads us directly to a Greek formulation and justification of the Jewish messianic hope, a hope which we have found veiled but strongly present in Philo's writings. Whether Philo went privately all the way with this reasoning or not, certainly his remarks about the succession of empires must have suggested to a contemporary reader what it has suggested to us, that the rule of Rome itself was something to be taken and endured for the time, since like all others it must be transitory.[68]

A state is thus the direct product of the Logos: for that reason it ought to conform to the Logos. This it can and should do primarily in

68. This theory of the flux of the Logos has very considerable possibilities philosophically. Aside from the reconciliation of the notion with the rule of God, the Logos in the Heraclitean sense is as good a term as any of the modern ones to describe the material-immaterial substrate of phenomena toward which modern science is tending. The theory that this becomes temporarily concentrated in different spots and periods of humanity is quite the most plausible one I know to account not only for the rise and fall of empires and civilization, but also for the amazing concentrations of other types of genius than the military and political. Why the Periclean Age, or Fifteenth Century Tuscany, or Elizabethan England? Economic interpretations utterly fail to account for the concentration of supreme genius represented by these terms. Its sudden disappearance is just as unaccountable. Of course the "cycles of the Logos" is a theory which, for us as for Philo and Heraclitus, is a myth, but no more mythical than modern attempts to construct a whole out of the scattered hints of modern physics, and of all these myths this one seems best to deserve being called ὁ εἰκὼς μῦθος.

its legal system, for while a state is made up of dwellings, inhabitants, and laws,[69] its being is fundamentally in its laws.

I have elsewhere discussed Philo's notion of natural law, and need not go into details here.[70] In substance Philo thought of the Absolute as being the "archetypal pattern of laws, just as the conceptual sun is of the sensible sun, for from the invisible source the conceptual sun furnishes visible brilliance to the sun that is seen."[71] God is not Himself law, for that would be too specific a formulation to be associated with the Absolute. But He is the pattern and source of law, which gets its first and highest expression in the Logos as it streams from Him, the Law of all other things. The law of the state is always to be tested by its conformity with this supreme Law. But the great difficulty is how to get a body of state law which will stand such a test. From the point of view of state law, Philo uses the familiar Stoic definition: law is a logos or formula ordaining what is to be done and prohibiting what is not to be done.[72] This definition is also applied to the law of Nature, which is "the Logos of Nature ordaining what must be done, and prohibiting what must not be done."[73] It is this Logos of Nature, the ὀρθὸς λόγος, which is the source of all other laws.[74] Philo did not mean this literally. Unfortunately it is an ideal, not a reality, that the Logos is the source of civil law. Even in Athens and Sparta, fine laws as these cities had, the civil laws were not the ideal, he points out, and the sage had frequently to disregard them, look beyond them to the higher law itself.[75] This was precisely the position taken in all Greek legal tradition. Always there was the desire to make the written law what it ought to be, a codification of what was true, right, just, the will of the gods, but always there recurred the sense of failure in a given body of laws.[76] Sometimes the law allowed a scoundrel to live with impunity, and sometimes an innocent man was legally guilty. As Aristotle said, "According to the written law he is liable and has committed an offence, but according to the truth he has committed no offence, and this sort of problem is a matter of equity."[77] The matter was much discussed in Philo's day.[78] In fact

69. Post., 52.
70. See my By Light, Light, Chap. II.
71. Spec., i, 279.
72. Praem., 55.
73. Jos., 29; Mig., 130. For Stoic parallels see SVF, III, 314, 315, 332. But the definition must not be taken as exclusively Stoic, for see Arist., Rhet., 1373b 19 f. On confusing Philo's notion of the Law of Nature with the Stoic see reference in note 70.
74. Prob., 47.
75. Ibid.
76. Hirzel, Themis, Dike, und Verwandtes, 108 ff., treats this very well.
77. Rhet., i, 13; 1374a 36 f. See this entire chapter.
78. Cicero, Repub., ii, 43.

only the Jewish Law was in Philo's mind a reliable codification of the law of Nature, the Logos, and even the Mosaic codification, I have shown, was to him quite inadequate, as a code, for man's higher development.[79] All other human systems were to him the product of human contingency, and so were best to be described as an "addition" to nature,[80] with the plain implication that like any addition to perfection they were essentially inferior and marring. Laws of men are a superfluity (περισσός), for that "arrogance" is a superfluity by which deceit is introduced into what should be an unerring life. By it various civil laws are introduced, with the result that instead of a universal observance of "the true standards of right" (τὰ αὐτὰ δίκαια) men follow custom (ἔθος), without once dreaming of "the universal and unchanging laws of Nature" (τὰ κοινὰ τῆς φύσεως καὶ ἀκίνητα νόμιμα).[81] Indeed Philo states the ideal of a society regimented by natural law usually when he is protesting against the fact that such regimentation is completely lacking in actual states.

State organization as it appears among the various peoples is an "addition" to Nature which has sovereign power over all things. For this world is the Megalopolis, or Great City, and uses a single constitution and a single law, and this is the Logos of Nature which enjoins what is to be done, and prohibits what is not to be done. But the variously situated states are unlimited in number and use different constitutions and dissimilar laws; for the different states various customs and laws have been invented and enacted in addition [to the law of Nature]. Now the cause [of such disparity] is the lack of intermingling and of social life not only between Greeks and barbarians, or barbarians and Greeks, but also within a single race between people of the same kin. Men seem to lay the blame [for their lack of intercourse or their bad laws] where it does not belong, as they point to bad times, failure of crops, poverty of soil, or to their geographical location by the sea or inland, or on an island or the mainland, or some other such geographical factor. But they do not mention the true reason, their greed and faithlessness toward each other, which lead them, since they are not pleased with the laws of Nature, to decree as "laws" whatever the crowd unites in supposing will be of public benefit. Thus naturally the individual constitutions are an "addition" to the one constitution of Nature; for the civic laws are "additions" to the right reason (ὀρθὸς λόγος) of Nature, and the politician is an addition to the man who lives according to Nature.[82]

79. See my *By Light, Light,* Chap. III and passim.   80. See above, p. 35.
81. *Agr.,* 43.   82. *Jos.,* 28–31.

Similarly in a long discussion of the unreliability of our perceptions Philo's chief illustration of human fallibility is the extreme divergence of civil laws in the various parts of the world, so that nothing is thought good by some that is not condemned as evil by others. In such a state of affairs the man who accepts blindly the traditions and laws of his own environment is little better than a slave. In this passage Philo's only conclusion is that we must suspend judgment upon specific definitions of the good, since even philosophers are in disagreement upon every essential point.[83] He contrasts the laws of a given tribe with those of the Olympians.[84] Human society is so corrupted by "arrogance," which leads men into mutual injustice, tyranny, and oppression, that true law like the Mosaic Code could not be given in a city, and had to be promulgated in the desert.[85] In contrast to the law of Moses the laws of other people seemed to be motivated by a myriad of pretexts, such as wars, tyrannies, or other contingencies, or by the fact that people had discarded true law in time of luxurious prosperity, and come into a state of insolence (ὕβρις), the antithesis of law.[86] Nor was it only the formulated laws of states which Philo disapproved. One who preferred customs (ἔθη) to laws was again only revealing his "arrogance." The inspiration of both customs and laws lay alike in the inadequacy of ordinary men to develop true principles for society.[87]

That is, Philo is consistently dualistic in his view of human nature and of the two laws to which man is subject. On the one hand, by virtue of his divine mind, man is naturally a citizen of the Cosmopolis, subject to the divine laws of Nature. As a man of material nature he is just as naturally given to producing civil law, and subject to its authority. But while the two laws are both in a sense the product of Nature, there is usually no lineal connection, much as there should be, between civic law as it is and natural law. Our civic law is actually a travesty rather than a reflection of Nature. Bréhier[88] and Cohn[89] agree in feeling a similarity between Philo's argument and that of Callicles in Plato's *Gorgias*

83. *Ebr.*, 192 ff. A similar contrast is being made in *QG*, iv, 184, but the medieval Latin translation differs so much from the Armenian that we cannot be sure of Philo's original meaning.

84. *Conf.*, 152. 85. *Decal.*, 2 ff. See above, pp. 33 ff.

86. *Mos.*, ii, 12 f.

87. *Mut.*, 103 f. On the relation of ἔθη to νόμοι in Greek tradition see Hirzel, *Themis, Dike, und Verwandtes*, 378–380.

88. *Les Idées*, 14, n. 1.

89. In *Philos Werke* (Bibliography no. 492), I, 165, n. 1.

(483*b*), where the contention is that law is made by the timid majority to protect themselves from the aggressiveness of a powerful few. But I cannot see any deep similarity; quite the reverse, it seems to me that Philo is as far as possible from the position of Callicles, and that it is such men as he and the tyrannies they advocated which Philo was most especially denouncing. Callicles wanted the strong man free to express his selfishness to the full, and so he disliked civic law. Philo thought that law was perverted more by selfish tyrants than by any other one force in society, and classed democratic legislation with the laws of tyrants only because he felt that the weak individuals in the multitude were largely kept from tyrannical extravagances by their weakness rather than by any virtuous scruples. It is the selfish ambition of man against man, including the tyrant against his fellows, of tribe against tribe, state against state, which makes it impossible for true law to exist in cities.

The actual facts of civic life were thus grim, and it was these facts which made Philo sympathize with the ascetics who felt that the only solution was to run away. Yet the city is truly a product of the Logos, and as such it has great ideal possibilities. For all his realistic descriptions of society as it was, he was certain that if the commonwealth were properly organized it had all the inspiring and educating possibilities for the individual which Plato saw in it. States with a fine constitution, he says, teach the primary virtues, intelligence, justice, and piety.[90] He has the figure so familiar in Plato that the law of the city, when right, is a physician prescribing what is beneficial for the people even if it is distasteful.[91] He tells how the cities of Palestine came into existence: originally a farming people, living scattered on their holdings, in course of time the Jews were brought together by increasing social feeling and friendliness (κοινωνία καὶ φιλία), and built cities.[92] Such a process he does not here regard to be unique with the Jews, for he describes it as "quite what was to have been expected," though it was the absence of precisely these virtues which made city life in general appear to him in other moods to be the source of civic turmoil and lawlessness.

So, aside from Philo's own natural gregariousness, there was a theoretical value to the city: if it could by wise leadership be made to conform to its possibilities it was in itself one of the most powerful of all influences for good among men. Hence his demand that the philoso-

90. *Praem.*, 66.   91. *Jos.*, 63, 75 ff.   92. *Spec.*, ii, 119.

pher who would lead the full life busy himself in civic affairs. The rounded experience of the mystic will bring him back after his experiences in the immaterial realm to take full responsibility and leadership in his social environment.

The warfare between statesman and philosopher in Philo's own life was thus a reflection of a greater warfare, that between the material and the immaterial. Philo's problem was solved, ideally, by first completing his heavenly virtue and then by bringing that virtue back to men on earth. As he stated it over and again, it was the problem of the warfare of two citizenships, that in the heavenly and that in the worldly city. Phrased in this way, the problem was obviously common to Philo and Augustine. Was this a matter of chance, the fact that both drew upon a Platonism colored by Stoic terms, so that both men, without interrelation, spoke of the heavenly city as the true state, and the earthly as an imitation? If Philo can be shown to have had any real place, direct or indirect, as a source for Augustine, his importance in the history of political thought would, by that fact alone, be manifest.

This particular relationship was studied some years ago by Leisegang.[93] The most important single figure for the heavenly city in Augustine, Leisegang indicates, is the Pauline contrast between Hagar and Sarah in Gal. iv, 21 ff. A study of this in Paul and Augustine shows that Augustine has complicated the comparison by introducing a middle city, a copy of the heavenly city, while the earthly city is a copy of the copy. This, Leisegang says, is a turning into Platonism of a comparison which in Paul had no Platonic reference or meaning. Here I do not follow Leisegang. Paul seems Platonic in at least the possible origins of his allegory, while Augustine, introducing the more complicated gradations, seems more definitely Neo-Platonic.[94]

However that may be, Leisegang shows that Philo presents also the same allegory of Hagar and Sarah, and that Augustine and Philo resemble each other at precisely the point where Paul seemed different. In other similes Philo develops the contrast even more clearly:

This is why all who are Sages by the standards of Moses are represented as sojourners. For their souls never go out as emigrants from heaven to found

93. Hans Leisegang, "Der Ursprung der Lehre Augustins von der Civitas Dei," *Archiv für Kulturgeschichte*, XVI (1926), 127–158.

94. Philo shows, of course, many traces that he is just on the eve of the more fully developed Neo-Platonism which we know from the next century.

a colony, but their way is to come to earthly nature as tourists who desire only to see and learn. So when they have stayed a while in their bodies and beheld through them all that sense and mortality has to show, they make their way back to the place from which they set out at the first. To them the heavenly region, where their citizenship lies, is their native land; the earthly region in which they became sojourners is a foreign country. For surely, when men found a colony, the land which receives them becomes a native land instead of the mother city, but for tourists the land which sent them forth is still the mother to whom also they long to return.[95]

The same contrast appears elsewhere, especially in *De Opificio Mundi*,[96] where, over against the material world, stands the Logos, of which the world is an imitation, while the Logos itself is an imitation of God, so that this world, for Philo as for Augustine, is an imitation of an imitation. And not only are the general notions the same; Leisegang has parallels with Augustine for almost every Philonic term in this discussion. Also he shows close parallels in other matters: of the angels, who, with God, are citizens of the higher world; in the way both writers connect the heavenly city with the Garden of Eden, or Paradise; in the way both consider men to be of three types according to the three worlds, and in the identification of the Epicureans with those who live in the lower world, the Stoics with those in the middle world, along with the obvious implication that the higher world, the world of Forms and immateriality, was the world of the Platonists.

Leisegang has compared Philo and Augustine on many points, but in general has contented himself with paralleling the "Grundgedanke" of the two, and says, reasonably, that to work out the comparison in all details would require an extended study. He closes his article by asking how Augustine, who knew no Greek to speak of, could have got this idea, and with such richness of detail, from Philo. His answer is convincing: Augustine was the convert and pupil of Ambrose, who, more than any other Latin writer was steeped in Philo, even to the point of having been called *Philo latinus*. Indeed it had been Ambrose's Philonic allegories of the Old Testament which had first broken through Augustine's Manichaeism. Leisegang goes on and briefly shows that the "Grundgedanke," with a great deal of the detail common to Augustine

95. *Conf.*, 77, 78. Philo seems here especially to have in mind the "city of the body" as the lower city, not the civic organization. He probably is including both in the material as contrasted with the immaterial.

96. *Opif.*, 16–25. Cf. *Prov.*, ii, 55; *Som.*, i, 46; *LA*, iii, 1 ff.

and Philo, is to be found in Ambrose, and in him first among the Latin Fathers. His conclusion therefore seems inevitable, that, whether *originally* done by Philo or not, the Greek Jews had taken over these states, the Epicurean, Stoic, and Platonic, and by identifying them with proof texts for the old and new Jerusalem, had made them part of Hellenistic Judaism. Ambrose took the idea from Philo. Augustine took it from Ambrose, and made it into one of the most influential interpretations of life and society ever to sway the human mind.

It would then appear that Philo's conflict of loyalties had a great background, and a mighty future, as well as a vivid present in Philo's own soul.

CHAPTER V

KINGSHIP

PHILO'S own relations to political life in theory and practice, if our interpretations have been correct, were stormy, contradictory, and real. It remains to speak of his theories for the organization of the state. In only one form of government, monarchy, did he seem to put much hope.[1]

This I say in spite of the fact that he almost invariably calls democracy the best form of government. But when we examine Philo's statements about democracy several interesting things become clear. For he praises democracy, "the best of constitutions," in many passages, as it manifests itself both in the soul of the individual, and in the state,[2] yet the term democracy is not used as Plato uses it, nor as we use it. Popular sovereignty, which Plato called democracy, is for Philo the lowest type of state organization, one which he called ochlocracy, mob rule.[3] In Philo's opinion the ideal democracy recognizes that every individual has rights which are respected, yet every individual is subject to the rule of law and justice; and this law and justice exist as a datum, not of popular whims, but of God or Nature. To him the wish of the multitude is, by definition, contrary to the Law of Nature. Tyranny and absolute sovereignty are equally hated.[4] But what then was democracy as he

1. The most important discussion of Philo's remarks about kings and kingship is by I. Heinemann, *Philons Bildung*, 182–202. As in all the subjects treated in this excellent book, Heinemann's chief concern is to ascertain whether Philo's ideas of kingship are derived predominantly from Greek or Jewish thought. He concludes that there is more specifically Greek than Jewish material in this case, but that the two traditions were here very close together, so much so that it is frequently difficult to tell from which source Philo is drawing. On this point the reason for the closeness of the two traditions might have been illuminated for him from my "Kingship in Ancient Israel," *Journal of Biblical Literature*, XLVIII (1929), 169–205. Heinemann draws exclusively, for Philo's remarks on kingship, from *De Specialibus Legibus*, and so concludes that when we discuss the subject we must be very careful in any attempt "aus seinen Angaben auf die praktische Durchführbarkeit, geschweige auf die tatsächliche Durchführung seiner Ideale zu schleissen" (p. 202). We must indeed be "vorsichtig" in drawing any scholarly conclusions, but I do not think, in view of Philo's statements, that Heinemann has fully understood Philo in stopping where he does.

2. *Virt.*, 180; *Spec.*, iv, 237; *Immut.*, 176; *Agr.*, 45 ff. See Geiger, 52–59; but Geiger has not distinguished between Philo's praise of democracy "in the soul" and his more literal intentions in speaking of government.

3. *Conf.*, 108 ff. Philo's various denunciations of ochlocracy are collected and discussed by Geiger, 53 f. Oligarchy is in *Decal.*, 135 f., 155 likewise thrown out.

4. *Abr.*, 46, 242; cf. *LA*, iii, 79 and the many references to tyranny, all unfavorable, given in Leisegang's *Index*, 787 f.

described it? In his recent careful analysis of the subject Langstadt[5] is clearly right in concluding that to Philo democracy was really Plato's ideal Politeia, the subjection of the mob to the firm rule of a philosopher king. It was not the royal person which Philo desired so much as the royal function and activity by which the king introduced equality (ἰσότης) into society. Those who have most carefully investigated the secrets of Nature, he says, have handed down to us the notion of the importance of equality in the cosmos, and of equality as the mother of justice. Equality makes the universe into a cosmos, cities into the best of all constitutions, a democracy; it makes bodies healthy and souls virtuous.[6] It will be recalled that fluctuations within the Logos, which cause the rise and fall of cities and empires, are governed, Philo thinks, by a fundamental cosmic democracy within the Logos itself.[7]

Philo's ideal is, then, a state based fundamentally upon the cosmic virtue of ἰσότης. He sketches an ideal state in describing the Essenes whose education brings the members to love of God, love of virtue, and love of man. Love of God leads man to intellectual and philosophic achievement, love of virtue to personal virtues, and love of man to the social virtues, benevolence (εὔνοια), equality (ἰσότης), and fellowship beyond verbal description (ἡ παντὸς λόγου κρείττων κοινωνία).[8] That is, the Essenes are an ideal community in which every man is a philosopher, and so has little need for the philosopher king to introduce ἰσότης and κοινωνία. But in the state as ordinarily understood, the ideal organization would require a philosophic ruler, else all would be lost.

Clearly what Philo says about democracy is more properly considered with his remarks about kingship. But it is interesting to inquire how Philo came to call such a government "democracy" when it does not correspond at all to the general use of the term in ancient tradition. Langstadt has published an extremely interesting parallel from the pseudo-Platonic *Menexenos*, 238B–239A, in which a polity based upon ἰσότης is described, one ruled over by a king, but called by some people a democracy. He sees that the author of this treatise is like Philo, further, in that both look back to a primitive time in history when the ideal

5. Erich Langstadt, "Zu Philos Begriff der Demokratie," *Occident and Orient, Studies . . . in honor of Haham Dr. M. Gaster's 80th Birthday*, London, 1937, 349–364. I agree with almost everything said in this essay, and have drawn freely on it for these paragraphs.

6. *Spec.*, iv, 237. The idea is again Pythagorean-Platonic.

7. *Immut.*, 176; see above, pp. 76 ff.

8. *Prob.*, 83 ff. Cf. *Virt.*, 119. Langstadt, *op. cit.*, 354 ff.

was achieved, in Philo's case under Moses and the earlier patriarchs. But Langstadt is aware that Philo's insistence upon praising democracy in terms of ideal kingship is so great an expansion of this passage that the passage alone can hardly be used as adequate explanation of Philo's peculiar and constant usage.

A more likely source of Philo's ideal democracy is to be found in his own political environment, to which we have already seen he was keenly sensitive. For Philo lived in the only age in history when monarchy and kingship were masking under the pose of democracy. The imperial rule of Augustus and Tiberius, under which Philo must have done most of his writing, presented itself as only the archonship in the Roman Republic, or, for one writing in Greek, in the Roman Democracy. It is interesting to turn from Philo to Dio Cassius, and see how Dio describes the rule of Augustus. Dio records, in Book LII, a conference in which Augustus, before taking over the state, consulted with his two friends Agrippa and Maecenas. Agrippa[9] begged him to preserve the Republic, the τῶν δήμων κατάστασις or δημοκρατία, and not to change to monarchy. Maecenas,[10] however, goes into a long oration in praise of monarchy in which he adapts to Roman conditions Plato's ideal aristocracy or monarchy, with many echoes of the Hellenistic theory of royalty. The single ruler must be just, law abiding, the true pilot of the ship of state, one who works with a properly selected senate, equestrian order, and other officials, and has a well disciplined army and an equitable system of taxation. He must be generous, open minded, modest, working always for peace at home and abroad, a personal model in every way to his subjects. He may refuse to take the title of king, but under other titles must actually be the king in the fullest sense. Such a man would be truly and inevitably regarded as the "father" and "savior" of the people. The alternative is either mob rule, which Maecenas like Plato and Agrippa calls "democracy," or else some usurper's tyranny. But in one place, where he has been talking of the organization of the state under monarchy, with the proper men selected to carry out the various functions of government, Maecenas says:

In this way each class of citizens will zealously discharge the duties which devolve upon them and will readily render to one another such services as are due, and will thus be unaware of their inferiority when one class is at a

9. Dio Cass., LII, §§ ii–xiii.   10. Ibid., LII, xiv–xl.

disadvantage as compared with another, *and all will gain the true democracy and the freedom which does not fail* (καὶ τὴν δημοκρατίαν τὴν ἀληθῆ τήν τε ἐλευθερίαν τὴν ἀσφαλῆ κτήσονται). For the boasted freedom of the mob proves in experience to be the bitterest servitude of the best element to the other and brings upon both a common destruction; whereas this freedom of which I speak everywhere prefers for honour the men of prudence, awarding at the same time equality (τὸ ἴσον) to all according to their deserts, and thus gives happiness impartially to all who enjoy this liberty.[11]

Augustus, of course, followed Maecenas' advice. The government he set up was, says Dio, "strictly speaking" a monarchy[12] in contrast with what had been a "democracy in the strict sense of the term" before.[13] The emperors, he says, built up their power by taking all the "democratic titles" (τὰ δημοκρατικὰ ὀνόματα),[14] that is, the titles of offices in the Republic. And Augustus wished, even after his supremacy had been ratified by the senate and people, to be considered a democrat (δημοτικός).[15] The matter is finally summed up by Dio in the following terms:

In this way the power of both people and senate passed entirely into the hands of Augustus, and from his time there was, strictly speaking, a monarchy; for monarchy would be the truest name for it, no matter if two or three men did later hold the power at the same time. The name of monarchy, to be sure, the Romans so detested that they called their emperors neither dictators nor kings nor anything of the sort; yet since the final authority for the government devolves upon them, they must needs be kings. The offices established by the laws, it is true, are maintained even now, except that of censor; but the entire direction and administration is absolutely in accordance with the wishes of the one in power at the time. And yet, in order to preserve the appearance of having this power by virtue of the laws and not because of their own domination, the emperors have taken to themselves all the functions, including the titles, of the offices which under the republic (δημοκρατία) and by the free gift of the people were powerful, with the single exception of the dictatorship.[16]

Dio is important in reminding us that the Greek word for the Latin "Republic" was "Democracy." It is common knowledge that the Empire was commonly called the *res publica* by earlier imperial writers. So

11. Dio Cass., LII, xiv, 4, 5. (Cary's translation in the Loeb Series.) It is notable that like Philo the true test of democracy-monarchy was that it put ἰσότης or τὸ ἴσον into society.
12. Ibid., LII, i, 1.   13. Ibid., LIII, i, 3.   14. Ibid., LIII, xviii, 2.
15. Ibid., LIII, xii, 1.   16. Ibid., LIII, xvii, 1–3.

do both Tacitus[17] and Suetonius[18] speak, and legal language long kept the same usage.[19] Since this is true, Greek writers who wished to abuse mob rule could hardly berate democracy in the traditional way, else people might think it a slur on the Roman government. And just as obviously it was excellent politics to praise monarchy or kingship as the ideal polity, doing it, as the Romans themselves would have had to do, in the form of praise of ideal democracy. We need not then be confused any longer by Philo's language. To him "ochlocracy" was anathema. The ideal government was monarchy in its Roman form of "democracy," kingship in its best sense, and it is as kingship that we shall discuss it hereafter.

Much of Philo's theory of the king has already appeared in connection with his discussions of Joseph.[20] It has been seen that his thought of the king was determined by the current hellenistic notions best preserved in the Neo-Pythagorean fragments on kingship, and that in presenting the ideal prefect in an allegory of Joseph Philo used almost every aspect of the royal theory, even to calling the ruler θεός, to show how Joseph was the true pattern for the ruler to follow. More directly stated, he wanted the prefect to be a ruler after the categories of the kingly ideal, and forced the details of that ideal into the traditional narrative of the career of Joseph so that the gentile reader might suppose that the real source of the conception was in the Jewish Bible, and that Roman rulers might feel themselves in sympathy with Jews.

But the theory appears in many other connections in Philo's writings, the more important of which must be recalled. God is the ideal king, for example. This I have already discussed at length elsewhere,[21] and so will here quote but a single instance, one not previously cited. God, says Philo,

has no such autocratic rule as a despot, but exercises the beneficent (εὐεργε-τικόν) rule characterized by a power which is uniformly merciful and gives

17. See *Annales*, I, 12 and passim.

18. See for example *Caligula*, 26. In *Divus Augustus*, 28, Augustus despaired, it is said, of "restoring the republic," and took the primacy only to establish the Republic on a safe and permanent basis.

19. See for example the Lex de imp. Vesp. v. 16. 119 Br.; in J. N. Madvig, *Die Verfassung und Verwaltung des römischen Staates*, I, 541. It is one of the many accurate reflections of Philo's usage in Bellier's dedication, quoted in the Appendix (see below, pp. 121 ff.), that Bellier refers to the French kingdom of the XVI. century as the *Republique*.

20. See above, pp. 44 ff.   21. See my *By Light, Light*, chapter I.

security (σωτήριον). As such he does away with the fear we might have toward him as a despot, while he puts into the soul the love and good will which go to a Benefactor (εὐεργέτης).[22]

So Philo goes on to describe God as characterized by the royal virtue of love for man (φιλανθρωπία).[23] Clearly Philo used such royal titles as Savior (Σωτήρ) and Benefactor (Εὐεργέτης) in terms of the current philosophy of kingship, according to which the ideal king produces love (φιλία) and good will (εὐνοία) instead of fear, and rules by attracting his subjects rather than by compelling them.[24]

Again, the king figure is often used in Cynic-Stoic fashion to describe the sage, for as the ideal king is a sage, every sage is essentially a king, since kingliness is a matter of character, not of external position.[25] The kingliness of a private citizen has little practical importance beyond making him a complete individualist as over against the government. But the fact that the king must ideally be a sage is quite the notion of the Pythagorean fragments.[26] One of Philo's passages explains the kingliness of the sage on the ground that he is properly a citizen of heaven (the universe) and hence lives and rules himself according to the Law of Nature. As such he gets the title king. It is obvious that to Philo and his audience the term king properly meant not anyone with royal power or title, but one who ruled according to the Law of Nature.[27] Again he says that it would not entitle the conqueror to be called king even if he conquered all the world, and went on, as is impious to suggest, to conquer the heavens also. Much more does the title belong to one who is in intimate relations with God, has "kinship with the Unbegotten" (ἡ πρὸς τὸν ἀγένητον οἰκειότης), or God as his portion (ὁ θεὸς κλῆρος).[28] We infer again that the true king in society is incarnate Wisdom, in close relations with God. Regardless of his social rank, the sage is royal because he is eternally ordained by Nature as royal,[29] which brings in again the association of the king with the Law of Nature. Like the authors of the Pythagorean fragments, Philo adds the king's proper education to his natural endowment, as a most important part of his equipment.[30] One of the most extensive discussions points out that

22. *Plant.*, 90.
23. Ibid., 92.
24. See also above, p. 61.
25. *QG*, iv, 76.
26. Sthenidas, *ap.* Stobaeus, IV, vii, 63: Χρὴ τὸν βασιλέα σοφὸν ἤμεν, κτλ. See my "Hellenistic Kingship," 73 ff.
27. *Agr.*, 41 ff., especially 65 f.
28. *Plant.*, 66–68.
29. *Mut.*, 151.
30. *Spec.*, ii, 20–22.

the sage is not just a prince, but is "prince of princes, and he is divine and king of kings, best and magnanimous, who has been ordained not by men but by God."[31] He alone can be a king who is clever (or handsome, ἀστεῖος) and beloved by God: for kingship is "the best of arts," and is to be ascribed to a man on the same basis as we should call a man a pilot, physician, or musician, that is on the basis of his being a master of his art. For, as Philo paraphrases Plato, to put the tools of those trades into untrained hands is not to make a man worthy of one of those titles. A man is not a pilot, for example, merely because he happens to be trying to steer a ship; rather is he a pilot who knows how to do so, whether he have a ship or not. So "he only can be called a king who has skill to rule" (rex dicendus solus peritus). When God sees a mind properly purified He gives it the gift of Wisdom, and having so given reckons the man who has it in the company of the greatest princes and kings. That is, kingship is essentially a gift of God. And one of the primary qualities of this gift is constancy, so that the law the king ordains is not changing like human law but enduring. Most of this, as applied to the sage in private station, has only figurative significance. Yet the king philosophy itself comes out in its essential features as a conception very definitely formulated in Philo's mind.

The reason why the king and the sage are ultimately identical Philo explains very well. Wisdom is the "art of arts." The great artist is recognizable, he says, in whatever medium. It made no difference whether Pheidias worked in brass, ivory, or gold, the art of Pheidias was always recognizable because it was the same art in each medium. So the art of the sage, which is to make things like Nature, can be applied in various media, in piety, natural science, meteorology, ethics, politics, economics, banqueting, kingship, or legislation.[32] The point is that if a real sage is at work the result in any case will be an exhibition of the "art of arts," the comprehension of Nature and the power of making things resemble Nature.

God's selection of a man for the kingly office, like all of God's elections, is not always clearly recognizable. Consequently many usurpers get into office. Yet Philo never lost faith that a man properly selected by the voting constituency would be confirmed by an added vote from

---

31. QG, iv, 76: "princeps principum, isque divinus, et rex regum, optimus et generosus, qui non ab hominibus, sed a deo ordinatus sit." There is Greek for part of the passage in Harris, Fragments, 36.

32. Ebr., 88–92.

God which would make him one elect (ἐκλογή) from the human race.[33] Moses became king, but he did so not in the usual way of getting control of the army and navy, the infantry and cavalry; instead, "he was elected by God with the voluntary concurrence of his subjects, for God worked in the subjects to bring them to make this voluntary choice."[34] The same contrast between the selection of Moses and the spirit of Roman imperial elections is brought out again, with the addition that Moses was chosen "because of his virtue and nobility and his never failing good will to all, and because God who loves virtue and nobility gave it to him as a fitting reward."[35]

From Philo's figurative use of the king to describe the rule of the mind over the lower elements in man's constitution much can also be learned of his political ideas. In one passage he depicts the lawlessness that can arise in a herd or flock when the herdsman loses control.[36] The ideal state of the herd, or of a kingdom on that analogy, appears to involve arrangement, order, steadiness, organization (τάξις, εὐκοσμία, εὐστάθεια, διάκρισις); but this is all destroyed when the herdsman is weak. The ideal rulership, "rulership with reason, by which law and justice are honored," is something that brings social salvation (σωτήριον). Again Melchizedek, as type of the mind, is King of Peace,[37] the priest-king. The king is the one who promulgates laws (νόμων εἰσηγητής). In contrast with the tyrant, who introduces lawlessness and rules only by grievous force, the king

resorts first to persuasion rather than commands, and then afterwards enjoins such things as will enable the ship, the living being, to make life's voyage successfully, piloted by the good pilot, right reason (ὀρθὸς λόγος).[38]

Philo is here following political imagery closely, even though the ship of state is the individual man (τὸ ζῷον). In both of these passages the ideal rulership is distinguished for its being in harmony with law. As

---

33. *Spec.*, iv, 157.   34. *Praem.*, 54.   35. *Mos.*, i, 148; cf. *Som.*, ii, 243.

36. *Som.*, ii, 152–154. Comparison of the rulership of the mind to the king was an ancient commonplace. See the Appendix to my *By Light, Light*, and, for instance, Seneca, *Epist.*, 114, 24: Animus noster modo rex est, modo tyrannus. Rex, cum honesta intuetur, . . . ubi vero inpotens, cupidus, delicatus est, . . . fit tyrannus.

37. Cf. Dio, *Orat.*, I, 75.

38. *LA*, iii, 79 f. Heinemann, in *Philos Werke* (Bibliography no. 492), III, 111, n. 1, has correctly paralleled this passage with Xenophon's *Cyropaed.*, I, iii, 18; Polybius, IV, 3; Dio Chrys., *Orat.*, I–IV: but I cannot see why he deduces from these parallels that Philo had his notion from Stoicism. The Stoics taught a very similar doctrine, but the idea is no more recognizably Stoic in Philo than it is in Xenophon.

such it is rulership with logos (σὺν λόγῳ), or in harmony with "right reason" (ὀρθὸς λόγος), the Law of Nature; with this statement goes another, that kingship is rulership according to law (ἀρχὴ νόμιμος).[39] The kingly office is a divine gift especially associated with law, so that, as every man should consecrate his gifts to God, the king should dedicate his legal authority and leadership.[40] By his administration the good ruler imitates God in putting harmony, equality, social-mindedness (κοινωνία), and order into the state.[41]

There are a great many additional details which show Philo's complete familiarity with and acceptance of the current theory of kingship as formulated by the Neo-Pythagorean fragments. All property is in the royal name, not just that which is collected in taxes and which lies in the king's treasury. For even the private savings of every subject are properly the king's. So all are his servants, though the king treats the court servants as such in a distinctive way. Ultimately all are servants, and apparently slaves, of the king.[42] The proverbial right of the king to the lion's share appears,[43] though the true king, far from taking advantage of this right to rob his subjects, will in time of need consider even the property peculiarly his own as not his own but public property.[44] The king is apt to enjoy founding new cities. He does so in accordance with the king's great love of honor (κατὰ πολλὴν φιλοτιμίαν βασιλέως). Love of honor (φιλοτιμία), a familiar part of any description of the king, is here explained:

The king claims autocratic power, and is at the same time magnificent in his ideas (τὸ φρόνημα λαμπρός), and so adds fresh luster to his good fortune.[45]

The good king is merciful and considerate toward every individual who comes to him, particularly toward the unfortunate, the widow, and

39. *Fug.*, 10.   40. *Mut.*, 221.
41. *Spec.*, iv, 187 f.   42. *Plant.*, 54–57.
43. *Opif.*, 56 f. Cf. Diotogenes, *ap.* Stobaeus, IV, vii, 26; Ecphantus, *ap.* ibid., IV, vii, 64. See my "Hellenistic Kingship," 70, 76.
44. *Spec.*, iv, 159. Cf. Diotogenes' king (see preceding note) who will be κοινωνατικὸς περὶ τὰ χρήματα.
45. *Opif.*, 17; cf. *Mos.*, i, 275. The term is used in praise of Ptolemy Philadelphus in *Mos.*, ii, 29. The love of being honored, which was one of the most obvious characteristics of an ancient king, was always having to be rationalized by those idealizing monarchy. So Dio Chrys. (*Orat.*, I, 27) says: φιλότιμος ὢν τὴν φύσιν καὶ εἰδὼς ὅτι τοὺς ἀγαθοὺς πεφύκασιν οἱ ἄνθρωποι τιμᾶν, ἧττον ἐλπίζει τιμᾶσθαι ἂν ὑπὸ ἀκόντων ἢ παρὰ μισούντων φιλίας τυγχάνειν. Diotogenes wrestles with the same word in *Stob.*, IV, vii, 62. The word could of course be used in a good sense as ambition.

orphan.[46] He is warned that it is better to receive suppliants for his favor than men bringing "gifts."[47] The obligation to care in mercy for his flock, especially for the weaklings, is the notion behind the conception of the king as the good shepherd which we have already frequently encountered. It is commonly so developed in Greek sources.[48] But there is nothing in Greek literature that I know which specifies the fatherless and widows. The Christian king in the Middle Ages was always presented with these as his special obligation, much as Philo has done. This specific duty seems to me, especially in view of its later history, to be an important addition to the Greek theory from Hebrew tradition,[49] and it is interesting to see that if it was not Philo's own contribution, it originated in his environment of Hellenistic Judaism.

The king is thus benevolent to his people because he is their father:

The ruler ought to stand before his subjects just as a father does before his children, that he also may be honored in turn as by his own children. Thus good rulers, to tell the truth, are the universal fathers of cities and tribes, and display a good will the equal, sometimes the superior, of that of parents. But those people who get great ruling power at the price of the ruin and loss of the subjects he [Moses] called not rulers but enemies, since they act the part of implacable enemies.[50]

The fatherhood of the king is likewise based upon the fatherhood of God along with the other divine characteristics of rulership. The phrase

46. *Decal.*, 40–43; *Spec.*, iv, 170 ff., esp. 176. See I. Heinemann, *Philons Bildung*, 193–199.

47. Fragment, *ap.* Harris, *Fragments*, p. 105. Cf. Diotogenes, *ap.* Stob., IV, vii, 62: εὐχάριστον δ' ἤμεν δεῖ μὴ ποττὸ μέγεθος ἀποβλέποντα τᾶς τιμᾶς, ἀλλὰ ποττὸν τρόπον καὶ τὰν προαίρεσιν τῶ τιμέοντος.

48. See Dio Chrys., *Orat.*, II, 77. He describes the king as being τοῖς ἀσθενέσιν ἀρήγοντα; cf. ibid., I, 15 ff., espec. 20: ἀνάγκη τὸν ἥμερον καὶ φιλάνθρωπον βασιλέα μὴ μόνον φιλεῖσθαι ὑπ' ἀνθρώπων, ἀλλὰ καὶ ἐρᾶσθαι. ταῦτ' οὖν εἰδὼς καὶ φύσει τοιοῦτος ὤν, ἵλεων καὶ πρᾷον παρέχει τὴν ψυχὴν πᾶσιν.

Diotogenes, *ap.* Stob., IV, vii, 62: δεῖ δὲ τὸν ἀγαθὸν βασιλέα βοηθατικόν τε ἤμεν τῶν δεομένων καὶ εὐχάριστον.

He will be ἀβαρέα . . . μάλιστα ποττὼς μήονας καὶ καταδεεστέρως ταῖς τύχαις.

Charondas is closest to Philo of them all when he says: Let rulers ἐπαρκείτωσαν τοῖς διὰ τύχην πενομένοις; Stob., IV, ii, 24 (ed. Wachs. et Hense, IV, 152, l. 11).

49. Exod. xxii, 22–24; Deut. x, 18; xxiv, 17; xxvii, 19; Ps. xciv, 6; Is. i, 17, 23; x, 2; Ezek. xxii, 7; Zech. vii, 10. On this subject see H. Bolkestein, *Een geval van sociaal-ethisch syncretisme*, Amsterdam, 1931 (*Mededeelingen der k. Akademie van Wetenschappen te Amsterd.*, Afdeeling Letterkunde, LXXII, Ser. B, 1); and the review by H. Windisch, *Theologische Literaturzeitung*, LVII (1932), 194–196.

50. *Spec.*, iv, 184. On the king as father see Diotogenes, *ap.* Stob., IV, vii, 62 (ad fin.); Sthenidas, *ap.* Stob., IV, vii, 63. See my "Hellenistic Kingship," 73 ff. Dio Chrys., *Orat.*, I, 22: πατέρα δὲ τῶν πολιτῶν καὶ τῶν ἀρχομένων οὐ λόγῳ κεκλῆσθαι μόνον, ἀλλὰ τοῖς ἔργοις τοῦτο ἐπιδείκνυσθαι.

universal father (πατὴρ κοινός) used by Philo in the foregoing quotation is a reflection of the traditional language used to describe Zeus, the πατὴρ κοινὸς ἀνθρώπων καὶ θεῶν,[51] and it is in his fatherhood as well as in his other aspects that the earthly king is to imitate him. The notion is most succinctly stated by Sthenidas:

The king would best imitate God by . . . evincing a fatherly disposition to those beneath him. For it is in this way that the first God is recognized as father of gods and men.[52]

In view of the fact that the fatherhood of the king was a familiar teaching in antiquity, it is interesting to note that Philo's form of presenting it indicates that his source, or mode of thinking, was definitely Pythagorean. This is clear from a comparison of one of his statements with a passage of Dio Chrysostom. In describing God as ruler and model for the king Philo points out that God is

a king exercising a kindly and legal rulership. . . . But there is no title more fitting for a king than "father." For what in family relationships parents are to the children, that the king is to the state, and God is to the world, since He attunes two most beautiful things in an indissoluble union by the immovable laws of Nature, namely rulership with protecting care.[53]

Dio describes Zeus:

He is called king by virtue of his rulership and power; he is called Father, it seems to me, because of his protecting care and kindness; he is called Guardian of the City by virtue of his law and public benefaction, etc.[54]

Dio's passage is quite familiarly Stoic in form: an allegorical interpretation is being suggested for each of a large number of names or epithets of the god.[55] Philo's formulation is just as Pythagorean as Dio's is Stoic. For Philo's comparison is expressed in a mathematical proportion: what the father is to his children that the king is to the state, and that God is to the world;[56] and the ruling and providential aspects are attuned into

51. Dio Chrys., *Orat.*, II, 75. Zeus is commonly called "father of gods and men" from Homer down.
52. See note 50, above; cf. Dio Chrys., *Orat.*, I, 37, 39.
53. Fragment *ap.* Eusebius, *Praep. Evang.*, VIII, xiv, 2, 3.
54. *Orat.*, I, 40.
55. On such Stoic allegory see Arnim, *SVF*, II, Frags. 1021, 1062, 1076; also 528 at end.
56. Cf. Diotogenes, *ap.* Stobaeus, IV, vii, 61: ἔχει δὲ καὶ ὡς θεὸς ποτὶ κόσμον βασιλεὺς ποτὶ πόλιν, καὶ ὡς πόλις ποτὶ κόσμον βασιλεὺς ποτὶ θεόν.

an indissoluble unit. But both think of the rulership of God as a union
of forceful rulership with "protecting care."[57] That is, the notion itself
seems to be peculiar to neither school, though Philo is expressing himself in Pythagorean terms.

It seems to me to have been a favorite detail in discussing kingship to
bring out the fact that the king is quite independent of any of his subjects. Philo alludes to this kingly quality in two passages.[58]

The notion of the king as Savior (σωτήρ) does not appear in any of
Philo's stated descriptions of the kingly office, but was axiomatic with
him. In the section on the Roman emperor it will appear that Philo
knew and used that title,[59] while God as ruler is Savior and Benefactor
throughout his writings.[60] God's rule is always saving (σωτηρίως).[61]
The human mind, when as king it rules with logos and honors law and
right, is a thing which saves (σωτήριον), while anarchy is a menace
(ἐπίβουλον). Proper government always affects the salvation of the citizens.[62] In the kingship of the Patriarchs the notion is so blended with
their mystic saving power that the passages cannot be used for the philosophy of kingship without care. But it is at least significant that the
royal saving power could thus easily be given a mystical interpretation.

In using the notion that the king should be the official high-priest of
the realm Philo makes an interesting innovation. Diotogenes had stated
that the task of the ruler was three-fold: he must act as military leader
and as supreme judge, and he must worship the gods.[63] In his *Life of
Moses* Philo describes Moses as primarily the king, and makes the priest-
hood a very important part of his function.[64] But in one place he makes
the surprising statement:

Nothing is more pleasant or distinguished than to serve God, which sur-
passes even the greatest kingship; and the first kings seem to me to have been
at the same time chief priests, by which they made clear in a practical way
that those ruling over others must for themselves dutifully worship God.[65]

57. Cf. *BGU*, 372, i, 12 (Second Century after Christ): ἡ τοῦ αὐτοκράτορος περὶ πάντας
κηδεμονία.
58. *Plant.*, 51: βασιλέα οὐδενὸς δεῖσθαι: cf. Frag. *ap.* Harris, *Fragments*, 104. Harris
compares this latter with the primitive Byzantine gnomon as restored by C. Wachsmuth: θεὸς
δεῖται οὐδενός· σοφὸς δὲ δεῖται μόνου θεοῦ. The king imitates God by being ὀλιγοδεέα in
Sthenidas, *ap.* Stobaeus, IV, vii, 63.
59. *Flac.*, 74, 126; *Legat.*, 22.   60. E.g., *Opif.*, 169; *LA*, ii, 56.
61. E.g., *Conf.*, 98; *Abr.*, 70; *Jos.*, 149; *Decal.*, 60, 155; *Praem.*, 34.
62. *Jos.*, 149; *Decal.*, 14.   63. *Ap.* Stobaeus, IV, vii, 61.
64. See my *By Light, Light*, 189 ff.
65. *QE*, ii, 105. Harris, *Fragments*, 68: οὐδὲν οὔτε ἥδιον οὔτε σεμνότερον ἢ θεῷ δου-

The notion that the king was the chief priest is founded in Pythagorean thought upon the king's divinity. The term divinity had of course a great range of meaning in antiquity, and certainly no one thought, in calling the king "god," that he was actually the supreme Being. To the Pythagoreans the king's divinity consisted in his being a sort of demigod, or as one ancient statement puts it:

The Pythagoreans posited between God and the human race a distinct third class, his august majesty the king, or the Sage, since Homer first put the king between gods and men, and represented the Sage as preceding the king in honor.[66]

Delatte is certainly right in saying that this is an expansion of a conception which Iamblichus[67] reports from Aristotle:

Aristotle records in the treatise on the Pythagoreans that, in their very secret teachings, they observed some such distinctions as follow: of the reasoning animal there is God as one sort, man as another, and a third which is of the sort represented by Pythagoras.

The following quotation from Ecphantus, which I have hitherto overlooked, is an excellent statement of what the divinity of the king meant to Pythagoreans:

Upon earth men are something exiled, a type of existence much inferior to the purer nature and made heavy with much earth. Accordingly men would scarcely have been elevated from the mother [Earth?] unless a divine form, something breathed into the pitiable animal, had bound it with the more exalted part, indicating the holy aspect of the begetter, since it is impossible for that aspect itself to be seen. Man has the highest nature of anything on earth, but more godlike is the king who claims the lion's share in that more exalted part of our common nature. He is like the others with respect to his tabernacle (σκᾶνος), since he has come into being out of the same material; but he was made by the supreme Craftsman, who, in fabricating the king, used Himself as the archetype.[68] . . . Oh that it had been possible to take from human nature the necessity of any obedience. For this [necessity] is a remnant of that earthly meanness according to which anything animate is

λεύειν, ὁ καὶ τὴν μεγίστην βασιλείαν ὑπερβάλλει· καὶ μοι δοκοῦσιν οἱ πρῶτοι βασιλεῖς
ἅμα καὶ ἀρχιερεῖς γενέσθαι, δηλοῦντες ἔργοις, ὅτι χρὴ τοὺς τῶν ἄλλων δεσπόζοντας
δουλεύειν τοῖς λατρεύουσι θεῷ.

66. *Schol. in Homer, Il.* A, 340: b. From Delatte, *Études sur la littérature Pythagoricienne,*
120 f. (See Dindorf, *Scholia Graeca in Hom. Il.,* III, 55.)

67. *De Pythagorica Vita,* VI, 31.   68. There is certainly a hiatus in the text here.

subject to death, and so must share in it [obedience]. But if anyone anywhere were so composed within himself that he was more divine than is true of other animate beings, he would have had no need whatever of obedience.[69]

Here it is plain that the divinity or semi-divinity of the king was for Pythagoreans a concept with definite religious and mystic possibilities. But they had no notion of identifying the king with supreme deity. The king could and should be for the people a saving link to God, showing them a much larger share of divine nature than was given to any private citizens.

Philo has statements in which he seems to go quite as far as Ecphantus in recognizing the king's divine nature. Melchizedek, he says, can be the great combination of king, priest, and Logos, "for he has the Really Existent as his portion, and thinks about Him in a way that is high, exalted, and sublime."[70] An ideal king he speaks of as one in whom Sophia was long a guest, if not a permanent resident,[71] which would be but another form of expressing the Pythagorean notion that the king was incarnate Logos or animate law (νόμος ἔμψυχος). Philo's attitude is best summarized in a fragment preserved by Antony:

In his material substance (οὐσία) the king is just the same as any man, but in the authority of his rank he is like the God of all. For there is nothing upon earth more exalted than he. Since he is a mortal, he must not vaunt himself; since he is a god he must not give way to anger. For if he is honored as being an image of God, yet he is at the same time fashioned from the dust of the earth, from which he should learn simplicity to all.[72]

In this Philo has almost accepted the full measure of royal divinity as described by Ecphantus, and has gone as far probably as most intelligent pagans of his day went. The distinction is carefully being made,

---

69. Stobaeus, *Anthol.*, IV, vi, 22 (ed. Wachsmuth et Hense, IV, pp. 244 f.). Several lines of this are quoted by Clemens Alexandrinus as from Eurysus the Pythagoraean: *Stromata*, V, v, 29, 1 f. (ed. Stählin, II, p. 344, ll. 19 ff.). This quotation by Clemens is extremely important since it shows first that the idea was current among Pythagoreans in general, and second that the material was current at least as early as the second or early third centuries.

70. *LA*, iii, 82.   71. *Plant.*, 169.

72. *Melissa*, Ser. CIV; Mangey, II, 673. This is one of the many fragments which Harris (*Fragments*, 106) for some reason "thought it not worth while to print." The fragment reads: Τῇ μὲν οὐσίᾳ ἴσος τοῦ παντὸς ἀνθρώπου ὁ βασιλεύς, τῇ ἐξουσίᾳ δὲ τοῦ ἀξιώματος ὅμοιός ἐστι τῷ ἐπὶ πάντων θεῷ· οὐκ ἔχει γὰρ ἐπὶ γῆς αὐτοῦ ὑψηλότερον. χρὴ τοίνυν καὶ ὡς θνητὸν μὴ ἐπαίρεσθαι, καὶ ὡς θεὸν μὴ ὀργίζεσθαι. εἰ γὰρ καὶ εἰκόνι θεϊκῇ τετίμηται, ἀλλὰ καὶ κόνει χοϊκῇ συμπέπληκται, δι' ἧς ἐκδιδάσκεται τὴν πρὸς πάντας ἁπλότητα. Οὐσία, which I have translated "material substance" obviously is used in that Stoic sense of the word here.

however, between the divinity of the king's rulership, which is an image of God, and his material nature (οὐσία). The point is that he draws the line at just the point Ecphantus does, for while the king is θεός for both, Ecphantus points out the human and material σκᾶνος as Philo does the human οὐσία. The two terms seem to me to mean the same thing.[73] But it will appear that for Philo and his Christian successors the distinction was used in a way Ecphantus did not dream.

One final detail in the kingly theory, of importance for later Christian speculation, is to be found in Philo's remarks about tyrants. Tyrants, he says, are permitted by God, like earthquakes and plagues, as a punishment for the wickedness of a nation. The implication is that, bad as they are, they are still put in office by God, and function as God's elect. In themselves they are wicked men, but they are kept in office by God as a state hires an executioner, who is usually a depraved individual but has his function in society. When the tyrant has done his devastating work in the wicked state he perishes with the society he has afflicted.[74] This also seems to me an idea which is foreign to Greek political thinking. Philo appears to have had it from Jewish tradition, where political difficulties, captivities, oppressive rulers, were interpreted consistently as being a form of divine punishment which God visits even upon his chosen people if they offend him. The prophets who announced this interpretation of evil rulers insisted that the only way out was by moral reform on the part of the people, not resistance to the oppressor, or tyrannicide. It is most interesting that this Jewish idea, worked into the body of Greek political tradition by Philo or his group, was reflected in Paul's unqualified assertion that the "powers that be are ordained by God," and that Philo's own statement was quoted by Eusebius, and became an important part of later Christian political philosophy. Its especial elaboration by Melanchthon for the Lutherans will be at once recalled.

Now that we have Philo's political theory in mind it is interesting to see how he used it when he was addressing his Roman rulers. In Chapter I Philo's two works of apology, *In Flaccum* and *Legatio ad Gaium,* were shown to be realistic, if subtle, attempts to threaten the prefect and

73. It will be recalled (see above, p. 58) that in discussing Joseph for gentiles Philo stopped at this same point and made the same distinction, while he has fearlessly called the true sage divine in virtue of his kingly nature (see above, p. 92).

74. Fragment, *ap.* Eusebius, *Praep. Evang.,* VIII, xiv, 37–41 (393c ff.).

emperor with disaster if they did not respect Jewish "rights." The political theory of the documents was not discussed, but we can now recognize that it is always the kingly ideal which, in one way or another, is held up before the rulers when they are addressed directly, as when presented in the allegory of Joseph. Roman sovereigns must respect Jewish rights; but Philo knows no political concept other than that of true kingship to offer them as their guide in office.

In discussing the prefect the ideal is brought out in the contrast between Flaccus under Tiberius, when he quite fulfilled all human dreams, and Flaccus under Gaius, when he illustrated the faults of the tyrant and usurper. When Flaccus was first appointed prefect of Egypt by Tiberius

he was astute and persistent, keen at grasping and executing what was desirable, skilled at speaking and at discovering what had not been spoken. So in every way in a short time he came to be at home in Egyptian affairs, which are complicated and variegated, difficult to master even for men who make that their professional task from an early age.[75]

Philo explains that Flaccus became so proficient in his work that the clerks, to whom reference was usually made by governors for expert and detailed information, became superfluous. Flaccus also took up the regulation of the finances of the country. To do this is not in itself a token of the "ruling soul" (ψυχὴ ἡγεμονική), he says, but Flaccus went on and gave evidence of the more brilliant and royal nature (λαμπροτέρα καὶ βασιλικὴ φύσις), which was displayed first in the fact that he carried himself personally with great distinction (σεμνότερος); second, he himself decided the more important suits, in connection with which he humbled the overweening; third, he suppressed all suspicious and riotous meetings. So did he fill the city and region with good order (εὐνομία). In addition he was very discreet in his handling of the army.[76] All of these aspects of rule have become thoroughly familiar in the theoretical discussion of government. Philo was convinced that his notions were not mere theory, but could be worked out in practice, and that they would mean the εὐνομία of the country if they were actually applied. The state of Egypt under Flaccus' early rule was a case in point. The horrors of Egypt when Flaccus ceased to fulfill this ideal need not be described again.

75. *Flac.*, 2 f.   76. Ibid., 1–5.

Of course the theory would be only partially exemplified in a prefect who had to work under a human superior. It was more fully represented in Tiberius and Augustus. Tiberius

for twenty-three years dominated land and sea, and allowed no spark of war to smoulder anywhere, but with an open hand he lavishly dispensed peace and its benefits to the end of his life. He was of the noblest ancestry from both parents, surpassed all his contemporaries in sagacity and forcible speaking. He lived to a fine old age, though he had the maturity of judgement of an old man while he was still young.[77]

Augustus was even nearer the ideal. Philo did not hesitate to say of him that he "surpassed human nature in all the virtues," though it is notable that, to use the distinction Philo made above,[78] he surpassed not in his material nature (οὐσία) but in his actions and qualities, elsewhere called εὐπραγία, or τὰ ἀξιώματα καὶ αἱ τύχαι.[79] This notion is now elaborated to show that Philo means by Augustus' "virtues," first, the fact that he founded his title and power alike by the magnitude of the autocratic rulership he achieved and by the καλοκἀγαθία he displayed; second, the fact that he brought peace to the Empire when it was distracted by civil wars, in the course of which he led the cities into liberty, made disorder into order, and took the wild nations and filled them with gentleness and harmony, so that instead of a single Greece there were many by his spreading Greek civilization in the most important parts of the barbarian world. He was a man of peace, he gave every man his due (i.e., he was just), he scattered lavish favors, and throughout his life he held back for himself nothing that was good or fine. In all ways he was Benefactor (εὐεργέτης) for forty-three years. The entire civilized world, with the single exception of the Jews, recognized in him a person equal to the Olympians, and decreed honors to him, dedicated games to him, triumphs, statues, and the like, in spontaneous recognition of his divinity.[80] At the end he left all in peace, εὐνομία, and harmony; the Greeks

77. *Legat.*, 141 f., abridged. The last detail is one not mentioned in other accounts of kingship which I have seen. One is reminded alike of the Jewish thought that old age is a divine seal of approval, and the Aristotelian notion that true happiness cannot be said to have been realized by one who died young. Even more striking is the reminiscence of the young "Self-Taught," the savior endowed with divine wisdom from infancy, so that when presented with teachers they proved less wise than the child. I suspect that it is the latter notion at which Philo is hinting.

78. See the fragment quoted above, p. 99.   79. Cf. *Legat.*, 140.

80. Ibid., 143–151.

and barbarians, the armies and private citizens were in mutual concord.[81]

So Philo claims to have found the ideal ruler realized in both Augustus and Tiberius. Indeed he represents the Romans in official circles as fully acquainted with the royal philosophy and aware of the necessity of living up to it. From this point of view he contrasts Gaius with the magnificent performances of his predecessors. Gaius has not only failed to follow their example, he insists, but has thus failed in spite of explicit precept. For Philo sees fit to idealize the highly dubious character of Macro, in spite of his admitted lack of sagacity, and to make him into that wise and philosophic counsellor of royalty whom philosophers always were advising kings to find and follow if the kings could not themselves be sages. Macro appears in Philo's description almost ridiculously devoted to the task of making Gaius into the model king. Gaius must first be made to look and act the part, Macro thinks. Accordingly when he saw him asleep at a banquet he would go and waken him, partly for Gaius' protection and partly for the sake of what was proper for royal dignity. He would nudge him if he was misconducting himself by looking excitedly at the dancers, or dancing with them; or if Gaius were laughing out like a schoolboy at low or scurrilous mimes instead of smiling with restraint in superior fashion (σεμνότερον); or if he showed himself to be carried away by the music of singers and dancers to the extent of sometimes singing with them.[82]

When he reclined beside Gaius at a banquet Macro, according to Philo, would preach to him as follows:

You ought not to be like any of the people here, or any other men, in respect to what strikes the eye or the ear or any of the other senses, but you ought to excel in every aspect of your life as much as you are marked off from the rest of mankind in your good fortune. For it would be strange for the ruler of earth and sea to be conquered by singing and dancing or ribald jesting, or the like, and not always and everywhere to bear in mind that he is the ruler, like a shepherd or keeper of a flock, and take to himself whatever is beneficial, whether found in word or deed. . . . When you are present at a contest, whether theatrical, gymnastic, or horseracing, pay not so much attention to what is done as to the correctness with which they do it, while you reason

81. *Legat.*, 8.
82. Ibid., 42, somewhat paraphrased. On Gaius' lasciviousness and especially his love of theatrical singing and dancing see Suetonius, *C. Caligula, passim,* especially 11, 54; Dio Cassius, LIX, ii, 5; v, 5.

thus with yourself: "If such people, in matters which bring not only no profit to human life, but nothing beyond delight and pleasure at the spectacle, take all this trouble in order to be praised and admired and to win rewards, honors, crowns, and public acclaim, what ought he do who is the expert in the highest and greatest art of all?" And rulership (ἡγεμονία) is the greatest and best art of all, for the result of it is that every good and deep-soiled land, whether level or hilly, is cultivated, and every sea is navigated without danger by the laden ships of merchandise as they execute the exchange which countries carry on in those things that will be especially beneficial, for they desire mutual relations (κοινωνία), and take what they themselves need in exchange for what they have in excess. Envy never yet ruled the whole inhabited world, nor yet any of its great divisions, as all of Europe or Asia, but like a venomous serpent Envy hides in a hole, going into such restricted places as a single individual or house, or if excessively inflated, into a single city. But it never attacks the larger circle of a whole nation or country, especially since your truly august family began its universal rule. For that family has sought out from our midst whatever is apt to become injurious, and has driven it into exile to the extremities, even to the last recess of Tartarus; at the same time, those profitable and beneficial things which were in a sense driven fugitive, the family has brought back from the ends of the earth and sea to restore them to our inhabited world. All these things are now entrusted to your single hand to govern. So since you have been escorted by Nature to the stern of the most exalted ship, and have had the helm put into your hand, you must guide the common ship of mankind safely (σωτη-ρίως) and take your joy and pleasure in nothing more than in benefiting (εὐεργετεῖν) your subjects. There are various contributions which the different citizens are compelled to bring into the cities; but no contribution is more fitting a ruler than to bring in good counsels concerning his subjects, to carry out what they properly desire, to bring out good things lavishly with a liberal hand and mind, saving only those things which ought to be held back out of prudence for unknown contingencies for the future.[83]

"The unhappy man," Philo continues, "kept dinning such remarks into his ears in the hope of improving Gaius." If Philo is right, and Macro did thus belabor Gaius, we cannot blame Gaius too severely for resorting to murder to be rid of him. Yet whether Macro ever made such a speech or not, it is highly valuable to us. If it was only idealistic rhetoric for Philo to indulge in such speculation, it was, or would have been, quite as idealistic and rhetorical for Macro, as the event bitterly

83. *Legat.*, 43–51.

proved. Philo could himself hardly have had opportunity to know what passed between Gaius and Macro in these private conversations. Philo could not have offered the speech as a literal report from Macro. What Philo is doing is fairly obvious. In the relative security of Claudius' rule, he is himself taking the opportunity to invent this speech for Macro so that he could state at length his own philosophy of kingship. He has been too clever to state it as his own, for that would have been an impertinence. But under the mask of Macro, whose lack of tact cost him his life, Philo can give a picture of Gaius as having gone wrong in directly flouting the true philosophy of kingship, and no Roman could accuse Philo of himself reading the emperor a lesson. The point is hardly worth laboring at this stage, but a careful reader of what we have collected from Philo's own casual statements and from his Neo-Pythagorean prototypes must see that the passage is an extended and careful statement of the philosophy of kingship which Philo always held.[84] It seems to me that Philo is quite in earnest: he saw no other salvation for society except that it have an emperor who was literally the fulfilment of hellenistic dreams of the ideal king. The Jews were at one on at least this point with their Greek neighbors.

Philo presents the other side of the theory just as clearly. Gaius' failure to fulfil this ideal is shown to be the cause of his degeneration.[85] First Gaius resents Macro's trying to teach the science of ruling. Who ever taught it to Macro? Gaius regards himself as being now quite beyond any man's instruction. He is steeped in the long tradition of government of his family, the members of which on both sides had won dictatorial powers.[86] Further, Gaius thinks that in him is the inherited royal character, the explanation of which is that

84. That Philo has used Macro simply as the mouthpiece of his own ideal for the emperor is strengthened by comparison with other accounts. Tacitus describes Macro as an unmitigated villain: *Annal.*, vi, 45, 48. That Gaius killed him for being a nuisance and scold is Philo's own invention, apparently, for there were other ways of getting rid of his presence if he were considered on other points a valuable man. Dio Cass., LIX, x, 6, says that he had been appointed prefect of Egypt by the emperor just before Gaius murdered him: it would look as though there might have been some real cause for killing him.

85. Philo is remarkably similar to Suetonius and Dio Cassius, especially the former, in his portrait of Caligula, even as concerns the emperor's type of thinking, and hence his account would seem to be a true one. Gaius' early popularity, especially in the East, is described by both Philo and Suetonius with the same enthusiasm and much similar detail. The same is true of the accounts of the universal concern over Gaius' illness.

86. In Gaius' early years he seems to have been fond of calling himself "autocrat"; Dio Cass., LIX, xvi, 2. But as he advanced in madness this term sounded too human, and so was abandoned: πάντα μᾶλλον ἢ ἄνθρωπος αὐτοκράτωρ τε δοκεῖν εἶναι ἤθελε; ibid., xxvi, 8.

there are certain royal potencies (δυνάμεις βασιλικαί) in the sperm of rulers from their first ejection. For as the bodily and spiritual resemblances are preserved in form and shape and motion, in actions and activities, within the seminal principles (λόγοι σπερματικοί), so it is likely that resemblance with respect to leadership would be sketched at least in outline in the same seminal principles.[87] Who then would dare to teach me when even before my birth, while I still lay in the womb, nature's workshop, I was framed into an autocrat? It is ignorance teaching one who knows! Where do private citizens get the slightest right to peek into the purposes of a ruling soul (ἡγεμονικὴ ψυχή)? Yet in their shameless presumption they dare act as hierophants and mystagogues of the secrets of rulership though they are barely listed among the initiates.[88]

This is a statement of the current royal philosophy in the form which we have seen Philo can use for allegorizing the Patriarchs, and which he has admitted in theory for kings. But when Gaius bases his claim to royal right not on his official position, but on his peculiar nature and constitution, Philo regards it as sacrilege. Again when Marcus Silanus, the emperor's father-in-law, repeated Macro's mistake and tried to become Gaius' mentor, Gaius resented the admonitions on the ground, Philo says, that he himself embodied the four virtues of wisdom, control, courage, and justice in the superlative degree.[89] And Silanus, like Macro, was put out of the way.

These murders, together with the earlier one of the co-emperor, the young Tiberius, were by no means popular, says Philo, but came to be generally condoned, the executions of Macro and Silanus for their presumption, that of young Tiberius as forestalling possible civil wars between the two emperors later. For "that rulership cannot be shared is an unchangeable law of Nature."[90]

Gaius had only begun setting himself off from other men. He no longer thought it right that he should abide within the limits of human nature, but began to lift his head in aspiration of being recognized as a god.[91]

---

87. On the λόγοι σπερματικοί, a spiritual quality in the seed by which resemblance was passed on from one generation to the next, see Max Heinze, *Die Lehre vom Logos* (1872), 107–125; Hans Meyer, *Geschichte der Lehre von den Keimkräften* (1914), 5–75. The idea was primarily Stoic, but was widely adopted by other schools. On Gaius' glorifying and deifying his ancestors see Suetonius, *Caligula*, 23.

88. *Legat.*, 54–56.   89. Ibid., 64.
90. Ibid., 68: ἀκοινώνητον ἀρχή, θεσμὸς φύσεως ἀκίνητος.
91. Ibid., 75.

Philo goes on to give Gaius' reasoning on the subject according to what he says was the popular rumor (φασίν).[92] Gaius reasoned from the familiar comparison of kings to herdsmen that the shepherd is never himself a sheep, and so he, as herdsman of the human herd, is not a human being (κατ' ἄνθρωπον), but has received a greater and more divine allotment (μείζων καὶ θειότερα μοῖρα).[93] Gaius seems to have been himself not clear as to just what this meant, Philo thinks. It was nothing but applying to himself the hellenistic and oriental theory. But it is interesting that this theory itself was open to some variety of interpretation. Gaius began, says Philo, by identifying himself with the demigods Dionysus, Heracles, and the Dioscuri,[94] and holding himself quite superior to such figures as the heroes Trophonius, Amphiaraus, and Amphilochus.[95] He distinguished himself even beyond any of the demigods, for he took the honors due each, and said all belonged together to him. He appropriated to himself not only their honors but their personalities,[96] which appropriation he proclaimed by wearing their insignia. Then, not satisfied with the demigods, he went on to identify himself with the Olympians, Hermes, Apollo, and Ares.[97]

Such identifications reflect popular religions rather than philosophy. But Philo represents Gaius as going on to the philosophical position of claiming that he was the animate law (νόμος ἔμψυχος). The form in which Philo says this is his assertion that Gaius abrogated the laws of the Jews and other people arbitrarily, for he regarded himself as the law (νόμον ἡγούμενος ἑαυτόν).[98] Philo is apparently condemning Gaius for claiming the most proper function of a ruler, as Philo himself usually stated it. But a closer examination shows that Philo is criticizing Gaius not for adopting the theory, but for perverting it. For as Gaius understood and applied the theory, it meant the enslavement of the subjects by the abolition of their legal rights altogether. The monarchs who preceded Gaius, Philo has been careful to indicate, had properly fulfilled the ideal, for instead of making their rule mean the general abro-

---

92. *Legat.*, 76.

93. Ibid. Dio Cassius, LIX, xxvi, 5 (cf. 8), says of Gaius that he ἠξίου μὲν γὰρ καὶ πρότερον ὑπὲρ ἄνθρωπον νομίζεσθαι. Suetonius, *Caligula*, 22: "nec multum afuit quin statim diadema sumeret speciemque principatus in regni formam converteret. Verum admonitus, et principum et regum se excessisse fastigium, divinam ex eo maiestatem asserere sibi coepit."

94. Cf. Suetonius, *Caligula*, 22, Dio Cassius, LIX, xxvi, 6.

95. *Legat.*, 78.   96. Ibid., 80.   97. Ibid., 93.

98. Ibid., 119: "Thinking himself to be Law he abrogated the enactments of the lawmakers of every state as empty talk."

gation of law they had ruled with equity and laws (σὺν ἐπιεικείᾳ καὶ μετὰ νόμων). The true "animate law" must always be law-abiding (νόμιμος), and hence just (δίκαιος), by being able to correct existing law when necessary, but in general by guaranteeing established legal tradition. His undoubted power to abrogate and alter existing laws was to be used only in necessity. Philo could hardly regard as a necessitous change in law the flouting of Jewish legal tradition in order to enforce Gaius' claims to divinity.[99] That is, Philo is deploring the abuse, not the correct application, of the theory of "animate law."

Philo has not dared to make this criticism of Gaius only on the basis of his high-handed treatment of Jewish rights. The Romans themselves had keen recollection of Gaius' abuse of the principle. Suetonius records Gaius' resentment against his grandmother Antonia for giving him advice. Gaius remarked, "Let her remember that all things which have to do with all men (*omnia et in omnis*) are permitted to me."[100] Again Suetonius says:

As if he were going to abolish every function of the science of the lawyers he would often boast about them, "By Hercules I shall see to it that they can not give a single opinion not based upon myself."[101]

Dio Cassius[102] gives a specific instance when Gaius applied this principle of legal autonomy. On one occasion the Senate wanted to do the same thing (abuse Tiberius) as Gaius had been doing. Gaius rebuked them: "I, as autocrat, am permitted to do this, which for you would be not only a crime but impiety." Philo still has his audience well in mind,

99. I think Hirzel (Ἄγραφος Νόμος, *Abhandlungen d. sächsischen Gesellschaft, Philol.-hist. Classe*, XX, 52, n. 3) is wrong when he classifies this statement with Eurip., *Suppl.*, 429 ff., and Antiphon, *De Caede Herod.*, 12–14. These passages describe the tyrant as one who uses the legal framework for his own advantage, which is not what Philo is saying. The passage which Hirzel quotes with these from Aristotle (*Polit.*, III, 1288a 3) is on the contrary like Philo and unlike the others.

100. *Caligula*, 29.

101. Ibid., 34: "De iuris quoque consultis, quasi scientiae eorum omnem usum aboliturus, saepe iactavit, se mehercule effecturum ne quid respondere possint praeter eum." The sentence is a difficult one. One would rather expect *ipsum*, if *eum* is not the corruption of some totally different word. The *praeter* is also extremely difficult, unless it is taken as I have done as a reflection of the νόμος ἔμψυχος theory. By that the sentence means that Gaius abolished legal science, which pronounced opinions on the basis of precedent and principle, and put his own person in its place. He was the basic referent of all specific legal opinion. That is to make Suetonius say exactly what Philo says in his phrase: νόμον ἡγούμενος ἑαυτόν. The obvious parallel is the statement of Cicero quoted above, p. 54: "suam vitam, ut legem, praefert suis civibus."

102. LIX, xvi, 2.

it is clear. He has classed the abrogation of Jewish legal tradition with a general policy of Gaius which Romans themselves had had cause to resent, and at the same time he has emphasized the value of the true theory of kingship, which insisted that the genuine "animate law" was strictly law-abiding, and guaranteed the rights of subjects. Philo is no Macro in manner of addressing his Roman rulers, but he is for that reason all the more successful in driving "Macro's" ideas home.

Philo's argument throughout this section of *Legatio* is that Gaius, if he wanted to liken himself to the demigods or gods, might have done so by imitating their virtues, such as their incessant labors for mankind,[103] their brotherly love and equality which is the source of justice (ἰσότης, ἥτις ἐστὶ πηγὴ δικαιοσύνης),[104] or their giving men gifts which eased human labor and made happiness. But Gaius has not imitated the demigods in these respects. He has not reproduced Hermes as the swift herald of good tidings; he has not been a radiation of lawfulness.[105] or a healer of mankind like Apollo. He was unlike Ares in being a coward and in lacking the helpful and peaceable side of Ares' work, which latter Philo forces in by rather amusing etymology.[106] The fundamental difficulty, according to Philo, was that Gaius did not recognize that one cannot make such a counterfeit image of the form of a god or of God as is possible with money.[107]

Gaius, then, should be compared with none of the gods or demigods, for he shares neither their nature, their being, nor their purposes.[108]

However much this premature adoption by Gaius of the hellenistic theory of kingship may have been foreign to Roman tradition, Philo's description of Gaius' conduct (which corresponds to the less systematic statements of Suetonius and Dio Cassius) makes it perfectly clear that Gaius was only taking the old theory literally, as countless monarchs in the East had done before him. Philo's objection is of course not from the point of view of the Roman, though he speaks as far as possible in a

---

103. Cf. the king as φιλόπονος in Dio Chrysostom, *Oratio*, I, 21, and on the kingship of Heracles in general see ibid., 59–84.

104. *Legat.*, 85.

105. Ibid., 103. The notion that the rays of Apollo are rays of lawfulness is implied rather than expressed, but seems to me quite clear. It is a shame, Philo says, to wear Apollo's radiant crown, imitating the sun, when not the sunlight but darkness is fit for *lawless* deeds.

106. Ibid., 112 f.   107. Ibid., 110.

108. Ibid., 114: μήτε φύσεως μήτε οὐσίας ἀλλὰ μηδὲ προαιρέσεως τετυχηκότα τῆς αὐτῆς.

way to recall to his Roman readers their own objections to Caligula, but
from the point of view of the religious Jew. To this he skillfully brings
around the argument. For hoary and familiar as the identification of a
ruler with deity might be, and much as the Jews themselves had
adopted of the current theories of kingship in the East, they had never
taken this last step. Augustus and Tiberius might be divine in office and
in function, but the Jew, for reasons of his own, refused to admit divinity in them. For Philo says that what Jewish Law Gaius tried to destroy
was not non-essential,

but the greatest point of all, for he had deified, at least in appearance, the
nature of man, which has come into existence and will perish, into the nature
which has no beginning or end. And this the Jewish nation judged to be the
most horrible form of sacrilege.[109]

That is, Philo persists to the end in refusing to allow the Greek and
Roman in politics to use the word "divine" with the same freedom he
himself uses it for the Patriarchs. Yet I cannot read *Legatio* with a sense
that I am reading "mere" theory. Philo draws a very fine line between
the true "animate law" and the "counterfeit" one. But I am confident
that if Philo was ready to face death rather than endure the "counterfeit," he was just as sincere in believing that the salvation of society lay
in the true king.

But why did Jews like Philo, who described the king in exactly the
same terms as the Pythagoreans, refuse, when claimed for an actual
Roman emperor, to recognize the divinity they otherwise theoretically
admitted? The conventional answer to this question is that worship of
the king, or any form of veneration which indicated that the king was
super-human, was an offence against Jewish, and later against Christian, monotheism. However true this may have been for orthodox Jews,
for Philo and the Christians it seems to me very dubious. In the first
place, it is certain that no intelligent Greek or Roman dreamed that in
calling the king "divine," and giving him ritualistic tribute, he was
identifying the king with supreme deity, or setting up a rival or parallel
to the Creator and Lord of the universe. "Divine," θεῖος, is really a
word which must often be translated by our word "godly," a word
which etymologically might give as much offence when applied to a human being as "divine" has done. Yet "godly" can be used by us freely

109. *Legat.*, 118.

because it has no such technical association with monotheism as our "divine." The Greek could use "divine" absolutely, as the adjective from ὁ θεός, the word for the one supreme God; or he could use it loosely as the adjective of θεός without the article, when it implied no greater divinity than Philo associated with the Patriarchs, and Christians with the saints, conceptions which in their minds did not in the least qualify their monotheism. The Greek or Roman would express reverence to a "godly man" in cult form in accordance with his religious terminology without prejudicing his monotheism, just as, again, Christians, still monotheists, venerated the Virgin and saints. Such is the practice of Shintoism today, a practice which in politics conservative Christians still refuse to understand. The king was, in the terms of Ecphantus, "more divine" than other men because he had a larger share than they of that "divine part" which had been breathed in lesser measure into everyone. The king's saving and governing power over men rested upon that *quantitative* distinction from them. Philo in the Mystery applied all these categories to the Patriarchs quite as literally as does Ecphantus to the king, and, as a result, is caught at least once *praying* to Moses.[110] Refusal to do as much for the emperor, then, was not a reservation from the point of view of monotheism, but was simply a refusal to recognize that in a given pagan emperor was to be found the "more divine thing." Philo has spoken of the dead Augustus and Tiberius as highly as could any gentile. Yet he praises Augustus for not insisting upon recognition as a divinity, and would obviously have refused to revere his statue just as emphatically as the statue of Gaius.

Hellenistic Jewish description of the Patriarchs, men "more divine than we are," was later paralleled in Christian reverence for the saints. The Church, which refused in face of torture to permit sacrifice to the emperor, came to encourage liturgical reverence at shrines of the Virgin, and certainly came nearer to fully deifying the Virgin than paganism ever did to fully deifying one of the emperors. When Ecphantus burned a pinch of incense before an image of his king or emperor he had no more idea that he was worshipping the supreme deity in this act than have Christians when they light a candle before an image of the Virgin or one of the saints: he would have been completely baffled at the Christian distinction which made one a breach of monotheism and the other not. He would have been just as puzzled at Philo, who ac-

110. By *Light, Light,* 233.

cepted all his statements about the ideal king and applied them to Moses and Abraham with a literalness with which Ecphantus himself probably never applied them to anyone; who went on to center his religious loyalties and experience in Moses as Ecphantus never dreamed of doing in any ruler; and who yet insisted that what he was doing did not break his monotheism, while he would rather die than practise polytheism by sacrificing to the emperor with Ecphantus.

Frankly, Ecphantus' perplexity is quite my own, for in spite of the statements and sincerity of both Philo and the later Christians I cannot see any more than the Romans how monotheism was at all the issue. For if they defined monotheism as belief that there was only one Being above men to whom men might direct their devotions, then in practice neither Philo nor the Christians were monotheists. If their monotheism meant that they admitted only a single supreme deity, along with whom were lesser divine beings, angels, "more divine men" on earth or in heaven, then they were monotheists as Ecphantus himself was a monotheist; and if their worship included veneration to the lesser divine beings, then their worship was, in essence if not in form, that of Ecphantus.

Modern psychology has taught us that when human logic breaks down as Philo's logic has done, we must look for some motive or emotion which has invaded the problem from outside the ideas being discussed. Actually, it seems to me, the arbitrary point at which the process of hellenization stopped for the Jews was not arbitrary at all, but had several definite causes.

First there was the real, if irrational, feeling, with Jews as later with Christians, that a dead saint is more holy than a living one, and hence that after death he can be recognized as "more divine" in a way impossible during his life. The term "divine Sage" of pagan speculation was likewise applied, if to any individual at all, to men safely removed by centuries from curious scrutiny. So Philo might well have talked about Abraham and Moses in language which he had to contradict for his contemporaries. This is a consideration which may have affected his attitude toward the emperor, but other considerations seem to me more important.

Secondly, Philo's deepest religious instincts were involved in this refusal to put Gaius, or even Augustus, really on a level with the Jewish Patriarchs. To do so would have been to abandon the last stronghold of

Jewish religious particularism. If terms used for Moses and his law could be applied to any Roman emperor, the unique value of Judaism would have been gone, and the *raison d'être* of the distinct race with it. Not monotheism, but religious Judaism, must have perished with such a concession.

Thirdly, with this went an equally important motive in the refusal, the instinct of Jewish patriotism. How much Philo resented being ruled by Roman conquerors has clearly appeared. In the allegories of Joseph for the inner circle of his own people there is a venom which shows that the suicidal patriotism of the Jews of his day burned in Philo no less hotly because its light was kept skillfully hid from Roman eyes. How could such a patriotism be expected to reason so logically that it was ready to admit that a gentile autocrat over Jewish liberties shared in divine nature? That Roman rule could be recognized as a divine dispensation to discipline the faithful for a time was entirely possible, and Philo and his friends intended to start no armed revolt. But death itself was better than admitting that these rulers, like Moses, had the "greater share of divine nature" which made them saviors of the human race. Jews could take many hellenistic ideas into their religion, but not divine kings when they were Greeks or Romans who ruled over the Jews by force.

It was not monotheism which was the issue, clearly, and I can think of no other motive than this politico-religious one as the reason why Jews stopped at this point in their hellenization. No more than monotheism can I believe that the issue was the Jewish detestation of images. The Jew was not asked, be it remembered, to go into pagan temples to venerate the emperor's statue with pagan rites. He was asked to put the image into his own synagogues, and show respect to it in his own fashion. Discovery of Jewish art has recently taught us that by not more than a century after Philo's time, and perhaps before him, hellenized Jews were making the freest use of pagan images in their catacombs and synagogues. We are even told in the Talmud[111] that rabbis of the late First and early Second Centuries put various images, including

111. J. D. Eisenstein, "Maẓẓah," *The Jewish Encyclopedia*, VIII, 394: "In the house of R. Gamaliel the perforations of the maẓẓot represented figures. . . . The figures were those of animals, flowers, etc. Artistic perforation was later prohibited as it consumed too much time and caused fermentation. Baytus ben Zonin suggested stamping the maẓẓah with ready-made figured plates, but was opposed on the ground that no discrimination must be made in favor of any particular kind of perforation (Pes. 37a). R. Isaac b. Gayyat says the figures represented Greeks, doves, and fishes."

those of Greeks (surely Greek gods), upon their sacred mazzoth. Again if Jews could put images of Nike, Demeter, Tyche, Helios, Orpheus, and Ares in their synagogues, why not an image of the emperor, unless it was precisely the emperor whom they did not wish fully to recognize? That is, in another aspect of their hellenization the Jews have again stopped short, logic or no logic, at precisely the same point. And again we must conclude that it was not the use of images any more than it was the idea of divinity in humanity which they refused to accept, but the Roman emperor as the realization of the kingly ideal for Jews. Indeed, the very fact that they completely accepted the pagan theory of kingship made their rejection of Roman imperial divinity all the more essential. For if God could give to man his true royal representation from gentile stock, Judaism as a religion and race alike had become meaningless. The Jew of that feverish day could, in the long run, take anything else from the gentiles, even death, but not this.

The power of an idea to survive is not determined by its logical origins. The new religion which regarded itself as the true or completed Judaism carried over from Judaism both the idea of the saving power of divinity in humanity and the prejudice against associating this idea with the Roman emperor. To say nothing of the blending of humanity and divinity in Jesus Christ, the Christian veneration of the Virgin and soon of the great company of saints belied their political logic in which humanity and divinity were still kept in sharp contrast. Similarly Christians could use images, but not images of the emperor. Christians followed Hellenistic Jews in regarding "the powers that be," however malevolent, as "ordained by God," and they had no inclination, when the Empire became Christian, to modify the pagan theory of kingship otherwise than to discard such statements of the emperor's relation to God as would imply an emperor cult. For the traditional distinction was so fundamental a part of the Christian heritage from Judaism that Christians insisted, when they came into power, upon changing the formula of "divine nature" to "divine right," in order that the "divinity that doth hedge a king" might never imply such veneration as was given to images of the Virgin and the saints.

What it is interesting to see is that the arbitrary logic of Christianity, which took ancient theories of the king on every point but the king's personal divinity, was itself a part of the Christian heritage from Judaism. When Philo refused to concede any measure of divinity to the

Roman emperor which would imply veneration, and led his friends to Rome to try to get his attitude sanctioned by Gaius, it little appeared that the successors of this group in Christianity would ultimately be victorious, and force the distinction upon the Empire, so that monarchy for the next fifteen hundred years would keep the kingly ideal of the ancients, but keep also the modification which the racial feeling of Hellenistic Jews had required.

There is one more aspect of Philo's ideas of kingship which must be examined. For over against the claims of the Roman emperors Philo himself occasionally gives us a glimpse of a still higher type of king for whom he was looking, that figure which is usually called the Messiah. An ideal warrior and king was to come who would "subdue great and populous nations."[112] Philo has little to say about the Messianic hope, but what he does say shows that there was much more thought of it than he dares write. In his scarcely veiled vituperation of the Roman rule at Alexandria, as he wrote it under cover of an allegory of Joseph for the faithful in the *Allegory,* he has been seen to remind them quietly of the true Herdsman who was to lay the ax at the very roots.[113] Somewhat more openly, but still kept well within the generalities, is the discussion of the promised "Man" in *De Benedictionibus,* printed by Cohn as a part of *De Praemiis et Poenis.* Philo has been describing the golden age of the future. At that time the enemies of the Jews (the "pious") may try to rise against them, but when they see that the Jews have the alliance of the Just One or Justice (ὁ δικαίος or τὸ δίκαιον),[114] the gentiles (the "wicked") will drop their arms and flee. For Virtue is in itself invincible. So the promised Man will come, lead the armies, and conquer all men. The Greek is obscure as to whether Philo here means τοῦ δικαίου as the genitive of the masculine or of the neuter. Is he referring to "the Just One" (God or the Messiah), or to "Justice"? Leopold Cohn took it as a reference to God,[115] but it seems rather a parallel of the ἀρετή of the next line, the ultimately invincible force. The promised Man, who is mentioned almost immediately, is apparently the bringer, the incarnation of this ἀρετή. At least that is a possible interpretation of the passage.

The difficulties continue in that the next sentence is quite unintelli-

---

112. *Praem.,* 95.   113. See above, p. 24.   114. *Praem.,* 93.
115. Gloss in *Philos Werke* (Bibliography no. 492), *ad loc.*

gible in the manuscripts. The τοῦτο with which §97 begins must be changed into τούτους or τοῦτον, and there is nothing to show which is right. §97 is a description of the coming to "these people" (the Jews, the pious ones) of the royal prerogatives of splendor (σεμνότης), impressiveness (δεινότης), and benefaction (εὐεργεσία) in the age after this "war." That is, the royal power comes to "these people" if we read τούτους; it will come to the Man himself if we read τοῦτον. Cohn prefers to read the plural, Bréhier[116] the singular. My feeling is that Cohn is right, for throughout the treatise Philo's "Messianic Age," to which he is constantly reverting, is seen from the point of view of the race. The ideal man is described as being superior to the city only to show that the ideal race is superior to every other race, and so, by traditional logic of Philo's day, ought to have the rulership over all other peoples.[117] The scattered race is to be gathered together again.[118] It is the race as a whole which will "at that time" be so well regulated in the cities, so successful in the country, that the Jews will be the world's bankers, lending money to all people everywhere.[119] The virtue of this race will even influence the animal kingdom, to the extent of bringing in that peaceful era which the prophet described when the lion should lie down with the lamb. Philo is not content with so simple a statement of the hope. With him it will be a time when bears, lions and leopards, and those beasts found in India, elephants and tigers, will at the approach of men wag their tails like Maltese lap-dogs with a cheerful motion.[120] The passage would then seem to be a picture of the coming of the race as a whole into royal power.

With this passage should be compared the very similar one in the companion piece, *De Exsecrationibus*. But at once the question arises whether these statements are sincerely meant, represent any essential part of Philo's thinking, or are mere statements made *ad hoc*, traditional flourishes for his conservative audience. Such was the opinion of Drummond,[121] Bréhier,[122] and Bousset,[123] to name but a few. Only Gfrörer[124] a century ago took Philo seriously on this matter. None of these had in mind as a Messianic passage the poignant reference to the

---

116. *Les Idées*, 5 f.   117. *Praem.*, 114.
118. Ibid., 117; cf. *Exs.*, 164.   119. *Praem.*, 106 f.
120. Ibid., 89. It is notable that Philo seems to have known nothing of African elephants.
121. *Philo Judaeus*, II, 322.   122. *Les Idées*, 4.
123. *Religion des Judentums* (1926), 439.
124. *Philo und die jüdisch-alexandrinische Theosophie* (1835), I, 494–534.

coming Husbandman and his pruning in the Allegory.[125] Taking *De Benedictionibus* and *De Exsecrationibus* by themselves it might be possible to believe that the passages were unconnected with the rest of Philo's thinking, and had no important part in it.[126] But even if these passages could not be harmonized with the rest of Philo's writing, it is rather wooden merely on that account to deny to Philo any real Messianic hope. People who have limited their hearts' desires to the logical possibilities of a system have lived only in the imaginations of historians.

It does not appear, however, that the Hope was left as unconnected with the rest of his thought as it has been taken to be. For Philo has given us broad hints as to how the Hope was to be integrated even with his Mystery. The great Age is to begin with a sudden transformation of the Jewish character everywhere. Up to that time they will have been scattered and enslaved, which I take to be Philo's way of expressing the fact that they will still be living subject to other nations' rulership. The great era will be introduced by the "collective transformation of all the race into virtue" (ἀθρόα πρὸς ἀρετὴν μεταβολή), which will so amaze their present rulers that they will let the Jews go free, since the masters themselves will be ashamed to govern people so obviously their superiors.[127] The Jews will then arise as a body and come together from all over the earth to a single place (obviously Palestine) under the leadership of a vision which they, but no one else, can see. It is a vision of "something more divine than human nature" (θειοτέρα ἢ κατὰ φύσιν ἀνθρωπίνην), which apparently means a vision of a "Man" who is beyond human nature and will lead them all together.[128] Such a blessed experience comes to the Jews partly because of the mercy of God, partly because of the *prayers of the Patriarchs* of old whose intercession is obviously still continued for their descendants, and partly because of the great change which has come upon those (Jews) who are in a position to make promises and agreements, namely the change from a life which had no direction (ἐξ ἀνοδίας) "into the Road, whose end is no less than the pleasing of God as sons please a father."[129] We are really in the Mystery again.[130] The point is that when enough Jews who are in po-

125. *Som.*, ii, 64; see above, p. 24.
126. On the treatises *Bened.* and *Exs.*, see my "Philo's Exposition of the Law and his De Vita Mosis," *Harvard Theological Review*, XXVII (1933), 109–125.
127. *Exs.*, 164. 128. Ibid., 165. 129. Ibid., 167.
130. Philo is certainly making a reference to the Mystery in §§162–164 when he describes δυνάμεις which come from God to men to lead them up into τὴν πρὸς τὸν αὐτοῦ λόγον συγγένειαν, ἀφ᾽ οὗ καθάπερ ἀρχετύπου γέγονεν ὁ ἀνθρώπινος νοῦς.

litical power and responsibility have become transformed into Jews of
the mystic Goal, then, by the mercy of God and the prayers of the saints
(the Patriarchs), all Jews will suddenly experience the same transformation, and will come out of their present slavery, their political bond-
age. The world will watch with wonder as they gather from the corners
of the earth to return, under the leadership of their Guide, to their own
place. Then will come the happy Age, with enemies discomfited, and
the Jews in such peace and prosperity as their ancestors have never experienced. The great Ax has indeed laid them low now, but it has not
cut the root of Judaism as Philo elsewhere promises it will cut the root
of the other "trees." The old Jewish root is left, and from it will miracu-
lously spring up a new and mighty trunk.[131]

The Messianic hope is indeed integrated with Philo's mystic concepts,
surprisingly so in a treatise which in general moves on a "normative"
level. Taking this passage with the reference to the Husbandman in *De
Somniis* it seems to me that Philo's Messianic hope was a very vital part
of his thought. It is not surprising that we get so little expression of it
from a man as prominent politically as Philo; rather the wonder is that
Philo's "caution" has put even this much of it in writing. My own guess
is that we have in this hope with its peculiar mode of fulfillment the
real answer to the question why Philo felt himself, in spite of his mystic
leanings, so powerfully driven into political life. He says that only as
the men in a position to make "promises and treaties" for the Jews became Jews who had really conquered in the Mystery could the great
relief come for the people. The mercy of God, the prayers of the Patriarchs, these were important, of course. But the decisive thing which
made these divine mercies available was the presence of Mystic leaders
in practical politics for the Jewish people. This may well have been
Philo's sense of call. It was truly a despairing ambition to try to live the
mystic life in Roman Alexandria. But only as he, Philo, faced this calling with the courage of his embassy to Gaius, could the rest of the Jews
hope for the deliverance of the great Age to come. He, or men greater
than he, must be the political "saviors" of the Jews.

The notion opens up a great many interesting suggestions for the interpretation of the Mystery. For our present political purposes it is sufficient that Philo has definitely committed himself to the dream of the
Messianic Age familiar to all Jews at the time, an age which will be

131. *Exs.*, 166 to end.

marked by the complete political rout of all other peoples under the inspired leadership of a Man who will lead the armies and put the ax to the root of the false growth of the Gentiles. And in that Age the dream of the ideal kingship, whether in the person of the Man or in the race, will be realized. That dream of a rulership which can make all society, even the animal and vegetable kingdoms, perfect, can bring universal "salvation," is not vain. Some day the true splendor (σεμνότης) will bring in humility (αἰδώς), impressiveness (δεινότης) will bring fear (φοβός), benefaction (εὐεργεσία) will bring good will (εὔνοια).

Philo's political philosophy, in theory and practice, has appeared sufficiently clearly. He thought of rulership in hellenistic fashion as being ideally a representation of God's rule to men, and of the ruler, if he were truly fit for his task, as being in a special relation with God. But in practical political situations his Judaism kept him from going all the way with this theory. No gentile ruler, however godlike, could be recognized as being of divine "nature." Philo's notions are interesting as his own, but much more so as there can be little doubt that he represented the thinking of Hellenistic Jews on the subject. Philo's acceptance of the theory of the king's divine right and prerogative, together with his rejection of the king's divine person, is precisely the distinction drawn by early Christian Apologists. It is the political philosophy which, far from being of no practical importance, had the power ultimately to check the tendencies manifest in Aurelian and Diocletian, become the official philosophy of the Christian Empire, write itself into the laws of Justinian, and so set the pattern of royalty down into the Twentieth Century.

Most interesting it is to see that with this political philosophy went also the Jewish hope of the Messiah who was to come and bring in the truly divine rulership. For the dream of a fully divine king, whom the Greeks tried to see in such characters as Alexander and Demetrius Poliorcetes, and the Persians in Cyrus, was the dream of the Jew none the less because he scorned the claims of Roman emperors to divinity. To the Jew as to the Greek, the only true government was the rule of God; but for the Jew the rule of God could never be accomplished until a miracle should happen and the Messiah come. Similarly the Christians, however loyal they might be to their divinely accoutered James, Louis, Friedrich, or Nicholas, knew that the governments of this world were but expedients of God, sooner or later to be replaced by the ideal rule of God's truly divine representative. What those Christians did not know was that their thoughts about the king, his dignity, his legal power, his individual personification of the state, his duties, his privileges, and his ultimate inadequacy and transitoriness, were all worked out by the forgotten Jews of the Diaspora as they struggled to adapt their Jewish heritage to the daring claims of hellenistic and Roman royalty.

APPENDIX

AN interesting attempt to apply the political philosophy of Philo in the sixteenth century is represented in the dedication of Bellier's French translation of Philo.[1] The volume is now so rare that it seems of value to append a translation.

To my Lord PHILIPPE HURAUT, *knight, Lord of Chiverni, one of the King's Privy Council, and Chancellor of his order: Pierre Bellier his humble servant.*

Sir, knowing that from your earliest age you have always borne deep affection for letters, and even more now when your house is equipped and embellished with an exceedingly beautiful, rich, and rare library, where all authors are gathered; I have dedicated to you the fruit of this my work: to the end that the Republic of France should recognize you always for one who takes in his safekeeping virtue, science, and the men who dedicate themselves to them. Happy the Republic in which such magistrates flourish, who cherish and love those who work for her. I present to you, then, this great and divine Philo in French, like a secretary of Moses; a man of whom they say in a common proverb: "Either Plato philonizes, or Philo platonizes": to such an extent are the sayings and the words of these two divine men similar. This is commonly said: but, as for me, it seems to me that, so much as the body is more excellent than the shadow which follows it, so much is Philo more excellent than Plato; for Philo mounts to the peak of divinity and gives to it from within, but Plato approaches only to the extent that he drew up the larger part of his divine statements from the ancestors and forerunners of Philo in the voyage he made to Egypt. Philo was Alexandrian by nationality, and Hebrew by race, one of the first and renowned priests. He flourished at the time of Caius Caligula, to whom he was, with others, sent to Rome as an ambassador, to reveal to him the wrongs that were being done to the Jews in Alexandria; but that was not without danger to his person, indeed to all his race; for (as he tells in the book entitled: Concerning the Virtues, and Embassy to Gaius) *thinking to*

1. See the Bibliography, no. 481. This dedication was pointed out to me by Mr. Goodhart. It is interesting to note also, in view of this dedication, that in Mr. Goodhart's collection is a copy of the Geneva, 1613, edition of Philo (see the Bibliography, no. 398), bound for Louis XIII and bearing his rare coat of arms.

*have found a judge just and equal to all parties, he fell into the hands
of an enemy and accuser. And what is more this did not exasperate him
so much as the mad idea which that stupid beast had fixed in his head,
namely that he was God: he wished, as such, to have himself adored by
all the inhabited world. He had even commanded that they should set
up within the secret oratory of the Temple at Jerusalem a statue bearing
this inscription: Caius, the new Jupiter. Philo, having heard this, was
so astonished and overcome, that, abandoning all human hopes, he
came to say that it was necessary to await divine aid, since that of men
had failed. This dictum did not remain without effect: for some time
afterward (as Josephus recounts at length), that Emperor who was impious and wicked, drunken and sordid, a devourer of the people (Emperor, say I, by title, not in fact), was taken out of this world by his
subjects. So divine justice, which has an eye on human affairs, did not
give him the leisure to execute his enterprise. That is the tragedy which
the great power of God allotted to him, that power which cut him off
and hounded him down: as since the creation of the world, such, or
similar, fates have come to those who, having set themselves up as governors of the gentle and humane flock of men, instead of good governors have shown themselves tyrants. I shall not hold you with a longer
discourse, my Lord, knowing well that Philo's life and deeds are well
enough known to you. I have only at the end a word to say to you in
Philo's name: for he begs you very strongly to make a report of a little
verbal request to the council of the King: little, I say, in words, but of
very great consequence, being a matter of the peace and repose of all of
poor France, which is afflicted by evils from on high because of the
execrable blasphemies pronounced daily, on every occasion, against the
honor of God. The request tends to this, that, for the means and reasons
deduced at length in Philo's treatise on the second commandment of
the Decalogue, the Edict of the late magnanimous King Francis, ances-
tor of our most illustrious King, against those who take the name of
God in vain, and blaspheme it, be renewed and very strictly enforced.
Philo expects indeed that this request will be granted to him by the
King, as being the justest and most reasonable of all those which one
could present him. There is only one difficulty implicit in the execution
of this. If it should please you, my Lord, to take the trouble—or rather
pleasure (for there is only pleasure in whatever one does for the honor
of God)—to have the magistrates and judges of the provinces com-*

manded to keep their eyes carefully on the carrying out of the said
Edict; and that along with this the sacred Sunday and day of rest be
solemnized duly and in accordance with its majesty; then there would
be hope that God would make peace with us. In doing this, all things
would be changed into a better condition. Instead of our having, as
heretofore, the seasons of the year disarranged and debauched, not keeping at all their proper nature and quality, it will render them regular
for us, ready and eager to perform the service to which they are des-
tined. So that when they do their duty, it would not be for the advantage of our enemies, since we should have none, but for our profit; along
with this the earth, being well seasoned by them, would not deceive our
good hopes, producing only a fourth part of what we would expect, but
would repay with very great interest that which will have been lent
her. In place of war, it would grant us much-desired peace; in place of
sterility, abundance of goods; in place of sickness, health; in place of
pestilence, a good and salubrious air; in place of enmity and estrange-
ment, friendship and communion; and so many murders would not be
committed daily, which, without doubt, according to the word of God,
derive only from the said blasphemies: as Moses says that the knife will
not go out of the house of him who takes the name of his Lord God in
vain. In short, heaven, the stars, the air, and the earth, common mother
of all, would smile upon us, and would furnish for us gladly what before she gave grudgingly and as by constraint and with regret. By this
means the time of Saturn and the golden age of the good King Francis,
author of this Edict, of which we speak, would come to flourish. This
is not by any means a fabricated tale, but the oracle and express wish of
God, as those know who have tasted not merely with the edge of the
lips the sweet and savorous beverage of Wisdom, but who have savored
and imbibed it well. At Paris, the first of August, 1575.

PHILO

THE PORTRAIT TYPE OF PLATE I CHRISTIANIZED

From a IX. century Ms. in the Bibliothèque Nationale.
See Bibliography, no. 56, and page v.

A

GENERAL BIBLIOGRAPHY

OF PHILO JUDAEUS

HOWARD L. GOODHART

AND

ERWIN R. GOODENOUGH

PREFACE

THE objectives of any bibliography are simply stated, completeness, accuracy, and convenience of arrangement.

Completeness did not seem to us to involve the including of incidental or conventional references to Philo such as appear in all popular works on the early history of Judaism or Christianity, or on the history of philosophy. Accordingly, though personal judgment had to rule arbitrarily in many cases, it seemed worth while to list only such items from modern times as showed evidence of some study of Philo. But a "Philo item" is by no means always shown to be such directly in the title. To list completely all mention of Philo in scholarly discussion of early Christianity, for example, would in itself be an extended problem, to be dealt with only by one working systematically in that field and with an eye to that particular point. The same is true of Philo's place in Greek philosophy, in Hebrew tradition, and in ecclesiastical tradition. Quite apart, then, from inevitable cases of oversight, the lists in many of the sections which follow are offered only as a suggestive beginning for one interested in tracing what scholars have considered to have been the influence of Philo in the various fields.

As to accuracy, in spite of our manifest debt to predecessors, we have spent so much time in trying to identify erroneous titles from former bibliographies that we have spared no pains ourselves to make each title complete and exact. We have ourselves seen every item which we list without comment. Items inaccessible to us are listed with the source of our entry: "From no.—" means that we have taken the title as we list it from the item which has that number in this Bibliography; "From U.C." means that the title so marked is from the Union Catalogue of America; "B.M.," British Museum Catalogue; "B.N.," the Catalogue of the Bibliothèque Nationale; "Heinsius," or "Kayser," the annual German *Bücher-Lexikons*.

Similarly we do not hope to have done more than approximate a solution of the problem of arrangement. Classification of titles so greatly contributes to the usefulness of a bibliography that classification had to be attempted here. But it was extremely dubious in many cases where to put an item, and again personal judgment had to take the place of any definite criterion. By making cross references we have tried to indicate the more obvious cases in which items are important for more than one category; but all students of Philo know that valuable comment upon almost any Philonic doctrine may appear in a secondary work which deals primarily with any other aspect of his teachings. One using the Bibliography should therefore be warned not to assume that titles in a given classification exhaust the literature, even the literature in this Bibliography, on that subject. The titles are arranged chronologically within each section; when two or more titles in the same group appeared in the same year they are listed alphabetically by author.

Items marked with an asterisk (*) are a part of Mr. Goodhart's private collection; of those marked with a dagger (†) he has a photostat. He will be glad to have scholars use the collection for works not otherwise accessible and to lend any but a few of the books to College or University Libraries. We shall try to keep the Bibliography growing through the years, and shall be grateful for notice of publications from authors, as well as for suggestions of titles which should have been included here.

H. L. G.
E. R. G.

New York, September, 1937.

CONTENTS

ABBREVIATIONS AND TITLES' OF THE EXTANT
TREATISES ATTRIBUTED TO PHILO

Abr. On Abraham (Colson and Whitaker, VI). *De Abrahamo* (Cohn and Wendland, IV). Βίος σοφοῦ τοῦ κατὰ διδασκαλίαν τελειωθέντος ἢ νόμων ἀγράφων <τὸ πρῶτον> ὅ ἐστι περὶ Ἀβραάμ.

Aet. On the Eternity of the World. *De aeternitate mundi* (VI). Περὶ ἀφθαρσίας κόσμου. Περὶ τῆς τοῦ κόσμου γενέσεως (MS. M of Cohn and Wendland).

Agr. On Husbandry (III). *De agricultura* (II). Περὶ γεωργίας.

Animal. Alexander, or That Dumb Animals have Reason. *Alexander, sive de eo quod rationem habeant bruta animalia.* Ὁ Ἀλέξανδρος ἢ περὶ τοῦ λόγου ἔχειν τὰ ἄλογα ζῷα (Eusebius). (Found only in Armenian and Aucher's translation.)

Antiq. Antiquities. *Historia ab initio mundi usque ad David regem. De successione generationum. Liber Philonis Antiquitatum.*

Cher. On the Cherubim, and the Flaming Sword, and Cain the First Man Created out of Man (II). *De cherubim* (I). Περὶ τῶν Χερουβὶμ καὶ τῆς φλογίνης ῥομφαίας καὶ τοῦ κτισθέντος πρώτου ἐξ ἀνθρώπου Κάϊν.

Conf. On the Confusion of Tongues (IV). *De confusione linguarum* (II). Περὶ συγχύσεως διαλέκτων.

Cong. On Mating with the Preliminary Studies (IV). *De congressu eruditionis gratia* (III). Περὶ τῆς πρὸς τὰ προπαιδεύματα συνόδου.

Cont. On the Contemplative Life. *De vita contemplativa* (VI). Περὶ βίου θεωρητικοῦ ἢ ἱκετῶν (Περὶ ἀρετῶν τὸ τέταρτον). Ἱκέται ἢ περὶ ἀρετῶν δ' (C).

Decal. On the Decalogue (VII). *De decalogo* (IV). Περὶ τῶν δέκα λόγων οἳ κεφάλαια νόμων εἰσίν. Εἰς τὴν δεκάλογον Μωσέως (AP). Περὶ νόμων ἰδέας (M).

Deo On God. *De deo* (found only in Armenian and Aucher's translation).

Det. That the Worse is Wont to Attack the Better (II). *Quod deterius potiori insidiari soleat* (I). Περὶ τοῦ τὸ χεῖρον τῷ κρείττονι φιλεῖν ἐπιτίθεσθαι.

Immut. On the Unchangeableness of God (III). *Quod deus sit immutabilis* (II). Ὅτι ἄτρεπτον τὸ θεῖον. Ὅτι ἄτρεπτόν ἐστι τὸ θεῖον λόγος θ' (U).

Ebr. On Drunkenness (III). *De ebrietate* (II). Περὶ μέθης λόγος πρῶτος. Περὶ μέθης λόγος ιβ' (U). Περὶ μέθης (GH).

Exs. On Curses. *De exsecrationibus* (V). Περὶ ἀρῶν.

Flac. Against Flaccus. *In Flaccum* (VI). Εἰς Φλάκκον. Φλάκκος ψεγόμενος

---

1. English titles are taken from the Colson and Whitaker edition of Philo in the *Loeb Classical Library* (no. 437) as far as that work is completed. Following the English title is the number of the volume in which the treatise is to be found. Latin and Greek titles are taken from the Cohn and Wendland edition (no. 431). The Latin title is followed by the number of the volume in which the treatise appears. Significant variants in the Greek titles are given together with the MS. authority.

(G = Phot. Bibl. cod. 105). Φίλωνος ἱστορία πάνυ ὠφέλιμος καὶ τῷ βίω χρήσιμος τὰ κατὰ τὸν Φλάκκον ἤτοι περὶ προνοίας (A).

Fug. On Flight and Finding (V). *De fuga et inventione* (III). Περὶ φυγῆς καὶ εὑρέσεως. Περὶ φυγάδων (H).

Gig. On the Giants (II). *De gigantibus* (II). Περὶ γιγάντων. Περὶ γιγάντων λόγος η' (U).

Heres Who is the Heir of Divine Things (IV). *Quis rerum divinarum heres* (III). Περὶ τοῦ τίς ὁ τῶν θείων ἐστιν κληρονόμος καὶ περὶ τῆς εἰς τὰ ἴσα καὶ ἐνάντια τομῆς.

Jona On Jona. *De Jona* (found only in Armenian and in Aucher's translation).

Jos. On Joseph (VI). *De Josepho* (IV). Βίος πολιτικοῦ ὅπερ ἐστὶ περὶ Ἰωσήφ.

LA Allegorical Interpretation of Genesis, I, II and III (I). *Legum allegoria*, i, ii, iii (I). i) Νόμων ἱερῶν ἀλληγορίας τῶν μετὰ τὴν ἑξαήμερον τὸ πρῶτον (UF). . . . τὸ δεύτερον (L). ii) Εἰς τὸ ποιήσωμεν βοηθὸν κατ' αὐτόν (M). Τὴν μετὰ τὴν ἑξαήμερον (A). iii) Νόμων ἱερῶν ἀλληγορία δευτέρα (APBH).

Legat. Legation to Gaius. *Legatio ad Gaium* (VI). Ἀρετῶν πρῶτον ὅ ἐστι τῆς αὐτοῦ πρεσβείας πρὸς Γάϊον. Περὶ ἀρετῶν καὶ πρεσβείας πρὸς Γάϊον (H). Ἱστορία πάνυ χρήσιμος καὶ ὠφέλιμος περὶ τῶν κατὰ τὸν Γάϊον καὶ τῆς αἰτίας τῆς πρὸς ἅπαν τὸ Ἰουδαίων ἔθνος ἀπεχθείας αὐτοῦ (A). Γάιος ψεγόμενος (Phot. Bibl. cod. 105).

Migr. On the Migration of Abraham (IV). *De migratione Abrahami* (II). Περὶ ἀποικίας.

Mos. Moses I and II (VI). *De vita Mosis,* i, ii (IV). i) Περὶ τοῦ βίου Μωυσέως λόγος πρῶτος. Περὶ τοῦ βίου Μωσέως λόγος πρῶτος: θεολόγου καὶ προφήτου (H). . . . θεολογίας καὶ προφητείας (L). ii) Περὶ τοῦ βίου Μωσέως λόγος δεύτερος (BEMH). Περὶ τῆς τοῦ Μωυσέος νομοθετικῆς (P). At §66 of *Mos.* ii MSS. and some editions begin a third book, λόγος γ' (BEMG). Περὶ τοῦ βίου μωσέως λόγος τρίτος (ss. περὶ ἱερωσύνης λόγος τρίτος) (H). Περὶ ἱερωσύνης λόγος γ' (VO).

Mund. On the World. *De mundo.* Περὶ κόσμου. (Printed in Mangey, no. 404, II, and Richter, no. 413, VI. See below, p. 145.)

Mut. On the Change of Names (V). *De mutatione nominum* (III). Περὶ τῶν μετονομαζομένων καὶ ὧν ἕνεκα μετονομάζονται.

Opif. On the Account of the World's Creation Given by Moses (I). *De opificio mundi* (I). Περὶ τῆς κατὰ Μωυσέα κοσμοποιίας. Περὶ τῆς τοῦ Μωσέως κοσμοποιίας λόγος Δ' (G).

Plant. Concerning Noah's Work as a Planter (III). *De plantatione* (II). Περὶ φυτουργίας Νῶε τὸ δεύτερον. Περὶ φυτουργίας το δεύτερον Νῶε λόγος ια' (U).

Post. On the Posterity of Cain and his Exile (II). *De posteritate Caini* (II). Περὶ τῶν τοῦ δοκησισόφου Κάιν ἐγγόνων καὶ ὡς μετανάστης γίγνεται.

Praem. On Rewards and Punishments. *De praemiis et poenis* (V). Περὶ ἄθλων καὶ ἐπιτιμίων.

Provid. On Providence I and II. *De providentia* i, ii. Τὰ περὶ προνοίας (Eusebius). (Found only in Armenian and Aucher's translation.)

Prob. That Every Virtuous Man is Free. *Quod omnis probus liber sit* (VI). Περὶ τοῦ πάντα σπουδαῖον ἐλεύθερον εἶναι. Ὅτι πᾶς ἀστεῖος ἐλεύθερος (Τ).

QE Questions and Answers on Exodus I and II. *Quaestiones et solutiones in Exodum,* i, ii. Τὰ ἐν Ἐξαγωγῇ ζητήματά τε καὶ λύσεις (Eusebius). (Found only in Armenian and Aucher's translation.)

QG Questions and Answers on Genesis I, II, III, and IV. *Quaestiones et solutiones in Genesim,* i, ii, iii, iv. Τὰ ἐν Γενέσει ζητήματά τε καὶ λύσεις (Eusebius). (Found only in Armenian and Aucher's translation; Books i–iii were translated from Aucher's Latin by Yonge in no. 475, IV.)

Sac. On the Birth of Abel and the Sacrifices Offered by Him and His Brother Cain (II). *De sacrificiis Abelis et Caini* (I). Περὶ γενέσεως Ἀβελ καὶ ὧν αὐτός τε καὶ ὁ ἀδελφὸς αὐτοῦ Κάϊν ἱερουργοῦσιν.

Samp. On Sampson. *Sine preparatione de Sampsone* [*sermo*] (found only in Armenian and in Aucher's translation).

Sobr. On the Prayers and Curses Uttered by Noah when He Became Sober (III). *De sobrietate* (II). Περὶ ὧν νήψας ὁ Νῶε εὔχεται καὶ καταρᾶται. Περὶ ὧν ἀνανήψας ὁ νοῦς (νῶε in mg.) εὔχεται καὶ καταρᾶται (G). Περὶ τοῦ ἐξένηψε Νῶε (Η).

Som. On Dreams, that They are God-sent, I and II (V). *De somniis,* i and ii (III). Περὶ τοῦ θεοπέμπτους εἶναι τοὺς ὀνείρους.

Spec. On the Special Laws, I, II, III (VII) and IV. *De specialibus legibus,* i, ii, iii, iv (V). Περὶ τῶν ἐν μέρει διαταγμάτων (R only).

Spec. i. On the Special Laws that Fall under the Two Heads of the Ten Commandments One of which is Directed against the Acknowledgment of Other Sovereign Gods Save the One, and the Other against Giving Honors to the Works of Men's Hands.[2] Περὶ τῶν ἀναφερομένων ἐν εἴδει νόμων εἰς δύο κεφάλαια τῶν δέκα λογίων, τό τε μὴ νομίζειν ἔξω τοῦ ἑνὸς θεοὺς ἑτέρους αὐτοκρατεῖς καὶ τὸ μὴ χειρόκμητα θεοπλάστειν.

   a. §§ 1–12. On Circumcision. *De circumcisione.* Περὶ περιτομῆς.

   b. §§ 13–65. On Monotheism. *De monarchia,* I.[3] Οἱ περὶ μοναρχίας νόμοι (RF). ... λόγοι (Vindob.). Περὶ μοναρχίας (ΑΗ). Περὶ μοναρχίας λόγος πρῶτος (L).

   c. §§ 66–78. On the Temple. *De templo.* Περὶ ἱεροῦ (RF). Περὶ μοναρχίας ἔτι (Α). Περὶ μοναρχίας λόγος β΄ (L).

   d. §§ 79–130. On Priests. *De sacerdotibus.* Περὶ ἱερέων.

---

2. In the following subdivisions of *Spec.* the Cohn and Wendland edition frequently omits the Latin titles. In such cases these are taken from the Mangey edition. In the present instance a Latin title is lacking in both editions. The English titles are translated here from the Greek where the Loeb edition is still incomplete.

3. In Mangey *De templo* and *De sacerdotibus* are included under *De monarchia,* II. In MS. L *De templo* is called *De monarchia* II, whereas in A it is called *De monarchia* I "continued." C.–W., no. 431, omit the title *De monarchia* II altogether.

e. §§ 131–161. On the Honoraria of Priests. *De sacerdotum honoribus*.[4] Γέρα ἱερέων. Περὶ τοῦ τίνα γέρα ἱερέων (H). Τίνα γέρα ἱερέων (A).

f. §§ 162–256. On Victims for Sacrifices. *De victimis*.[5] Περὶ ζῴων τῶν εἰς [τὰς] ἱερουργίας καὶ τίνα τῶν θυσιῶν [τὰ] εἴδη (R). Περὶ τῶν εἰς τὰς ἱερουργίας ζώων καὶ τίνα τῶν θυσιῶν τὰ εἴδη (F, cf. Eusebius). Περὶ ζώων τῶν εἰς τὰς θυσίας καὶ τίνα τῶν θυσιῶν τὰ εἴδη (A).

g. §§ 257–345. On Sacrifices. *De sacrificantibus*. Περὶ θυόντων. §§ 285–345 have the title Τὰ ἄλλα περὶ τὸ θυσιαστήριον (R). Τὰ ἄλλα τὰ περὶ τὸ θυσιαστήριον (AH). Τὰ ἄλλα τὰ περὶ τὸν βωμόν (F).

g.[2] §§ 280–284. On not Carrying the Hire of a Harlot into the Temple. *De mercede meretricis non accipienda in sacrarium*. Περὶ τοῦ μίσθωμα πόρνης εἰς τὸ ἱερὸν μὴ κομίζειν (R om F). Περὶ τοῦ ... μὴ προσδέχεσθαι (ceteri).

Spec. ii, a. §§ 1–38. On the Special Laws that Fall under Three of the Ten General Commandments; namely, the Third on the Duty of Keeping Oaths, the Fourth on Reverencing the Sabbath Day, and the Fifth on Honoring Parents. *De specialibus legibus quae referuntur ad tria decalogi capita, videlicet tertium, quartum, quintumque, De jureiurando religioneque, De sacro sabbato, De honore habendo parentibus*. Περὶ τῶν ἀναφερομένων ἐν εἴδει νόμων εἰς τρία γένη τῶν δέκα λογίων, τὸ τρίτον, τὸ τέταρτον, τὸ πέμπτον· τὸ περὶ εὐορκίας καὶ σεβασμοῦ τῆς ἱερᾶς ἑβδόμης καὶ γονέων τιμῆς.

b. §§ 39–40. On the Number Seven. *De septenario*, part I. Περὶ ἑβδόμης (mg R mg M). Περὶ τῆς ἑβδόμης (F).

c. §§ 41–223. On the Ten Festivals. *De septenario*, part II, *De festis diebus ut numero decem sint*. Περὶ τῶν δέκα ἑορτῶν (mg M Tisch.). Περὶ τῶν ἑορτῶν ὡς εἰσὶ τὸν ἀριθμὸν δέκα (F om R).

c.[2] §§ 215–223. On the Festival of the Baskets. *De cophini festo*. Καρτάλου πανήγυρις (add. mg M only).

d. §§ 224–262. On Honoring Parents. *De parentibus colendis*. Περὶ γονέων τιμῆς.

Spec. iii, a. §§ 1–64. On the Particular Laws which Come under Two of the Ten general Commandments; namely, the Sixth against Adulterers and all Licentiousness, and the Seventh against Murderers and all Violence. *De specialibus legibus, quae referuntur ad duo decalogi capita, sextum septimumque. Contra moechos omnesque libidinosos, et contra homicidas omnemque violentiam*. Περὶ τῶν ἀναφερομένων ἐν εἴδει νόμων εἰς δύο γένη τῶν δέκα λογίων, τὸ ἕκτον καὶ τὸ ἕβδομον, τὸ κατὰ μοιχῶν καὶ παντὸς ἀκολάστου καὶ τὸ κατὰ ἀνδροφόνων καὶ πάσης βίας.[6]

b. §§ 65–71. On Debauching a Virgin. *De stupro*. Περὶ φθορᾶς.

c. §§ 72–82. On Illicit Intercourse between Betrothed Persons. *De concubitu intercepto*. Περὶ ὑπογαμίου.

4. Mangey has *De praemiis sacerdotum*.
5. Mangey has *De animalibus idoneis sacrificio, deque victimarum speciebus*.
6. §§ 52–64 have the title in Mangey, *De adulterio;* Περὶ μοιχαλίδος (add. S mg M, om. ceteri).

d. §§ 83–119. Against Murderers. *De homicidas.* Κατὰ ἀνδροφόνων. Περὶ ἀνδροφόνων (A).

e.[7] §§120–136. On Unintentional Murder. *De caede nolente animo facta deque asylis.* Περὶ ἀκουσίου φόνου.

f.[8] §§137–143. Against Those who Kill Servants. *De caede in servo perpetrata.* Κατὰ τῶν οἰκέτας κτεινόντων (F). Περὶ τῶν οἰκέτας κτεινόντων (SAH[2] mg M mg G).

g.[9] §§ 144–168. Against Dumb Beasts which Cause Death. *De animalibus brutis, quae mortis sunt causae.* Κατὰ ζῴων ἀλόγων ἃ παραίτια γίνεται θανάτου. Περὶ ταύρου ἀνδροφόνου (S mg M).

h. §§ 169–200. On Women not Being Shameless. *Ne impudenter se gerant foeminae.* Περὶ τοῦ μὴ ἀναισχυντεῖν γυναῖκας.

Spec. iv. On the Special Laws which Come under Three of the Ten General Commandments; namely, the Eighth against Stealing, the Ninth against Bearing False Witness, and the Tenth against Coveting; and on the Laws which Come under Each Commandment; and on Justice which is in Harmony with all the Ten Oracles, and which is the [Objective] of that Code as a Whole. *De specialibus legibus, quae pertinent ad tria capita decalogi, nimirum octavum, nonum et decimum; De non committendis furti, falsi testimonii et concupiscentiae criminibus. Quin et de justitia, quae cum omnibus in universum decalogi praeceptis cognationem habet.* Περὶ τῶν ἀναφερομένων ἐν εἴδει νόμων εἰς τρία γένη τῶν δέκα λογίων, τὸ ὄγδοον καὶ τὸ ἔνατον καὶ τὸ δέκατον, τὸ περὶ τοῦ μὴ κλέπτειν καὶ <μὴ> ψευδομαρτυρεῖν καὶ μὴ ἐπιθυμεῖν, καὶ περὶ τῶν εἰς ἕκαστον ἀναφερομένων, καὶ περὶ δικαιοσύνης, ἣ πᾶσι τοῖς δέκα λογίοις ἐφαρμόζει, ὅ ἐστι τῆς ὅλης συντάξεως <τέλος>.

a.[10] §§ 1–40. On Theft. *De furto.* Περὶ κλοπῆς.

b. §§ 41–54. Thou Shalt not Bear False Witness. *Non perhibebis falsum testimonium.* Οὐ ψευδομαρτυρήσεις.

c. §§ 55–78. On the Office and Character of a Judge. *De judice.* Τὰ πρὸς δικαστήν. Κεφάλαια νόμων τὰ πρὸς τὸν δικαστήν (F). Τὰ περὶ δικαστοῦ (H).

d.[11] §§ 79–135. Thou Shalt not Covet. *Non concupisces.* Οὐκ ἐπιθυμήσεις.

---

7. This and the following section carry no separate title in Mangey. The Latin titles are taken from the Richter edition (no. 413).

8. See the preceding note.

9. §§147–168 have in Mangey the title, *De puteis;* Περὶ ὀρυγμάτων (add S mg M).

10. In the editions of Mangey and Richter this section is further divided as follows: §§7–10, Against Housebreakers, *De murorum profossoribus,* Κατὰ τοιχωρύχων; §§11–12, On the Theft of a Sheep or Bull, *De furto ovis et bovis,* Περὶ κλοπῆς προβάτου καὶ βοός; §§13–19, On Kidnappers, *De plagiariis,* Περὶ ἀνδραποδιστῶν; §§20–25, On Damage, *De damno,* Περὶ βλάβης; §§26–29, On not Setting Fire to Brambles Carelessly, *De igne inter sentes non accendendo,* Περὶ τοῦ μὴ ἀπερισκέπτως πῦρ ἐξάπτειν ἀκάνθαις; §§30–40, On Deposits, *De depositis,* Περὶ παρακαταθηκῶν. The Greek titles are found in S (add) and M (mg).

11. The editions of Mangey and Richter, following MS. S of Cohn, subdivide this section as follows: §§100–104, On Animals, *De animalibus,* Περὶ ζώων; §§105–108, What Quadrupeds are Clean, *De quadrupedibus mundis,* Τετραπόδων ὅσα καθαρά; §109, What Beasts are not Clean, *De quadrupedibus immundis,* Τετραπόδων τὰ μὴ καθαρά; §§110–112, What Aquatic Animals are Clean, *De aquatibus mundis,* Περὶ ἐνύδρων καθαρῶν; §§113–115, On Reptiles,

e.[12] §§ 136–150. On Justice I. *De justitia* I. Περὶ δικαιοσύνης.

f. §§ 151–237. On Justice II. *De justitia* II. On the Creation of Magistrates. *De constitutione principum.* Κατάστασις ἀρχόντων. Περὶ καταστάσεως ἀρχόντων (mg MFGA).

Virt. On Virtues which, among Others, Moses Discussed; or on Courage, Piety, Benevolence, and Repentance. Περὶ ἀρετῶν ἃς σὺν ἄλλαις ἀνέγραψε Μωυσῆς, ἤτοι περὶ ἀνδρείας καὶ εὐσεβείας καὶ φιλανθρωπίας καὶ μετανοίας (V).[13]

a. §§ 1–50. On Courage. *De fortitudine.* Περὶ ἀνδρείας.

b. §§ 51–174. On Humanity. *De humanitate.* Περὶ φιλανθρωπίας. Περὶ εὐσεβείας καὶ φιλανθρωπίας (HP). The treatise on Piety is lost.

c. §§ 175–186. On Repentance. *De paenitentia.* Περὶ μετανοίας.

d. §§ 187–227. On Nobility. *De nobilitate.* Περὶ εὐγενείας.

De reptilibus, Περὶ ἑρπετῶν; §§116–118, On Flying Creatures, *De volatilibus,* Περὶ πτηνῶν; §§119–123a, On Carcasses and Bodies Torn by Wild Beasts, *De morticinis et a feris discerptis,* Περὶ θνησιμαίων καὶ θηριαλώτων; §§123b–135, On the Soul of Man, *De anima hominis,* Περὶ ψυχῆς ἀνθρώπου.

12. The subtitles of Mangey and Richter in this section are: §§143–148, That Nothing is to be Added to or Taken from the Law, *Ne quid adjiciatur vel detrahatur,* "Ὅτι οὐ δεῖ προστιθέναι ἢ (MS. καὶ) ἀφαιρεῖν; §§149–150, On not Moving Landmarks, *Ne transferantur termini,* Περὶ τοῦ μὴ παρακινεῖν ὅρια.

13. The title here given is that of Cohn, who very properly included the little treatise *De nobilitate* as a part of *Virt.* and then altered the manuscript title which read: Περὶ τριῶν ἀρετῶν, ἤτοι περὶ ἀνδρείας καὶ φιλανθρωπίας (or εὐσεβείας καὶ φιλανθρωπίας) καὶ μετανοίας, *De tribus virtutibus: sive de fortitudine et humanitate et paenitentia.*

I. MANUSCRIPTS OF PHILO

SOURCES OF MANUSCRIPT INFORMATION

The following catalogue has been compiled from museum catalogues, from the Prolegomena *of the Cohn and Wendland edition (no. 23) and other indirect sources, and from a direct examination of particular codices. Sources which are used only once or twice are described in full under the first codex where the work is cited. Other sources, cited more frequently, are referred to by author and number according to the list which follows:*

1. Montfaucon, Bernard de, *Bibliotheca Coisliniana, olim Segueriana, sive mss. omnium graecorum, quae in ea continentur, accurata discriptio,* Paris, 1715.
2. Morelli, Jacob, *Bibliothecae Regiae Divi Marci Venetiarum custodis Bibliotheca manuscripta Graeca et Latina,* I, Bessani, 1802.
3. Hardt, Ign., *Catalogus codicum manuscriptorum Bibliothecae Regiae Bavaricae* (Munich, K. Hof- und Staats-Bibliothek), I. *Catalogus codicum mss. graec. Bibl. R. Bav.,* Munich, parts 1–5, 1806–1812.
4. Miller, E., *Catalogue des mss. grecs de la bibliothèque de l'Escurial,* Paris, 1848.
5. *Index to the Additional MSS. in the British Museum and Acquired in the Years 1783–1835,* London, 1849.
6. Coxe, Henry, *Catalogus codicum MSS. in collegiis aulisque Oxoniensibus,* Oxford, 1852, Part II.
7. Coxe, Henry, *Catalogi codicum manuscriptorum Bibliothecae Bodleianae,* Oxford, 1853–1885.
8. Macray, William, *Catalogi codicum manuscriptorum Bibliothecae Bodleiana,* Oxford, V, 1862–1898.
9. *Catalogue of the MSS. Preserved in the Library of the University of Cambridge,* Cambridge, 1856–1867, Vol. IV.
10. Tischendorf, Constantinus, *Philonea, inedita altera, altera nunc demum recte ex vetera scriptura eruta,* Leipzig, 1868.
11. Stevenson, Henry, Sr., *Bibliotheca apostolica Vaticana codicibus mss. recensita iubente Leone XIII Pont. Max. edita: Codices manuscripti Palatini graeci Bibliothecae Vaticanae,* Rome, 1885.
12. Harris, J. R., *Fragments of Philo Judaeus,* Cambridge, 1886.
13. Omont, Henri, "Catalogue des mss. grecs des bibl. des Pays-Bas," *Centralblatt für Bibliothekswesen,* IV (1887), 185–214.

14. Cohn, Leopold, *Philonis Alexandrini libellus de opificio mundi,* Vratislavia (Breslau), 1889. See no. 425.

15. Wendland, Paul, *Neu entdeckte Fragmente Philos,* Berlin, 1891. See no. 427.

16. Papadopoulos-Kerameus, A., Ἱεροσολυμιτικὴ βιβλιοθήκη ἤτοι κατάλογος τῶν ἐν ταῖς βιβλιοθήκαις τοῦ ἁγιωτάτου ἀποστολικοῦ τε καὶ καθολικοῦ ὀρθοδόξου πατριαρχικοῦ θρόνου τῶν Ἱεροσολύμων καὶ πάσης Παλαιστίνης ἀποκειμένων Ἑλληνικῶν κωδίκων, St. Petersburg, I–IV, 1891–1899.

17. Graux, Charles, and Martin, Albert, *Notices sommaires de mss. grecs d' Espagne et de Portugal,* Paris, 1892.

18. Cohn, Leopold, "Die Philo-Handschriften in Oxford und Paris," *Philologus,* LI (1892), 266–275.

19. Cohn, Leopold, "Zur indirekten Ueberlieferung Philos und der älteren Kirchenväter," *Jahrbücher für protestantische Theologie,* XVIII (1892), 475–492.

20. Conybeare, Fred C., *Philo about the Contemplative Life,* Oxford, 1895. See no. 429.

21. Stornajolo, Cosimus, *Apostolicae Vaticanae codices mss. recensiti iubente Leone XIII Pont. Max., codices Urbinates graeci Bibliothecae Vaticanae,* Rome, 1895.

22. Lambros, S., *Catalogue of the Greek MSS. on Mt. Athos,* Cambridge, I, II, 1895, 1900.

23. Cohn, Leopold and Wendland, Paul, "Prolegomena," *Omnia opera Philonis Alexandrini, quae supersunt.* Berlin, I–VI, 1896–1915. See no. 431.

24. Holl, K., *Die Sacra Parallela des Johannes Damascenus,* Leipzig, 1897. (*Texte und Untersuchungen zur Geschichte der altchristlichen Litteratur,* XVI, N. F. I.)

25. James, M. R., *The Western MSS. in the Library of Trinity College Cambridge,* Cambridge, 1900.

26. Karo, G. and Lietzmann, J., "Catenarum graecarum catalogus," *Nachrichten von der Königlichen Gesellschaft der Wissenschaften zu Göttingen, Philologisch-historische Klasse,* 1902, 1–66, 299–350, 559–620.

27. Martini, E., *Catalogo di manoscritti greci esistenti nelle biblioteche italiane.* II: *Catalogus codicum graecorum qui in Bibliotheca Vallicellana Romae adservantur,* Milan, 1902.

28. Cohn, Leopold, "Beiträge zur Textgeschichte und Kritik der philonischen Schriften," *Hermes,* XXXVIII (1903), 498–545.

29. Martin, A., and Bassus, D., *Catalogus codicum graecorum Bibliothecae Ambrosianae,* Milan, 1906, I, II.

30. *Catalogue of Additions to the MSS. in the British Museum in the years 1900–1905*, London, 1907.

31. James, M. R., *A Descriptive Catalogue of the MSS. in the Library of Corpus Christi College Cambridge*, Cambridge, II, 1912.

32. James, M. R., *A Descriptive Catalogue of the McClean Collection in the Fitzwilliam Museum*, Cambridge, 1912.

33. Rahlfs, Alfred, *Verzeichnis der griechischen Handschriften des Alten Testaments*, Berlin, 1915. (*Nachrichten von der Gesellschaft der Wissenschaften zu Göttingen. Philologisch-historische Klasse, 1914, Beiheft.*)

34. Lewy, Hans, "Neu gefundene griechische Philonfragmente," *Sitzungsberichte der Preussischen Akademie der Wissenschaften. Philosophisch-historische Klasse*, 1932, 72–84. See no. 438.

GREEK MANUSCRIPTS

GREEK MANUSCRIPTS, A.

The Manuscripts listed in this section under family groups are those discussed and classified into families by Cohn and Wendland (no. 23). The group headed C.-W., Family A, or C.-W., Family B, thus includes the manuscripts they classify as in Family A or B. The first manuscript of each group is, unless otherwise indicated, the one they selected as the best text of that group.

C.-W., FAMILY A.

35. *Monacensis gr.* 459, formerly *Augustanus*, parchment, 474 larger size folios, XIII. century, beautifully written, in two hands (fols. 1–332r in first hand, fols. 333r–474v in second hand). Specimen of text in Tischendorf, no. 10.

Contains: 1. *Spec.* i, a; 2. *Spec.* i, b; 3. *Spec.* i, c; 4. *Spec.* i, e; 5. *Spec.* i, f; 6. *Spec.* i, g; 7. *Mut.;* 8. *LA* iii; 9. *Heres;* 10. *Praem.;* 11. *Exs.;* 12. *Virt.* a; 13–15. *Mos.* i, ii, iii; 16. *Opif.;* 17. *Decal.;* 18. *Spec.* iv, f; 19. *Prob.;* 20. *Cont.;* 21. *Spec.* i, g^2; 22. *Spec.* iii; 23. *Jos.;* 24. *Flac.;* 25. *Legat.;* 26. *Spec.* iv, c, *Virt.* b and beginning of *Virt.* c; 27. *Sac.;* 28. *Cher.;* 29. *Agr.;* 30. *Immut.;* 31. *Gig.;* 32. *Migr.;* 33. *Cong.;* 34. *LA* i; 35. *LA* ii; 36. *Som.* i; 37. *Som.* ii; 38. *Abr.*

See C.-W., no. 23, I, iv–vii; Conybeare, no. 20, p. 2; catalogue, no. 3, pt. 4.

36. *Matritensis Est.* 11, *gr.* 2a, 40, paper, 509 folios, XVI. century (ἐν Ῥόδῳ αφή).

Contains: the same treatises as no. 35, from which it is derived, but in a different order.

See C.-W., no. 23, I, viii; Martin, no. 17, pp. 13-17.

37. *Palatinus gr.* 183, formerly *Iannotii* or *Manetti* then *Heidelbergensis* 183, paper, 577 small folios, XIV. century, mutilated at the end.

Contains: the same treatises in the same order as no. 35 from which it seems to have been copied.

See C.-W., no. 23, I, vii; Conybeare, no. 20, p. 3; Stevenson, no. 11.

38. *Vaticanus gr.* 380, parchment, XV. century. There are 3 paper fly leaves and one of parchment, containing a table of contents in both Greek and Latin. There are 235 numbered folios, but 21 is repeated and folios after 64 and 108 were left unnumbered. This codex is a companion to no. 39, having on fol. 1r a design by the same illuminator, and below the same coat of arms with the inscription in gold, NI·PAPE·V·[1]

Contains: the same treatises in the same order as no. 35, 1-23, but seems to have been derived from no. 37 since it follows a misplaced order of folios in the latter codex. Copied by Johannes Thessalus Seutariota.

See C.-W., no. 23, I, vii; Conybeare, no. 20, p. 3.

39. *Vaticanus gr.* 378, beautiful white parchment, 4 + 204 folios, XV. century, wide margins, titles in red ink, single column as also no. 38.[1] Copied by Johannes Thessalus Seutariota.

Contains: the same treatises in the same order as no. 35, 24-28.

See C.-W., no. 23, I, vii.

40. *Coislinianus* 43, parchment, XVI. century, written by Jacob Diassorinus in Italy.

Contains: the same treatises in the same order as no. 35, 1-23, but was apparently copied from no. 38.

See C.-W., no. 23, I, vii; Conybeare, no. 20, p. 2.

41. *Vaticanus gr.* 2174, paper, 231 folios, XVI. century, formerly *Colonna* 13.[2]

Contains: the same treatises in the same order as no. 35, 24-38, but was apparently copied from no. 39.

See C.-W., no. 23, I, vii; Conybeare, no. 20, p. 2.

42. *Ottobonianus gr.* 74, paper, XVII. century.

Contains: the same treatises as no. 35, 1-8, from which it is derived.

See C.-W., no. 23, I, viii.

---

1. Additional data for this and other codices have been obtained for the authors by Dr. C. W. Barlow who has recently inspected the Vatican MSS. of Philo.

2. See the preceding note.

C.-W., Family B.

43. *Venetus gr.* 42, parchment, in quarto, 142 folios, XII. century, written with great care, formerly owned by Cardinal Bessarion.[3]
Contains: *Mos., Virt.* a, *Jos., Abr.*
See C.-W., no. 23, IV, v–vi.

44. *Barberinus gr.* 556, formerly 226 and V. 52, paper, 363 folios, XV. century.
Contains: *Mos.* i (ending with τῶν ἱερῶν γραμμάτων μνημονεύσεται), *Mos.* ii; *Mos.* iii (ending with ἐσχάτους κακοδαίμονες), *Jos., Abr.* This is a copy of no. 43 though it seems to have been corrected to a text like that of no. 112.
See C.-W., no. 23, IV, v–vi; above, p. 140, n. 1.

45. *Vallicellianus* F9, paper, 4 + 310 folios, XVI. century, damaged by usage and moisture.
Contains: works of different authors; of Philo (fols. 287–290), *Jos.* (beginning with καὶ ξενιτείαν, τὴν εἰς τὸ ἁμαρτάνειν ἐκεχειρίαν), *Abr.* (τῶν ἱερῶν νόμων ἐν πέντε βίβλοις..., ...ἀλλὰ διὰ τὸ μὴ προσβέβλησθαι κακίαν).
See C.-W., no. 23, IV, v–vi; Martini, no. 27, cod. 78.

46. *Venetus gr.* 41, once owned by Bessarion, cardinal of Tusculum, paper, quarto, 360 folios, XIV. century. The text belongs to group A.
Contains: the same treatises as no. 35, except for *Sac., Cher., Agr., Migr., Cong., LA* i, ii; *Som.* i, ii, and *Abr.*, which it omits. The order of treatises differs from no. 35, to which the codex seems to be related. The codex was used by John Christopherson of Lancaster for his edition printed at Antwerp, 1553. See no. 450.
See C.-W., no. 23, I, x–xi; IV, xii; J. Morelli, no. 2, under Cod. XL.

47. *Vaticanus gr.* 152, formerly *Palatinus* 152, paper, octavo, 285 folios, XIV. century, text similar to no. 46.
Contains: *Mos.* iii (fols. 39r–69r).
See C.-W., no. 23, IV, xiii; cf. I, xxx; Stevenson, no. 11.

48. *Laurentianus conv. soppr.* 107, paper, XV. century.
Contains: the same treatises as no. 97, pt. III and in the same order.
See C.-W., no. 23, I, xxx.

C.-W., Family C.

49. *Parisinus gr.* 435, formerly *Regius* 2251, parchment, 175 largest size folios, XI. century, written in a neat but uncultured hand, specimen given in Conybeare, no. 20.

3. This is probably the codex listed by H. A. Omont, *Inventaire des MSS. grecs et latins donnés à Saint-Marc de Venise par le Cardinal Bessarion en 1468* (Paris, 1894), as no. 431.

Contains: *Abr., Jos., Mos.* i, *Virt.* b, c, d, three extracts from *Mos.* ii, *Legat., Cont.* One of the chief texts used by Turnebus, no. 391.

See C.-W., no. 23, IV, i; VI, xxxviii; Conybeare, no. 20, p. 1; Cohn, no. 28, p. 510. C.-W., *loc. cit.,* list this erroneously as *Regius* 2551.

C.-W., FAMILY D.

A Florilegium ascribed to John Damascene, composed probably in the sixth century, consisted of three books. The work was made up of selections from the Old and New Testaments and from the Church Fathers. The first book dealt with things divine, the second book with human affairs (περὶ συστά- σεως καὶ καταστάσεως τῶν ἀνθρωπίνων πραγμάτων). These two books were entitled τὰ ἱερά, "Sacred Things." The third book had to do with virtues and vices and bore the title τὰ παράλληλα, "The Parallels." Parts of this work, *The Sacred Parallels,* are preserved in numerous MSS. (see Holl, *Texte und Untersuchungen,* N.F. I, 1 and V, 2). Extracts from the first two books of the Sacred Parallels (the third book is lost) which also contain extracts from Philo are found in Group D. See C.-W., no. 23, I, lxiii–lxvii; Cohn, no. 19, pp. 480–490; Wendland, no. 15, pp. 18–20; Lewy, no. 34, p. 72.

50. *Coislinianus* 276 (Dᶜ), in quarto, 278 folios, X. century, formerly *Athous Laurae Monasterii,* preserved extracts from Parallels, Book I, with the title Ἰωάννου πρεσβυτέρου καὶ μοναχοῦ τῶν ἐκλογῶν βιβλίον πρῶτον. Contains: extracts from *Sobr., Opif., Mos., LA* iii, *Post., Cher., Mut., Ebr., QE, QG, Gig., Flac., Virt.* c.
    See C.-W., no. 23, I, lxv; Harris, no. 12, pp. ix, xix, 83–85; Cohn, no. 19, p. 480; Lewy, no. 34, p. 72 (who says that the codex is not collated).

51. *Hierosolymitanus S. Sep.* 15 (Dᴴ), parchment, XI. century, a compilation of Florilegia preserving parts of the Sacred Parallels, Book I. Contains: extracts from *Decal., Opif., LA* i, *Cher., Sac., Det., Post., Immut., Ebr.*
    See C.-W., no. 23, II, xii; IV, xxv; Cohn no. 19, pp. 485–490; Lewy, no. 34, p. 72; Papadopoulos-Karameus, no. 16, I, 65 ff.

52. *Vaticanus gr.* 1553 (Dᴷ), formerly *Cryptoferratensis,*[4] parchment, 1 + 280 folios, XII. century, preserved the Sacred Parallels, Book II, under the title Λεοντίου πρεσβυτέρου καὶ Ἰωάννου τῶν ἱερῶν βιβλίον δεύτερον, edited by Angelo Mai, *Scriptorum veterum nova collectio,* VII, 74–109. Contains: according to a list in vol. X, 379, of Mai's edition, extracts from Philo's *QE, QG, Spec.* iii. g, *Spec.* i. c, *LA* iii, iv, vii, viii, ix, xiii, from περὶ τῶν ἐν τῷ νόμῳ ζητημάτων, and *Quaestiones in Leviticum.*

---

4. Dr. Barlow, see note p. 140, reports that on fol. iv is to be read: τοῦτο τὸ βιβλίον ἦν (sic) τῆς μονῆς τῆς κρυπτωφέρρης.

A. PHILO: AS HE APPEARS OVER FORTY TIMES IN A IX. CENTURY MS.
IN THE BIBLIOTHÈQUE NATIONALE

See Bibliography, no. 56, and page v.

B. PHILO AND JOSEPHUS FROM THE SAME MS.

See C.-W., no. 23, I, lxv; Harris, no. 12, p. xix; Cohn, no. 19, p. 482; Lewy, no. 34, p. 72.

53. *Laurentianus pluteus* VIII. 22 (D^L), paper, XIV. century, preserves three mixed recensions of the Sacred Parallels arranged alphabetically according to authors cited. The first (fols. 46–73) is derived from a recension represented by nos. 58, 59, 60, and a recension represented by no. 57; the second is another mixed recension (fols. 1–45). Fols. 126–188 preserve the third mixed rescension.

See C.-W., no. 23, I, lxvi, lxix; Cohn, no. 19, p. 483; Lewy, no. 34, p. 72.

54. *Venetus Marcianus gr.* 138 (D^M), parchment, 293 folios, XI. century, preserves the same recension of the Sacred Parallels as nos. 56 and 53, fols. 46–73.

See C.-W., no. 23, I, lxv; Lewy, *ibid.*

55. *Venetus append. gr. class.* III. 4. 88. 3 (D^N), formerly *Nanianus* 228, paper, XVI. century, similar to no. 58.

See C.-W., no. 23, I, lxvi; Lewy, *ibid.*

56. *Parisinus gr.* 923 (D^P), formerly *Regius* 923, parchment, 394 largest size folios, IX. century, uncial, beautifully written, rubricated titles, miniature portraits of saints and others, including about forty-five of Philo, script retraced in places, specimen of codex in Harris, no. 12, some leaves missing. It preserves a recension of the Sacred Parallels similar to no. 53, fols. 46–73, under the title: τάδε ἐστὶν ἐν τῇδε τῶν παραλλήλων βίβλῳ περὶ τῆς τοῦ ἀνθρώπου πλάσεως.

Contains: extracts from *Opif., LA* i, iii, *Post., Ebr., Heres, Mut., Som.* i, *Abr., Jos., Mos.* i, *Decal., Virt.* a, *Praem., Flac., Legat., Gig.*

See C.-W., no. 23, I, lxv; Harris, no. 12, pp. vii–xxii, 89–95; Lewy, *ibid.;* Cohn, no. 19, p. 480.

57. *Berolinensis gr.* 46 (D^R), formerly *Rupefucaldinus, Claromontanus* 150, *Meermannianus* 94, *Phillippicus* 1450, parchment, 290 folios, XII. century, preserves a most copious recension of the Sacred Parallels, Books I, II, and some parts of Book III, under the title: Ἰωάννου πρεσβυτέρου καὶ μοναχοῦ τοῦ Δημασκηνοῦ τῶν ἐκλογῶν βιβλίον ά καὶ β'.

See C.-W., no. 23, I, lxv–lxvi; Harris, *ibid.;* Lewy, *ibid.;* Cohn, *ibid.;* Wendland, no. 15, p. 18.

58. *Vaticanus gr.* 1236 (D^V), paper, XV. century, preserves the "Vatican" recension of the Sacred Parallels. It gathers the three books into one book, as also nos. 54 and 56. Lequien's edition of the Sacred Parallels of John Damascene was taken from this codex with additions from no. 57. Less ample than no. 57.

See C.-W., no. 23, I, lxvi; Lewy, *ibid.;* Cohn, no. 19, p. 481.

59. *Ottobonianus gr.* 79, paper, XV. century, is the exemplar of no. 58.

See C.-W., no. 23, II, xi; Lewy, *ibid.*

60. *Ambrosianus* H 26, XV. century, is similar to no. 59.
    See C.-W., no. 23, *ibid.;* Lewy, *ibid.*

A number of Gnomologia Sacroprofana derive their materials in part from *The Sacred Parallels.* They are *Florilegium Parisinum* (no. 61), *Maximi Confessoris eclogae* (no. 62), *Antonii Monachi Melissa* (no. 66), *Joannis Georgidis gnomologium* (no. 70), *Florilegium Laurentianum* (no. 72). See C.-W., no. 23, I, lxvii–lxix; V, xvii; VI, xlvi–xlvii.

61. *Parisinus* 1168, XIV. century, unedited.
    Contains: extracts from *LA* i, *Sac., Flac., Legat.*
    See C.-W., no. 23, I, lxviii; VI, xl; Lewy, no. 34, p. 73.
62. *Berolinensis* 1609, formerly *Phillippicus* 1609, *Meermannianus* 348, parchment, XI. century.
    Contains: the same extracts as no. 61, published in Migne, *Patrol. gr.,* XCI, 721 ff. as *Maximi Confessoris eclogae.*
    See C.-W., no. 23, I, lxviii, Lewy, *ibid.*
63. *Barberinus* I, 158, XI. century, similar to no. 62, but seems to be a more ample recension.
    See C.-W., no. 23, II, xiii–xiv; Lewy, *ibid.*
64. *Laurentianus* IX, 29, similar to no. 63.
    See C.-W., no. 23, *ibid.*
65. *Vaticanus* 739, similar to no. 63.
    See C.-W., no. 23, *ibid.*
66. *Baroccianus* 143 (= Melissa Barocciana), parchment, 259 folios in quarto, XII. century, a few folios supplied here and there at a later date, perhaps XV. century, a compendium of citations from a very large number of authors divided into forty-eight chapters. This is the *Melissa Antonii Monachi,* ed. Gesner, 1546 (= Migne, *Patrol. gr.,* CXXXVI, 765 ff.).
    Contains: citations from Philo in chs. 2, 4, 5, 9–15, 18–24, 28, 29, 31, 32, 34, 36, 37, 39, 40, 45, 46.
    See C.-W., no. 23, I, lxviii; Lewy, no. 34, p. 53; Coxe, no. 7, pt. I, 245–247.
67. *Monacensis* 429, or *Melissa Augustana,* paper, 130 folios, XIV. century, written (A.D. 1346) by Nicephorus the priest in a small neat hand, titles and initials rubricated, with abbreviations. Very similar to no. 66.
    Contains: citations from Philo in chs. 2, 4, 5, 9–15, 18–25, 28, 31, 32, 34, 36, 38–40, 45–47, 49, 51–53, 55–56.
    See C.-W., no. 23, I, lxviii; Lewy, *ibid.,*[5] catalogue, no. 3, pt. 4.

---

5. Lewy numbers this codex 492, apparently by a reversal of digits.

68. *Patmiacus* 6, parchment, XII. century, similar to no. 66.
     See C.-W., no. 23, *ibid*.

69. *Hierosolymitanus* 225, XV.-XVI. centuries, similar to no. 66.
     See C.-W., no. 23, *ibid*.

70. *Parisinus* 1166, preserves the *Gnomologium Joannis Georgidis,* ed. Bois-
     sonade, *Anecd. Gr.* I, 1–108 (= Migne, *Patrol. gr.,* CXVII, 1057 f.).
     See C.-W., no. 23, *ibid*.

71. *Laurentianus* VI, 15, parchment, XI. century, similar to no. 70.
     See C.-W., no. 23, *ibid.;* Lewy, no. 34, p. 73.

72. *Laurentianus* LVII, 12, XV. century.
     Contains: twenty-five *sententiae Philoneae* from *Sac.,* and *Legat.* (fol.
     122r) under the title: Ἐκ τοῦ Φίλωνος τοῦ Ἑβραίου περὶ οὖ εἴρηται· ἢ
     Φίλων πλατονίζει ἢ Πλάτων φιλωνίζει.
     See C.-W., no. 23, I, lxix; VI, xxxix; Lewy, *ibid*.

73. *Vaticanus* 1354, XV. century, similar to no. 72.
     See C.-W., no. 23, *ibid*.

74. *Neapolitanus* IIIA, 15, XV. century, similar to no. 72.
     See C.-W., no. 23, *ibid*.

75. *Mazarineus* 611A, XVI. century, similar to no. 72.
     See C.-W., no. 23, II, xiv.

C.-W., FAMILY E.

76. *Oxoniensis Collegii Lincolniensis* 34, parchment, 280 largest size folios,
     XI.-XII. centuries.
     Contains: in the first part (fols. 1–140), Θεοδωρίτου περὶ προνοίας
     δεκάλογος; in the second part (fols. 141–280), *Mos.* i, ii, iii, *Virt.* a,
     Jos., Abr. (incomplete). Text similar to no. 43.
     See C.-W., no. 23, IV, vi–vii; Cohn, no. 18, pp. 270–272; Coxe, no. 6, I.

A work entitled περὶ κόσμου, attributed to Philo and first edited by Aldus
Manutius in 1497 (no. 387) together with works of Aristotle and Theophrastus, contains extracts from *Conf., Virt.* d, *Plant., Gig., Immut., Aet.* An epitome of this work is preserved in the following three codices which are collectively designated as E in C.-W., II. The text substantially agrees with nos.
110 and 80. See C.-W., no. 23, II, vi–viii; V, xv; VI, xxxiv.

77. *Vindobonensis philos. et. phil. gr.* 102, paper, 266 largest size folios, XV.
     century.
     Contains: Φίλωνος περὶ κόσμου (fol. 218r).

78. *Vaticanus gr.* 671, paper, XV. or XVI. century, similar to no. 77.

79. *Vaticanus Reginensis gr.* 123, paper, octavo, 339 folios, XV. or XVI. cen-
     tury, similar to no. 77.

C.-W., FAMILY F.

80. *Laurentianus plut.* LXXXV. 10, paper, 559 largest size folios, XV.–XVI. centuries, written in two hands. Fols. 1–2 give an index of the treatises. Contains: 1. *Mos.* i (the greater part supplied by the more recent hand); 2. *Virt.* a–c; 3–4. *Mos.* ii, iii; 5. *Spec.* iii; 6. *Praem.;* 7. *Opif.;* 8. *Spec.* iv. c; 9. *Jos.;* 10. *Abr.;* 11. *Virt.* b and first half of c; 12. *Spec.* iv. f; 13. *Prob.;* 14. *Cont.;* 15. *Decal.;* 16. *Spec.* i. a; 17. *Spec.* i. b; 18. *Spec.* i. c; 19. *Spec.* i. d; 20. *Spec.* i. e; 21. *Spec.* i. f; 22. *Spec.* i. g; 23. *Spec.* ii. a, b, and first part of c; 24. *Cong.;* 25. *Som.* i; 26. *LA* i, ii; 27. *Cher.* (lacks the last part); 28. *Sac.* (lacks the end); 29. *Det.;* 30. *Ebr.;* 31. *Sobr.;* 32. *Immut.;* 33. *Agr.* (lacks the end); 34. *Plant.;* 35. *Conf.;* 36. *Virt.* d (lacks the end). About 1550 A.D. Jacob Diassorinus added from the edition of Philo's works by Adrianus Turnebus, *Gig., Migr., Heres, Fug., Spec.* i, g², *Exs., Aet., Flac., Legat.* The text of this codex is related to no. 110.

See C.-W., no. 23, I, xx–xxiv; Conybeare, no. 20, p. 3.

81. *Vaticanus gr.* 379, owned by Nicolaus Sophianus at end of XVI. century, paper, 386 folios in quarto, XIV. century, badly worn so that the original writing has almost disappeared in many places. It agrees with no. 80 and in no instance has better readings.

Contains: of no. 80, treatises 5, 11, 15–20, 23–36. At the end is a work titled Ἐκ τῶν ἐν Ἐξόδῳ ἤτοι Ἐξαγωγῇ ζητημάτων καὶ λύσεων (ed. A. Mai, *Classic. Auct.* IV, 430–441; Grossmann, *Anecdoton graecum Philonis Judaei de Cherubinis,* Leipzig, 1856).

See Harris, no. 12, pp. 63–68; Tischendorf, no. 10, pp. 144–152; C.-W., no. 23, I, xxv–xxvii.

82. *Monacensis gr.* 113 (= *Boicus* 174 used by David Hoeschel), paper, 263 folios, XVI. century, script small and neat, rubricated titles and initials, corrections in the margins.

Contains: *Spec.* ii. b, c (first part).

See C.-W., no. 23, I, lxxiii (note), lxxviii; V, xxi–xxiii; catalogue, no. 3, pt. 2.

C.-W., FAMILY G.

83. *Vaticano-Palatinus gr.* 248, paper, 326 largest size folios, XIV.–XV. centuries.

Contains: 1–3. *Mos.* i, ii, iii; 4. *Opif.;* 5. *Decal.;* 6. *Spec.* iv, c; *Virt.* b and beginning of c; 7. *Spec.* iv, f; 8. *Prob.;* 9. *Cont.;* 10. *Spec.* i, g²; 11. *Spec.* iii; 12. *Jos.;* 13. *Sac.;* 14. *Cher.;* 15. *Agr.;* 16. *Plant.;* 17. *Immut.;* 18. *Ebr.;* 19. *Sobr.;* 20. *Conf.;* 21. *Abr.;* 22. *Flac.;* 23. *Legat.;* 24. *Virt.* a; 25. *Virt.* b with d; 26. *Fug.;* 27. *Heres;* 28. *Cong.;* 29. *Som.* i.

See C.-W., no. 23, I, xxxiv–xxxv; Conybeare, no. 20, p. 2.

C.-W., FAMILY H.

84. *Venetus gr.* 40, once owned by Bessarion, paper, 449 folios in quarto, XIV. century (apparently corrected in XV. century by a more scholarly hand, which supplied missing fols. 55, 56, 110, 111). Two quaternions were incorrectly bound so that fols. 59–66 should follow fols. 67–73.

    Contains: 1. *Opif.;* 2. *Decal.;* 3. *Spec.* iv. c; 4. *Virt.* b and beginning of c; 5. *Spec.* iv, f; 6. *Prob.;* 7. *Cont.;* 8. *Spec.* i, g²; 9. *Spec.* iii; 10. *Jos.;* 11. *Sac.;* 12. *Cher.;* 13. *Agr.;* 14. *Gig.;* 15. *Immut.;* 16. *Migr.;* 17. *Cong.;* 18. *Abr.;* 19. *Heres;* 20. *Som.* i; 21. *Praem.;* 22. *Exs.;* 23. *Virt.* a; 24. *Flac.;* 25. *Legat.;* 26–28. *Mos.* i, ii, iii; 29. *Virt.* d; 30. *Fug.;* 31. *Plant.;* 32. *Sobr.;* 33. *Conf.;* 34. *Aet.;* 35. *Det.;* 36. *Ebr.;* 37. *Spec.* i. a; 38–39. *Spec.* i. b; 40. *Spec.* i. e; 41. *Spec.* i. f; 42. *Spec.* i. g; 43. *LA* iii; 44. *Spec.* iii. d; 45. *Spec.* iii. f; 46. *Spec.* iii. b. Items 44–46 repeat material in item 9, but seem to come from a different source, perhaps one related to no. 46.

    See C.-W., no. 23, I, xi–xiv; Conybeare, no. 20, p. 2.

85. *Vaticanus gr.* 382, paper, XV. century, a copy of no. 84.

    See C.-W., no. 23, I, xiv.

86. *Monacensis gr.* 124 (= *Boicus* 52 used by Hoeschel), paper, 744 folios, XVI. century, in small neat hand, with rubricated titles and initials, copied from no. 84, and used by Friderick Pfeiffer for his edition of Philo.

    See C.-W., no. 23, I, xiv, lxxviii; Cohn, no. 14, p. xv; catalogue, no. 3, pt. 2.

87. *Venetus gr.* 39, parchment, 271 largest size folios, XV. century, beautifully written, once owned by Bessarion, a twin of, or copied from, no. 84.

    See C.-W., no. 23, I, xiv; Conybeare, no. 20, p. 2.

88. *Parisinus gr.* 434, once *Regius* 2250, paper, 433 folios in quarto, early XVI. century, written by various hands. In 1529 the codex came from Italy to the Royal Library of Fontainebleau. This codex, along with nos. 49 and 99, was used by Turnebus for his edition of Philo.

    Contains: the same treatises as no. 84, although the order varies somewhat.

    See C.-W., no. 23, I, xv; Conybeare, *ibid.;* Cohn, no. 28, p. 510.

89. *Genuensis Bibl. Congregationis Missionis urbanae* 39, paper, late XIV. century.

    Contains: the same treatises as no. 84.

    See C.-W., no. 23, I, xiv.

90. *Escurialensis* Y, I, 5, once at Mendoza, paper, 449 folios, XV. century. Its index lists 46 titles which clearly agree with no. 84, but the codex contains only the first twenty-three of these treatises, ending with *Virt.* a.

    See C.-W., no. 23, I, xv; Miller, no. 4, p. 262.

91. *Ottobonianus gr.* 48, paper, 626 folios, XVI. or XVII. century.
    Contains: the same treatises as no. 84, except for the omission of *Spec.*
    iii. h.
    See C.-W., no. 23, I, xiv; Conybeare, no. 20, p. 3.

92. *Leeuwardensis gr.* 40, once *Pelicerianus,* then *Claromontanus* 199, then
    Meermannianus 376, paper, 281 folios, XVI. century.
    Contains: treatises 1–9 and 11–13 of no. 84 and *Mos.* i, ii, iii, *Jos., Virt.*
    a, b, c, *Abr.,* and *Virt.* a, b, c repeated.
    See C.-W., no. 23, I, xv; IV, viii; Omont, no. 13, p. 20.

93. *Vaticano-Palatinus gr.* 311, paper in folio, 899 pages, XV.–XVI. centuries,
    written in two hands.
    Contains: in first hand the same treatises as no. 84; in second hand adds
    Mut.
    See C.-W., no. 23, I, xiv.

94. *Vaticanus Reginensis gr.* 94, paper, XVI. century.
    Contains: *Det.* (fols. 48–68).
    See C.-W., no. 23, I, xvi.

95. *Oxoniensis Collegii Novi* 143, paper, 396 largest size folios, XVI. century,
    apparently written by Arsenius, bishop of Monembasia. The first 181
    folios are closely related to no. 84.
    Contains (first 181 fols.): *Virt.* b, *Sac., Cher., Agr., Migr., Cong., Abr.,*
    Som. i, *Virt.* d, *Fug., Plant., Sobr., Conf., Aet.* The last 212 fols., prob-
    ably written by Bartolomeo Comparini, are closely related to no. 46.
    Contains (last 212 fols.): *Prob., Cont., Spec.* i. c, *Gig., Immut., Mut.,*
    LA ii, *Decal., Spec.* i. a, *Spec.* i. b, *Spec.* i. e; *Spec.* i. f, *Spec.* i. g, *Spec.*
    iii. a–c, *Opif., Heres, Praem., Exs., Virt.* a, *Spec.* iii. d, *Spec.* iv. f, *Flac.,*
    Legat.
    See C.-W., no. 23, I, xix; Conybeare, no. 20, p. 2; Coxe, no. 6, pt. I;
    Cohn, no. 18, p. 272.

C.-W., FAMILY K.

96. *Laurentianus conv. soppr.* 59, once belonged to the Abbey of Florence, no.
    2709, paper, octavo, 211 folios, XIV. century, written in various hands.
    Contains: (fols. 27–211) 1–2. *Mos.* i, iii (the last without separate title);
    3. *Mos.* i; 4. *Jos.;* 5. *Abr.;* 6. *Virt.* a (defective); 7. *LA* i (defective at the
    beginning); 8. *Cher.;* 9. *Sac.* (end of work is omitted and after a va-
    cant line is followed by) 10. *Det.* The codex falls into two parts, items
    1–6 and 7–10, which are related to nos. 110 and 80.
    See C.-W., no. 23, I, xxvii–xxviii; IV, ix.

97. *Laurentianus plut.* LXIX. 11, paper, 262 folios in quarto, XV. century,
    consists of three parts and is related to no. 96.

Contains: I. *Mos.* i, ii, iii, *Jos., Abr., Virt.,* a; II. *LA* i (divided into two parts), *Cher., Sac.* (defective); III. *Opif., Spec.* i, g², *Gig., Immut., Decal., LA* iii (defective). Part III agrees with no. 46.

See C.-W., no. 23, I, xxix.

98. *Matritensis* O, 17, paper, 661 largest size folios, XVI. century, written in two hands. The codex is copied from no. 97 and differs only in placing *Mos.* i, ii, iii at the end. Fols. 1–408 contain the Commentary on the Psalms by John Chrysostom.

See C.-W., no. 23, I, xxx f.

C.-W., FAMILY L.

99. *Parisinus gr.* 433, formerly *Regius* 1895, paper, 567 larger size folios in quarto, XVI. century, written by Nicolaus Sophianus. Its first thirty-three books follow the order of no. 84 to which the text is related. At the end *LA* i and *Spec.* ii. a are added from a different text. The text of the first part is corrected to that of the last part.

See C.-W., no. 23, I, xvi; Conybeare, no. 20, p. 2.

C.-W., FAMILY M.

100. *Laurentianus plut.* X, 20, once *Mediceus,* at one time owned by Franciscus Filelfus, parchment, 399 folios in duodecimo, early XIII. century, written by three hands in small script, specimen in Tischendorf, no. 10. It seems to have been copied from an uncial text. A. Cocchius, a Florentine physician, collated the codex with the Turnebus edition for Mangey in 1733.

Contains: 1. *LA* i; 2. *LA* ii; 3. *Sac.;* 4. *Cher.;* 5. *Agr.;* 6. *Immut.;* 7. *Gig.;* 8. *Abr.;* 9. *Migr.;* 10. *Cong.;* 11. *Som.* i; 12. *Opif.;* 13. *Decal.;* 14. *Spec.* i. a, b (first book); 15. *Spec.* ii; 16. *Spec.* iii; 17. *Spec.* iv; 18–20. *Mos.* i, ii, iii; 21. *Virt.* a; 22. *Jos.;* 23. *Prob.;* 24. *Cont.;* 25. *Flac.;* 26. *Legat.;* 27. *Aet.;* 28. *Plant.*

See C.-W., no. 23, I, xxxi; Conybeare, no. 20, p. 3.

C.-W., FAMILY N.

101. *Neapolitanus* II C 32, paper, small size, XV. century.

Contains: in fols. 150–190 extracts from *Cong., Som.* i, *Flac., Decal., Spec.* i, b, f, g², *Spec.* iii, *Mos.* ii, iii, *Praem., Opif., Spec.* ii. b–d, *LA* i, *Sac., Ebr., Heres, Cong., Jos., Ebr., Sobr., Immut., Plant., Conf., Virt.* d. The text is related to that of no. 80.

See C.-W., no. 23, I, lviii; II, ii–vi; III, xi; V, xiii; VI, xxxix.

C.-W., FAMILY O.

102. *Laurentianus plut.* X, 23, parchment, small size, XIV. century.
Contains: *Mos.* i, ii, iii; *Virt.* a, *Jos., Heres* (a part of which has been supplied from the Turnebus edition by Jacob Diassorinus). From *Jos.* on the text follows Family A. Cf. no. 113.
See C.-W., no. 23, III, i–iii; IV, v; Cohn, no. 19, p. 498.

103. *Bononiensis gr.* 3568, paper, 160 folios, XIV. and XV. centuries. Codex O in C.-W., no. 23, VI.
Contains: (Fols. 1–131) Josephus, *Bellum Judaicum;* (fols. 132–160) *Legat.*
See C.-W., no. 23, VI, xxxviii.

C.-W., FAMILY P.

104. *Petropolitanus* XX A a1, formerly of the Monastery of Vatopedi on Mt. Athos, paper, rectangular, 446 folios, XIII. or XIV. century; on fol. 1 appears 'Αρσενίου.
Contains: (listed on fol. 2v) 1. *Opif.;* 2. *Decal.;* 3. *LA* i, ii; 4. *Cher.;* 5. *LA* iii; 6. *Spec.* iv. c; 7. *Virt.* b; 8. *Spec.* iv. f; 9. *Prob.;* 10. *Cont.;* 11. *Spec.* i. g²; 12. *Spec.* iii; 13. *Jos.;* 14. *Sac.;* 15. *Gig.;* 16. *Immut.;* 17. *Migr.;* 18. *Abr.;* 19. *Heres;* 20. *Som.* i; 21. *Praem.;* 22. *Exs.;* 23. *Virt.* a; 24–26. *Mos.* i, ii, iii; 27. *Virt.* d; 28. *Conf.;* 29. *Aet.* Items 1–5 can be called a twin of no. 35. Items 6–29 are very similar to no. 84.
See C.-W., no. 23, I, xvii–xviii.

C.-W., FAMILY Q.

105. *Parisinus gr.* 2075, paper, 418 folios in octavo, XV. century.
Contains: *Prob.* (fols. 30r–45r).
See C.-W., no. 23, VI, i.

C.-W., FAMILY R.

106. *Parisinus gr.* 1630, once *Regius* 3502, paper, 91 folios in duodecimo, XIV. century.
Contains: extracts from *Virt.* c, *Opif., Sac., Plant., LA* i, *Aet., Immut., Post.* The exemplar used for these extracts was ancient and excellent.
See C.-W., no. 23, I, lvi–lviii; V, xv.

107. *Vaticanus gr.* 316, formerly 191, parchment, largest size for its period, IX. or X. century, a palimpsest, double column, neatly written.
Contains: extracts from *Migr., Jos., Mos.* i; parts of *Mos.* ii, *Spec.* ii. a, b, d; all of *Decal.* and *Spec.* i.

See Cohn, *Sitzungsberichte d. k. preuss. Akad. d. Wissenschaft,* I
(1905), 36–52.

C.-W., FAMILY S.

108. *Seldenianus* XII (= Coxe XI), parchment, 156 folios in small quarto,
X. or XI. century, well written in bold miniscule, evidently copied
from an uncial text, mutilated at the beginning and end. Specimen in
C.-W., V, pl. II.
Contains: *Spec.* iii (defective, begins προσαγωγὸν γὰρ μάλιστα ἐν τοῖς
τοιούτοις τὸ εὐῶδες), *Spec.* iv, *Virt.* a, b, c. On fol. 126 appears this
title, Φίλωνος περὶ γ′ ἀρετῶν, περὶ ἡμερότητος καὶ ἐπιεικείας, περὶ
τοῦ μὴ δεῖν ἐν ἡμέρᾳ τῇ αὐτῇ θυεῖν μητέρα καὶ ἔγγονον, διατὶ ἔγκυον
ζῶον προστάσσει μὴ θύεσθαι. The last six folios contain a commentary
on Philo's *de mandato decimo* with the title: Φίλωνος περὶ τῆς
δεκάδος εἰρημένου ἑρμηνεία.
See C.-W., no. 23, V, viii–x, pl. II; Coxe, no. 7, pt. I, pp. 590–591;
Cohn, no. 18, pp. 266–270.

C.-W., FAMILY T.

109. *Ambrosianus* D 27 (= Martin D 27 *sup.*), formerly T 218, paper, 1 +
131 folios in octavo, XV. century.
Contains: *Philonis quod omnis stultus servus est* (fols. 49–55), edited
from this codex by Angelo Mai (no. 411), and *Quod omnis urbanus
liber* (= *Prob.*).
See C.-W., no. 23, VI, i; Martin, no. 17, I, p. 224.

C.-W., FAMILY U.

110. *Vaticanus gr.* 381, paper, 3 + 217 folios in quarto, XIII. or XIV. century,
poorly written and very difficult to read, specimen in Tischendorf, no.
10. The text is of equal value with that of no. 80.
Contains: *Aet., LA* i, ii, *Cher., Sac.* (defective at the end), *Det., Post.*
(preserved only in this codex, is edited by Tischendorf, *op. cit.*), *Gig.,
Immut., Agr.* (defective), *Plant., Ebr.*
See C.-W., no. 23, I, xix–xx.

111. *Parisinus suppl. gr.* 1120, a papyrus discovered in Coptus, Upper Egypt,
1889, 44 leaves in octavo, VI. century according to U. Wilcken, written
by two hands in uncial. The text is related most closely to UF codices.
Contains: *Heres, Sac.* (frags.).
See C.-W., no. 23, I, xli–xlix; cf. III, iii–xi; see *Centralblatt für Bibliothekswesen,* XIV (1897), 396–397.

C.-W., FAMILY V.

112. *Vindobonensis theologicus gr.* 29, parchment, 249 largest size folios, XI.
century, written in a beautiful hand by Augerius Busbeckius at Constantinople, specimen at end of C.-W., no. 23, I.
Contains: *Opif.* only (first half) on fols. 147r–154v. Fol. 146v gives an
index of Philo's works as follows: *Opif., QG* i, ii, iii, iv, v, vi, *QE* ii, v,
Post., Decal., Spec. iii, iv. This list was evidently contained in the exemplar. On the same folio appears Εὐζόϊος ἐπίσκοπος ἐν σωματίοις
ἐνενεώσατο, written in the form of a Greek cross and seems to mean
that Euzoïus had the text transcribed from papyrus to parchment. The
exemplar therefore goes back to about A.D. 380 when Euzoïus was
bishop of Caesarea.
See C.-W., no. 23, I, iii, xxxv–xxxvii; Cohn, no. 14, pp. i–vii.

113. *Vindobonensis suppl. gr.* 50, once in the possession of John Alexander
Brassicanus, a lawyer, then at the Bibliotheca Windhagiana, parchment, 108 folios in quarto, XII. century. This codex is the exemplar of
the first part of no. 102 and of nos. 92, 114–117. Sometime in the XIII.
century the text of the codex was corrected throughout by a learned
scribe whose corrections depended on his own ingenuity rather than on
MS. authority. In many places he obscured the original text. The de-
pendent codices copy his corrections.
Contains: *Mos.* i, ii, iii, *Virt.* a, *Jos.*
See C.-W., no. 23, IV, ii–v; Cohn, no. 28, pp. 488–500.

114. *Venetus append. class.* XI, 31, once belonged to Gaspar Contarini, paper,
304 folios in quarto, XIV. century, written in small script with many
abbreviations.
Contains: the same treatises as no. 113, of which it is a copy.
See C.-W., no. 23, IV, iv–v; Cohn, *ibid.*

115. *Vindobonensis hist. gr.* 81 (bound with cod. 80), paper, 194 folios in
quarto, XV.–XVI. centuries, written by the hand of Arsenius, archbishop of Monembasia.
Contains: *Mos.* i, ii, iii (defective at the end), *Jos.* (defective at the beginning); *Abr.* The text of *Abr.* agrees with that of no. 43.
See C.-W., no. 23, IV, vii–viii; Cohn, *ibid.*

116. *Leidensis suppl. gr.* 105, once *Claromontanus* 198, then *Meermannianus*
375, paper, 115 folios in quarto, XVI. century.
Contains: *Mos.* i, ii, iii, *Virt.* a, *Jos., Abr.* The text of *Abr.* agrees with
that of no. 43.
See C.-W., no. 23, IV, viii; Cohn, *ibid.*

117. *Monacensis gr.* 19 (= *Boicus* 35 used by Hoeschel), paper, 496 largest
size folios, XVI. century.

Contains: the same as no. 116. The text of *Abr.* agrees with that of no. 43.

See C.-W., no. 23, IV, viii–ix; Cohn, *ibid.;* catalogue, no. 3, pt. 1.

C.-W., FAMILY Z.

118. *Mazarinaeus* 1310, paper, 34 folios in octavo, XIII. century, the order of the folios is disarranged.

Contains: *Mos.* i. The text agrees with no. 96.

See C.-W., no. 23, IV, xi.

119. *Laurentianus* XI, 13, paper, XIV. century, similar to no. 118.

See *loc. cit.*

120. *Coislinianus* 384, paper, XIV. century, similar to no. 118.

Contains: *Mos.* i on fols. 212–236.

See *loc. cit.*

GREEK MANUSCRIPTS, B.

THIS division contains manuscripts of Philonean treatises not classified, or not known, by Cohn and Wendland.

121. *Cantabrigiensis Collegii S. Trinitatis* B 9, 6, paper, 539 largest size folios, XV. and XVI. centuries, poorly written and of little value. The margins are full of emendations and conjectures, by two (?) hands.

Contains: *Opif., Decal., Spec.* iv, c, *Virt.* b, c, *Spec.* iv, f, *Prob., Cont., Spec.* i, *Spec.* i, g²; *Spec.* ii, *Jos., Sac., Cher., Agr., Gig., Immut., Migr., Cong., Abr., Heres, Som.* i, *Praem., Exs., Virt.* a, *Flac., Legat., Mos.* ii, *Virt.* d, *Fug., Plant., Sobr., Conf., Aet., Det., Ebr., Spec.* i, a, *Spec.* i, b, *Spec.* i, e, *Spec.* i, f, *LA* iii, *Mut., LA* ii, *LA* i, *Som.* ii.

See James, no. 25, pp. 264–267, Cohn, no. 14, p. xxx; Conybeare, no. 20, p. 2.

122. *Athous Iberorum Monasterii* 252, paper, 238 folios in quarto, XVI. century.

Contains: Item 1a, *Abr.;* item 1b, *Migr., Cong., Fug., Heres, Som.,* at the end of this item (fol. 146v) is the statement, τέλος τοῦ βιβλίου τοῦ ἱστορόκου Φίλωνος πραγματεία καὶ γράψιον τοῦ Ἰωσὴφ ἐκ πόλεως Σινόπης; item 6, extract from *Jos.* (fol. 178); item 14, extract from *Praem.*

See Lambros, no. 22, p. 66, cod. 4372.

123. *Athous Iberorum Monasterii* 267, paper, 257 folios in quarto, XVI. century.

Contains: *Opif., LA* i, ii, *Cher., Sac., Det., Agr., Plant., Ebr., Sobr.,*

Gig., Immut., Conf. (at the conclusion of which is the statement that this is the end of Philo's *Opif.*). Then follows *Spec.* i, g² (fol. 235v).
See Lambros, no. 22, p. 263 f., cod. 4387.

124. *Urbinas gr.* 125, paper (first two and last two folios parchment), 309 folios, XIII.–XIV. centuries, a miscellany of writings.
Contains: *Spec.* iii, *Mos.* i, ii, iii, *Virt.* a on folios 214–229v and 230–277; extracts from *Prob.* and *LA* ii on folio 306v, from *Prob.* on folio 308v. The text is derived from two or more exemplars.
See C.-W., no. 23, I, lix; IV, xii; VI, i–ii; no. 21, pp. 217–229.

125. *Hierosolymitanus* 23, formerly in the Library of the Sala Monastery, parchment, 408 folios, IX. century.
Contains: *Spec.* i, a (fols. 403–405).
See Papadopoulos-Kerameus, no. 16, III, p. 54.

126. *Athous Penteleemoni Monasterii* 741, paper, 230 folios, XVII. century.
Contains: *Spec.* i, b (bk. I) on fols. 1–3v.
See Lambros, no. 22, p. 423, cod. 6248.

127. *Oxyrhynchus Papyri* 1173 and 1356, 10 folios (17.5 × 15 cm.), III. century.
Contains: Parts of *LA* i, *Det., Ebr., Spec.* i, g², and parts of some treatise or treatises not elsewhere extant.
See Grenfell-Hunt, *Oxyrhynchus Papyri,* IX (1912), 16–29; XI (1915), 12–19.

128. *Papyrus della Società Italiana* 1207, frag. of 1 folio (numbered σπ, σπα, σπη, σπθ), II. century.
Contains: Last section of *Ebr.* (§223); and *Post.* (frags. of §§ 1, 31, 32, and 34).
See no. 439.

GREEK MANUSCRIPTS, C.

CODICES containing the seven Eusebian extracts from Philo's *De Vita Contemplativa* (*Cont.*) which are preserved in the works of the pseudo-Dionysius the Areopagite. In editing the text of *Cont.* Cohn and Ritter (C.-W., no. 23, VI) found these excerpts of considerable value. The manuscripts are here listed, including several not mentioned by Cohn and Ritter. Manuscripts of the early Latin translations are listed below with the Latin manuscripts.

129. *Vallicellianus* E 29, parchment, 4 + 167 folios, X. century.
Contains: Eusebian extracts from *Cont.*
See Martini, no. 27, cod. 69.

130. *Laurentianus S. Marci,* X. century.
Contains: Eusebian extracts from *Cont.* (fol. 215).
See C.-W., no. 23, VI, iii.

131. *Londiniensis Musei Britannici addit. gr.* 36821, parchment, 214 folios, X. century, written in well formed sloping minuscules with marginal gloss in small uncials, from the library of the Earl of Ashburnham. On fol. 214 is a note relative to the capture of Nauptria by the Turks, dated July(?) 1715. The codex is devoted to the works of pseudo-Dionysius the Areopagite.

Contains: Eusebian extracts from *Cont.* §§ 3, 4, 8, 10 with a note on the interpretations of Eusebius and others concerning the Therapeutae (fols. 198v–200).

See Catalogue, no. 30, pp. 234–236.[6]

132. *Londiniensis Mus. Brit. addit. gr.* 18231, X. century (A.D. 972).

Contains: Eusebian extracts from *Cont.* (fol. 12).

See C.–W., no. 23, VI, iii.

133. *Athous Vatopedii Monasterii* 159, parchment, 442 folios, XI. century.

Contains: Eusebian extracts from *Cont.* (item 8).

See Sophronios Eustratiades, *Catalogue of the Greek Manuscripts in the Library of the Monastery of Vatopedi on Mt. Athos,* Harvard University Press, 1924, 36.

134. *Oxoniensis Collegii Corporis Christi* 141, 125 large folios in quarto, XII. century.

Contains: Eusebian extracts from *Cont.* (fol. 1).

See Coxe, no. 6; C.–W., no. 23, VI, iii.

135. *Coislinianus* 86, parchment, 396 folios, XII. century.

Contains: Eusebian extracts from *Cont.* (fol. 394).

See Montfaucon, no. 1, p. 140; C.–W., no. 23, VI, iii.

136. *Parisinus* 440, XII. century.

Contains: Eusebian extracts from *Cont.* (fol. 178).

See C.–W., no. 23, VI, iii.

137. *Ambrosianus* H, 11 *sup.,* formerly T, 88, paper, 281 folios, XIII. and XIV. centuries. Works of Dionysius Areopagita.

Contains: Eusebian extracts from *Cont.* (fols. 214v–216).

See M.–B., no. 29, vol. I, 500–502.

138. *Vaticanus gr.* 374, paper, 4 + 246 folios, XIII.–XIV. centuries, original folio 246 lost, but text was copied on a more recent fly-leaf.

Contains: Eusebian extracts from *Cont.* (fols. 244–246).

See above, p. 140, n. 1.

139. *Vaticanus gr.* 504, parchment and paper, 4 + 197 folios, century? double col. in part.

---

6. *Londiniensis Mus. Brit. Addit.* 22350, parchment, XVI. century is listed in B.M. Catalogue as containing *omnia opera sancti Dionysii Areopagitae,* but this description frequently does not include the Eusebian extracts. See *Catalogue of Additions to the Mss. in the British Museum in the Years 1876–1881.*

Contains: same extracts as no. 128 (fols. 76–77).
See above, p. 140, n. 1.

140. *Ambrosianus* O, 82 *sup.,* formerly T, 231, paper, 4 + 77 folios, XV. century.
Contains: extracts from *Cont.* (fol. 38).
See M.–B., no. 29, vol. II, 681 f.

141. *Urbinas* 5, paper, 247 folios, XVII. century. In the first part of the codex are the works of Dionysius the Areopagite.
Contains: extracts from *Cont.* (fol. 247).
See Catalogue, no. 21, p. 13 f.

142. *Hierosolymitanus* 414, 138 folios, late XVII. century.
Contains: Eusebian extracts from *Cont.* (fols. 129–138).
See Papadopoulos-Kerameus, no. 16, I, 414.

GREEK MANUSCRIPTS, D.

CODICES containing *The Sacred Parallels*[7] and *Florilegia* (see Greek Manuscripts A, C.–W., Family D).

143. *Vaticanus* 1456, palimpsest, VIII. and IX. centuries.
Contains: *Sacred Parallels,* bk. II, closely related to no. 52; not yet collated.
See Lewy, no. 34, p. 72; Holl, no. 24, pp. 219–224.

144. *Atheniensis* 464, parchment, 214 folios (23 folios missing at the beginning, other folios missing in the middle and at the end), late X. century.
Contains: *Sacred Parallels,* similar to no. 145.
See Holl, no. 24, p. 138.

145. *Coislinianus* 294, parchment, 220 folios, XII. century.
Contains: a mixed recension of the *Sacred Parallels.* The authors including Philo, are arranged alphabetically under the various topics.
See Montfaucon, no. 1, p. 412; Harris, no. 12, p. xiii; Cohn, no. 19, p. 482; Lewy, no. 34, p. 72; Holl, no. 24, pp. 132–138.

146. *Constantinopolitanus Metochion* 274, XII. century.
Contains: extract from Bk. I of the *Sacred Parallels* with Philo citations, related to no. 51. It is so damaged by dampness that a complete numbering of the folios is impossible.
See Lewy, no. 34, p. 72 and note.

147. *Atheniensis* 32(?), 231 folios, XII. and XIII. centuries.
Contains: *Melissa* of Antonius Monachus (fols. 2–84v); The *Sacred Parallels,* book II (fols. 84v–158v).

---

7. *Coislinianus* 20 has at the beginning two leaves written in sloping uncials of the ninth century which evidently belonged at one time to a volume of the *Sacred Parallels.* See Harris, no. 12, pp. ix, xxii–iii.

See Holl, no. 24, pp. 339–342 who takes his data from Sakkelion in Δελτίον τῆς ἱστορικῆς καὶ ἐθνολογικῆς ἑταιρίας τῆς Ἑλλάδος, vol. II (1885–89), pp. 577 ff. Holl says that Sakkelion gives the number of the codex as 32, which however he does not find in Sakkelion's Catalogue of the Ἐθνικὴ Βιβλιοθήκη. Cf. Lewy, no. 34, p. 73.

148. *Matritensis* O, 5, paper, 397 folios, XVI. century.
     Contains: The *Sacred Parallels,* copied from no. 54.
     See Holl, no. 24, pp. 72–74.

149. *Athous Iberorum Monasterii* 330, paper, octavo, XVIII. century.
     Contains: Item 12, Γνῶμαι Βασιλείου, Φίλωνος τοῦ Ἰουδαίου, Θεο-
     δωρήτου Κύρρου καὶ ἄλλων.
     See Lambros, no. 22, p. 88, cod. 4450.

150. *Oxoniensis Bibl. Bodl. Clarkianus* 11.
     Contains: extract from Philo (fol. 63v) in a florilegium.
     See Coxe, no. 7, pt. I, index p. 949, under Philo.

GREEK MANUSCRIPTS, E.

Codices containing the *Catenae on the Octateuch.*
In the *Catenae on the Octateuch* (Ἐκλογαὶ εἰς ὀκτάτευχον), i.e. Genesis to Ruth, the extracts from Philo are distributed as follows: more than ten on Genesis from *QG*, more than ten on Exodus from *QE* and *Mos.,* i, three on Numbers from *Mos.,* iii, one on Deuteronomy from *QE*. On the following pages only the manuscripts on the Octateuch which contain the Philo extracts are listed; there are many others which do not contain them. The classification of the codices is taken from the work of Karo and Lietzmann on the Greek Catenae (K.–L., no. 26). See also C.–W., no. 23, IV, xxii f., xxvii; Wendland, no. 15, pp. 29–108; Cohn, no. 19, pp. 475–480; Rahlfs, no. 33, pp. 377 f.; below, Greek Manuscripts, F.

CLASS 1.

151. *Basiliensis Bibliothecae Universitariae* A N III, 13, formerly B, VI, 18,
     parchment, X. century (fols. 1–263), XIII. century (fols. 264–268),
     written in uncials.
     Contains: Catena on Gen. (fols. 1–215), on Ex. (fols. 216–268).
     See K.–L., no. 26, pp. 3–5; Lewy, no. 34, p. 73; Rahlfs, no. 33, p. 26.

152. *Leningradensis* (= *Petropolitanus*) 124, paper, 229 folios, XIII. century,
     double col., written in imitation of a X. century hand.
     Contains: Catena on Gen. (fol. 1); on Ex. (124v); Num. (165v);
     Deut. (185v).
     See K.–L., no. 26, pp. 3–5; Lewy, no. 34, p. 73.

CLASS 2.

153. *Mosquensis Bibliothecae Synod.* 385, parchment, 410 folios, X. century, written in red semi-uncials.
Contains: Catena on Gen.
See K.-L., no. 26, pp. 5–7; Lewy, no. 34, p. 73; Rahlfs, no. 33, p. 147.

154. *Barberinus gr.* 569, formerly 185, and VI. 8, paper, 269 folios, XVI. century.
Contains: Catena on Gen.
See K.-L., no. 26, pp. 5–7; Lewy, no. 34, p. 74; Cohn, no. 19, pp. 479 f., 491; Wendland, no. 15, p. 34, 42.

155. *Vaticanus Reginensis* 7, paper, 183 folios, XV. century.
Contains: Catena on Gen. 1_1–3_7 (fols. 1–63), edited by Pitra, *Analecta sacra specilegio solesmensi parata,* Paris, III, 1884, 599.
See K.-L., no. 26, pp. 3, 5–7; Rahlfs, no. 33, p. 246.

CLASS 3.

156. *Matritensis* O, 10, formerly O, 37, paper, 542 folios, XVI. century.
Contains: Catena on Gen. (fols. 1–261v).
See Rahlfs, no. 33, p. 119; K.-L., no. 26, p. 591.

CLASS 3a.

157. *Laurentianus acquis.* 44, parchment, 384 folios, X. and XI. centuries, folios 63–66, 155–158, 175–178, 283–286 supplied in XIV. century.
Contains: Catena on Gen. (fol. 1), on Ex. (112), Num. (221v), Deut. (268v).
See K.-L., no. 26, pp. 7–12; C.-W., no. 23, IV, xxii–xxiii; Rahlfs, no. 33, p. 62.

158. *Vaticanus* 1668, parchment, 358 folios, XII. century, purchased *ex libris Illm̄i Lelij Ruini epī Balneoregieñ 1622.*
Contains: Catena on Gen., very similar to the text of the Leipzig edition, no. 405.
See K.-L., no. 26, pp. 2, 7–12.

159. *Hierosolymitanus S. Sepulcri* 3, parchment, 170 folios, XII. and XIII. centuries.
Contains: Catena on Gen.
See K.-L., no. 26, pp. 7–12; Papadopoulos-Karameus, no. 16, vol. I, 15.

160. *Hierosolymitanus* 224, parchment, 73 folios, XI. century, similar in contents to no. 159.
See Papadopoulos-Kerameus, no. 16, vol. IV, 193.

161. *Parisinus* 129, formerly *Regius* 1888, *Mazarinaeus* 1401, paper, 539 folios, XIII. century, double col.

Contains: Catena on Gen. (fols. 20–174, order disarranged), on Ex. (175), Num. (335), Deut. (404v).

See K.–L., no. 26, pp. 7–12; C.–W., IV, xxii–iii; Rahlfs, no. 33, p. 199.

162. *Vallicellianus* C, 4 (= 30), paper, XIV. century (fols. 199, 214–419), XV. century (fols. 200–213), and XVI. century (fols. 420–494).

Contains: Catena on Pentateuch.

See no. 27, codex 30; K.–L., no. 26, pp. 7–13.

163. *Turicensis Bibliothecae Munic.* C 11, paper, 20 + 716 pages, XIII. century.

Contains: Catena on Gen. (page 1), on Ex. (177), Num. (387), Deut. (475).

See K.–L., no. 26, pp. 7–13; C.–W., no. 23, IV, xxii–iii.

164. *Vaticanus* 1684, paper, 206 folios, XV. century.

Contains: Catena on Gen., text very similar to that of the Leipzig edition, no. 405.

See K.–L., no. 26, pp. 2, 7–13.

CLASS 3b, 1.

165. *Venetus* 534, parchment, 297 folios, X. century, catenae written in the margins by first hand.

Contains: Catena on Gen. (fol. 7), on Ex. (74v), Num. (161), Deut. (204).

See K.–L., no. 26, pp. 7–13.

166. *Vaticanus Palatinus,* once *Heidelbergensis,* 203, parchment, 304 folios, XI. century, double col.

Contains: Catena on Gen. (fol. 23), Ex. 1–40$_{21}$ (176).

See K.–L., no. 26, pp. 7–13; Rahlfs, no. 33, p. 243.

167. *Monacensis* 82, paper, 485 folios, XVI. century.

Contains: Catena on Gen. (fol. 1), on Ex. (251) defective at end. Copied from no. 166.

See K.–L., *ibid.*

168. *Vaticanus* 748, paper, 295 folios, XIII. century.

Contains: Catena on Gen. (fol. 1), Ex. (78v), Num. (170v), Deut. (209v).

See K.–L., *ibid.*

169. *Taurinensis* B, III, 15, formerly B, V, 30, paper, 638 folios, XVI. century.

Contains: *Catena on Octateuch; Commentary of Procopius* on Gen. (fol. 512).

See Rahlfs, no. 33, p. 298; K.–L., *ibid.*

CLASS 3b, 2.

170. *Vaticanus* 747, parchment, 260 folios, XI. century, beautifully decorated with about 500 miniatures, catenae written in the margins.
Contains: Catena on Gen. (fol. 13), Ex. (72), Num. (beginning lost), Deut. (148) defective. The order of the folios must be restored thus: 13–146, 152–191, 148–151, 192–259.
See K.-L., no. 26, pp. 7–14; Rahlfs, no. 33, p. 255.

171. *Parisinus* 128, formerly *Regius* 1825, parchment, 610 pages, XII. century.
Contains: Catena on Gen. (p. 28), Ex. (187), Num. (374), Deut. (449).
See K.-L., no. 26, pp. 7–12, 14.

172. *Vindobonensis theol gr.* 7, paper, 132 folios, XV. century. On fol. 1 *ex libris Sebastiani Tengnageln J. V. D. Caes. Consiliar. et Bibliothecar.*
Contains: Catena on Gen.
See K.-L., *ibid.*

173. *Vaticanus* 383, parchment, 319 folios, XII. and XIII. centuries.
Contains: Catenae on Gen. and Ex.
See K.-L., *ibid.*

174. *Vaticanus* 746, parchment, folios 1–251 (vol. I), folios 252–508 (vol. II), XIII. century, decorated with about 300 fine miniatures very similar to those of no. 170.
Contains: Catena on Gen. (fol. 14), on Ex. (151), Num. (310 v), Deut. (374 v).
See K.-L., *ibid.;* Rahlfs, no. 33, p. 254 who dates the codex to XI. and XII. centuries.

175. *Londiniensis Mus. Brit. Burnianus* 34, paper, 319 folios, XV. century.
Contains: *Catenae on Octateuch,* perhaps copied from no. 171.
See K.-L., *ibid.;* C.-W., no. 23, IV, xxii–iii.

176. *Parisini* 130 and 132, formerly *Regii* 1889, 1872, paper, 288 + 421 folios, XV. century.
Contains: *Catenae on Octateuch* copied from no. 171.
See K.-L., *ibid.;* Rahlfs, no. 33, p. 199.

177. *Vaticanus* 2131, paper, 371 folios, XVI. century. *Jo. Matthaei Giberti episcopi Veron.*
Contains: Catena on Ex. (fol. 1), Num. (289) defective at end. Copied from no. 170.
See K.-L., *ibid.*

178. *Angelicanus* 114, 178 folios, XVI. century.
Contains: Catena on Gen., copied from no. 170.
See K.-L., *ibid.;* Rahlfs, no. 33, p. 233.

179. *Vaticanus* 1520, paper, 690 pages, XVI. century, with Latin title, *Octa-*

teuchus veteris testamenti collectitiis graecorum patrum sententiis interpretatus. ex Bibliothecha Regis Francorum erutus.
Contains: *Catenae on Octateuch,* apparently copied from no. 171.
See K.-L., *ibid.*

CLASS 3c.

180. *Monacensis* 9, parchment, 227 folios, XI. century, double col. On fol. 227 Crusius notes that he read the codex in the year 1576.
    Contains: Catena on Gen. (fol. 1), on Ex. (fol. 121).
    See K.-L., no. 26, pp. 7–12, 15; Rahlfs, no. 33, pp. 149–50.
181. *Venetus* 15, parchment, 400 folios, X. century, catenae written in the margins.
    Contains: Catena on Gen. (fol. 1), Ex. (105), Num. (216v), Deut. (283v).
    See K.-L., *ibid.;* Morelli, no. 2, cod. 15.
182. *Vaticanus* 1657, parchment, 245 folios, XI.(?) century, catena written in the margins. The following note appears at the beginning, *integra haec catena ex regis Francorum Bibliothecae codice transcripta habetur in cod. Vaticano num 1520 Zacagnius.*
    Contains: Catena on Gen. (defective at beginning and end). The rest of the Octateuch is without catenae.
    See K.-L., *ibid.;* Rahlfs, no. 33, p. 264.
183. *Barberinus* 474, formerly IV, 56, once belonged to Nicolai de Nicolis, later in the convent of St. Mark in Florence, parchment, 233 folios, XII. century. On fol. 1: "Caroli Senezza Thome filij 1635."
    Contains: Catena on Gen. (beginning defective), Ex. (fol. 53v), Num. (129v), Deut. (155). Index of Philo extracts (fols. 104–106). This codex differs somewhat from others of the same group.
    See K.-L., *ibid.,* C.-W., no. 23, III, xv; IV, xxiii; V, xv; above, p. 140, n. 1; Rahlfs, no. 33, p. 238.

CLASS 3d.

184. *Atheniensis* 43, formerly *Constantinopolitanus,* parchment, 254 folios, XI. century, catenae written in margins.
    Contains: Catena on Gen. (fol. 1), on Ex. (45), Num. (119), Deut. (145v). A primary MS. for the *Catena Lipsiensis* (no. 405).
    See K.-L., no. 26, pp. 7–12, 16; Lewy, no. 34, p. 73 n.; Rahlfs, no. 33, p. 6.
185. *Londiniensis Musei Britannici addit.* 35123, parchment, 472 folios, XII. (some parts added in XIII.) century, carelessly written by numerous hands, catenae in margins.

Contains: *Catenae on Octateuch*.
See K.-L., *ibid.;* Rahlfs, no. 33, p. 106.

186. *Parisinus* 131, formerly *Colbertinus* 1599, paper, 156 folios, XVI. century.
Contains: Catena on Ex. (beginning defective).
See K.-L., *ibid.;* Rahlfs, no. 33, p. 199.

187. *Parisinus* 161, formerly *Regius* 2911, parchment, 127 folios, XIII. century, palimpsest.
Contains: Catena on Gen. (1–34$_{26}$).
See Rahlfs, no. 33, p. 204; K.-L., *ibid.*

188. *Coislinianus* 5, parchment, 185 folios, XIII. century (1264).
Contains: Catena on Lev. (fol. 1), Num. (41), Deut. (86).
See K.-L., *ibid.;* Rahlfs, no. 33, p. 185.

189. *Coislinianus* 6, parchment, 276 folios, XIII. century, double col.
Contains: Catena on Num. (fol. 53), Deut. (126).
See K.-L., *ibid.;* Rahlfs, *ibid.*

190. *Mosquensis* 19, paper, 208 folios, XV. century (1475), double col.
Contains: Catena on Gen. (fol. 69v), Ex. (107–208). Lev.–Ruth without catena.
See K.-L., *ibid.;* Rahlfs, no. 33, p. 143.

191. *Escurialensis* Σ, I, 6, XVI. century (1586), perhaps copied from no. 176 according to Paul Wendland, *Aristeae ad Philocratem, Epistula, cum ceteris de origine versionis LXX interpretum testimoniis,* Leipzig, 1900, xiii.
Contains: Catenae on Gen. and Ex.
See K.-L., *ibid.;* Rahlfs, no. 33, p. 54.

UNCLASSIFIED.[8]

192. *Constantinopolitanus* μετόχιον τοῦ ἁγίου τάφου 224, parchment, 73 folios, XI. century.
Contains: Catena on Gen. 2$_8$–49$_{16}$.
See Rahlfs, no. 33, p. 90.

193. *Patmiacus* ᾽Ιωάννου τοῦ θεολόγου 216, parchment, 308 folios, XI. century.
Contains: Catenae (in margins) on Pentateuch.
See Rahlfs, no. 33, p. 218.

194. *Patmiacus* ᾽Ιωάννου τοῦ θεολόγου 217, parchment, 136 folios, XI. century.

8. We are unable to find out whether the following codices contain Philo extracts: *Lisbonensis* 540, paper, XVI. century, containing a catena on Gen. under the title, τοῦ σοφωτάτου Μαρκελλίνου ἀπὸ διαφόρων ἐξήγησις. *Lisbonenses* 669, 668, 671, 670, paper, XVI. century, containing a Commentary on Ex.–Deut. *Escurialensis* Σ, II, 17, paper, XVI. century, containing a catena on Gen. with the same title as *Lisbon.* 540. See Rahlfs, no. 33, pp. 54, 101.

Contains: Catenae (in margins) on Num. 2₁₆–Ruth.

See Rahlfs, no. 33, p. 218.

195. *Nikolsburgensis Dietrichsteinsche Schlossbibl.* II, 221, now *Vindobonensis,* parchment, 297 folios, and XII. century; on fol. 5 is read, τὸ προοί-μιον τοῦτο ἀνεγράφη ἔκ τινος βιβλίου εὑρισκομένου ἐν τῷ ἁγίῳ ὄρει. The prooemium is by Nicetas Serranus, on which there is this note, *Carolus Rymius Sacrae C.M. consiliarius et orator in Curia ottomania hunc librum Constantinopoli comparavit et prooemium ex codice vetere patriarchale rescribendum curavit Junuario 1573.* The codex was copied by μοναχῷ καὶ πρεσβυτέρῳ Συμεῶνι.

Contains: *Catenae on Octateuch* in the margins.

See Rahlfs, no. 33, p. 161; *Sitzungsber. d. Kais. Akad. d. Wiss., Philos.-hist. Cl.,* CXLVI (1903), 7, pp. 59–90, no. 19.

196. *Constantinopolitanus Bibl. Serail* 8, parchment, 568 folios, XII. century, with more than 300 pictures.

Contains: *Catenae on Octateuch.*

See Rahlfs, no. 33, p. 90.

197. *Sinaiticus gr.* 2, parchment, 209 folios, XII. century.

Contains: Catenae on Gen. 16₈–Lev.

See Rahlfs, no. 33, p. 285.

198. *Smyrnensis* Εὐαγγελικῆς Σχολῆς A–1, parchment, 262 folios, XII. century, 380 miniatures.

Contains: *Catenae on Octateuch.*

See Rahlfs, no. 33, pp. 293–4.

199. *Leidensis Voss. gr. in fol.* 13, paper, 367 folios, XIV. century.

Contains: *Catenae on Octateuch.*

See Rahlfs, no. 33, p. 93.

200. *Berolinensis Phillippicus* 1405, formerly *Pelicerianus* 10 or 11, *Claromontanus* 56, *Meermannianus* 33, paper, 321 folios, XVI. century (ca. 1540), written by Nicolaus Malaxas.

Contains: *Catenae on Octateuch.*

See Rahlfs, no. 33, p. 31.

201. *Toletanus* 9, 20, paper, 177 folios, XVI. century, once owned by Francis Xavier.

Contains: Catena on Gen. 1–3₁₅.

See Rahlfs, no. 33, p. 295.

202. *Oxoniensis Bibl. Bodl. Miscellaneus* 179, once *Claromontanus,* then *Meermannianus* Auct. T, 1, 1, paper, 262 large size folios, XVII. century, a collection from many authors made by Fronto Ducaeus(?).

Contains: a Catena on Gen., fols. 1–29.

See Coxe, no. 7, pt. I, 724.

203. *Alexandrinus Patr. Bibl.* 68, formerly *Cairensis.*
    Contained: Catena on Gen.
    See Rahlfs, no. 33, p. 88; cf. Lewy, no. 34, p. 74, note 1.

204. *Rumanianus* (Jassy?), a codex, which K. Ἐρβιτσιάνος [= Erbiceanu]
    seems to have treated in detail in the *Revista Theologica,* Jassy, I, 371.
    Contains: Catenae on the Pentateuch.
    See Rahlfs, no. 33, p. 281, who cites the catalogue of Erbiceanu as,
    Κατάλογος συνοπτικὸς τῶν χειρογράφων καὶ ἰδιογράφων, τῶν ἐν ταῖς
    βιβλιοθήκαις τῆς Ῥωμουνίας εὑρισκομένων: Ὁ ἐν Κωνσταντινουπόλει
    Ἑλληνικὸς Φιλολογικὸς Σύλλογος. Εἰκοσιπενταετηρίς 1861–1886.
    Παράρτημα τοῦ ιη΄ τόμου, Constantinople, 1888, 97–102.

GREEK MANUSCRIPTS, F.

CODICES containing the *Commentary of Procopius of Gaza on the Octateuch.*
In 1772/3 Nicephorus Theotokes published at Leipzig a catena on the Octateuch (no. 405) for the text of which he used *Atheniensis* 43 (no. 184), *Lon-
dinensis Archiepisc. Libr.* Lambeth Palace 1214 (catenae on Lev. to Ruth),
and *Monacensis* 358. The last named codex was actually an epitome of a
larger work on the Octateuch and omitted the names of many of the authors
from whom citations were taken. In cases where Nicephorus recognized that
some of these agreed more or less verbally with his other MSS. and were not
identified therein he printed them under the name of Procopius with a single
star added. To other citations he added the name of Procopius with a double
star. Still other passages from the Munich codex he labelled as anonymous.
The Munich codex is entitled, Ἀρχὴ σὺν θεῷ τῆς εἰς τὴν Γένεσιν τῶν
ἐκλογῶν ἐπιτομῆς Προκοπίου σοφιστοῦ and in the foreword the author
states that he has previously composed a larger work on the Octateuch in
which he assembled citations from various authors and that now on account
of the great compass of that work he has condensed it into a short and connected commentary. *Monacensis* 358 therefore represents a condensation of a
larger work which was entitled, Ἐκλογαί. L. Cohn believes that the larger
work was the compilation of Procopius (see no. 19, p. 477). In the epitome,
or commentary, Procopius added citations which were not in the larger
catena, as he himself says in the preface, προσθήσομεν δέ τι καὶ ἔξωθεν εἰς
τρανοτέραν ἔσθ᾽ ὅτε παράστασιν. On the basis of the Munich codex a Latin
translation was published in Zurich, 1555, by Conrad Clauser (or Claudius
Thrasybulus) and Hartmann Hamberger. In 1834 A. Mai, *Class. auct.* VI,
1–347, edited the commentary on Gen. 1–18₃ from *Vaticanus* 1441 (no. 213)
and two other later MSS. All of the previous Greek editions are combined in
Migne, *Patr. gr.* LXXXVII, 17–1220. See Rahlfs, no. 33, p. 379, note 4; 377,
note 2; Cohn, no. 19, pp. 475–80; above, Greek Manuscripts, E.

205. *Monacensis gr.* 358, parchment, 453 folios, XI. century, written with great care by Ἰω(άννης) νοτάριος. Once owned by παπᾶ Νικάνδρου ἀρχιδιακόνου.

Contains: Procopius' commentary. Nicephorus used this codex for his printed edition of the catena (no. 405).

See Cohn, no. 19, pp. 475–480; no. 23, IV, xxvii; Wendland, no. 15, p. 31; Lewy, no. 34, p. 74 (who numbers the codex 385 by error); Rahlfs, no. 33, p. 155 (who dates the MS. in the IX. century); and the preceding note.

206. *Athous* Κουτλουμουσίου 10, parchment, 360 folios, XI. century.

Contains: Procopius' commentary (beginning of codex defective).

See Rahlfs, no. 33, p. 15.

207. *Ambrosianus* Q96 sup., paper, 427 folios, XIII. and XIV. centuries.

Contains: Procopius' commentary on Gen. and Ex. (fols. 140–255). The text seems to be nearer to no. 205 than to nos. 210, 211, but actually represents a third type of text.

See Cohn, no. 19, p. 492 (note by Wendland); Rahlfs, no. 33, p. 131.

208. *Londiniensis Mus. Brit. addit.* 18232, paper, XV. century, once owned by Γεωργίου Κόμητος τοῦ Κορινθίου.

Contains: Procopius' commentary on Gen. (fols. 2–122).

See Rahlfs, no. 33, p. 104.

209. *Oxoniensis Bodl. Bibl. Canonicianus* 99, paper, 197 folios, late XV. century.

Contains: Procopius' commentary on Gen. (fols. 1–109).

See Rahlfs, no. 33, p. 171.

210. *Vindobonensis theol. gr.* 47, paper, 284 folios, XVI. century.

Contains: Procopius' commentary on Gen. (fols. 133–264). More closely related to the three Roman MSS. used by Mai for his edition of the commentary than to no. 205.

See Wendland, no. 15, pp. 31–32; Rahlfs, no. 33, p. 320.

211. *Vindobonensis theol. gr.* 68, paper, 315 folios, XVI. century.

Contains: Procopius' commentary on Gen. (fols. 1–136), similar to no. 210.

See Wendland, *ibid.;* Rahlfs, *ibid.*

212. *Berolinensis Phillippicus* 1426, formerly *Claromontanus* 93, *Meermannianus* 63, paper, 363 folios, XVI. century.

Contains: Procopius' commentary on Gen. 1–18_3.

See Wendland, *ibid.;* Rahlfs, no. 33, p. 32.

213. *Vaticanus gr.* 1441, paper, 135 folios, XVI. century, once owned by Cardinal Sirlet.

Contains: Procopius' commentary on Gen. 1–18_3, used by A. Mai for

his edition in *Class. Auct.* VI, pp. 1–347, cf. p. v f. (= Migne, *Patr. gr.* LXXXVII, 21–365).
See Rahlfs, no. 33, p. 263.

214. *Monacensis gr.* 51, paper, 471 folios, XVI. century.
Contains: Procopius' commentary on Gen. (fols. 214–320).
See Rahlfs, no. 33, p. 151.

215. *Salamantinus Bibl. Univ.* 1-1-5, paper, 46 quaternions, XVI. century, written by Nikolaos Turrianos.
Contains: Procopius' commentary on Ex.
See Rahlfs, no. 33, p. 282.

216. *Taurinensis Bibl. Naz.* B, III, 15. See no. 169.

217. *Alexandrinus Patr.-Bibl. gr.* 57, formerly *Cairensis* 84, and 776.
Contains: a mutilated copy of Procopius' commentary on Gen. and Ex.
See Lewy, no. 34, p. 74, note 1; Rahlfs, no. 33, p. 88.

218. *Alexandrinus Patr.-Bibl. gr.* 101, formerly *Cairensis gr.* 98, and 471.
Contains: a mutilated copy of Procopius' commentary on Gen. and Ex. (fols. 19–58).
See Lewy, *ibid.*, Rahlfs, *ibid.*

GREEK MANUSCRIPTS, G.

CODICES containing the *Catena of Nicetas Serranus on the Psalms.*[9]
Of the twenty-seven classes of catenae on the Psalms described by Karo and Lietzmann (K.-L., no. 26) classes VIII and IX contain the codices in which the catena of Nicetas is found. Of the following codices (nos. 219 to 228) all belong to class VIII except no. 227 which belongs to class IX and the last (no. 228) which belongs to class XXVII, and consists of miscellaneous codices. Philo is cited in these catenae, sometimes apparently without the name, in the prologue, on Ps. 103_{21}, and elsewhere(?). In nos. 223 and 220 the catena carries the title, Συναγωγὴ ἐξηγήσεων ἀπὸ διαφόρων ἁγίων πρῶν καὶ διδασκάλων εἰς τὴν βίβλον τῶν ψαλμῶν. συλλεγεῖσα παρὰ τοῦ ἱερωτάτου μρōπολίτου Ἡρακλείας κυ′ Νικήτα τοῦ τοῦ Σερρῶν.

219. *Athous Gregorii Monasterii* 5, paper, 270 folios, XIV. century.
Contains: Catena of Nicetas on Psalms 33–148.
See K.-L., no. 26, pp. 32–34; Rahlfs, no. 33, p. 9, who dates the codex in XVI. century; Lambros, no. 22, cod. 552.

9. *Cryptoferratensis* (= *Gotta Ferrata*) A, γ, II (listed as 11 by K.-L.), parchment, 366 folios, 1282 A.D., containing a Psalter with a commentary on Psalms 1–77 in Greek and Latin on the margins, is listed by K.-L. as a catena of Nicetas. It may contain Philo citations. See K.-L., no. 26, pp. 32, 35; Rahlfs, no. 33, p. 74.

220. *Vaticanus Palatinus* 247, parchment, 387 folios, XIII. (fols. 384–387, XIV.) century.

Contains: Catena of Nicetas on Psalms 1–76 (53–57₃ missing) with a prologue in which Philo is cited.

See K.-L., no. 26, pp. 32–34; Rahlfs, no. 33, p. 243.

221. *Mosquensis* 197, paper, 387 folios, XIII. century (1275).

Contains: Catena of Nicetas on Psalms with beginning (fol. 1) mutilated. Citation from Philo ?

See K.-L., *ibid.;* Rahlfs, no. 33, p. 145.

222. *Venetus* 536, paper, 443 folios, XIV. century, fols. 1, 440–443 are supplied.

Contains: Catena of Nicetas on Psalms, title Συλλογὴ τῶν εἰς τὸν ψαλτήριον ἐξηγήσεων. Philo is cited on fols. 332–333.

See K.-L., *ibid.*

223. *Londiniensis Mus. Brit. Harleianus* 5677, paper, 163 folios, XV. century.

Contains: Catena of Nicetas on Psalms 1–54 with prologue in which Philo is cited. Title same as no. 220.

See K.-L., no. 26, pp. 32–34; Rahlfs, no. 33, p. 110.

224. *Parisinus* 171, formerly *Colbertinus* 5062, paper, 36 folios, XVI. century.

Contains: Catena on Psalm 1 (frag.) with prologue in which Philo is cited.

See K.-L., *ibid.;* Rahlfs, no. 33, p. 205.

225. *Coislinianus* 190, parchment, 259 folios, XIII. century, palimpsest. The under-text, of the X. century, is a catena on the Psalms.

Contains: (upper-text) Catena of Nicetas on Psalms 80–150. Philo is not named among the authors listed on fol. 259.

See K.-L., *ibid.*

226. *Gothanus* I, 77 (given as 81 by K.-L.), parchment, 415 folios, XII. century.

Contains: Catena of Nicetas on Psalms 1–40₁₁.

See Rahlfs, no. 33, p. 73; cf. K.-L., no. 26, p. 35.

227. *Vaticanus Reginensis* 40, paper, 344 folios, XIV. century, a commentary of Hesychius on the margins.

Contains: Catena on Psalms. The Philo extracts from *LA,* i on Ps. 103₂₁₋₂₂ from this codex are printed by J. B. Pitra, *Analecta Sacra,* II, 310.

See K.-L., no. 26, p. 35; C.-W., no. 23, I, lix; Rahlfs, no. 33, p. 246.

228. *Laurentianus* V, 14, parchment, 433 folios, XI. and XII. centuries.

Contains: Catena on Psalms 77–112. An extract from *Mos.* i appears on fol. 336.

See K.-L., no. 26, p. 65; C.-W., no. 23, IV, xxiv; Rahlfs, no. 33, p. 65.

GREEK MANUSCRIPTS, H.

CODICES containing a *Catena on Proverbs* in which Philo is cited.
Of the numerous codices described by Karo and Lietzmann, no. 26, pp. 300–312, the following (nos. 229 to 234) are the only codices which appear with some certainty to contain Philonean extracts. Since the authors cited in this catena are frequently not named it is impossible to determine from general descriptions which contain Philonean extracts and which do not. It is quite probable that the Philonean extracts are to be found in other codices containing the catena on Proverbs.[10] A list of these codices is given by Rahlfs, no. 33, pp. 415–420.

229. *Vaticanus Reginensis 77*, paper, XVI. century, copied in 1598 from a Munich codex (no. 230? or no. 231?).
      Contains: Catena on Proverbs with a Latin translation by David Hoeschel. The catena contains an extract from *Sob.* and another extract not preserved in extant treatises of Philo. It reads, ὁ αὐτός: τὴν εὐκατάπρηστον ὕλην ἐπιμελὲς ἡμῖν ὅτι πορρωτάτω τοῦ πυρὸς ἀποτίθεσθαι.
      See C.-W., no. 23, II, xvii–iii; K.-L., no. 26, p. 304.
230. *Monacensis 32*, paper, 503 folios, XVI. century, written or owned by Michael Sophianus. Wendland thinks this codex may have been the exemplar of no. 229.
      Contains: Catena on Proverbs (fols. 1–86).
      See C.-W., no. 23, II, xviii, note 1; K.-L., no. 26, p. 304.
231. *Monacensis 561*, paper, pages numbered from 1 to 271, XVI. and XVII. centuries; on what would be page 273 begins folio number 137 which numbering continues up to 148. Karo-Lietzmann suggest that this codex is the exemplar of no. 229.
      Contains: Catena on Proverbs (pp. 1–271) with readings from another codex copied on the margins by David Hoeschel; also extracts made by David Hoeschel from another codex (fols. 137–148).
      See K.-L., no. 26, p. 304.
232. *Venetus 23*, parchment, XI. century (IX. century by K.-L.).
      Contains: A catena on Proverbs (fol. 101) arranged in alphabetical order without title, which, Morelli says, so far as the beginning is concerned agrees with the following, nos. 233, 234.
      See Morelli, no. 2, cod. 23; cf. K.-L., no. 26, p. 309 f.
233. *Laurentianus*,[11] a codex described by Bandini, *Catal.*, I, 252, entitled

---

10. Wendland mentions *Angelicanus* 113 (C.-W., no. 23, II, xvii, note 2) and *Vaticanus* 1802 (*Ibid.*, III, xvi) but does not state that they contain the Philo extracts. Both are described by K.-L., no. 26, pp. 304, 308.
11. The *Laurentianus* codex may be the one listed by Karo-Lietzmann as *plut.* VII, 30 and described by Rahlfs as of paper, 246 folios, A.D. 1323, catena on Proverbs 1–21$_{26}$ (fol. 113). See

Γνῶμαι συλλεγεῖσαι ὑπὸ κυρία μονάζοντος τοῦ Γεωργιδίου (sententiae collected by Dominus Monachus Georgidius).
See Morelli, *ibid*.

234. *Parisinus* 1166 (= no. 70) seems also to contain this catena.
See Morelli, *ibid*.

GREEK MANUSCRIPTS, I.

Codices containing a *Catena on the Song of Songs* in which Philo is cited. This catena is class V of Karo-Lietzmann and was published by John Meursius in 1617 (no. 400, pp. 1–74) under the name of Eusebius.

235. *Florentinus Riccardianus* 7 (K. I. 8), paper, 105 folios, XVI. century.
Contains: Catena on the Song of Songs (fols. 1–47v).
See K.-L., no. 26, p. 318; Rahlfs, no. 33, p. 69.
236. *Vindobonensis theol.* 258, formerly 186, paper, 68 folios, XV. and XVI. centuries.
Contains: Catena on Song of Songs.
See K.-L., no. 26, p. 319; Rahlfs, no. 33, p. 322.
237. *Ottobonianus* 305, paper, XVII. century.
Contains: Catena on Song of Songs.
See K.-L., *ibid*.
238. *Hierosolymitanus* 355, paper, 741 folios, XVII. century
Contains: Catena of Eusebius on the Song of Songs (fols. 608–697) in which there are Philo extracts.
See Papadopoulos-Kerameus, no. 16, IV, 310.
239. *Matritensis* 20, formerly 6, paper, 300 folios, XVI. century, written by Andreas Darmarius.
Contains: Catena on Song of Songs (fols. 1–48), ῥήσεις κατὰ μέρος Ἑβραϊκαὶ ὧν ἡ δήλωσις γέγραπται πρόχειρος, beginning, Ἱερουσαλὴμ ὅρασιν; and a second catena on the Song of Songs similar to Karo-Lietzmann class IV.
See Martin, no. 17, pp. 86–7; Rahlfs, no. 33, p. 122.

GREEK MANUSCRIPTS, J.

Codices containing the *Catena of Nicetas Serranus* (bishop of Heraclea) *on Luke* in which Philo is cited.
The title of this catena is, Συναγωγὴ ἐξηγήσεως εἰς τὸ κατὰ Λουκᾶν ἅγιον εὐαγγέλιον ἐκ διαφόρων ἑρμηνευτῶν παρὰ Νικήτα διακόνου τῆς τοῦ θεοῦ

K.-L., no. 26, p. 302; and Rahlfs, no 33, pp. 66 f. The same catena appears in *Parisinus* 999, paper, 182 folios, A.D. 1272, fol. 120.

μεγάλης ἐκκλησίας καὶ διδασκάλου γεγονυῖα. The work was divided into four books, as follows: I (Luke 1–6₁₆), II (6₁₇–11₂₆), III (11₂₇–18₁₇), IV (18₁₈–24₅₁). Philo is cited six times on Luke 12₁₇–19₂₂, and once on 22₁. The citations come from *QE, Sob., Decal., Spec.* ii, c, *Spec.* iii, a, d. A Latin version was made by B. Corderius (no. 461) from a Venetus codex of Bessarion (no. 246). The numerous codices in which the catena is found are described by K.-L., no. 26, pp. 577–581 according to which the following, nos. 240 to 248, are arranged. See also C.-W., no. 23, II, xv–xvii; V, xvi. For an investigation of the catena see J. Sickenberger in *Texte und Untersuchungen zur Geschichte d. altchrist. Lit.,* New Series VII (1902), 4.

CLASS 4a.

240. *Vaticanus* 1611, formerly at Monastery of Rossano, parchment, 320 folios, XII. century (A.D. 1116), on fol. 1, *Libro 33 santo nichira diacono.*
    Contains: Catena of Nicetas on Luke 1–24₅₁ (defective at the end). The catena is divided into four books.
    See K.-L., no. 26, pp. 577–580; C.-W., no. 23, II, xv f.; above, p. 140, n. 1.

241. *Athous Vatopedii* 457, parchment, 585 folios, early XIII. century. Fols. 62–70 should be read before fol. 55.
    Contains: Catena of Nicetas on Luke 12₃₂(*sic*)–24₅₁.
    See K.-L., *ibid.*

242. *Angelicanus* 100 (B. I. 4), parchment, 343 folios, XII. century.
    Contains: Catena of Nicetas on Luke 6₃₂–12₁₈.
    See K.-L., *ibid.*

CLASS 4b.

243. *Constantinopolitanus Metochion* 466, parchment, XII. and XIII. centuries.
    Contains: Catena of Nicetas on Luke 11–24. The first half of this catena is found in *Athous Iberorum* 371, fols. 1–409.
    See K.-L., no. 26, p. 581.

244. *Coislinianus* 201, paper, 605 folios, XV. century, copied apparently from the two parts of no. 243.
    Contains: Catena of Nicetas on Luke; the books are undivided.
    See K.-L., *ibid.*

245. *Parisinus* 208, paper, 460 folios, XIV. century.
    Contains: Catena of Nicetas on Luke 1–12₄₆.
    See K.-L., *ibid.*

CLASS 4c.

246. *Venetus* 494, paper, 58 folios, XIII. century, double col., once owned by Bessarion.

Contains: extracts from the catena of Nicetas on Luke. Philo cited on fol. 47.

See K.-L., no. 26, pp. 577–581.

247. *Monacensis* 33, paper, 397 folios, XVI. century.

Contains: extracts from the catena of Nicetas on Luke copied from no. 246.

See K.-L., *ibid.*

248. *Vaticanus* 759, paper, 261 folios, XVI. century.

Contains: extracts from catena of Nicetas on Luke 12_{82}–24 (fols. 94–96, 112v, 172v–173).

See K.-L., *ibid.*

GREEK MANUSCRIPTS, K.

CODICES containing catenae on Acts and the Catholic Epistles in which Philo is cited. Class a on the Acts and Class a on the Catholic Epistles of Karo-Lietzmann, no. 26, pp. 593–597, contain nearly the same codices. In the catenae of both classes a citation from Philo is to be found.

249. *Coislinianus* 25, parchment, X. century.

Contains: Catena of Andrea the Elder on Acts; and catena on the Catholic Epistles.

See Montfaucon, no. 1, p. 76; K.-L., no. 26, pp. 593, 597.

250. *Barbarinus* VI, 21, parchment, 295 folios, XI. century, double col., beautifully written.

Contains: Catenae on Acts and Catholic Epistles.

See K.-L., no. 26, pp. 594, 597.

251. *Oxoniensis Collegii Novi* 58, parchment, XIII. century.

Contains: Catenae on Acts and Cath. Epist.

See K.-L., *ibid.*

252. *Casanatensis* 1395, paper, 456 folios, XVI. century.

Contains: Catena on Cath. Epist.

See K.-L., *ibid.*

GREEK MANUSCRIPTS, L.

MISCELLANEOUS codices containing extracts from Philo. The general character of some of these codices cannot be determined from the data accessible to us. Several may be catenae or gnomologia; others are probably collections of miscellaneous texts.

253. *Vaticanus gr.* 1941, parchment, 293 folios, X. century; fols. 1–4, 291–3 are unrelated to the rest of the codex. On the bottom of fol. 5: "Messanae emi a Georgio Constantinop. VI kts. Octobris. M.O.LI."

Contains: *Chronicon Paschale;* a late hand has added the title, *Epitome temporum ab Adam usque ad Heracliam. Item Prolegomena quaedam de temporis ratione et celebratione Paschae. Imperfectus liber sed usque ad Olympiada 352 integer.* On fol. 5 is a citation from *Mos.* ii given in C.-W., no. 23, IV, 252 and note.
See *ibid.;* above, p. 140, n. 1.

254. *Coislinianus* 305, parchment, 340 folios, X. or XI. century.
Contains: extracts from Philo (fols. 235v–240).
See Montfaucon, no. 1, p. 241.

255. *Vindobonensis hist gr.* 67, parchment, XII. century, very poorly written.
Contains: extracts from *Decal., Spec.,* and *Prob.* on fols. 56–60.
See C.-W., no. 23, IV, xxii; V, xiv; VI, ii.

256. *Hierosolymitanus* 365, paper, 287 folios, XII.–XIII. century.
Contains: Commentary on the Tenth Commandment in which Philo is cited once (item 28). Cf. no. 277.
See Papadopoulos–Kerameus, no. 16, II, 481.

257. *Coislinianus* 37, parchment, 367 folios, XIII. and XIV. centuries.
Contains: a catena (?) in which Philo is cited. The citations are taken from the Bible, Church Fathers, and the Councils.
See Montfaucon, no. 1, p. 111.

258. *Escurialensis* X, I, 13, paper, 387 folios, XIV. century.
Contains: extracts from *Opif., Sac., Spec.* iv, f, *Agr., Immut., LA* ii, *Prob., Som.* i, *Cher., Spec.* iv, e, *Praem.* (fols. 226, 226v, 228, 228v, 229, 234, 238v).
See C.-W., no. 23, I, lx; V, xiv.

259. *Laurentianus* VI, 4, parchment, XIV. century, having 63 chapters of expositions of sacred precepts collected from the Bible and Church Fathers.
Contains: extract from *Mos.* i (fol. 73).
See C.-W., no. 23, IV, xxii.

260. *Oxoniensis Coll. B. Mariae Magdalenae gr.* 10, paper, 209 folios, late XIV. century, a codex of *Sententiae.*
Contains: Item 7, ἱστορία περὶ μαγνητίδος καὶ Χρυσοπόλεως διὰ στίχων πολιτικῶν (fol. 184v–291), beginning, μάγνησσα λίθος μέλαινα, βαρεία, τραχυτάτη λυσιτελὴς συνήσουσα καὶ πολυχρηστοτάτη. Among the numerous authors cited are John Damascene, Dionysius Areopagita, Anastasius, Aristotle, Didymus, Plutarch, Philo, etc.
See Coxe, no. 6, p. 5.

261. *Vaticanus Palatinus* 209, paper, 287 folios in quarto, XIV. century, the last folios are decorated on the bottom margins with pictures by different artists and with Arabic writing.

Contains: extracts from many authors; from Philo's *de pio vitae instituto veterum apud Hebraeos philosophorum* (fol. 185).
See Stevenson, no. 11, pp. 105–108.

262. *Darmstadiensis gr.* 2773, XIV.–XV. centuries, written in various hands.
Contains: extracts from *Mos.* i, *Spec.* i, b, *Cher.*, *Abr.*
See C.–W., no. 23, III, xii f.

263. *Ambrosianus* C 46 sup., paper, 2 + 173 folios, XV. century.
Contains: extract from *Mos.* i, beginning, αἴγυπτος μόνον σχεδὸν . . .
ending, ἀθρόος κατασκῆψαι (fols. 90v–91).
See M.–B., no. 29, vol. I, p. 178.

264. *Coislinianus* 122, paper, 415 folios, XV. century.
Contains: a catena(?) from various authors including Philo.
See Montfaucon, no. 1, p. 197.

265. *Coislinianus* 178, paper, 292 folios, XV. century.
Contains: a catena(?) from various authors including Philo.
See Montfaucon, no. 1, p. 238.

266. *Parisinus* 91, paper, quarto, 372 folios, XV. century.
Contains: extracts from Philo.
See *Codd. graeci MSS. Regiae Bibl. Borboninae descripti atque illustrati a Salvatore Cyrillo*, Naples, 1826–1832, II, 6.

267. *Sinaiticus* 327, paper, 275 folios, XV. century.
Contains: Item 15, extracts from Philo.
See V. Gardthausen, *Catalogus codicum graecorum Sinaiticorum*, Oxford, 1886, p. 67.

268. *Vaticano–Palatinus*, once *Heidelbergensis* 129, paper, 141 folios in octavo, late XV. century, *ex codicibus Parisios primum translatis, Heidelbergae postea redditis.*
Contains: a catena of ancient authors, extracts from *Opif.*, *Som.* ii on fols. 14, 24, 31v, 127v.
See Stevenson, no. 11, pp. 61–62; C.–W., no. 23, I, lix; III, xi f.

269. *Ambrosianus* E, 26 sup., formerly T, 71, paper, 3 + 204 folios, XVI. century.
Contains: extracts from Philo and others (fols. 101–109).
See M.–B., no. 29, vol. I, pp. 306–10.

270. *Parisinus* 2221, paper, XVI. century.
Contains: *Cont.* and *Jos.* (beginning).
See Conybeare, no. 20, p. 2; Cohn, no. 18, p. 274.

271. *Vindobonensis theol. gr.* 65.
Contains: extracts from *Cont.*
See C.–W., no. 23, II, i; under no. 282.

272. *Vindobonensis theol. gr.* 110.
     Contains: extracts from *Cont.*
     See C.-W., no. 23, II, i.

273. *Athous Iberorum Monasterii* 710 (of Lambros), paper, 144 folios in
     16mo., XVI. century.
     Contains: extracts from κατὰ Φίλωνα αἱ ἀληγορίαι τῶν δ' μεγάλων
     ποταμῶν (fols. 96–99v).
     See Lambros, no. 22, p. 210, cod. 4830.

274. *Athous Iberorum Monasterii* 139, paper, 169 folios in octavo, XVII. cen-
     tury.
     Contains: extracts from Φίλωνος περὶ τῆς πορείας τῶν Ἰουδαίων
     (fol. 169r), beginning, τὸν μὲν παλαιὸν αὐτοῖς πρόγονον ἀπὸ Χαλδαίων
     εἶναι; ending, κἀπὶ τοσοῦτον ὑπερβάλειν εἰς πολυανδρίαν καὶ μετὰ
     βραχέα φῆσιν....
     See Lambros, no. 22, p. 29 f., cod. 4259.

275. *Athous Iberorum Monasterii* 493, paper, 218 folios in quarto, XVIII.
     century.
     Contains: Item 16, extracts from Philo.
     See Lambros, no. 22, p. 154, cod. 4613.

276. *Athous Iberorum Monasterii* 1317, paper, 351 folios in octavo, XVIII.
     century.
     Contains: Item 51, extracts from *Mut.*
     See Lambros, no. 22, p. 263 f., cod. 5437.

277. *Cantabrigiensis Bibl. Univ.* Oo. VI. 91, a collection of various Greek
     MSS. (on paper in folio) made by Abenego Seller, consisting of several
     fasciculi some of which are numbered and most of them separately
     paged.
     Contains: (fasc. 28 a quire of 8 folios), Φίλωνος περὶ τῆς δεκάδος
     εἰρημένων ἑρμηνεία which begins, Φίλων τοὺς κατὰ Μωυσέα and
     breaks off with ἢ ἀριστερός, ἢ πη... This is the same Commentary
     on the Tenth Commandment preserved in nos. 118 and 256.
     See Catalogue, no. 9, pp. 506–513.

278. *Vaticanus* 163.
     Contains: an anonymous Byzantine Chronicle, which preserves an ab-
     stract of Old Testament history which represents in a closely parallel
     form a common part of other works closely related to one another.
     These go under the names of Symeon Logothetes, Leon Grammatikos,
     Theodosios Melitenos, and Julios Polydeukes. The name Julios Poly-
     deukes rests on a false title of Darmarios. The chronicle of pseudo-
     Polydeukes represents one recension of an original chronicle, while all
     of the others represent a second recension of which the chronicle of

Symeon Logothetes is primary. The original chronicle goes back perhaps to the last quarter of the fourth century. The Philo extracts preserved in this chronicle come from *QG* and are compared by Praechter with Aucher's Latin translation of the Armenian version. For the readings of *Vaticanus* 163 Praechter used a collation made by Dr. H. Graeven in Rome. The beginning of the Logothetes chronicle (not yet completely published) is to be found in the *Codices Mosquenses* of Georgius Monachus and is published in Muralt, *Georgios Monachos,* pp. 902–914. A recension of Georgius Monachus is to be found in *Vindobonensis hist. gr.* 40. For the editions of Leon, Theodosios, and Polydeukes see Krumbacher, *Gesch. d. byz. Litter.,* 136.

See Karl Praechter, no. 430.

GREEK MANUSCRIPTS, M.

CODICES containing collations of Philonean treatises.

279. *Leningradensis Bibl. Acad. Eccles.* 353, 28 folios.
Contains: *Variae lectiones ex codice Petropolitano ad Philonem* (i.e. a collation of no. 104) made by Chr. Fr. Matthaei.
See C.-W., no. 23, I, xvii, note; III, xxi.

280. *Lipsiensis cod. Tischend.* 60.
Contains: collations made by Tischendorf for Grossmann of *Parisini codices* of Philo. The codices investigated are: nos. 99 (with Mangey ed. II, 471 ff.), 88, 49, 106, *Coislinianus* 296 (and nine other codd. unspecified in the catal.), *Regius* 123 (in another hand).
See V. Gardthausen, *Katalog der Handschriften der Universitäts-Bibliothek zu Leipzig,* III. *Katalog der griechischen Handschriften,* Leipzig, 1898, 35, cod. 29; cf. Tischendorf, no. 10, p. v.

281. *Lipsiensis cod. Tischend.* 61.
Contains: collations by Tischendorf of "Italian codices" of Philo. The codices investigated are: nos. 100, 109, 78 (in another hand), *Burbonicus* I, B, 18 or XVI (title corrected by Tisch. to cod. *Neapol.* [= no. 101?], 114), *Laurent. pl.* XCI Sup. 10 (*sic!*) along with another *Laur. cod.,* and nos. 100, 81, 110, 166, 124, 83, 94, 85, 93, 174, 38, 219, 93, 110, 47, 68 (in another hand).
See V. Gardthausen, *op. cit.,* 36, cod. 30.

282. *Lipsiensis cod. Tischend.* 62.
Contains: collations for Tischendorf of Philo codices in Vienna. Codices investigated are: *Vindobonensis* 80, and 81 (= no. 115) collated with Mangey II, 80 ff., *Vindob. theol. gr.* 65, no. 110, *Vindob. theol.* 69, *suppl. Kollar,* 447 ff.
See *ibid.,* 37, cod. 31.

283. *Londinienses Mus. Brit. addit. 6447-6449, 6453, 6457.*
    Contains: collations of Philo's works by Mangey.
    See *BM Index,* no. 5, under "Philo Judaeus."
284. *Londiniensis Mus. Brit. addit. 6416.*
    Contains: "Various readings from an ancient codex of the Medicean Lib., Florence; collation with the Turnebus edition, 1552, by Antonius Cocchius, 1731." Fol. 72.
    See *BM Index,* no. 5, under "Philo Judaeus."
285. *Londiniensis Mus. Brit. addit. 6455.*
    Contains: collations of Philo together with brief notes on two Parisinae Catenae on Lev. to Ruth which contain Philo citations (nos. 188 ?, 189 ?).
    See Rahlfs, no. 33, p. 103, note 1; *BM Index,* no. 5, p. 93, under "Catena."
286. *Oxoniensis Bibl. Bodl. Adversaria Grabe 21.*
    Contains: Item 13 (fols. 74-96), *Varia ad Philonis editionem novam parandam,* beginning, *Collatio editionis Parisiensis cum cod. MS. collegii Lincolniensis* [xxxiv] (= no. 76).
    See Coxe, no. 7, pt. I, p. 865 f.
287. *Oxoniensis Bibl. Bodl. Rawlinsonianus B, 259,* paper, 113 folios, XVIII. century.
    Contains: Item 2 (fols. 33-47), *Collatio editionis Parisiensis operum Philonis Judaei cum codice in Bibl. Collegii Lincoln. Oxon. gr.* xxxiv (= no. 76).
    See Macray, no. 8, pt. V, p. 566.
288. *Parisinus suppl. gr. 867,* paper, XVIII. century.
    Contains: *Post.,* copied from no. 110; and *Philonis Judaei quaedam, cum collatione cod. Palat.* 152 (= no. 47), fols. 39 ff.
    See H. Omont, *Inventaire sommaire des mss. supplément grecs de la Bibliothèque Nationale,* Paris, 1883, 93.

GREEK MANUSCRIPTS, N.

CODICES which are not positively identified. Several of this group will probably have been described above under other designations.

289. *Bessarianus gr. 431.*
    Contains: "some of the treatises" of Philo.
    See H. Omont, *Inventaire des mss. grecs et latins donnés à Saint-Marc de Venise par le Cardinal Bessarion en 1468,* Paris, 1894.
290. *Boicus.*
    Contains: *Spec.* ii b, c, the text of which D. Hoeschel used for his edition (no. 397).
    See Tischendorf, no. 10, pp. xiii-xiv and note.

291. *Cahirinus* (= *Alexandrinus Bibl. Patriarchalis* ?), X. century.
Contains: extracts from Philo in a gnomologium.
See Tischendorf, no. 10, pp. xx, 152n.

292. *Codex Theodori Canteri Bibliothecae.*
Contains: *Spec.* ii, b, c, which Hoeschel used for his edition (no. 397).
On this codex Hoeschel makes the following notes: "codex Boicus (see
no. 290) et vetus, quem vir clariss. Andreas Schottus e nobilissimi et
eruditissimi Theodori Canteri Bibliotheca—misit"; and, "haec usque
ad finem in codice Boico et vetere desiderantur, suppleta ex recentiore
antigrapho eiusdem Th. Canteri."
See Tischendorf, no. 10, pp. xiii–xiv and note.

293. *Monacensis* 117, XV. or XVI. century. In addition to the golden verses
of Pythagoras and orations of Libanius and Julianus the codex.
Contains: *Spec.* ii b, c, which first appeared in the Hoeschel edition
(no. 397).
See Tischendorf, no. 10, pp. xii–xiii; cf. Rahlfs, no. 33, p. 152.

294. *Sirletanus* 26.
Contains: *Mos.*
This codex is listed in a Catalogue of the MSS. of Cardinal Sirlet con-
tained in *Escurialensis* X, I, 15 and described by Miller, no. 4, pp. 304 f.

295. *Sirletanus* 288.
Contains: extracts from Philo.
See under the codex above. The larger number of the *Sirletani* codices
are in the Vatican Library; a few are in the Escurial.

296 and 297. *Vaticani duo codices* used by A. Mai for his edition of the commentary of Procopius and still unidentified. The third was *Vaticanus*
1441 (no. 213).
See Rahlfs, no. 33, p. 379 n. 4.

LATIN MANUSCRIPTS

LATIN MANUSCRIPTS, A.

THE following Latin codices (nos. 298–319) are listed according to C.-W.
(no. 23), VI, xii–xvi with several codices added from M. R. James, *The Biblical Antiquities of Philo* (no. 477), 14–18. See also C.-W. (no. 23), I, l–lii.

Group 1, containing a portion of *QG*, a frag. of *Cont.* and the *Antiquitates*
of pseudo-Philo:

298. *Laurissensis,* now lost, which was said by John Sichardus (A.D. 1527) to
be a twin of the following codex.

299. *Cassellanus theol.* 4.3, formerly *Fuldensis,* parchment, square, 89 folios, XI. century.

300.* *Admontensis* 359 (now owned by H. L. Goodhart in New York), parchment, of large size, 98 folios, XI. century, carefully written.

301. *Monacensis lat.* 18481, formerly *Tegernseensis* 481, parchment, square, 137 folios, XI. century, beautifully written.

302. *Monacensis lat.* 4569, parchment, large size, 119 folios, XII. century.

303. *Monacensis lat.* 17133, parchment, large size, 125 folios, XII. century.

304. *Budapestinus lat. medii aevi* 23, parchment, rectangular, 149 folios, XII. century.

305. *Cusanus* 16, parchment, rectangular, 154 folios, XV. century (written in 1451 A.D. in the Monastery of Gottwice).

306. *Confluentinus.* G. 132, paper, square, 143 folios, late XV. century.

307. *Wirceburgensis* M. ch. f. 276, paper, 104 folios, XV. century (written in 1462 A.D.).

308. *Vaticanus lat.* 488, paper, larger size, 149 folios, XV. century.

Group 2, containing only the *Antiquitates* of pseudo-Philo:

309. *Cheltenhamensis* 461 or *Phillippicus* 461, parchment, rectangular, XII. century. On fol. 1 is read, *Codex sancti Eucharii primi Trevirorum Archiepiscopi. si quis eum abstulerit, anathema sit.*

310. *Vindobonensis lat.* 446, parchment, square, 53 folios, XIII. century.

311. *Wirceburgensis* M. ch. f. 210, paper, larger size, 232 folios, XV. century.

312. *Treverensis* 117, A.D. 1459, related to the following.

313. *Phillippicus* MS. 391, 92 folios, early XII. century, formerly belonged to Leander von Ess and has an old press mark C 1 (or C 7), and contains four extracts from *Antiquitates.*

314. *Cantabrigiensis McClean* 31, parchment, 260 folios, XIII. century, contains extracts from *Antiquitates* (fols. 15–260, interspersed with other materials).

315. [*Chronicle of Jerahmeel* in Hebrew, early XIV. century, contains large portions of *Antiquitates* translated, according to James, from a Latin text.]

Group 3, containing fragments of *QG*[12] and *Cont.:*

316. *Augustanus* 9, parchment, XII. century.

317. *Laurentianus* XII, 10, parchment, largest size, 300 folios, XV. century; most beautifully written for Matthew Corvinus King of Hungary.

318. *Urbinas lat.* 61, paper, 182 folios, XIV. century.

319. *Treverensis* 71, paper, larger size, 266 folios, XIV. century.

12. James (p. 14) says that there is a codex at Coblenz, containing *QG* only, about which he could obtain no particulars. It is probably no. 306 above.

Hieronimus de philone in katalo
go [...] illustrium.

PHYLO IVDEUS NA
TIONE ALEXANDRINVS.
de genere sacerdotu. ideirco a nob
inter scriptores ecclasticos ponit. qd
in libro que de prima Marci euange
liste apud alexandriam scripsit eccla. in
nror laude uersat est. ñ solu cos ibi sin
multis quoq preuenit esse comemorans.
& habitacula eor dies monasteria. [...] apparet
tale primu in xpm credentiu fuisse ecclam. q
les nunc monachi cu unitant & cupiunt. ut
nichil cuiqua ipm sit. null inter eos diues. null
paup. patrimonia egentib diuidunt. orationi
uacet & psalmis. doctrine qq & cotinentie. q les
& lucas refert primu hierosolime fuisse eden
tes. Aiunt hunc sub gaio caligula rome pericli
tatu. q legat gentis sue mult erat. cu seda ui
ce uenisset ad claudiu in eade urbe locutu
cu aplo petro eiq habuisse amicicias. & ob hac
causa etia marci discipuli petri ap alexandri
am sectatores ornasse laudib suis. Extant hui
pclara & innumirabilia opa. ui. v. libros moysi.

PHILO WEARING THE DRESS AND HAT OF A
MEDIEVAL JEW

From the Admont Ms., XI. century (Reduced).

See Bibliography, no. 300

LATIN MANUSCRIPTS, B.

Codices related to those of section A but not listed by Cohn and Wendland, or James.

320. *Escurialensis lat.* d II 5.
    Contains: (fols. 169–181) *Ex Philone Judeo character antiquissime eiusdemque apostolice ecclesie.* Begins, "cum de Esseis hactenus egerim," . . . ends, "summumque obtinet principatum"; (fols. 182–194) *De Aegyptiis illis quorum historiam philo judeus conscripsit, deque eorum vetustissimis iisdemque ecclesiasticis ritibus et cerimoniis.* This seems to refer to Philo's *Cont.*
    See P. Guillermo Antolin, *Catalogo de los códices Latinos de la Real Biblioteca del Escorial,* Madrid, 1910, I, 416 f.

321. *Berolinensis Görres* 132, paper, 144 folios, XV. century.
    Contains: (fols. 2–79v) *Antiquitates;* (fols. 114–143v) *QG.*
    See Fritz Schillmann, "Die Görreshandschriften," *Die Handschriften Verzeichnisse der Preussischen Staatsbibliothek zu Berlin,* Vol. XIV, *Lateinischen Handschriften,* Vol. III (Berlin, 1919), p. 187 f.

321a.* *Melk* 324, now in the H. L. Goodhart collection, parchment, 303 folios, double col., XV. century, written in a beautiful and calligraphic Gothic script in Austria, with two fine painted initials at the beginning.
    Contains: *Antiq.* (fols. 216–244).

322. *Vaticanus Ottobonianus lat.* 870, a miscellaneous codex in two vols. all of the XVI. century, vol. I (fols. 1–178), vol. II (fols. 179–361); once belonged to Joannes Angelus, duke of Altaemps.
    Contains: *Cont.* (fols. 240–258v).
    See above, p. 140, n. 1; cf. Conybeare, no. 20, p. 145, who thinks the text may be the "work of Lilius Typhernas, of the rest of whose Latin versions I have seen copies in the Barberini and Vatican Libraries [i.e. nos. 330 to 333]."

323. *Urbinas lat.* 73.
    Contains: a portion of *QG* and a frag. of *Cont.*
    See Conybeare, no. 20, p. 142.

324. *Vaticanus lat.* 382.
    Contains: a portion of *QG* and a frag. of *Cont.*
    See *ibid.*

LATIN MANUSCRIPTS, C.

Codices containing the Seven Eusebian Extracts from *Cont.* included in the works of Dionysius Areopagita (see above, Greek Manuscripts, C.).

325. *Oxoniensis Coll. S. Johannis Baptistae* 128, parchment, 237 small folios, early XI. century.
Contains: Item 8, Eusebian extracts from *Cont.*
See Coxe, no. 6, p. 38.

326. *Cantabrigiensis Coll. Trinitatis* B. 2, 31, parchment, 111 folios, XII. century, well written. From Christ Church, Canterbury.
Contains: Item 11, Eusebian extracts from *Cont.* (fol. 109v).
See James, no. 25, pp. 91–93.

327. *Cantabrigiensis Coll. Corp. Christi* D. 9, parchment, 2 + 195 folios in quarto, late XIII. century, double col., in a clear upright hand.
Contains: Item 5, Eusebian extracts from *Cont.* (fol. 121v).
See James, no. 31, p. 118 f.

328. *Oxoniensis Bibl. Bodl. Ashmoleanus* 1526, parchment, 186 small folios, XIV. century, fairly written, adorned with rubrics and painted capitals.
Contains: Eusebian extracts from *Cont.* (fols. 69d–70c).
See W. H. Black, *Cat. of the MSS. bequeathed unto the Univ. of Oxford by Elias Ashmole,* Oxford, 1845, p. 1437 f.

329. *Oxoniensis Bibl. Bodl. Miscell. Laudianus* 639, once *Guillermi Reynant,* then 1398, parchment, 6 + 139 folios, late XII. century, double col., well written.
Contains: Eusebian extracts from *Cont.* (fols. 110v–117).
See Coxe, no. 7, II, 462 f.

LATIN MANUSCRIPTS, D.

Codices containing the Latin translation of Lilius Typhernas.[13]

330–332. *Vaticani lat.* 180–185. Lilius Typhernas' Latin translation of Philo's works.
See C.-W., no. 23, I, lxxx; also no. 333.

333. *Barberinus lat.* 662, formerly 1782, later XIV. 35, paper, 1 + 498 + 1 pages, XVI. century. All evidence seems to show that this codex is a copy of nos. 330–332. On the shelf back are the words: *Philo Judaeus Alexandrinus cum Lylio Typhernate.* On fol. 1 is read: *D. Octavius Pretianus canonicus senen. dono dedit hunc librum nobis Franc. Mariae Piccolomineo episcopo Pientino et Ilcinensi septimo. Senis, die 23 aprilis 1579.* The codex represents vols. IV, V, and VI of a larger work.
Contains: (beside Prologues, Epistulae, Capitulae, and a Carmen) Vol. IV, *Liber post Hexaemeron et de creatione mulieris, Conf., Fug.,*

---

13. For David Hoeschel's translation of the *Catena on the Octateuch* see no. 229.

Spec. iv c, *Virt.* b, *De spiritu dei, Quod Noe factus est Sobrius,*[14] *Spec.* i a, *Spec.* i b, c, (d?), *Spec.* i e; Vol. V, *Liber de vita Sapientis, Jos., Cong., Som., Ebr., Quod ab ebrietate resipuit Noe;*[14] Vol. VI, *Migr.* i, ii; *De animalibus (Spec.* iv d?), *Flac., Legat., Som.*
See above, p. 140, n. 1.

334. *Bruxellensis lat.* 2938 (1117–18), paper, 354 folios, XVI. century (A.D. 1508, for on fol. 169v one reads, *Explicit Philonis primum volumen, traductum de graeco a Lilio Tyfernate ex archetype, scriptum anno 1508, 18 martii (10) aprilis.* On fol. 1 is the note, *Collegii Soc. Iesu Antverpiae D. P.).*
Contains: fol. 1, title and index (by André Schott ?); *Aet., Det., Plant., Sac., Cher., Spec., Spec.* iii, h.
See J. van den Gheyn, *Catalogue des mss. de la Bibliothèque royale de Belgique,* IV, Bruxelles, 1904, 350 f.

LATIN MANUSCRIPTS, E.

CODICES containing the *Interpretatio Hebraicorum Nominum* ascribed to Philo Judaeus.

335. *Brugiensis lat.* 91, parchment, 100 folios, XIII. century, double col., rubricated initials, decorated with arabesques, beautifully written.
Contains: "Some interpretations of Hebrew names with many other extracts both of Catholic and pagan *sententiae.*"
See *Catalogue des mss. de la Bibliothèque Publique de Bruges,* Bruges, 1859, 73–75.

336. *Engelbergensis lat.* 49, formerly 3/18, 119 folios, XII. century.
Contains: Item 13 (fols. 104–119), *Liber interpretationis Hebraicorum nominum editus a Philone Judaeo.*
See Benedictus Göttwald, *Catalogus codicum manu scriptorum in Bibliotheca Monasterii O. S. B. Engelbergensis in Helvetia,* [Frankfurt i. B.], 1891, 86–88.

LATIN MANUSCRIPTS, F.

Unidentified codex.

337. *Cluniacensis* 27.
Contains: "volumen in quo continetur historia Philonis judei" (= *Antiq.* ?).
See Leopold Delisle, "Catalogue de la Bibliothèque de Cluni au milieu du XIIᵉ siècle," *Inventaire des mss. de la Bibliothèque Nationale, Fonds de Cluni,* Paris, 1884, Appendix I, 339.

14. Which of these two represents our *Sobr.* has not been verified.

ARMENIAN MANUSCRIPTS

The following catalogue of Armenian codices has been compiled from the sources cited under various manuscripts and supplemented by valuable notes supplied with characteristic generosity by Father Nerses Akinian of the Community of the Mechitarists at Vienna. They are the results of his own investigations in Oriental libraries. Further research would no doubt increase the number of codices considerably. For the most recent treatment of the Armenian version of Philo, its date, and the place which it occupies in the "Graecophile" literature of Armenia see Lewy, no. 443, pp. 1–24. We are indebted for the compilation of this material to Professor Robert P. Casey of Brown University.

338. *Edschmiatzin* 1500, formerly 944, paper, 1188 folios, 38 × 26 cm., written A.D. 1282 in the "round hand" (*Bolorgir*) by the learned historian Mechitas of the monastery of Ayrivank in the province of Sisuan. In addition to almost all of the known Armenian translations from Greek literature, both patristic and philosophic, it
Contains: *Provid.* (fols. 370–388), *Animal.* (1–121), *Abr.* (388–392v), *Cont.* (392v–401v), *LA* i, ii (401v–412v), *QG* (412v–466), *QE* (466–481), *Spec.* i, d, e (481–484v), *Spec.* i, g (484v–487v), *Decal.* (482v–494v), *Spec.* iii, a (494v–497), *Samp.* (497–501), *Jona* (501–507); *Deo* (507).
See Lewy, no. 443, p. 4.

339. *Edschmiatzin* 2101, formerly 2093, A.D. 1223, "the oldest [Armenian] MS. of Philo," written in the "round hand."
Contains: *Provid.* (fol. 87).
See Lewy, *op. cit.* p. 6, n. 22.

340. *Edschmiatzin* 2100, formerly 2092, paper, small square octavo, A.D. 1325, written in a large neat cursive hand. It is signed by Karapet the elder who wrote it at the request of the Vardapet Kirakos.
Contains: *QG* (fols. 3–112v), *LA,* i, ii (113), *Provid.* (159v), *Animal.* (264v), *Abr.* (313).

341. *Edschmiatzin* 2051 (of Kharenian's Catalogue), completed in March A.D. 1342 by the same scribe as no. 340 and is a companion codex to the same.
Contains: the Armenian treatises of Philo not listed under no. 340.

342. *Edschmiatzin* 2057 (Lewy lists as 2507), formerly 2509, A.D. 1328. The scribe was Jacob Krakatzi of Jermaghbiur in Cilicia.
Contains: the same treatises as no. 338 and in the same order, except that *Cont., Abr.* and *LA,* i, ii follow at the end.

343. *Edschmiatzin* 2046.2 (of Kharenian's Catalogue), paper in folio, written in A.D. 1329 at Cracow, Poland, in a good cursive hand. This codex is not listed by Akinian or Lewy.

Contains: "the whole of the Armenian version of Philo." [Cf. no. 338.]

See Conybeare, no. 20, p. 154.

344. *Edschmiatzin* 2056, formerly 2088, A.D. 1646 (Akinian), 1649 (Lewy).

Contains: copy of no. 338.

345. *Edschmiatzin* 2595, A.D. 1785, a copy of no. 353.

Contains: the same treatises as No. 338 and in the same order, except that the first four follow the rest.

346. *Edschmiatzin* 3932, A.D. 1275.

Contains: *Jona* (fols. 299–324).

See Lewy, no. 443, p. 5.

347. *Edschmiatzin* 3935, XIII. or XIV. century.

Contains: *Jona* (fols. 277–301).

See *ibid*.

348. *Edschmiatzin* 2058, formerly 2090, XIV. century.

Contains: (treatises not listed).

See *ibid*. p. 6, n. 22.

349. *Bzomar* (a monastery in the Lebanon) 330, XIII. century, a considerable number of folios missing at the beginning.

Contains: the same treatises as no. 338, except *Abr., Cont.* and *LA,* i, ii. The treatises are abbreviated copies of a codex similar to no. 338.

350. *Venice, San Lazzaro* 1040, 317 folios, written in A.D. 1296 by the royal scribe for Hethŏum II, the Rubenite king of Armenian Cilicia.

Contains: "a Philonian corpus."

See Lewy, no. 443, p. 4; Conybeare, no. 20, p. 154.

351. *Paris Arm.* 159, paper, 426 pages, XVIII. century, a copy of no. 350.

See F. Macler, *Catalogue des mss. arméniens et georgiens de la Bibliothèque Nationale,* Paris, 1898, 86.

351a. *Paris arm.* 303, paper, 11 pages, XIII. century.

Contains: fragment of *Provid.,* i.

352. *Venice, San Lazzaro.* "A codex of the Mechitarist library in Venice, written, as the colophon proves, by Vartan, a disciple of John Erzukatzi, during the latter's life time. This teacher was born about A.D. 1250, and died about 1326. Therefore this codex must belong at least to the beginning of the fourteenth century. It is written in a good cursive hand, on paper. This description only applies to the first half of the volume, which however contains the D.U.C. [*Cont.*] with certain other treatises. The rest of the codex is by a later and unknown hand."

See Conybeare, no. 20, p. 155.

353. *Jerusalem* (Library of the Armenian Patriarchate in the Convent of St. James) 333, A.D. 1298, written by Wahram Sarkawag in the Monastery of Armen in the Cilician Taurus.
    Contains: the same treatises as no. 338 and in the same order, except that the first four of 338 are at the end.

354. *Jerusalem* 157, A.D. 1758, a copy of no. 343.

355. *Istanbul* (Library of the Armenian Patriarchate, Church of the Trinity) 69, A.D. 1291, Aucher's cod. B, a copy of no. 353.

356. *Constantinople* (Armenian National Library) 69, XVI. century. Its exemplar was written in A.D. 1298.

357. *Constantinople* 114, A.D. 1668.
    Contains: Philo's treatises with scholia.

358. *Djulfa* (near Ispahan Library of the Armenian Monastery) 186, listed in S. Ter-Avetissian's manuscript catalogue, seen by Akinian in Tiflis in 1925, XVI. century.
    Contains: *LA* i, ii (fragmentary text).

359. *Istanbul* 114, XVIII. century.
    See Lewy, no. 443, p. 5.

360. *Jerusalem* 1331, XIV. century.
    See Lewy, no. 443, p. 6, note 22.

361. *Edschmiatzin* 465, XVII. century.
    Contains: quotations from Philo (fols. 291–295v).

362. *Tabriz* VI, 51, XVII. century.
    Contains: a short catena of Philonic quotations (fols. 350–357).
    See H. Adjarian, *Katalog der armenischen Handschriften in Tabris*, Vienna, 1910, 117.

363. *Tübingen cod. arm* Ma. XIII, 97, XVIII. century.
    Contains: a catena of philosophic opinions on the definition and nature of substance (fol. 102).
    See Fink, F. N. and Gjandschezian, L., *Verzeichnis der armenischen Handschriften der Königlichen Universitätsbibliothek*, Tübingen, 1907, 150.

Scholia were made probably in the thirteenth century to assist Armenian students of Philo. They throw some light on the history of Armenian scholarship in that period, but appear to have little textual value. They are found in the following codices:

364. *Edschmiatzin* 1672, XII. century.
365. *Edschmiatzin* 1897, XII.–XIII. centuries.
366. *Edschmiatzin* 437, XIII. century.

THE FIRST MENTION OF PHILO IN AN
ENGLISH MANUSCRIPT (LINE 7)

From a Ms. of King Alfred's translation of Orosius.

See Bibliography, no. 378.

367. *Edschmiatzin* 59, XV. century.
368. *Edschmiatzin* 2379, XVII. century.
369. *Edschmiatzin* 598.
370. *Edschmiatzin* 1138.
371. *Edschmiatzin* 1449.
372. *Edschmiatzin* 1448.
373. *Edschmiatzin* 1879.
374. *Edschmiatzin* 2595.
375. *Bzomar* 153.
376. *Vienna, Mechitaristenkloster* 47.

See for a discussion of these scholia Dashian, *Katalog der armenischen Handschriften in der Mechitaristen-Bibliothek zu Wien*, Vienna, 1895, 222–224; Akinian, *Introduction to the Book of Causes*, Vienna, 1922, 96 ff. (In modern Armenian.)

MISCELLANEOUS MANUSCRIPTS

377. *Ambrosianus* N, 66 sup., paper 8 + 89 folios, XVI. century.
Contains: *Notulae* in Latin on various authors including Philo, Diodorus, Theophrastus, etc.
See M.-B., no. 29, vol. II, 657 f.
378. *Cottonianus Tiberius* B, 1, parchment, 162 folios, XI. century.
Contains: King Alfred's "The Seven Books of Orosius." In a. vi. 3 (= Orosius vii. 5) is an account of Philo's embassy to Gaius.
See no. 1449.
379. *Creuzeranus* 897.
Contains: *De Plotino et Philone Judaeo* (fol. 63).
See *Die HSS. der Grossherzöglich–Badischen Hof- und Landesbibliothek in Karlsruhe*, Karlsruhe, IV, 1896.
380. *Gotingensis Michaelis* 323.
Contains: N. Gobet, "Réflexions sur ce que Philon dit de la circoncision." (*Briefe*, Bd. IV, fols. 155–156.)
See W. Meyer, *Verzeichnis der Handschriften in preussischen Staate* I, iii, *Göttingen*, Berlin, 1894, III, 230.
381. *Londiniensis Mus. Brit. Sloanianus* 3088, XVII. century.
Contains: (fol. 105) "Observatio H. Broughton ad citationem Philonis Judaei."
See E. J. L. Scott, *Index to the Sloane MSS. in the British Museum*, London, 1904.

382. *Londiniensis Mus. Brit. addit.* 6416.

Contains: (fol. 83) "Letter of John Mitchell to Dr. Magnay (*sic*) respecting a MS. of Philo Judaeus, Sept. 4, 1739."

See *B.M. Index,* no. 5, under "J. Mitchell."

383. *Londinienses Mus. Brit. addit.* 6446, 6447.

"Ericus Bengelius, Bp. Sincopensis, Annotationes in Philonem Judaeum."

See *B.M. Index,* no. 5, under "E. Bengelius."

384. *Londiniensis Mus. Brit. addit.* 6450.

"Treatise concerning the author of the books that go under Philo's name by Bp. Chandler."

See *B.M. Index,* no. 5, under "Bp. Chandler."

385. *Londiniensis Archiepisc. Lib. Lambeth Palace* 930.

Contains: Item 43, "Dr. Wm. Lloyd, bishop of Coventry and Litchfield's letter to Archbishop Tenison concerning the writings of Philo the Jew, the Λογος, etc. Aug. 7, 1697."

See *Catalogue of the Archiepiscopal MSS. in the Library at Lambeth Palace,* London, 1812.

386. *Londiniensis Archiepisc. Lib. Lambeth Palace* 953.

Contains: Item 54, "Bishop Lloyd to Dr. Allix concerning his notes about the Messiah and Dr. Chandler's Book about Philo. July 12, 1697." See *ibid.*

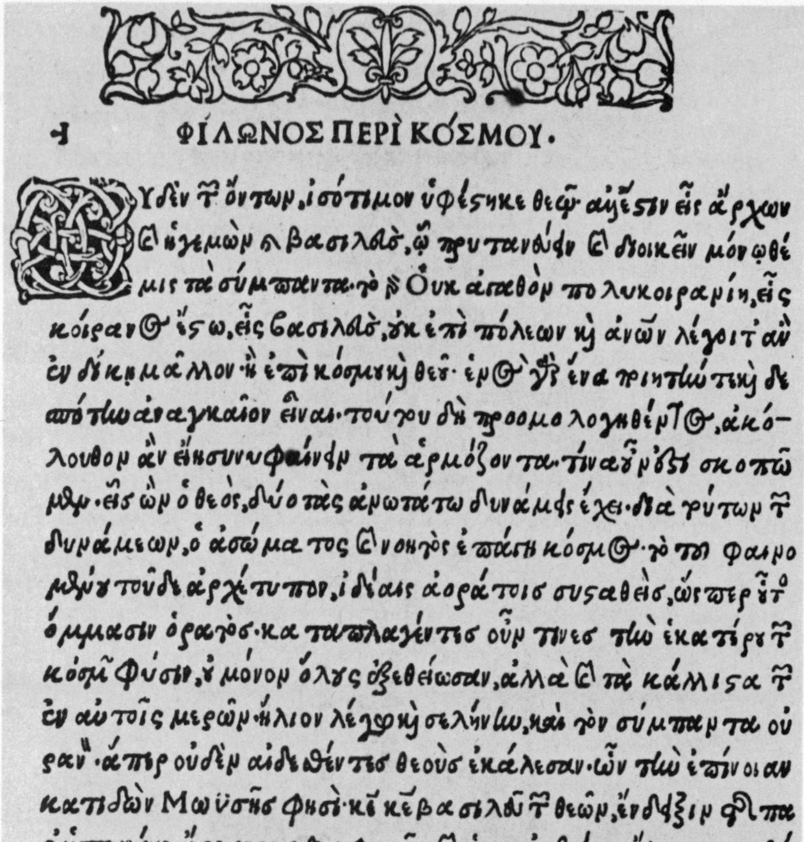

Οὐδὲν τῶν ὄντων, ἰσότιμον ὑφέστηκε θεῷ αὐξῆσιν εἰς ἄρχων ἡγεμὼν ἢ βασιλεὺς, ᾧ πρυτανεύειν τε καὶ διοικεῖν μόνῳ θέμις τὰ σύμπαντα...

[...Greek text continues...]

EE iiii

THE FIRST PRINTED TEXT OF PHILO (REDUCED)

See Bibliography, no. 387.

II. EDITIONS AND TRANSLATIONS OF PHILO[1]

A. GREEK TEXTS

387.* *Aristotelis Opera,* 1st edit., Venetiis, Aldus Manutius, II, February 1497, folios 225-236.
The first edition in print of any portion of the works of Philo under the title of Φίλωνος περὶ κόσμου. (Hain 1657.)
Contains: *Mund.*

388.* *Aristotelis de mundo libellus,* G. BUDAEO *interprete Philonis Judei itidem de mundo libellus ab eodem traductus. Quibus adjecti sunt iidem Graeci . . . restituti,* Parisiis, in Aedibus Ascensianis, [1526?], 8vo.
Contains: *Mund.*

389.* *De mundo Aristotelis lib. I., Philonis lib. I.,* GULIELMO BUDAEO *interprete. Cleomedis lib. II., Georgio Valla interprete.* ’Αριστοτέλους περὶ κόσμου . . . Φίλωνος ’Ιουδαίου περὶ κόσμου . . . *Ad haec Scholion doctiss. in Aristotelis libellus de mundo, Simone Grynaeo authore,* Basileae, Ioan. Valderus, March, 1533, 8vo, sigs. B₈r–Δ₇v, Greek and Latin.
Contains: *Mund.*

390. "Philonis Judaei liber de mundo, graece et latine, GUIL. BUDAEO interprete," in Μικροπρεσβυτικον, *Mikropresbutikon, veterum quorundam breuium theologorum, sive episcoporum, sive presbyterorum,* Basileae, apud H. Petri, 1550, folios 389-409.
Reprinted in *Budaei Opera* (T. I. p. 458-70); and in Guiliaume Budé, *Lucubrationes variae cum ad studiorum rectam institutionem ac philologiam . . . quibus adjunximus epistolarum ejusdem latinarum ac Graecarum libros VI non omissis iis quae ex graecis in latinam linguam convertit,* Basiliae, 1557. (From no. 528 and B.M.)

391.* Φίλωνος ’Ιουδαίου εἰς τὰ τοῦ Μωσέως, κοσμοποιητικά, ἱστορικά, νομοθετικά. Τοῦ αὐτοῦ Μονοβίβλα. *Philonis Iudaei in libros Mosis, de mundi opificio, historicos, de legibus. Eiusdem libri singulares,* [edidit ADR. TURNEBUS], 1st edit., Parisiis, Adrianus Turnebus, 1552, folio, pp. [12], 736, [38].
Contains: *Opif., LA* i, iii (ii), *Cher., Sac., Det., Agr., Plant., Ebr.,*

---

1. Including all works ascribed to Philo except the forgery of Giovanni Nanni, for which see below, nos. 1587-1596.

Sobr., Gig., Immut., Conf., Abr., Migr., Cong., Fug., Heres, Jos., Som. i, Mos., Virt. b, *Spec.* iv e, f, *Virt.* a, *Decal., Spec.* ii a, iii, i, *Prob., Cont., Virt.* d, *Praem., Exs., Aet., Flac., Legat.*

392. *Interpretatio linguarum: seu, de ratione conuertendi & explicandi autores tam sacros quàm prophanos, libri tres. Ad finem Obadias Propheta Hebraicus, uersus & explicatus. Philonis Iudaei de judice liber graecè & latinè,* by LAVRENTIVS HVMFREDVS, Basilae, Hieronymus Frobenius and Nic. Episcopius, 1559, 594–605.
Contains: *Spec.* iv, c.

393.* Ἀριστοτέλους καὶ Φίλωνος περὶ κόσμου, Parisiis, Conradus Neobar, 1560, 8vo, folios 31r (23)–59v.
Contains: *Mund.*

394.* *Optimates, sive de nobilitate, eius'que antiqua origine, natura, officiis, disciplina, & recta ac Christiana institutione libri tres.* LAVRENTIO HVMFREDO *autore. Adiunctus est propter utilitatem & affinitatem argumenti, Philo Iudaeus de nobilitate, graecè & latinè: Eodem interprete,* Basileae, Ioannes Oporinus, 1560, 357–381, 8vo.
Contains: *Virt.* d.

395. *Epistolae duae, una: Q. Ciceronis ad M. Tullium, de petitione consulatus. Altera . . . His accesserunt . . .* PETREII *notae ad quoddam* Προλεγομενον *Philonis, de officio judicis,* [with the text], etc., ff. 59, apud A. Wechelum: Parisiis, 1564. (From B.M.)
Contains: *Spec.* iv c.

396. *Philonis Iudaei . . . liber de nobilitate, ex graeco in latinum conuersus ab* HERMANNO NEHEMIO *. . . Accessit praetereà contextus graecus, eiusdemque logica analysis, & breuis explicatio: Item carmen elegiacum in laudem uerae nobilitatis, ab eodem conscriptum in eandem ferè sententiam,* Basileae, Leonhardus Ostenius, 1581, folios 39, 16½ cm.
Contains: *Virt.* d.

397. *Philonis Judaei opuscula tria: 1, Quare quorundam in sacris literis mutata sint nomina. 2, De formatione Euae ex Adami latere; & de vtriusque lapsu. 3, Somniorum Iosephi, Pharaonis, pincernaeque ac pistoris, allegorica expositio. Graece nunc primum edita, studio & opera* DAVIDIS HOESCHELII *. . . Notatiunculis alicubi illustrata. Bibliotheca Augustana,* Francofurdi, Ioannes Wechelus, 1587, pp. [viii], 277.
Contains: *Mut., LA,* ii, *Som.,* ii.

398.* Φίλωνος Ἰουδαίου ἐξηγητικὰ συγγράμματα . . . *Philonis Iudaei opera exegetica in libros Mosis, de mundi opificio, historicos, & legales, quae partim ab* ADRIANO TVRNEBO *. . . partim à* DA-

VIDE HOESCHELIO . . . *edita & illustrata sunt. Accessêre extra superiorum ordinem eiusdem Philonis sex opuscula quorum alia sunt* ἐπιδεικτικὰ, *alia* διδασκλικὰ, *alia denique historica res quae Iudaeis auctoris aeuo contigêre describentia, nunc graecè & latinè in lucem emissa ex accuratissima* SIGISMVNDI GELENIJ *interpretatione cum rerum indice locupletissimo,* Coloniae Allobrogum (Geneva), Petrus de la Rouiere, 1613, pp. 10, 904, 24, folio, Greek and Latin in parallel columns.

Contains: *Opif., LA* i, iii (ii), *Cher., Sac., Det., Agr., Plant., Ebr., Sobr., Gig., Immut., Conf., Abr., Migr., Cong., Fug., Heres, Ios., Som.* i, *Mos., Virt.* b, *Spec.* iv e, f, *Virt.* a, *Decal., Spec.* ii a, iii, i, *Prob., Cont., Virt.* d, *Praem., Exs., Aet., Flac., Legat., Mut.* (Ped. Morello interprete), *LA* ii (iii), *Som.* ii, *Mund.* (Gulielmo Budaeo interprete).

399. *Philo Judaeus de septenario ejusdem fragmenta II. e libro de providentia. Omnia e codicibus manuscriptis nunc primum edita a* DAV. HOESCHELIO, Augustae Vindelicorum (Augsburg), 1614, 4°. (From no. 528 and B.M.)
Contains: *Spec.* ii b and c, Frags. (*Prov.*).

400. *Eusebii, Polychronii, Pselli, in Canticum Canticorum expositiones graece.* JOANNES MEURSIUS *primus nunc e tenebris eruit, publicavit,* Lugduni Batavorum (Leyden), Ex officiona Elzeviriana, Typis Godefredi Basson, 1617, 4°.
Contains: Frags. (See Greek Manuscripts, I.)

401. *Philonis Judaei liber de virtutibus et legatione ad Gajum; graece,* Paris, Joh. Libert, 1626, 4°. (From no. 528.)
Contains: *Legat.*

402. Φίλωνος ’Ιουδαίου Συγγράμματα. *Philonis Iudaei, omnia quae extant opera. Ex accuratissima* SIGISMVNDI GELENII, *& aliorum interpretatione, Partim ab* ADRIANO TVRNEBO . . . *partim à* DAVIDE HOESCHELIO . . . *edita & illustrata. Huic nouissimae editioni accessere Variae lectiones & elegantissimus eiusdem Philonis, de septenario libellus, & de providentia dei fragmenta, cum rerum indice locupletissimo,* Lutetiae Parisiorum, 1640, pp. iv, 1200, 69, folio, Greek and Latin in parallel columns.
A reprint of the 1613 edition, adding *Sept.* (Fed. Morello interprete) and Frags. (Fed. Morello interprete).
*Another printing, Francofurti, Jeremias Schrey and Heinrici Joh. Meyer, 1691, with the same pagination.

403. *Philonis Iudaei liber de nobilitate e graeco conuersus carmine per* IOHANNEM CORVERVM *Ruremundanum. Additus est idem liber & graecè ex collatione optimi exemplaris eiusdem Corueri opera*

emendatus, & latinè LAVRENTIO HVMFREDO interprete, Colonia (Cologne), apud Maternum Cholinum, 1664 (1564?), pp. [40], 4°.
Contains: Virt. d.

404.* Φίλωνος τοῦ Ἰουδαίου τὰ εὑρισκόμενα ἅπαντα. Philonis Judaei opera quae reperiri potuerunt omnia. Textum cum MSS. contulit, quamplurima etiam è Codd. Vaticano, Mediceo, & Bodleiano, scriptoribus item vetustis, necnon catenis graecis ineditis, adjecit, interpretationemque emendavit, universa notis & observationibus illustravit THOMAS MANGEY, London, William Bowyer, 1742, 2 vols., pp. xxix, 736, [12]; 692, [12], Greek and Latin in parallel columns.
Contains: I, Opif., LA, Cher., Sac., Det., Post., Gig., Immut., Agr., Plant., Ebr., Sobr., Conf., Migr., Heres, Cong., Fug., Mut. (Ped. Morello interprete), Som.; II, Abr., Jos., Mos., Decal., Spec. i, ii a–c, iii, iv, Virt. a–c, Praem., Exs., Virt. d, Prob., Cont., Aet., Flac., Legat., Mund. (Gulielmo Budaeo interprete), Frags.

405.* Σειρὰ ἑνὸς καὶ πεντήκοντα ὑπομνηματίστων εἰς τὴν ὀκτάτευχον καὶ τὰ τῶν βασιλείων ἤδη πρῶτον τύποις ἐκδοθεῖσα ἀξιώσει μὲν τοῦ εὐσεβεστάτου καὶ γαληνοτάτου ἡγεμόνος πάσης οὐγκροβλαχίας κυρίου κυρίου Γρηγορίου Ἀλεξάνδρου Γκίκα ἐπιμέλεια δὲ ΝΙΚΗΦΟΡΟΥ ΙΕΡΟΜΟΝΑΧΟΥ ΤΟΥ ΘΕΟΤΟΚΟΥ (NICEPHORUS HIEROMONACHUS THEOTOKOS), Leipzig, 1772–73, 2 vols.; see, e.g., I, 185, 187 f., 191, 218, 219 f., 221 f., 223 f., 225, 228 f., 251–254, 272, 307, 325–327, 331 f., 339, 346 f., 350, 397, 399, 403, 428 f., 458–462, 477, 481.
Contains: Frags.

406. Liber de virtutibus sive de legatione ad Caium imperatorum, ed. S. FR. N. MORUS, Leipzig, Klaubarth, 1781, pp. 86, 8vo. (From no. 532.)
Contains: Legat.

407.* Philonis Iudaei opera omnia, graece et latine, ad editionem Thomae Mangey collatis aliquot Mss. edenda curavit AVGVSTVS FRIEDERICVS PFEIFFER, Erlangae, Wolfgang Walther, 1785–92, 5 vols., 8vo, Greek and Latin on opposite pages.
Contains: I, Opif., LA; II, Cher., Sac., Det., Post., Gig., Immut.; III, Agr., Plant., Ebr., Sobr., Conf., Migr.; IV, Heres, Cong., Fug., Mut.; V, Som., Abr.
A second edition, Erlangen, Libraria Heyderiana, 1820.

408.* Chrestomathia Philoniana sive loci illustres ex Philone Alexandrino decerpti et cum animadversionibus editi a IOANNE CHRISTIANO GUIL. DAHL, Hamburg, Karl Ernst Bohn, 1800, pp. xvi, 310, Greek text, Latin notes.
Contains: excerpts from various works.

409.* Chrestomathiae Philonianae pars altera sive Philonis Alexandrini li-

belli illustres adversus Flaccum et de legatione ad Caium cum animad-versionibus editi a IOANNE CHRISTIANO GUILIEL. DAHL, Hamburg, Karl Ernst Bohn, 1802, pp. x, 424, Greek text, Latin notes. Contains: *Flac., Legat.*

410. *De Philonis Iudaei et Eusebii Pamphili scriptis ineditis aliorumque libris ex armeniaca lingua convertendis dissertatio cum ipsorum operum Philonis ac praesertim Eusebii speciminibus scribente* ANGELO MAIO, Mediolani, Regiis Typis, 1816, 1–28.
Contains: *Virt.*

411.* Φίλωνος τοῦ 'Ιουδαίου περὶ ἀρετῆς καὶ τῶν ταύτης μορίων. *Philonis Iudaei de virtute eiusque partibus. Invenit et interpretatus est* AN-GELVS MAIVS . . . *Praeponitur dissertatio cum descriptione librorum aliquot incognitorum Philonis cumque partibus nonnullis chronici inediti Eusebii Pamphili et aliorum operum notitia e codicibus armeniacis petita,* Mediolanus, 1816, Regiis Typis, 2 vols., pp. lxxx, 28; viii, 68.
Contains: *Virt.*
(Part I of Mai's *Philonis Iudaei, Porphyrii Philosophi, Eusebii Pamphili Opera Inedita.*)
† Reviewed by Raoul-Rochette, *Journal des Savans,* 1817, 227–238.

412.* *Philonis Iudaei de cophini festo et de colendis parentibus, cum brevi scripto de Iona. Editore ac interprete* ANGELVS MAIVS, Mediolanus, Regiis Typis, 1818, pp. xx, 36.
Contains: *Spec.* ii, c, d, and the "Appendix" to *Jona* (= Aucher, p. 612). (Part I of Mai's *Philo et Vergilii interpres.*)

413.* *Philonis Iudaei opera omnia. Textus editus ad fidem optimarum editionum,* edited by [C. E. RICHTER], Leipzig, E. B. Schwickert, 1828–1830, 8 vols., Greek text, Latin for Armenian. (*Bibliotheca Sacra patrum Ecclesiae Graecorum, Pars II.*)
Contains: I, *Opif., LA, Cher., Sac., Det.;* II, *Post., Gig., Immut., Agr., Plant., Ebr., Sobr., Conf., Migr.;* III, *Heres, Cong., Fug., Mut., Som.;* IV, *Abr., Jos., Mos., Decal., Spec.* i a–g^1; V, *Spec.* i g^2, ii, iii, iv, *Virt.* a–c, *Praem., Exs., Virt.* d, *Prob., Cont.;* VI, *Aet., Flac., Legat., Mund.,* Frags., *QG,* i, ii; VII, *QG,* iii, iv, *QE, Samp., Jona., Deo;* VIII, *Provid., Animal.*

414. "De cophini festo," "De honorandis parentibus," "Ex opere in Exodum selectae quaestiones," in A[NGELO] M[AI], *Classicorum auctorum e vaticanis codicibus editorum,* Rome, Typis Vaticanis, IV, 1831, 402–447. (Greek and Latin.)
Contains: *Spec.* ii, c (214–224), d, *QE* ii, 62–68.

415. "Λεοντίου πρεσβυτέρου καὶ 'Ιωάννου τῶν ἱερῶν βιβλίον δεύτερον," in

A[NGELO] M[AI], *Scriptorum veterum nova collectio e vaticanis codicibus edita*, Rome, Typis Vaticanis, VII, 1833, 83–109.
Contains: Frags.

416. "Προκοπίου χριστιανοῦ σοφιστοῦ εἰς τὴν Γένεσιν τῶν ἐκλογῶν ἐπιτομή," in A[NGELO] M[AI], *Classicorum auctorum e vaticanis codicibus editorum*, Rome, Typis Vaticanis, VI, 1834, 1–347.
Contains: Frags.

417. "Συναγωγὴ ἐξηγήσεων εἰς τὸ κατὰ Λουκὰν ἅγιον εὐαγγέλιον," in A[NGELO] M[AI], *Scriptorum veterum nova collectio e vaticanis codicibus edita*, Rome, Typis Vaticanis, IX, 1837, 626–674.
Contains: Frags.

418. *Catenae in Evangelica . . . Lucae et . . . Joannis . . . Edidit* J[OHN] A[NTHONY] C[RAMER], 1841, 8vo. (From B.M.)
Contains: Frags.

419.* *Des Juden Philo Buch von der Weltschöpfung, herausgegeben und erklärt von* J. G. MÜLLER, Berlin, G. Reimer, 1841, pp. vi, 465.
Contains: *Opif.* (pp. 47–110).

420.* *Philonis Iudaei opera omnia ad librorum optimorum fidem edita, Editio Stereotypa*, Leipzig, Carolus Tauchnitius, 1851–53, 8 vols., 12mo, Greek text, Latin for Armenian.
A reprint of no. 413 with the same contents. Reprinted, Leipzig, Otto Holtze, 1880–1893.

421. *Anecdoton graecum Philonis Judaei de cherubinis: Exod. 25, 18*, by CHRISTIAN GOTTLOB LEBERECHT GROSSMAN (here Christianus Aenotheus Orthobius), Lipsiae, Edelmann, [1856], pp. 21.
Contains: *QE*, ii, 62–68, with notes.

422.* *Philonea, inedita altera, altera nunc demum recte ex vetere scriptura eruta. Edidit* CONSTANTINUS TISCHENDORF, Lipsiae, Giesecke et Devrient, 1868, pp. xx, 155, 2 plates, Greek text only except in the *QE* where the Latin text is also found.
Contains: *Spec.* ii. a–d, *Post., QE* ii (7 questions).

423.† "Die unter Philon's Werken stehende Schrift ueber die Unzerstörbarkeit des Weltalls nach ihrer ursprünglichen Anordnung wiederhergestellt und ins Deutsche übertragen," by JACOB BERNAYS, *Philologische und historische Abhandlungen der Königlichen Akademie der Wissenschaften zu Berlin, aus dem Jahre 1876*, Berlin, 1877, 209–278, Greek and German.
Contains: *Aet.*
† Reviewed by Th.-H. Martin, *Revue critique d'histoire et de littérature*, XI, ii (N.S. IV) (1877), 275–278.

424.* *Fragments of Philo Judaeus: Newly edited by* J. RENDEL HARRIS,

Cambridge (England), University Press, 1886, pp. xxiii, 110, with two facsimiles, Greek and Latin.

Contains: Frags.

Reviewed in *The Athenaeum*, 1887, ii, 47.

425.* *Philonis Alexandrini libellus de opificio mundi, edidit* LEOPOLDUS COHN, Vratislaviae (Breslau), Wilhelm Koebner, 1889, pp. [vi], lviii, [2], 108. (*Breslauer philologische Abhandlungen*, IV, 4.)

Contains: *Opif.*

Reviewed by B., *Literarisches Centralblatt für Deutschland*, [XLI] (1890), 590–591; by C. Haeberlin, *Wochenschrift für klassische Philologie*, VII (1890), 453–455; †by [Paul] Wendland, *Berliner philologische Wochenschrift*, X (1890), 237–242; by Siegfried Reiter, *Zeitschrift für die österreichischen Gymnasien*, XLII (1891), 982–985; by E. Schürer, *Theologische Literaturzeitung*, XVI (1891), 139–141.

426.* *Philonis de aeternitate mundi, edidit et prolegomenis instruxit* FRANCISCUS CUMONT, Berlin, George Reimer, 1891, pp. xxix, 76.

Contains: *Aet.*

Reviewed by E. Schürer, *Theologische Literaturzeitung*, XVI (1891), 441–443; by P. Wendland, *Berliner philologische Wochenschrift*, XI (1891), 1029–1035; by R. Ausfeld, *Neue philologische Rundschau*, 1892, 290–298; by Leopold Cohn, *Wochenschrift für klassische Philologie*, IX (1892), 262–266; and by Siegfried Reiter, *Zeitschrift für die österreichischen Gymnasien*, XLIII (1892), 17–20.

427. *Neu entdeckte Fragmente Philos: nebst einer Untersuchung über die ursprüngliche Gestalt der Schrift de sacrificiis Abelis et Caini*, by PAUL WENDLAND, Berlin, 1891, pp. x, 152.

Contains: Frags.

†Reviewed by F. C. Conybeare, *The Academy*, XL (1891), 482–483; †by [Franz] Cumont, *Berliner philologische Wochenschrift*, XI (1891), 1484–1490; by Johannes Dräseke, *Wochenschrift für klassische Philologie*, VIII (1891), 1206–9; by L., *Revue critique d'histoire et de littérature*, XXV, ii (N.S. XXXII) (1891), 503–4; by H. v. Arnim, *Deutsche Litteraturzeitung*, XIII (1892), 400–402; by C. Bigg, *The Classical Review*, VI (1892), 24; by Whlrb., *Literarisches Centralblatt für Deutschland*, [XLIII] (1892), 22–23; and by C. O. Zuretti, *Rivista di filologia e d'istruzione classica*, XXI (1893), 162–164.

428.* "Deux traités de Philon: Φίλωνος περὶ τοῦ τίς ὁ τῶν θείων ἐστὶν κληρονόμος ἢ περὶ τῆς εἰς τὰ ἴσα καὶ ἐναντία τομῆς.

Φίλωνος περὶ γενέσεως Ἄβελ καὶ ὧν αὐτός τε καὶ ὁ ἀδελφὸς ἱερουργοῦσι.

Traités réédités d'après un papyrus du VIe siècle environ par" V.

SCHEIL, *Mémoires publiés par les membres de la Mission Archéologique Française au Caire,* Paris, IX (1893), pp. vii, 151–215.
Contains: *Heres* and *Sac.*

429.* *Philo about the Contemplative Life, or the Fourth Book of the Treatise Concerning Virtues, critically edited with a defence of its genuineness* by FRED[ERICK] C. CONYBEARE, Oxford, Clarendon Press, 1895, pp. xvi, 403, facsimile frontispiece.
Contains: *Cont.*
Reviewed in *The Athenaeum,* [LXVIII, ii] (1895), 712–713; †by Alfred W. Benn, *The Academy,* XLVIII (1895), 228–229 (see Conybeare's answer, †*ibid.,* 274); by M. F., *Literarisches Centralblatt für Deutschland,* [XLVI] (1895), 1490–1491; by Samuel Macauley Jackson, *The Presbyterian and Reformed Review,* VI (1895), 769–773; †by E[mil] Schürer, *Theologische Literaturzeitung,* XX (1895), 385–391, 603–604; †by P[aul] Wendland, *Berliner philologische Wochenschrift,* XV (1895), 705–712; †by James Drummond, *The Jewish Quarterly Review,* VIII (1895–1896), 155–172; by A. E. Brooke, *The Classical Review,* X (1896), 262–263; by F. Cumont, *Revue de l'instruction publique (supérieure et moyenne) en Belgique,* XXXIX (1896), 16–19; by John Gibb, *The Critical Review,* VI (1896), 37–41; by C. Siegfried, *Deutsche Litteraturzeitung,* XVII (1896), 129–132; by Joseph Viteau, *Revue de philologie, de littérature et d'histoire anciennes,* N.S. XX (1896), 67–68; by A. H., *Zeitschrift für wissenschaftliche Theologie,* XL (1897), 154–158; by A. C. Headlam, *The English Historical Review,* XII (1897), 325–330; and by P. L[ejay], *Revue critique d'histoire et de littérature,* XXXI, i (N.S. XLIII) (1897), 489–491.

430.† "Unbeachtete Philonfragmente," by KARL PRAECHTER, *Archiv für Geschichte der Philosophie,* IX (1896), 415–426.

431.* *Philonis Alexandrini opera quae supersunt,* ediderunt LEOPOLDVS COHN et PAVLVS WENDLAND, Berlin, Georg Reimer, 1896–1930, 7 vols. in 8. I, by Cohn; contains: *Opif., LA, Cher., Sac., Det.* II, by Wendland; contains: *Post., Gig., Immut., Agr., Plant., Ebr., Sobr., Conf., Migr.* III, by Wendland; contains: *Heres, Cong., Fug., Mut., Som.* IV, by Cohn; contains: *Abr., Jos., Mos., Decal.* V, by Cohn; contains: *Spec.* i, ii, iii, iv, *Virt., Praem., Exs.* VI, Cohn and SIGOFREDVS REITER; contains: *Prob., Cont., Aet., Flac., Legat.* VII, *Indices ad Philonis Alexandrini opera,* by IOANNES LEISEGANG, in two parts, Berlin, Walter de Gruyter & Co.
Vol. I reviewed by †J. R. Asmus, *Wochenschrift für klassische Philologie,* XIII (1896), 1166 f.; by F. C[umont], *Revue de l'instruction publique (supérieure et moyenne) en Belgique,* XXXIX (1896), 353–355;

by M. F., *Literarisches Centralblatt für Deutschland*, [XLVII] (1896), 1512 f.; by Henri Weil, *Revue critique d'histoire et de littérature*, XXX, i (N.S. XLII) (1896), 323–325; by Fred. C. Conybeare, *The Classical Review*, XI (1897), 66 f.; †by Freudenthal, *Monatsschrift für Geschichte und Wissenschaft des Judenthums*, XLI (1897), 178–180; by G. Heinrici, *Theologische Literaturzeitung*, XXII (1897), 211–215; by Siegfried Reiter, *Zeitschrift für die österreichischen Gymnasien*, XLVIII (1897), 42–47; by C. Siegfried, *Deutsche Litteraturzeitung*, XVIII (1897), 489–491; and by Otto Stählin, *Berliner philologische Wochenschrift*, XVII (1897), 583–588.

Vols. I and II reviewed by J. Sitzler, *Neue Philologische Rundschau*, 1898, 271–273; by C. O. Zuretti, *Rivista di filologia e d'istruzione classica*, XXVI (1898), 159 f.; and by von Dobschütz, *Historische Zeitschrift*, LXXXII (N.F. XLVI) (1899), 111–118.

Vol. II reviewed by J. R. Asmus, *Wochenschrift für klassische Philologie*, XV (1898), 89–98; by G. Heinrici, *Theologische Literaturzeitung*, XXIII (1898), 233–236; by C. Siegfried, *Deutsche Litteraturzeitung*, XIX (1898), 577–579; by Otto Stählin, *Berliner philologische Wochenschrift*, XVIII (1898), 355–357; and by Siegfried Reiter, *Zeitschrift für die österreichischen Gymnasien*, L (1899), 20–22.

Vol. III reviewed by J. R. Asmus, *Wochenschrift für klassische Philologie*, XVI (1899), 708–714; by J. Sitzler, *Neue Philologische Rundschau*, 1899, 343 f.; by O. Zuretti, *Rivista di filologia e d'istruzione classica*, XXVII (1899), 304 f.; by G. Heinrici *Theologische Literaturzeitung*, XXV (1900), 657–662; and by v[on] D[obschütz], *Historische Zeitschrift*, LXXXVIII (N.F. LII) (1902), 158.

Vol. IV reviewed by J. Sitzler, *Neue Philologische Rundschau*, 1902, 601–603; by Otto Stählin, *Berliner philologische Wochenschrift*, XXII (1902), 1191–1194; by Rudolf Asmus, *Wochenschrift für klassische Philologie*, XX (1903), 1054 f.; and by G. Heinrici, *Theologische Literaturzeitung*, XXVIII (1903), 77–82.

Vols. IV, V, VI, reviewed by M.F., *Literarisches Zentralblatt für Deutschland*, XLVI (1915), 692 f.

Vol. V reviewed by v[on] D[obschütz], *Historische Zeitschrift*, CXIX (1907), 435 f.; by Otto Stählin, *Berliner philologische Wochenschrift*, XXVII (1907), 1345–1350; and by J. Sitzler, *Neue Philologische Rundschau*, 1908, 457–460.

Vols. V and VI reviewed by Martin Dibelius, *Wochenschrift für klassische Philologie*, XXXIII (1916), 607–611.

Vol. VI reviewed by Otto Stählin, *Berliner philologische Wochen-*

schrift, XXXVIII (1918), 1201–1205; and by v. Dobschütz, *Historische Zeitschrift,* CXX (3. F. XXIV) (1919), 540 f.

Vol. VII reviewed by Otto Stählin, *Philologische Wochenschrift* XLVII (1927), 8–13 (Nachtrag, 281 f.); by Wilhelm Crönert, *Gnomon,* IV (1928), 571–577; †by I. Heinemann, *Monatsschrift für Geschichte und Wissenschaft des Judentums,* LXXIII (1929), 439–441, LXXV (1931), 76 f.; by Robert Philippson, *Archiv für Geschichte der Philosophie und Soziologie,* XXXIX (N.F. XXXII) (1930), 319 f.; by Wilhelm Crönert, *Gnomon,* VII (1931), 170–172; by F. Perles, *Orientalistische Literaturzeitung,* XXXVI (1933), 102 f.

432. *Philonis Alexandrini opera quae supersunt, ediderunt* LEOPOLDVS COHN et PAVLVS WENDLAND, Berlin, Georg Reimer, 1896–1915, 6 vols.

Editio Minor containing the text as published in the foregoing, vols. I–VI, but omitting the Prolegomena and Apparatus criticus.

Vol. I reviewed by C. Siegfried, *Deutsche Litteraturzeitung,* XVIII (1897), 491; by Otto Stählin, *Berliner philologische Wochenschrift,* XVII (1897), 583–588.

Vols. I and II reviewed by J. Sitzler, *Neue Philologische Rundschau,* 1898, 271–273.

Vols. IV, V, and VI reviewed by M. F., *Literarisches Zentralblatt für Deutschland,* LXVI (1915), 692 f.

433.* *Philon: Commentaire allégorique des saintes lois après l'oeuvre des six jours: texte grec, traduction française, introduction et index, par* ÉMILE BRÉHIER, Paris, Alphonse Picard et fils, 1909, pp. 330, Greek and French on opposite pages. (Hippolyte Hemmer et Paul Lejay, *Textes et documents pour l'étude historique du christianisme,* 9.)

Contains: *LA,* i, ii, iii.

Reviewed by Paul Wendland, *Theologische Literaturzeitung,* XXXV (1910), 521.

434.* *Oxyrhynchus Papyri,* IX, *edited with translations and notes by* ARTHUR S. HUNT, London, Oxford University Press, 1912, § 1173, pp. 16–29;* *ibid.,* XI, London, 1915, edited by B. P. GRENFELL and A. S. HUNT, § 1356, pp. 12–19.

Contains: excerpts from *LA* i, *Det., Ebr., Spec.* i, g^2.

435.† "Übersehenes," by M. WELLMANN, *Hermes,* LII (1917); see 128–129.

Contains: Frags.

436.* *Philonis de opificio mundi, testo riveduto da* N. FESTA, Rome, A. Sampaolesi, 1922–1923, pp. 44, 122, Greek and Italian text, with commentary.

437.* *Philo, with an English translation by* F[RANCIS] H[ENRY] COL-
SON *and* G. H. WHITAKER, London and New York (Cambridge,
Mass.), 1929—, 7 vols. now published, the Greek and English text on
opposite pages. (*The Loeb Classical Library.*) Mr. Whitaker cooper-
ated in editing through volume V; since his death the series is being
completed by Mr. Colson.
Contains: I, *Opif., LA;* II, *Cher., Sac., Det., Post., Gig.;* III, *Immut.,*
Agr., Plant., Ebr., Sobr.; IV, *Conf., Migr., Heres, Cong.;* V, *Fug.,*
Mut., Som.; VI, *Abr., Jos., Mos.;* VII, *Decal., Spec.* i, ii, iii.
†Vols. I and II reviewed by Otto Stählin, *Philologische Wochenschrift,*
L (1930), 225–227.
†Vols. I, II, III reviewed by I. Heinemann, *Monatsschrift für Ge-*
schichte und Wissenschaft des Judentums, LXXVI (1932), 263–265.
Vol. III reviewed by Otto Stählin, *Philologische Wochenschrift,* LI
(1931), 1473–1476.
Vol. IV reviewed by Otto Stählin, *Philologische Wochenschrift,* LIII
(1933), 177–179.
438. "Neue Philontexte in der Überarbeitung des Ambrosius. Mit einem
Anhang: Neu gefundene griechische Philonfragmente," by HANS
LEWY, *Sitzungsberichte der preussischen Akademie der Wissen-*
schaften, Jahrgang 1932, Philosophisch-historische Klasse, 1932, 23–84.
Contains: Frags.
*Reprinted, Berlin, 1932, pp. 64.
*Reviewed by I. Heinemann in no. 537, LXXVI (1932), 265, and in
Gnomon, IX (1933), 670–671; and †by Robert Devreesse, *Revue bib-*
lique, XLII (1933), 136–137.
439.* "Philon. de ebr. § 223—de poster. Cain. § 34," *Papiri greci e latini,*
Florence, XI, 1935, § 1207, pp. 90 f. (*Pubblicazioni della Società Ita-*
liana.)
Contains: *Ebr.* § 223, *Cain.* § 34.
439a. Früchtel, L., "Griechische Fragmente zu Philons Quaestiones in Gene-
sin et in Exodum," *Zeitschrift für die alttestamentliche Wissenschaft,*
LV (N.F. XIV) (1937), 108–115.
Contains: Frags.

B. ARMENIAN TRANSLATIONS

440.* *Philonis Iudaei sermones tres hactenus inediti I. et II. De providentia,*
et III. De animalibus, ex armena versione antiquissima ab ipso origi-
nali textu graeco ad verbum stricte exequuta, nunc primum in Latium
fideliter translati, per P. JO: BAPTISTAM AUCHER, Venice, Typis

Coenobii PP. Armenorum in Insula S. Lazari, 1822, pp. xi, 178, added title page in Armenian, Latin and Armenian in parallel columns.

Contains: *Provid.* and *Animal.*

441.* *Philonis Iudaei Paralipomena armena. Libri videlicet quatuor in Genesin. Libri duo in Exodum. Sermo unus de Sampsone. Alter de Jona. Tertius de tribus angelis Abraamo apparentibus. Opera hactenus inedita ex armena versione antiquissima ab ipso originali textu graeco . . . nunc primum in Latium fideliter translata per* P. JO. BAPTIS-TAM AUCHER, Venice, Typis Coenobii PP. Armenorum in Insula S. Lazari, 1826, pp. v, 630, 4to, added title page in Armenian, Latin and Armenian in parallel columns.

Contains: *QG, QE, Samp., Jona., Deo.*

442. *Sermons of Philo the Hebrew, translated by our Ancestors, the Greek text of which has come down to us* (Armenian), Venice, Typography of the Mechitarists, 1892.

Contains: *Cont., Abr., LA, Decal., Spec.* (selections).

443.* *The Pseudo-Philonic de Jona*, Part I, *The Armenian Text with a Critical Introduction, by* HANS LEWY, London, Christophers, 1936, pp. 24, 49. (Kirsopp and Silva Lake, *Studies and Documents*, VII.)

C. LATIN TRANSLATIONS

444. *Philonis Judaei quaestiones centum et duae, et totidem responsiones morales super Genesin, latine, ex editione* AUG. JUSTINIANI, Paris, 1520, folio. (From no. 528.)

Contains: *QG.*

445.* *Philonis Iudaei Alexandrini, libri antiquitatum. Quaestionum et solutionum in Genesin. De essaeis. De nominibus Hebraicis. De mundo,* GVLIELMO BVDAEO *interprete,* [edited by J. Sichardus], Basileae, Adamus Petrus, August, 1527, folio, pp. viii, 142.

Contains: *Antiq., QG,* iv, 154–245, *De Essaeis, De Nominibus Hebraicis* ("Divo Hieronymo interprete"), *Mund.*

446. *Philonis Judaei quaestionum et solutionum in Genesim liber,* Basle, Henricus Petrus, 1538.

Contains: *QG,* iv, 154–245.

447.* *De mundo Aristotelis lib. I., Philonis lib. I.,* GVLIELMO BVDAEO *interprete. Ocelli Lucani veteris philosophi libellus de vniversi natura,* Parisiis, [Conradum Neobar], 1541, 8vo, 24r–44v.

Contains: *Mund.*

448. "Philonis Judaei antiquitatum biblicarum liber, quaestionum et solutio-

num in Genesin liber, liber de statu Essaeorum i. e. Monachorum, qui temporibus Agrippae regis monasteria sibi fecerunt; de nominibus hebraicis N. et V. Testamenti liber, latine," in Μικροπρεσβυτικον, Mikropresbutikon, *Veterum quorundam breuium Theologorum, sive Episcoporum, sive Presbyterorum,* Basileae, apud H. Petri, 1550, folio, 295–388. (From no. 528 and B.M. *Cat.*)

Contains: *Antiq., QG, De Essaeis, De Nominibus Hebraicis.*

449.* *Antiquitatum variarum autores,* Lugd. (Lyons), Seb. Gryphius, 1552, 16mo, 86–245; cf. 84 f.

Contains: *Antiq.*

Erroneously listed in the Catalogue of the British Museum as a "Berosus" item because one of the treatises included is the Berosus forgery of Nanni. See below Section XXXIII.

Another edition, *ibid.,* 1560.

450.* *Libri quatuor.* I. *De mundi fabricatione, quae est à Moyse descripta.* II. *De decem praeceptis, quae capita legum sunt.* III. *De magistratu seu principe deligendo.* IV. *De officio Iudicis, iam primum de graeco in latinum conuersi:* JOANNE CHRISTOPHORSONO *Anglo interprete,* Antwerpia, Joannes Verwithaghen, 1553, pp. [24], 149, [8].

Contains: *Mund., Decal., Virt.* iv. f, e.

451.* *Philonis Iudaei, scriptoris eloquentissimi, ac philosophi summi, lucubrationes omnes quotquot haberi potuerunt, nunc primum Latinae ex Graecis factae per* SIGISMUNDUM GELENIUM, *addito in fine rerum memorandarum indice foecundisimo,* Basilaea, Nicolaus Episcopius, iuniore, 1554, 4 preliminary leaves, pp. 651, 11 leaves of Index.

Contains: *Opif., LA, Cher., Sac., Det., Agr., Plant., Ebr., Sobr., Gig., Immut., Conf., Abr., Migr., Cong., Fug., Heres, Jos., Som.* I, *Mos., Virt.* b, *Spec.* iv. e, f, *Virt.* a, *Decal., Spec.* ii. a, iii. a, i, *Prob., Cont., Virt.* d, *Praem., Exs., Aet., Flac., Legat.*

Reprinted, *Lugduni (Lyons), Theobaldus Paganus, 1555; *Basileae, Nic. Episcopius Iun., 1558, 2 vols.; *Basileae, Nic. Episcopius, Iun., 1561; *Lugduni (Lyons), Nicol. Petronillus, 1561, 2 vols.

452.* *Philonis Iudaei de vita Mosis, lib. III,* ADR. TVRNEBO *interprete,* Parisiis, Adr. Turnebus, 1554, pp. [iv,] 156, 8vo.

Contains: *Mos.*

453. *Philonis Iudaei de divinis decem oraculis, quae summa sunt legum capita, Liber* IOHANNE VAEURAEO *interprete,* Lutetiae (Paris), apud Carolum Stephanum, 1554, pp. 72.

Contains: *Decal.*

454.* *Iosephi patriarchae vita a Philone Hebraeo graecè composita; et a* PETRO FRANCISCO ZINO *Canonico Veronensi in latinum con-*

uersa: In qua optimi viri civilis forma describitur, Venetiis, Christophorus Zanetus, 1574, 63 folios, 8vo.
Contains: *Jos.*

455.* *Exempla tria insignia naturae, legis, et gratiae, cùm in vita Iosephi patriarchae, & magni Mosis à Philone Hebraeo; tum à D. Gregorio Nyssae Pontifice, in forma perfecti hominis Christiani ad Olympium Monachum; eleganter expressa.* PETRO FRANCISCO ZINO, *Canonico Veronensi interprete,* Venetiis, Bologninus Zalterius, 1575, 175 folios, 8vo.
Contains: *Jos., Mos.* i, ii (ii and iii).

456. *Philonis Judaei liber singularis, quare quorundam in scripturis sacris mutata sint nomina. Ex interpretatione* F. MORELLI, Lutetiae, apud F. Morellum, 1593, pp. 77. (From B.M.)
Contains: *Mut.*
Another edition, 1598 (from no. 528).

457.* *Historia antiqua,* by BEROSVS, [Rome ?], ex Bibliopolio Commeliniano, 1599, 8vo, 41–118.
Contains: *Antiq.*

458. "Philonis Judaeus, de vita Mosis libri III," *Viri clariss.* ADRIEN TVRNEBI . . . *Opera nunc primum ex bibliotheca amplissimi viri:* STEPHANI ADRIANI F. TVRNEBI *in vnum collecta, emendata, aucta & tributa,* Argentorati (Strassburg), L. Zetzner, 1600, II, 105–138. (From the Library of Congress Catalogue and no. 528.)
Contains: *Mos.*

459.* *Philonis Iudaei, de septenario, liber singularis. In hoc, praeter mystici huius numeri arcana pleraque, feriarum etiam maximè solennium ceremoniae in lege olim obseruatae accuratè exponuntur.* FEDERICVS MORELLVS . . . *nunc primum latine vertit notísque illustrauit,* Lutetiae (Paris), Federicus Morellus, 1614, pp. 52, [4].
Contains: *Spec.* ii b and c, Frags.

460.* *Opera Philonis Iudaei exegetica in libros Mosis, de mundi opificio, historicos, & legales, quae partim ab* ADRIANO TVRNEBO . . . *partim à* DAVIDE HOESCHELIO *ex Augustana, edita & illustrata sunt. Accessere extra superiorum ordinem eiusdem Philonis sex opuscula, quorum alia sunt* ἐπιδεικτικά, *alia* διδασκαλικά, *alia denique historica, res quae Iudaeis auctoris aeuo contigere describentia, nunc nouiter additis marginalibus in lucem emissa ex accuratissima* SIGISMVNDI GELENII *interpretatione, cum rerum indice locupletissimo,* Antwerp, Iohannes Keerbergius, 1614, pp. [xiv], 812, [45]. A reprint of the Latin translation in no. 398.
Contains: *Opif., LA,* i, iii (ii), *Cher., Sac., Det., Agr., Plant., Ebr.,*

*Sobr., Gig., Immut., Conf., Abr., Migr., Cong., Fug., Heres, Jos., Som.
i, Mos., Virt.* b, *Spec.* iv. e, f, *Virt.* a, *Decal., Spec.* ii a, iii, i, *Prob.,
Cont., Virt.* d, *Praem., Exs., Aet., Flac., Legat., Mut.* (Ped. Morello
interprete), *LA* ii (iii), *Som.* ii, *Mund.* (Guilielmo Budaeo interprete).

461.* Corderius, Balthasar, *Catena sexaginta quinque graecorum patrum in
S. Lucam,* Antwerp, 1628; see the *Index patrum* at the beginning, s.v.,
sig. **₅ r and v and pages 426b, 451a–453b, 480b, 535b–539b.
Contains: Frags. (Cf. Greek Manuscripts, J.)

See also nos. 388, 389, 390, 392, 394, 396, 398, 402, 403, 404, 407, 413, 414, 420,
422, 424, 440, 441.

D. DUTCH TRANSLATIONS

462. *Alle de Werken van Flavius Josephus, Behelzende twintigh Boecken Van
de Joodsche Oudheden, 't verhaal van zyn eigen Leeven . . . Waarby
komt Het Gezantschap van Philo aan den Keizer Kaligula. Alles uyt
de Overzettinge van den Heere D'Andilly in 't Nederduytsch overge-
bragt door* W. SÉWEL. *Nógh zyn daarby gevoegt de Vyf Boeken van
Egesippus Van de Joodsche oorlogen, en de Verwoestinge van Jerusalem,* Amsterdam, Pieter Mortier, 1704, II, 759–782.
Contains: *Legat.*
Republished, Amsterdam, 1722, II, 759–782; and 1732, II, 775–790.

463. *Historie der Jooden, of alle de Werken van Flavius Josephus . . . naar
't Fransch van den Heere D'Andilly vertaald door Willem Sewel;
Sedert naar 't Griecksch overzien, verbeterd, enz. door* SIGEBERT
HAVERKAMP, Amsterdam, Marten Schagen, 1737, 1165–1360.
Contains: *Legat., Flac.*

464. *Alle de Werken van Flavius Josephus, naar het Griecksch in 't Engelsch
gebragt en Verkort . . . uit het Engelsch in het Nederduitsch Vertaald,*
Amsterdam, J. van Gulik, 1780, II, 618–646.
Contains: *Legat.*

465. *Alle de Werken van Flavius Josephus, met aanmerkingen uitgegeeven,
door* J. F. MARTINET, Amsterdam, Allart and Holtrop, VIII, 1787,
293–467.
Contains: *Legat., Flac.*

E. ENGLISH TRANSLATIONS

466.* *The Nobles, or of Nobilitye. The original nature, dutyes, right, and
Christian Institucion thereof three bookes. Fyrste eloquentlye written
in Latine by* LAWRENCE HUMPHREY . . . *late englished.*

Whereto, for the readers commoditatye, and matters affinitye, is coupled the small treatyse of Philo, a Jewe. By the same Author out of the Greeke Latined, nowe also Englished, London, Thomas Marshe, 1563, 8vo, Aa₁r–Aa₇iv.
Contains: *Virt.* d.

467.* *The Works of Josephus. With great diligence Revised and Amended, according to the Excellent French Translation of Monsieur AR-NAULD D'ANDILLY. Also the Embassy of Philo Judaeus, to the Emperor Caius Caligula, Never Translated before,* London, 1683, pp. [xii], 855, [33].
Contains: *Legat.* (pp. 828–854).
Frequently republished.

468. *The Works of Josephus Epitomized, from the Greek original; the two Books against Appion; the Martyrdom of the Maccabees; and the Embassy of Philo to the Emperor Caius Caligulo,* [ANONYMOUS], London, 1701; 2nd edit., revised, London, 1702. (From Watt, *Bibliotheca Britannica,* Edinburgh and London, 1824.)

469.* *The Works of Flavius Josephus: Translated into English by* SIR ROGER L'ESTRANGE . . . *All Carefully Revis'd, and Compar'd with the Original Greek. To which are added, two Discourses, and several Remarks and Observations upon Josephus, together with Maps, Sculptures, and Accurate Indexes,* London, Richard Sare, 1702, 1075–1106.
Contains: *Legat.*
This work was frequently reprinted: London, 1709, 1716, *1725, 1733, 1739, *1755; Edinburgh, 1751, 1762; Dundee, 1766; Aberdeen, 1768.

470. *A Compleat Collection of the Genuine Works of Flavius Josephus, Faithfully Translated from the original Greek,* by H. JACKSON, London, D. Henry, 1732, 750–774.
Contains: *Legat.*

471. *The Works of Flavius Josephus,* translated by HUDSON, edited by John Court, London, R. Penny and J. Janeway, 1733, 791–836.
Contains: *Legat.*
Frequently reprinted, for example, *London, 1754.

472.* *The Whole Works of Flavius Josephus . . . translated from the Original Greek by* CHARLES CLARKE, London, printed for John Walker, 1785, 665–690.
Contains: *Legat.*

473. *The Works of Flavius Josephus,* translated by [EBENEZER THOMPSON and WM. CHAS. PRICE], York, L. Pennington, later G. Walker, IV, 1792, 262–339.
Contains: *Legat.*

THE FIRST PRINTED ENGLISH TEXT OF PHILO

See Bibliography, no. 466.

474.* *The Whole Genuine and Complete Works of Flavius Josephus, the Learned and Authentic Jewish Historian, and Celebrated Warrior . . . also a continuation of the History of the Jews from Josephus down to the present . . .* by GEORGE HENRY MAYNARD, London, printed for C. Cooke, [ca. 1793], 500–517 (519).
Contains: *Legat.*

475.* *The Works of Philo Judaeus, the contemporary of Josephus, translated from the Greek,* by C. D. YONGE, London, Henry G. Bohn, 1854–1855, 4 vols. (*Bohn's Ecclesiastical Library.*)
Contains: I, *Opif., LA, Cher., Sac., Det., Post., Gig., Immut., Agr., Plant., Ebr., Sobr.;* II, *Conf., Migr., Heres, Cong., Fug., Mut., Som., Abr., Jos.;* III, *Mos., Decal., Spec.* i, ii, iii, iv, *Virt.* a–c, *Praem., Exs., Virt.* d, *Prob.;* IV, *Cont., Aet., Flac., Legat., Mun.,* Frags., *QG,* i, ii, iii. Vols. I–III reprinted from stereotype plates, London, 1900, (and New York) 1894, 1899.
Reviewed in no. 582.

476.† "Philo Concerning the Contemplative Life," translated by F[RED.] C. CONYBEARE, *The Jewish Quarterly Review,* VII (1894–1895), 755–769.
Contains: *Cont.*
Reviewed by A. C. Headlam, *The English Historical Review,* XII (1897), 325–330.

477.* *The Biblical Antiquities of Philo, now first translated from the old Latin version by* M. R. JAMES, London and New York, 1917, pp. vi, 280. (Society for Promoting Christian Knowledge, *Translations of Early Documents,* series I.)
Contains: *Antiq.*
Reviewed by R. G. Bury, *The Classical Review,* XXXII (1918), 132–133; by D. D. D., *Revue Bénédictine,* XXXIII (1921), 64–65; and by Riessler, *Theologische Quartalschrift,* CII (1921), 219–221.

478.* *Philo Judaeus, On the Contemplative Life. Translation, Notes, and an Essay on Philo's Religious Ideas,* by FRANK WILLIAM TILDEN, Bloomington, Indiana, 1922, pp. 37. (*Indiana University Studies,* 52.)
Contains: *Cont.*

479.* *Two Men of Alexandria: Philo, born B.C. 20. Origen, born A.D. 185; some of their shorter sayings and incidental side issues, collected and translated by* HERBERT GAUSSEN, *with a preface by* J. F. Bethune-Baker, London, Heath Cranton Limited, 1930, 5–43.
Contains: Extracts from various works.

See also nos. 434, 437.

F. FRENCH TRANSLATIONS

480. *Aristote, du Monde. Philon, du Monde. Songe de Scipion. Le tout* [or rather the first only] *mis nouvellement de grec en francois.* [The two last from the Latin: the former from the translation of Philo's "περι ἀφθαρσίας κόσμου" by G. Budé, with his interpolations . . .], by PIERRE DE TOURS, Lyon, 1542, pp. 95. (From B.M.)
Contains: *Mund.*

481.* *Les oeuvres de Philon Iuif, autheur tres-eloquent, et philosophe tres-graue. Contenans l'interpretation de plusieurs diuins & sacrez mys-teres, & l'instruction d'un chacun en toutes bonnes & sainctes moeurs. Mises de grec en françois, par* PIERRE BELLIER, Paris, Nicolas Chesneau, 1575, 30 preliminary leaves, pp. 468, 8vo, pp. 265–300 mis-bound.
Contains: *Opif., LA* i, *Plant., Mos., Virt.* b, *Spec.* iv e, f, *Virt.* a, *Decal., Spec.* ii a, iii, i, *Prob., Cont., Virt.* d, *Praem., Exs., Aet., Flac., Legat.*
*Reprinted, Paris, Michel Sonnius, 1598, pp. 528, 8vo. No. 528 lists also an edition, Paris, 1588, 8vo.

482.* *Les Oeuvres de Philon Iuif, Autheur tres-eloquent, & Philosophe tres-graue. Contenant l'interpretation de plusieurs diuins, & sacrez mys-teres, & l'instruction d'un chacun en toutes bonnes & sainctes moeurs. Translatées de grec en françois, par* PIERRE BELLIER . . . *Reueuës, corrigées & augmentées de trois liures, traduits sur l'original Grec, Par* FED. MOREL, Paris, David Gilles, 1612, pp. [xiv], 1236, [100], 8vo.
Contains: *Opif., LA, Mos., Virt.* b, *Spec.* iv. e, f, *Virt.* a, *Decal., Spec.* ii a, iii, i, *Prob., Cont., Virt.* d, *Praem., Exs., Aet., Flac., Legat., Agr., Plant.*
No. 528 lists also an edition, Paris, Chr. Chappellain, 1612.

483. *Histoire des Juifs, ecrite par Flavius Joseph, sous le titre de* Antiquitez judaiques, *traduite sur l'original grec revue sur divers manuscrits, par* Monsieur ARNAULD D'ANDILLY, Paris, Pierre le Petit, II, 1668, 477–520.
Contains: *Legat.*
*Republished Bruxelles, Eugene Henry Fricx, 1684, 5 vols.; see V, 437–508. Frequently reprinted.

484. *Le livre de Philon, de la Vie contemplative, traduit sur l'original grec, avec des observations où l'on fait voir que les Thérapeutes dont il parle étoient chrétiens,* by BERNARD DE MONTFAUCON, Paris, L. Guérin, 1709, pp. 303. (From B.N. and B.M.)
Contains: *Cont.*
No. 528 lists the translator of *Cont.* in this edition as Thom. d'Acquin.

485. "Des Esséniens, fragments traduits de Philon," *Oeuvres de* RACINE *avec les notes de tous les commentateurs. Cinquième édition publiée par L. Aimé Martin, avec des additions nouvelles,* Paris, V, 1844. (From B.M.)
Contains: Fragments from Philo's writings about the Essenes.

486.* *Philon d'Alexandrie. Écrits historiques. Influence, luttes et persécutions des Juifs dans le monde romain,* par FERDINAND DELAUNAY, Paris, Didier et Cie, 1867, *2nd edit., Paris, Didier et Cie, 1870, pp. xvi, 389.
Contains: *Flac.,* (pp. 201–269); *Legat.,* (pp. 271–389).
Reviewed by Ad. Franck in "Rapport verbal," *Séances et Travaux de L'Académie des Sciences Morales et Politiques, Institut Impérial de France,* XII (1867), 1–8, 139–144.

See also no. 433.

G. GERMAN TRANSLATIONS

487. *Philo vom Leben Moses, das ist: von der Gottesgelahrheit und dem prophetischen Geiste,* [ANONYMOUS], Dresden, 1778, pp. 262.
Contains: *Mos.*

488. *Die Gesandtschaft an den Cajus: Aus dem Griechischen des Philo übersetzt,* by JOHANN FRIEDRICH ECKHARD, Leipzig, Dyk, 1783, pp. [xvi], 151.
Contains: *Legat.*

489.* *Bibliothek der griechischen und römischen Shriftsteller über Judenthum und Juden, in neuen Uebertragungen und Sammlungen* by [ISAAK] M[ARCUS] I[OST], Leipzig, Oskar Leiner, 1865–72, 4 vols. (Ludwig Philippson, A. M. Goldschmidt, L. Herzfeld, *Schriften herausgegeben vom Institute zur Förderung der israelitischen Literatur*).
Contains: I, *Mos.;* (II, Josephus); III, *Opif., LA, Cher.;* IV, *Sacr., Det., Post., Gig., Immut.*

490.* *Ueber die Philanthropie des mos[aischen] Gesetzes. Von Philo, übersetzt und erläutert,* by M[ORITZ] FRIEDLÄNDER, Wien, M. Waizner, 1880, pp. iv, xv, [17]–71.
Contains: *Virt.,* b and c.

491. *Die Essener nach Josephus und Philo (aus dem Griechischen übersetzt) mit Einleitung zur Geschichte der Übergangsperiode,* by OSKAR WALDECK, Wien, Herm. Liebermann, 1885, pp. 32, 26. (Oskar Waldeck, *Volksausgabe des jüdisch-hellenistischen Schriftthums der drei vorchistlichen Jahrhunderte,* III, IV).
Contains: The Fragments on the Essenes from Eusebius.

492. *Die Werke Philos von Alexandria in deutscher Übersetzung*, edited by LEOPOLD COHN, continued by I. HEINEMANN, Breslau, M. and H. Marcus, 1909–29, vols. I–V, translations by various scholars. (Leopold Cohn, I–III, I. Heinemann, IV, V, *Schriften der jüdisch-hellenistischen Literatur*, I–V.)

Contains: I, *Opif.* and *Abr.* (J. Cohn), *Jos.* (L. Cohn), *Mos.* (B. Badt), *Decal.* (L. Treitel); II, *Spec.* (I. Heinemann), *Virt.* and *Praem.* (L. Cohn); III, *LA* (I. Heinemann), *Cher.* (L. Cohn), *Sacr.* and *Det.* (H. Leisegang); IV, *Post., Gig.,* and *Immut.* (H. Leisegang), *Agr.* and *Plant.* (I. Heinemann); V, *Ebr.* and *Sobr.* (Maximilian Adler), *Conf.* (Edmund Stein), *Migr.* (Posner), *Heres* (Joseph Cohn).

Vol. I reviewed by Paul Heinisch, *Theologische Revue,* VIII (1909), 302 f.; †by [I.] Heinemann, *Monatsschrift für Geschichte und Wissenschaft des Judentums,* LIV (1910), 504–510; by G. Heinrici, *Theologische Literaturzeitung,* XXXV (1910), 195–198; by —l —u., *Literarisches Zentralblatt für Deutschland,* LXI (1910), 1216 f.; by Eb. Nestle, *Berliner philologische Wochenschrift,* XXX (1910), 1277–1280; by E. Weber, *Theologisches Literaturblatt,* XXXI (1910), 121–126.

Vol. II reviewed by Heinisch, *Theologische Revue,* X (1911), 382; by G. Heinrici, *Theologische Literaturzeitung,* XXXVI (1911), 713–715; by —l —u., *Literarisches Zentralblatt für Deutschland,* LXII (1911), 866 f.; by Eb. Nestle, *Berliner philologische Wochenschrift,* XXI (1911), 1333–1335; by Weber, *Theologisches Literaturblatt,* XXXII (1911), 512 f.

Vol. III reviewed by Paul Heinisch, *Theologische Revue,* XIX (1920), 48 f.; by Georg Helbig, *Theologische Literaturzeitung,* XLV (1920), 30; by —l —u., *Literarisches Zentralblatt für Deutschland,* LXXI (1920), 737 f.; by Weber, *Theologisches Literaturblatt,* XLI (1920), 388 f.; by Georg Grützmacher, *Die Theologie der Gegenwart,* XV (1921), 117–119; and by Otto Stählin, *Philologische Wochenschrift,* XLI (1921), 721–729.

Vol. IV reviewed by Georg Helbig, *Theologische Literaturzeitung,* XLIX (1924), 54 f.; and by Weber, *Theologisches Literaturblatt,* XLVII (1926), 278 f.

Vol. V reviewed by I. Heinemann in no. 537, LXXIII (1929), 442; †by Otto Stählin, *Philologische Wochenschrift,* XLIX (1929), 1318–1326; †by G. A. van den Bergh van Eysinga, *Nieuw Theologisch Tijdschrift,* XVIII (1929), 274 f.; by Hans Leisegang, *Theologisches Literaturblatt,* LI (1930), 12; †by Otto Michel, *Theologische Literaturzeitung,* LV (1930), 225; and by H. Drexler, *Gnomon,* VIII (1932), 155–162.

493.* *Philon von Alexandrien von den Machterweisen Gottes: eine zeitgenös-*

*sische Darstellung der Judenverfolgungen unter dem Kaiser Caligula.
Übersetzt, bearbeitet und eingeleitet von* HANS LEWY, Berlin,
Schocken Verlag, 1935, pp. 85.
Reviewed by E. R. Goodenough, *Journal of Biblical Literature,* LV
(1936), 245 f.

See also no. 423.

H. HEBREW TRANSLATIONS

494. מִן הַיּוֹרֵשׁ דִּבְרֵי אֱלֹהִים. Prag, 1830, pp. [vii], 92.
   Contains: *Heres.*

495. מלאכות לקיום מאת ידידי' האלכסנרוני (so) המכונה פילון
   Philo an Cajus [aus welcher Sprache?], hebräisch von M. MENDEL-
   SON. (From Moritz Steinschneider, *Catalog der Hebräischen Hand-
   schriften in der Stadtbibliothek zu Hamburg und der sich anschlies-
   senden in anderen Sprachen,* Hamburg, 1878.)
   Contains: *Legat.*

496. הַמַּלְאָכוּת *Die Sendung Philon's an Caj. Caligula. Aus dem Griechischen Philon's in's Deutsche von J. F. Eckhard, und daraus in's Hebräische,* by MARD. AH. GINZBURG (GÜNZBURG), Wilna, 1837.
   (From no. 528.)
   Contains: *Legat.*
   Republished (edited by J. B. Schwartzberg), Warsaw, 1894, pp. 76,
   with titles in Russian.

497.* *Philonis Judaei de vita Mosis. Hoc est de theologia et prophetia idio-
   mate graeco olim descripta et in tres libros divisa, nunc autem in linguam
   hebraicam translata auctaque cum notis in usum lectorum; nec non
   adnexus liber quartus continens Decalogum, quod est juris summa-
   rium ab eo ipsius auctore alibi interpretatum. His libellus quintus additus est de Essaeis et Therapeutis, in unum congessit et edidit in lucem
   impensis propriis* JOSEPHUS FLESCH, Prague, M. I. Landau, 1838,
   pp. xiv, 192, (2), 40, (4), added title page in Hebrew.
   Contains: *Mos., Decal.,* Selections on the Essenes and Therapeutae.
   Reviewed by Goldenthal, *Sitzungsberichte der kaiserlichen Akademie
   der Wissenschaften. Philosophisch-historische Classe,* II, i (1849), 124–
   130.

498.* *Writings of Philo of Alexandria translated from Greek into Hebrew;*
   Book I, *On the Creation of the World translated by* ISAAK MANN,
   with Introduction and notes by MOSES SCHWABE, Jerusalem, 1931,

title and text in Hebrew. (*Philosophic Library* published by Judah Yunovitch.)

Contains: *Opif.*

Reviewed by †T. F. Perles, *Orientalistische Literaturzeitung,* XXXVI (1933), 103.

I. HUNGARIAN TRANSLATIONS

499.* *Alexandriai Philo Jelentése a Caius Caligulánál járt küldöttségről. Legatio ad Caium. Görögből forditotta* SCHILL SALAMON, Budapest, 1896, pp. xiii, 100. (*Az Izr. Magyar Irodalmi Társulat Kiadványai,* IV.)

Contains: *Legat.*

J. ITALIAN TRANSLATIONS

500. *La vita di Mosè* (*scritta da Filone*) *volgarizzata* by SEBAST. FAUSTO DI LONGIANO, Venedig, Valgrisi, 1548, 8vo. (From no. 528.)

Contains: *Mos.*

501. *La Vita di Mosè, composta da Filon Giudeo in lingua greca, e tradotta da* GIVLIO BALLINO *in volgare Italiana,* Venetia, Nicolò Beuilocqua, 1560, pp. viii, 211.

Contains: *Mos.*

502. *Discorso vniversale di M. Agostino Ferentilli* . . . *Aggiuntavi La Creatione del Mondo, descritta da Filone Hebreo, et tradotta da* M. AGOSTINO FERENTILLI, Vinetia, Gabriel Giolito di Ferrarii, 1570, pp. xvi, 231, viii, 48, 8vo. (1570 edit. from no. 528.)

Contains: *Opif.* (with separate title page).

Other editions, *ibid.,* *1572; *1573, *1574, 1575, 1578.

503. *Il ritratto del vero e perfetto gentiluomo espresso da Filone Ebreo nella vita di Giuseppe Patriarca, e fatto volgare da* PIET. FRANC. ZINO, Venedig, 1574, Giolito, 4°. (From no. 528.)

Republished, Venedig, Bolognin Zaltiero, 1574, 12mo; and with *La forma del perfetto Christiano descritta da S. Gregorio Vescovo Nisseno, fratello del Grande Basilio,* Venedig, Franc. Rampazetto, 1575, 8vo. (From no. 528.)

504. *Volgarizzamento del trattato di Filone Ebreo su la virtu e le sue specie, giusta il testo Greco recentemente scoperto e pubblicato dal Ch. Sig.* AB. MAI, Milan, Carlo Dova, 1817, pp. vi, 32.

Contains: *Virt.*

505. *Trattato della virtù e delle sue specie, sia poi di Filone, oppur di Ge-*

misto Pletone, giusta il testo greco discoperto e publicato dal ch. Mai, venne tradotto in italiano dal Cav. LUIGI ROSSI, Milan, Dova, 1817, 8vo. (From no. 528.)
Contains: *Virt.*

506. *Trattato del rispetto ai genitori. Traduzione dal Greco de Philone,* Milan, 1819, 8vo. (From no. 528.)
Contains: *Spec.,* ii d.

507. *Filone Giudeo delle Legazione a Gajo, volgarizzamento* by G. BELLONI, 1828. (*Collana degli Antichi Storici Greci volgarizzati,* Storici Minori, Milano, 1819–36, tom. 2.) (From B.M.)
Contains: *Legat.*

508. "Sul debito che hanno i figliuoli d'onorare i genitori trattatello di Filone Giudeo," *Sulla educazione dei figliuoli dialogo del Cardinale* GIACOMO SADOLETO *recato in italiano con annotazioni,* 2nd edit., Pesaro, Annesio Nobili, 1834, 181–204.
Contains: *Spec.,* ii d.

509.* *Vita di Moisè scritta da Filone Ebreo in lingua greca e recata in italiano da* GIULIO BALLINO, Padova, Tipografia Bianchi, 1857, pp. viii, 219.
Contains: *Mos.*

510.* *Vita di Moisè scritta da Filone Ebreo con altri aurei trattatelli dello stesso autore aggiunti in questa, recato in italiano da* GIULIO BALLINO, Ancona, 1861, pp. viii, 268.
Contains: *Mos., Spec.,* ii. d[1].

511. *Trattato del rispetto ai genitori. Versione di* ANT. ZACCARIA, Lucca, 1876, pp. 15. (From Attilio Pagliaini, *Catalogo Generale della Libreria Italiana,* 1903, E–O, 97.)
Contains: *Spec.,* ii. d.

512. *Lettera del re Agrippa a Cajo Caligola Imperatore scritta in ebraico da Filone Ebreo, e tradotta in latino da S. Gelenio, e dal latino in volgare da* . . . G. D. BERTOLI, [edited by P. and G. Rota], S. Vito, [1885], pp. 19. (From B.M.) Pagliani, see preceding item, spells the author BARTOLI.
Contains: *Legat.,* 276–349.

See also no. 436.

K. RUSSIAN TRANSLATIONS

513. *Filon Iudeianin o Subbote i prochikh vetkhozavetnykh prazdnikakh* (Philo Judaeus on Sabbath and other Old Testament holidays), translated from the Greek by the Hiero-monk GEDEON, Moscow, 1783.

L. SPANISH TRANSLATIONS

514. *Herve Estoico o el Hombre Libre; Discurso in que se prueba, que no puede haber verdadera libertad, donde no domina la virtud; escrito in Griego por Filon, traducido al Espan.* etc. by EM. JOS. FD. VINGOY, Madrid, 1789. (From no. 528.)
Contains: *Prob.*

M. SWEDISH TRANSLATIONS

515.* *Philo Judaeus om Essaeerne, Therapeuterne och Therapeutriderna, Judarnas förföljelse under Flaccus och Legationen till Cajus Caligula, samt smärre, spridda Utdrag ur Philos, före Christi offentliga uppträdande, till större delen åtminstone affattade, gammaltestamentliga, Allegoriska Skrifttolkningar, ordnade och rubricerade efter det hufvudsakliga af innehållet, och såsom omedvetne nytestamentliga läror samt synbara, högre förberedelser för Christendomen, flerstädes med Evangelii dogmer och bud jemnförde och sammanställde,* by I. BERGGREN, Söderköping, N. F. Tengzelius, 1853, pp. xx, 288.
Contains: *Prob., Cont., Flac., Legat.,* and a large miscellaneous selection of passages from other works.

III. BIBLIOGRAPHIES OF PHILO

516.* Gesnerus, Conradus, *Bibliotheca uniuersalis, siue catalogus omnium scriptorum locupletissimus, in tribus linguis, latina, greca, & hebraica: extantium & non extantium, ueterum & recentiorum in hunc usque diem, doctorum & indoctorum, publicatorum & in bibliothecis latentium. Opus nouum, & non bibliothecis tantum publicis priuatisue instituendis necessarium, sed studiosis omnibus cuiuscunque artis aut scientiae ad studia melius formanda utilissimum,* Tiguri (Zurich), Christophorus Froschouer, 1545, 559v–560v.

517.* Bellarminus, Robertus, *De scriptoribus ecclesiasticis liber unus. Adiunctis indicibus vndecim, & breui chronologia ab orbe condito usque ad annum MDCXII. Ultima editio à mendis praecedentium sedulò ac diligenter expurgata. Cum appendice philologica & chronologica R. P. Philippi Labbe, Biturci,* Paris, 1658.
Contains on pp. 33–34 among the writers "Testamenti veteris" a brief summary of the life of Philo and a list of his writings quoted from the edition printed in Basil in 1561.

518.* Labbe, Philippus, *De scriptoribus ecclesiasticis, quos attigit Eminentiss. S.R.E. Card. Robertus Bellarminus, philologica et historica dissertatio,* Paris, 1660, II, 214–220, 785–788; see also I, 439, 626, 705, II, 48, 97, sig. Ss[1]v.

519.* Georgius, Theophilus, *Allgemeines europäisches Bücher-Lexicon, in welchem nach Ordnung des Dictionarii die allermeisten Autores oder Gattungen von Büchern zu finden,* Leipzig, 1742–58, 5 vols. and three supplements bound in four; III, 210; V, 305; Suppl. I, 287; Suppl. II, 262; Suppl. III, 265.

520.* Harles, Theophilus Christophorus, *Introductio in historiam linguae graecae,* Altenburg, 1778, 326–330.

521. Struvius, Burcardus Gotthelf, *Bibliotheca historica* (edit. and enlarged by Christi. Gottlieb Buderus and Ioannes Georgius Meuselius), Leipzig, I, ii, 1784, 239, 255, 257.

522.* Brunet, J.–C., fils, *Manuel du libraire et de l'amateur de livres,* Paris, 1810, 3 vols. in 5; II, i, 283; III, ii, 385.

523.* Federici, Fortunato, *Degli scrittori greci e delle italiane versioni delle loro opere,* Padua, 1828, 233–236.

524.† Hoffmann, S[amuel] F[riedrich] W[ilhelm], *Lexicon bibliographicum, sive index editionum et interpretationum scriptorum graecorum tum sacrorum tum profanorum,* Leipzig, III, 1836, 225–233.

525.† Georgii, Johann Christian Ludwig, "Ueber die neuesten Gegensätze in

Auffassung der alexandrinischen Religionsphilosophie, insbesondere des Jüdischen Alexandrinismus, eine historisch-theologische Untersuchung," *Zeitschrift für die historische Theologie,* IX (N.F. III) (1839), iii, 3–98; iv, 3–98.

526.* Engelmann, Wilhelm, *Bibliotheca scriptorum classicorum et graecorum et latinorum. Alphabetisches Verzeichniss der Ausgaben, Uebersetzungen und Erläuterungsschriften der griechischen und lateinischen Schriftsteller, welche vom Jahre 1700 bis zu Ende des Jahres 1846 besonders in Deutschland gedruckt worden sind,* Leipzig, 1847, 159 and *Supplement-heft,* 1853, 44.

527.* Brunet, Jacques-Charles, *Manuel du libraire et de l'amateur de livres,* Paris, 5th edit., IV, i, 1863, 614 f.; VI, 1865, 35.

528.* Fürst, Julius, *Bibliotheca Judaica. Bibliographisches Handbuch der gesammten jüdischen Literatur mit Einschluss der Schriften über Juden und Judenthum und einer Geschichte der jüdischen Bibliographie. Nach alfabetischer Ordnung der Verfasser,* Leipzig, III, 1863, 87–94.

529.† Graesse, Jean George Théodore, *Trésor de livres rares et précieux, ou nouveau dictionnaire bibliographique,* Dresden (also Geneva, London, and Paris), V, 1864, 269–271.

530.† Freudenthal, [J.], "Zur Geschichte der Anschauungen über die jüdisch-hellenistische Religionsphilosophie," *Monatschrift für Geschichte und Wissenschaft des Judenthums,* XVIII (1869), 399–421.
Published separately, Breslau, 1869, pp. 23.

531. Bursian, Conrad, *Jahresbericht über die Fortschritte der classischen Alterthumswissenschaft,* 1873—.
In connection with the bibliographical studies, systematic notice of titles has been regularly published under the separate title: *Bibliotheca philologica classica. Verzeichniss der auf dem Gebiete der classischen Alterthumswissenschaft . . . Beiblatt zum Jahresbericht über die Fortschritte der classischen Alterthumskunde,* 1874—. See each installment at Philo's name in the section devoted to Greek Authors.

532.* Preuss, E., *Bibliotheca scriptorum classicorum herausgegeben von Wilhelm Engelmann. Achte auflage, umfassend die Literatur von 1700 bis 1878, neu bearbeitet,* Leipzig, I, 1880, 546–548.

533.* Müntz, Eugène, and Fabre, Paul, *La Bibliothèque du Vatican au XVe siècle d'après des documents inédits,* Paris, 1887, 276 f., 280, 334, 335. (*Bibliothèque des Écoles Françaises d'Athènes et de Rome,* 48.)

534. Cohn, Leopold, "The Latest Researches on Philo of Alexandria," *The Jewish Quarterly Review,* V (1892–1893), 24–50.
*Reprinted, London, 1892, pp. 29.

535.* Chevalier, Ulysse, *Répertoire des sources historiques du Moyen Age.*

. . . *Bio-bibliographie, nouvelle édition refondue, corrigée et considé-rablement augmentée*, Paris, II, 1907, 3648–3651.

536.† Klussmann, Rudolf, *Bibliotheca scriptorum classicorum et graecorum et latinorum*, Leipzig, I, ii, 1911, 130–135.

537.† Heinemann, I., "Hellenistica," *Monatsschrift für Geschichte und Wissenschaft des Judentums*, LXVII (1923), 278–287; LXXIII (1929), 425–443; LXXVI (1932), 263–269.

538.* British Museum, *Short-title Catalogue of Books printed in France and of French Books printed in other countries from 1470 to 1600 now in the British Museum*, London, 1924, 350.

539.* Ueberweg, Friedrich, *Grundriss der Geschichte der Philosophie*, Berlin, 5 vols., I. *Die Philosophie des Altertums*, by Karl Praechter, 12th edit., 1926, 572–578, 181*–183*; see Index for this and Vols. II and III. Reviewed in no. 537, LXXIII (1929), 442 f.

540.† Marouzeau, J., *Dix années de bibliographie classique, bibliographie critique et analytique de l'antiquité greco-latine pour la période, 1914–24*, Paris, I, *Auteurs et Textes*, 1927, 276–277.
Continued to date as an annual volume with the title *L'Année philologique*. See each s.v. "Philo." See also the sections on Philosophy and History of Religion.

541. Nock, A. D., "Bibliography: Graeco-Roman Egypt: A. Papyri, § 2. Religion, Magic, Astrology," *The Journal of Egyptian Archaeology*.
Since Volume XVII (1931) Nock has been devoting a valuable paragraph to current Philonic literature in this annual bibliography.

542.† Lebreton, Jules, "Bulletin d'histoire des origines chrétiennes, I. Philon," *Recherches de science religieuse*, XXIII (1933), 331–338.

543.* Marcus, Ralph, "Recent Literature on Philo (1924–1934)," *Jewish Studies in Memory of George A[lexander] Kohut*, New York, 1935, 463–491.
*Reprinted, New York, 1935, pp. 29.

544.* Shunami, Shlomo, *Bibliography of Jewish Bibliographies*, Jerusalem, 1936, 223.

545. *Biblica*.
In the annual "Elenchus Bibliographicus," XX, § 3, is listed from year to year current bibliography on "Philo et Iosephus."

See also nos. 593, 626, 631, 658, 1156.

IV. GENERAL STUDIES ON PHILO

546.* Volterranus, Raphael, *Commentariorum Vrbanorum,* Lugduni (Lyons), Sebastianus Gryphius, 1552, col. 561 f. (sig. A3r).

547. Gaddius, Iacobus, *De Scriptoribus, tomus secundus. In hoc haud pauca continentur ad politicam & naturalem philosophiam; ad theologiam tum Christianam, tum ethnicam, ad historiam multiplicem . . . ad criticam & poëticam artem spectantia,* Lugduni (Lyons), 1649, pp. 386.

548. Rabanus (Maurus), "Liber sive epistola contra Iudaeos," in Petrus Franciscus Chiffletius, *Scriptorum veterum de fide catholica quinque opuscula,* Divione (Dijon), 1656; see 315.

549.* Hankius, Martin, *De romanarum rerum scriptoribus,* Leipzig, 1669–1675, 2 vols., II, 44–100.

550. Honorius Augustodunensis, "De luminaribus ecclesiae," "Gemma animae," in *Maxima bibliotheca veterum patrum et antiquorum scriptorum ecclesiasticorum,* revised by Margarino de la Bigne, Lugduni (Lyons), XX, 1677; see 1028, 1128.

551. Cudworth, Ralph, *The True Intellectual System of the Universe,* London, 1678.
Frequently republished. See the Index in Vol. III of the edition of London, 1845, where is also translated the essay of Mosheim, no. 557.

552. Hoffmann, J., *Philonem, Josephum, etc. historice exhib.,* Rudolst., 1687. (From no. 535.)

553.* Relandus, Hadrianus, *Antiquitates sacrae veterum Hebraeorum, breviter delineatae,* 3rd edit., Trajectum (Utrecht), 1717, 152, 263, 266, 285, 303, 316 f., 336, 338, 341, 356 f., 367, 382, 454, 474, 477 f., 492, 507, 509, 512, 516, 518.

554.* Cave, Guilielmus, *Scriptorum ecclesiasticorum historia literaria, a Christo nato, usque ad saeculum XIV. facili methodo digesta, & nunc auctior facta, qua de vita illorum ac rebus gestis,* Coloniae Allobrogum (Geneva), 1720, 14–16.

555. Scharbau, Henrico (I.G. ?), "De Philone," *Judaismus detectus,* Lübeck, 1722, 98–104.

556. Mosheim, Johann Lorenz von, "De Philone," in his translation and annotation of Ralph Cudworth, *Systema intellectuale hujus universi,* Jena, 1733; see 2nd edit., Lugduni Batavorum (Leyden), I, 1773, 828–839. See no. 551.

557.* Brucker, [Johann] Iacob, *Historia critica philosophiae,* II: *Ab initiis monarchiae romanae ad repurgatas vsque literas,* Leipzig, 1742; see (Gen.) 691–693, (Essenes) 759–788, (Therapeutae) 797–812, (Creation) 883–886, (Powers and Kabbala) 842, 903, 945 f., 966–968, (Angels) 894, (Incorruptibility of the world) 909; VI (V): *Appendix*, Leipzig, 1767, (Therapeutae) 452–457.

558.† Crellius, Samuel, "De Philone," in Io. Ludovicus Uhlius, *Thesaurus epistolicus lacrozianus*, I, 1742, 97–114.

559.* Senensis, Sixtus, *Bibliotheca sancta criticis, ac theologicis animadversionibus, nec non duplici adjecto Sacrorum Scriptorum elencho adaucta et inlustrata a Fr. Pio-Thoma Milante*, Naples, 1742, I, 457–461 and *passim*.
*First edition, *Bibliotheca sancta . . . ordinis Praedicatorum, ex praecipuis catholicae ecclesiae autoribus collecta*, Venetia, Francisus Franciscius Senensem, 1566.

560.* Petavius, Dionysius, *Opera de theologicis dogmatibus, in hac novissima editione auctius*, Venice, 1745, 6 vols. in 3; I, 2, 11, 14, 29 f., 34, 52, 63, 85, 90, 93, 117–119, 127, 129, 135, 139, 151, 157, 159, 161–163, 172, 174, 188, 190, 202, 244, 245, 251, 253, 261, 263, 277, 280 f., 305, 314, 331 f., 336, 339; II, 18, 37, 88 f., 262, 301 f., 317, 442; III, 1, 2, 69, 71, 84, 94, 114 f., 119 f., 123 f., 126, 138, 140 f., 146 f., 150, 157, 160, 162, 166, 168, 172 f.; V, 74, 117, 354, 409, 430 f.; VI, 45, 61, 91, 106–108, 125, 208, 249, 265, 276, 280.
See "De Trinitate," I, ii, in the edition of Franciscus Antonius Zacharia, II, Venice, 1757, 19.

561.† Jöcher, Christian Gottlieb, "Philo Senior" and "Philo, von Alexandria," *Allgemeines Gelehrten-Lexicon*, Leipzig, 1751, III, 1527 f.

562.* Moréri, Louis, *Le grand dictionnaire historique, ou le mélange curieux de l'histoire sacrée et profane*, Paris, 1759, 10 vols.; VIII, 293.

563. Lumper, Gottfried, *Historia theologico-critica de vita, scriptis atque doctrina sanctorum patrum aliorumque scriptorum ecclesiasticorum*, Augustae Vindelicorum (Augsburg), I, 1783, 475–491.

564. Michaelis, Johann David, *Einleitung in die göttlichen Schriften des Neuen Bundes*, 4th edit., Göttingen, 1788, II; see Index and 1244–1251.

565. Stahl, E. H., "Versuch eines systematischen Entwurfs des Lehrbegriffs Philo's von Alexandrien," in Johann Gottfried Eichhorn, *Allgemeine Bibliothek der biblischen Litteratur*, IV, v, Leipzig, 1793, 767–890.

566.* Fabricius, Ioannus Albertus, *Bibliotheca graeca, sive notitia scriptorum veterum graecorum*, 4th edit. by Gottlieb Christophorus Harles, Hamburg, IV, 1795, 721–750. See also Index Vol. (Leipzig, 1838), s.v. "Philo."
The first edition was 14 vols., 1705–28.

567. Buhle, Johann Gottlieb, *Lehrbuch der Geschichte der Philosophie und einer kritischen Literatur derselben*, Göttingen, IV, 1799, 69–141.

568.* Matter, Jacques, *Essai historique sur l'école d'Alexandrie, et coup d'oeil* *comparatif sur la littérature grecque, depuis le temps d'Alexandre le Grand jusqu'a celui d'Alexandre Sévère,* Paris, 1820, 2 vols.; I, 16, 22 n., 59, 76, 184, 188, 223–227, 279; II, 141, 143 f., 149, 173, 183, 185 f., 259 f., 267, 273, 282.

A second edition in 3 vols., entirely revised, *Histoire de l'école d'Alexandrie comparée aux principales écoles contemporaines,* Paris, 1840–48.

569.* Gfrörer, August, *Philo und die alexandrinische Theosophie, oder vom Einflusse der jüdisch-ägyptischen Schule auf die Lehre des Neuen Testaments,* Stuttgart, 1831, 2 vols., pp. xliv, 534, 406. (*Kritische Geschichte des Urchristenthums,* I, i, ii.)

Second unchanged edition, *ibid.,* 1835, with title, *Philo und die jüdisch-alexandrinische Theosophie.*

Reviewed in *Jahrbücher für wissenschaftliche Kritik,* 1883, ii, 717–720.

570.* Dähne, August Ferdinand, *Geschichtliche Darstellung der jüdisch-alexandrinischen Religions-Philosophie,* Halle, 1834, 2 vols., pp. xx, 497; viii, 266.

Reviewed by [Ferd. Chr.] Baur, *Jahrbücher für wissenschaftliche Kritik,* 1835, ii, 737–743, 745–765, 769–792.

571. Ritter, [August] Heinrich, *Geschichte der Philosophie alter Zeit,* Hamburg, IV, 1834, 418, 487 f., 493, 510, 561, 567 f., 579. (*Geschichte der Philosophie,* IV.)

*English translation by Alexander J. W. Morrison, *The History of Ancient Philosophy,* IV, London, 1846; see 407–478 for character, life and doctrines; 479 f., doctrines of Philo compared with those of Pythagorean philosophers; 482–484 with those of Appolonius; 507 f., with those of Plutarch; 542, 550, 557, 561, 563, 587, doctrines of Philo approved or rejected by Plotinus.

572. Sarazin, A. H., *De philosophica Philonis Judaei doctrina,* Strasbourg, 1835, pp. 39. (From no. 535.)

573. Denzinger, Henr., *Diss. De Philonis philosophia et schola judaeor. alexandrina,* Diss., Herbipoli, 1840, pp. 162. (From no. 532.)

574. Muralt, Edward von, *Beiträge zur alten Literatur; oder Untersuchungen über Philo, Plinius I., Ptolemaeus, Dionysius Areopagita, Hephaestio, Porphyrius, Basilius, Olympiodor und Theodorus Metochita, nach St. Petersburger Handschriften nebst Copien einiger unedirten griechischen Inschriften,* St. Petersburg, 1844, pp. [66]. (From U.C.)

575.* Vacherot, E., *Histoire critique de l'école d'Alexandrie,* Paris, I, 1846, 125–167.

576.† Daehne, F., "Philon (Philo Judaeus)," in J. S. Ersch and J. G. Gruber, *Allgemeine Encyklopädie der Wissenschaften und Künste,* Leipzig, Sect. III, Vol. XXIII, 1847, 435–454.

577. Wolff, M., *Die philonische Philosophie in ihren Hauptmomenten darge-stellt* (früher in der "Sulamith" abgedrukt), Leipzig, 1849. (From no. 528.)

*Second, enlarged edition, *ibid.*, Gothenburg, 1858, pp. x, 61.

578. Noack, Ludwig, "Der Jude Philon von Alexandrien und seine Weltan-sicht," *Psyche*, II, 1851, 4–7.

579.† Rubinsohn, Theophilus, "Philo and his Opinions," *The Christian Re-view*, XVIII (1853), 119–135.

580.† Darling, James, "Philo Judaeus," *Cyclopaedia Bibliographica*, I–Z, 1854, 2361 f.

581.* Kingsley, Charles, *Alexandria and her Schools. Four Lectures delivered at the Philosophical Institution, Edinburgh,* Cambridge (England), 1854, 79, 81, 85–94, 105, 152.

582. [Anonymous], "Philo Judaeus and Alexandrian Jewish Theology," *The Eclectic Review*, N.S. X (1855), 602–613.

583. Döllinger, Joh. Jos. Ign., "Das alexandrinische Judenthum Philo," *Hei-denthum und Judenthum. Vorhalle zur Geschichte des Christenthums,* Regensburg, 1857, 836–848.

584. Jost, J. M., *Geschichte des Judenthums und seiner Secten,* Leipzig, I, 1857, 99–108, 344–361, 367–393. (*Schriften herausgegeben vom Institut zur Förderung der Israelitischen Literatur.*)

585. Müller, J. G., "Philo und die jüdisch-alexandrinische Religionsphilo-sophie," in J. J. Herzog, *Real-Encyklopädie für protestantische The-ologie und Kirche,* 1st edit., Gotha, XI, 1859, 578–603.

586.† Holmes, Peter, "Philo or Philon," in John Kitto, *A Cyclopaedia of Biblical Literature,* 3rd edit. by William Lindsay Alexander, Edin-burgh, 1862, III, 515–517.
Frequently reprinted.

587. Schultz, "Die alexandrinische Religionsphilosophie," Gelzer's *Monatsb.,* octobre 1864. (From no. 626.)

588.† Ceillier, Remy, "Philon le Juif," *Histoire générale des auteurs sacrés et ecclésiastiques,* new edit., by . . . Bauzon, Paris, I, 1865, 309–313.
An earlier edition 1729–1783. (From B.N.)

589.* Keim, Theodor, "Die jüdische Aufklärung. Philon der Alexandriner," "Die Essäer," *Geschichte Jesu von Nazara in ihrer Verkettung mit dem Gesammtleben seines Volkes,* Zürich, I, 1867, 208–225, 282–306; see also 9–11, 634.

590. Ewald, Heinrich, *Geschichte des Volkes Israel,* 3rd edit., Göttingen, VI, 1868, 257–312.

591. Hausrath, A., *Neutestamentliche Zeitgeschichte,* Heidelberg, II, 1872, 126–179.

592.† Prowett, Charles Gipps, "Philo the Jew," *Fraser's Magazine,* N.S. X (1874), 186–200.

593. Schürer, Emil, *Lehrbuch der neutestamentlichen Zeitgeschichte,* Leipzig, 1874.
Later editions: *Geschichte des jüdischen Volkes im Zeitalter Jesu Christi,* Leipzig, 1886–90; *ibid.,* 1901, 1898; **ibid.,* 1901–1911.
*English translation (of the second edition) by John MacPherson, Sophia Taylor, and Peter Christie: *A History of the Jewish People in the Time of Jesus Christ,* Edinburgh, 1890–93, two divisions in five vols. (plus index vol.). (T. T. Clark, *Foreign Theological Library,* N.S. XLI, XLIII, XXIII, XXIV, XXV.)
See § 34, "Philo the Jewish Philosopher," in all editions except the first, 1874 (§ 32, "Die jüdische Philosophie. Philo").

594. Thorelli, Jöns Jönsson, *Alexandrinaren Filo och hans lärer,* Diss. (Lund), Malmö, 1874, pp. 46. (From Aksel G. S. Josephson, *Avhandlinger ock Programm . . . under Åren 1855–1890,* Uppsala, [1891–93], 230.)

595.* Joël, M., "Ueber Philo, den hervorragendsten Vertreter der jüdisch-alexandrinischen Geistesrichtung," *Beiträge zur Geschichte der Philosophie,* Breslau, 1876, II. Four sections of this volume are paged separately. See the last section, 12–33.

596.* Drummond, James, *Philo, and the Principles of the Jewish-Alexandrine Philosophy,* London and Manchester, 1877, pp. 28.

597.† [Worman, James H.], "Philo, the Jew," *Methodist Quarterly Review,* LX (4th S. XXX) (1878), 121–141.

598.† C[ook], K[eningale], "A Contemporary of Jesus," *The University Magazine,* V (1880), 392–410, 598–622, 728–746.

599. Reuss, Eduard, *Die Geschichte der heiligen Schriften Alten Testaments,* Braunschweig, 1881, 674–676, 697–702.

600.† H., "Filone Alessandrino," *Il Vessillo Israelitico,* XXX (1882), 33–35, 72–74. (A final installment was promised but not printed.)

601.† Nicolas, Michel, "Études sur Philon d'Alexandrie," *Revue de l'histoire des religions,* V (1882), 318–339; VII (1883), 145–164; VIII (1883), 468–488, 582–602, 756–772.

602. Zöckler, [Otto], "Philo von Alexandreia," in J. J. Herzog, *Real-Encyklopädie für protestantische Theologie und Kirche,* edited by Alb[ert] Hauck, 2nd edit., Leipzig, XI (1883), 636–649.
Revised in third edition, edited by Albert Hauck, Leipzig, XV, 1904, 348–362.

603. Schmidt, Paul Victor, *Libellus historico-criticus in quo quomodo ultimis a. Chr. saeculis Judaismus cum paganismo coaluerit Philonis theosophiae ratione sub finem habita,* Leipzig, 1884, pp. 81.

Reviewed by D. Otto, *Wochenschrift für klassische Philologie*, II (1885), 1387–1390.

604. Harnack, Adolph von, *Lehrbuch der Dogmengeschichte*, 1st edit., 1885; 4th edit., Tübingen, I, 1909, 121–132. (*Sammlung Theologischer Lehrbücher*.)

English translation (of the third edition, Freiburg i.B., 1888) by Neil Buchanan, *History of Dogma*, London and Edinburgh, I, 1894, 107–116. (T. K. Cheyne and A. B. Bruce, *Theological Translation Library*, II.)

605.* Bigg, Charles, *The Christian Platonists of Alexandria, being the Bampton Lectures of the year 1886* . . . *reprinted with some additions and corrections*, Oxford, 1913, 31–53 and *passim*.

606.* Edersheim, A., "Philo," in William Smith and Henry Wace, *A Dictionary of Christian Biography, Literature, Sects and Doctrines*, London, IV, 1887, 357–389.

607.* Drummond, James, *Philo Judaeus; or, the Jewish-Alexandrian philosophy in its development and completion*, London, 1888, 2 vols., pp. viii, 359; 355.

Reviewed in *The Athenaeum*, [LXI, ii] (1888), 769 f.; in *The Spectator*, LXI (1888), 1411–1413; by E. Schürer, *Theologische Literaturzeitung*, XIII (1888), 489–491; in *The Nation*, XLIX (1889), 297; and in no. 608.

608. Porter, F. C., "Philo, and his Latest Interpreter," *New Englander and Yale Review*, L (N.S. XIV) (1889), 127–139.

609.† [Anonymous], "Philo," in John M'Clintock and James Strong, *Cyclopaedia of Biblical, Theological, and Ecclesiastical Literature*, New York, 1891, VIII, 110–116.

610. Renan, Ernest, *Histoire du peuple d'Israël*, Paris, V, 1893, 345–380.

611.† Montefiore, C. G., "Florilegium Philonis," *The Jewish Quarterly Review*, VII (1894–1895), 481–545.

612.† Renan, Ernest, "Philon d'Alexandrie et son oeuvre," *La revue de Paris*, I (1894), 37–55.

613. Kleffner, Ant. Ign., "Philo," in Wetzer and Welte, *Kirchenlexikon*, 2nd edit. by Joseph Hergenröther and Franz Kaulen, Frieburg im Breisgau, IX, 1895, 2031–2037.

614. Bussell, F[rederick] W[illiam], *The School of Plato: Its Origin, Development, and Revival under the Roman Empire*, London, 1896, 193–207.

615.* Herriot, Édouard, *Philon le Juif: essai sur l'école juive d'alexandrie*, Paris, 1898, pp. xix, 366.

The preface contains bibliographical lists.

Reviewed in *The Athenaeum*, 1898, ii, 63 f.; by J. R. Asmus, *Wochen-*

schrift für klassische Philologie, XV (1898), 567–579; *by Leopold Cohn, "Philo von Alexandria," *Neue Jahrbücher für das klassische Altertum,* I (1898), 514–540; by M. F., *Literarisches Centralblatt für Deutschland,* [XLIX] (1898), 727 f.; by H. G., *Revue des études grecques,* XI (1898), 350 f.; by A. L., *Revue critique d'histoire et de littérature,* XXXII, i (N.S. XLV) (1898), 264–266; by C. Siegfried, *Deutsche Litteraturzeitung,* XIX (1898), 579–581; by P. Wendland, *Berliner philologische Wochenschrift,* XVIII (1898), 330–333; by Is. van Dijk, *Museum: Maandblad voor philologie en geschiedenis,* VII (1899), 58–61; and †by Louis Saltet, "Philon le Juif a propos d'un livre récent," *Revue des questions historiques,* LXV (N.S. XXI) (1899), 214–226.

616. Trubetzkoï, S. N., "Philon und seine Vorläufer" (Russian), *Voprosy filosofii i psikhologii,* VIII (1898), 813–866 and IX (1898), 138–183.

617.† Blum, Eugène, "Philon d'Alexandrie," *La grande encyclopédie,* Paris, [1899], XXVI, 698–705.

618.† [Anonymous], "Philos Leben, Wirken und Einfluss," in Adolf Brüll's *Populär-wissenschaftliche Monatsblätter zur Belehrung über das Judentum für Gebildete aller Konfessionen,* XX (1900), 35–37.
A report of the substance of a lecture by Salomon Kaufmann.

619. Pfleiderer, Otto, *Das Urchristentum, seine Schriften und Lehren,* 2nd edit., Berlin, 1902, II, 1–16, 25–54.

620. Pitkin, Walter Boughton, "Philo Judaeus," *The Hartford Seminary Record,* XIII (1902–1903), 304–311.

621. Caird, Edward, "The Philosophy and Theology of Philo," *The Evolution of Theology in the Greek Philosophers,* Glasgow, 1904, II, 184–209. (The Gifford Lectures delivered in the University of Glasgow in Sessions 1900–1 and 1901–2.)

622.* Drummond, James, "Philo," in James Hastings, *A Dictionary of the Bible,* Extra Volume, New York and Edinburgh, 1904 (frequently reprinted with later dates, e.g. *1928), 197–208.

623.† Treitel, L[eopold], "Die religions- und kulturgeschichtliche Stellung Philos," *Theologische Studien und Kritiken,* LXXVII (1904), 380–401. Reprinted in no. 643, 66–84.

624.* Siegfried, Carl, "Philo Judaeus," *The Jewish Encyclopedia,* New York, X, 1905, 6–15.

625.* Martin, Jules, *Philon,* Paris, 1907, pp. 303. (*Les grands philosophes.*) Reviewed in no. 627.

626.* Bréhier, Émile, *Les idées philosophiques et religieuses de Philon d'Alexandrie,* Paris, 1908, pp. xiv, 336. (Étienne Gilson, *Études de philosophie médiévale,* VIII.)
*Second edition (reprint with revised bibliography), 1925.

Reviewed by E. Tz., *Revue critique d'histoire et de littérature*, XLIII, i, or N.S. LXVII (1909), 29–30; and in nos. 627, 543.

627.† Dauriac, Lionel, "Philon d'après deux ouvrages récents," *Revue des études juives*, LV (1908), 37–47.

628.† Inge, W[illiam] R[alph], "Alexandrian Theology," in James Hastings, *Encyclopaedia of Religion and Ethics*, New York and Edinburgh, I, 1908, 308–319, esp. 309–312.

629. Arnim, Hans von, "Die europäische Philosophie des Altertums," *Allgemeine Geschichte der Philosophie*, Berlin and Leipzig, 1909, 265–271. (Paul Hinneberg, *Die Kultur der Gegenwart*, I, v.)

630.* Guthrie, Kenneth Sylvan Launfal, *The Message of Philo Judaeus of Alexandria*, London, 1909, pp. 96.

631.* Bentwich, Norman, *Philo-Judaeus of Alexandria*, Philadelphia, 1910, pp. 273; bibliography, 263–265.

632.* Bréhier, Émile, "Philo Judaeus," *The Catholic Encyclopedia*, New York, XII, [1911], 23–25.

633.* Caraccio, Marcello, *Filone d'Alessandria e le sue opere*, Padova, 1911, pp. 96, 31.

634.* Herzog, Karl, *Spekulativ-psychologische Entwicklung der Grundlagen und Grundlinien des philonischen Systems*, Diss. (Erlangen), Nürnberg, 1911, pp. v, 127.
Republished as a monograph, Leipzig, 1911.

635.* Louis, M., *Philon le Juif*, Paris, 1911, pp. 62.
Reviewed by Adalbert Schulte, *Theologische Revue*, X (1911), 479 f.

636.† Marshall, J. T., "The Odes and Philo," *The Expositor*, 8. S. I (1911), 385–398, 519–536.

637.* Oesterley, W. O. E. and Box, G. H., *The Religion and Worship of the Synagogue: An Introduction to the Study of Judaism from the New Testament Period*, 2nd and rev. edit., London, 1911, 7, 44 f., 116–120, 139, 204, 207 f.

638. Zöckler, Otto, "Philo of Alexandria," *The New Schaff-Herzog Encyclopedia of Religious Knowledge*, New York and London, IX, [1911], 38–42.

639. Lesêtre, H., "Philon," in F. Vigouroux, *Dictionnaire de la Bible*, Paris, V, 1912, 300–312.

640. Stegmann, Otto, *Die Anschauungen des Mittelalters über die endogenen Erscheinungen der Erde*, Diss. (Tübingen), Leipzig, 1913, 7–9.

641. Windisch, [Hans], "Philo," in Friedrich Michael Schiele and Leopold Zscharnack, *Die Religion in Geschichte und Gegenwart*, 1st edit., Tübingen, IV, 1913, 1500–1502.

642. Strathmann, H., *Geschichte der frühchristlichen Askese bis zur Entstehung des Mönchtums*, Leipzig, I, 1914, 83–157.

643.* Treitel, Leopold, *Philonische Studien,* edited by M. Brann, Breslau, 1915, pp. vii, 130.
Reviewed by J. W. Rothstein, *Berliner philologische Wochenschrift,* XXXV (1915), 1268–1270.

644. Heinemann, Fritz, "Philos Bedeutung für die abendländische Geistesgeschichte," *Neue Jüdische Monatshefte,* III (1918–1919), 424–430.

645. Bouillon, Léon, *Quod Philo Alexandrinus vixerit tempore belli judaici defendet,* Thèse (Montauban), Monte Albano (Montauban), 1919, pp. 58.

646. Staerk, W., *Neutestamentliche Zeitgeschichte,* Berlin and Leipzig, 1920, II, 123–131, 145–149. (*Sammlung Göschen.*)

647.* Treitel, L[eopold], *Gesamte Theologie und Philosophie Philo's von Alexandria,* Berlin, 1923, pp. 150.
†Reviewed by I. Heinemann, *Monatsschrift für Geschichte und Wissenschaft des Judentums,* LXVII (1923), 281–282; by Joachim Jeremias, *Theologisches Literaturblatt,* XLIV (1923), 264–265; by Hans Leisegang, *Theologische Literaturzeitung,* XLVIII (1923), 199–201; and by —l., *Jeschurun,* XII (1925), 336.

648. Fahsel, Kaplan, "Philo der Jude," *C[entral] V[erein]-Zeitung. Blätter für Deutschtum und Judentum. Organ des Central-vereins deutscher Staatsbürger jüdischen Glaubens,* III (1924), 753.

649.* Fairweather, William, "The Jewish Hellenist Philo of Alexandria," *Jesus and the Greeks; or, Early Christianity in the Tideway of Hellenism,* Edinburgh, 1924, 159–216.
Reviewed by Marcus in no. 543, p. 464.

650.* Jackson, F. J. Foakes-, "Philo and Hellenistic Judaism," *Studies in the Life of the Early Church,* New York, 1924, 25 f.

651. Heinemann, Fritz, "Philo von Alexandria" ("Gestalten der Spätantike," II), *Der Morgen,* I (1925), 480–495.

652.* Schlatter, A[dolf], *Geschichte Israels von Alexander dem Grossen bis Hadrian,* 3rd edit., Stuttgart, 1925, 295–305.

653. Buber, Martin, "Philon und Cohen," *Juedische Rundschau,* XXXIII (1928), 463.

654.* Moore, George Foot, *History of Religions,* New York, I, rev. edit., 1932, 381, 385, 531–533; II, 1928, 50, 58–62, 72, 87, 90, 126 f., 137 f., 140 n., 141 n., 161, 274. (*The International Theological Library.*)

655.* Kershner, Frederick D[oyle], "Philo," *Pioneers of Christian Thought,* Indianapolis, 1930, 19–42.

656. Leisegang, [Hans], "Philo, 1. von Alexandria," in Hermann Gunkel and Leopold Zscharnack, *Die Religion in Geschichte und Gegenwart,* 2nd edit., Tübingen, IV, 1930, 1193–1197; see also "Philo v. Alexandria" in the *Registerband,* Tübingen, 1932, 651.

657. Stein, Edmund, "Filon z Aleksandrji, Czlowiek, Dziela i Nauka filozoficzna, (Philo of Alexandria; the Man, his Work and Philosophical Teaching)," *Pisma Institutu Nauk Judaistycznych w Warzawie IV Sepher ha-Yobel likbod Dr. Mordechai Zeeb Braude*, 1931, 1–138. (From Marcus in no. 543, p. 477.)
Reviewed by W. Auerbach, *Kwartalnik klasyczny. Warszawa, Nakladem polsk. towarzystwa filologicznego*, VIII (1934), 150 f. (From Bursian, no. 531, Bibliotheca, LXI [1934], 46.)

658.* Boughton, Jesse Scott, *The Idea of Progress in Philo Judaeus*, Diss. (Columbia), New York, 1932, pp. ix, 291.
Reviewed by Marcus in no. 543, p. 480 f.

659.* Heinemann, Isaak, *Philons griechische und jüdische Bildung. Kulturvergleichende Untersuchungen zu Philons Darstellung der jüdischen Gesetze*, Breslau, 1932, pp. 598.
†Reviewed by I. Heinemann, *Monatsschrift für Geschichte und Wissenschaft des Judentums*, LXXVI (1932), 267–269; by A. Posner, *Revue des études juives*, XCIII (1932), 98–102; by G. A. van den Bergh van Eysinga, *Nieuw theologisch Tijdschrift*, XXI (1932), 370–373; †by E. R. Goodenough, "The Education of Philo," *The Journal of Religion*, XIII (1933), 93–95; †by Jules Lebreton, *Recherches de science religieuse*, XXIII (1933), 331–334; †by Herbert Preisker, *Theologische Literaturzeitung*, LVIII (1933), 46–47; by S. Krauss, *Orientalistische Literaturzeitung*, XXXVII (1934), 519–523; †by Hans Leisegang, *Göttingische gelehrte Anzeigen*, CXCVI (1934), 130–141; and *by Marcus in no. 543, pp. 478–480.

660.* Pál, Vidor, *A görög és a zsidó gondolat találkozása Philon bölcseletében*, (*Elsö rész*), Budapest, 1932, pp. 29. (*Különlenyomat a Magyar Zsidó Szemle XLIX. évfolyamából.*)

661. Tollinton, R[ichard] B[artram], *The Alexandrine Teaching on the Universe, Four Lectures*, London, [1932], pp. 181.

662.* Trotti, Giovanni, *Filone Alessandrino*, Roma, 1932, pp. 58. (*Scuola di Filologia Classica della R. Università di Roma*, I, 2, 1.)
†Reviewed by E[rnesto] B[uonaiuti], *Religio: Rivista di studi religiosi*, X (1934), 280.

663. Bardy, G., "Philon le Juif," *Dictionnaire de théologie catholique*, Paris, XII, i, 1933, 1439–1456.

663a. Klausner, Joseph, *Philosophers and Thinkers: Investigations and Researches*, Tel-Aviv and Jerusalem, I, 5694 [1933/4], pp. viii, 244. In Hebrew. From the following review, which states that Philo is one of four philosophers discussed.
Reviewed by Israel Efros in *The Jewish Quarterly Review*, XXVIII (1937), 135–136.

664. Heinemann, Isaak, *C.-V. Zeitung. Blätter f. Dtschtum u. Judent. Org. d. Centralverein. d. Staatsbürg. jüd. Glaubens,* XIV (1935), No. 20, 2 Beibl., 1. (From *Bibliographie der deutschen Zeitschriften-Literatur,* LXXVII [1935], 546.)

664a.* Knox, W. L., "Pharisaism and Hellenism," in H. Loewe, *Judaism and Christianity,* London and New York, [1937], II, 61–111.

See also nos. 743–745, 772, 782, 784, 786, 906, 965, 1043.

V. JEWS IN GREEK AND ROMAN SOCIETY

665. Wesseling, Peter, *Diatribe de Judaeorum archontibus ad inscriptionem Berenicensem, et Dissertatio de evangeliis jussu Imp. Anastasii non emendatis in victorem Tunnunensem,* Trajecti ad Rhenum (Utrecht a. R.), 1738, pp. [xii], 173.

666. Vesterboe, Martinus, *Suetonius, Dio Cassius, Josephus et Philo, in imperio Caji Caligulae invicem et cum aliis comparati,* Hafniae, 1797. (From B.M.)

667.* Milman, Henry Hart, *The History of the Jews. From the Earliest Period Down to Modern Times,* London, 1829. See the 4th edit., London, 1866, II, 120, 121 n., 133–152.

668.† Frankel, [Z.], "Die Diaspora zur Zeit des zweiten Tempels," *Monatsschrift für Geschichte und Wissenschaft des Judenthums,* II (1853), 409–429, 449–463.

669.† Frankel, [Z.], "Die Juden unter den ersten römischen Kaisern," *Monatsschrift für Geschichte und Wissenschaft des Judenthums,* III (1854), 401–413, 439–450.

670.† [Frankel, Z.], "Das Alterthum über Judenthum und Juden," *Monatsschrift für Geschichte und Wissenschaft des Judenthums,* V (1856), 81–94.

671.† [Frankel, Z.], "Juden und Judenthum nach römischer Anschauung," *Monatsschrift für Geschichte und Wissenschaft des Judenthums,* IX (1860), 125–142.

672.† [Graetz, H.], "Die judäischen Ethnarchen oder Alabarchen in Alexandria," *Monatsschrift für Geschichte und Wissenschaft des Judenthums,* XXV (1876), 209–224, 241–254, 308–320.

673.† [Graetz, H.], "Präcisirung der Zeit für die, die Judäer betreffenden Vorgänge unter dem Kaiser Caligula," *Monatsschrift für Geschichte und Wissenschaft des Judenthums,* XXVI (1877), 97–107, 145–156.

674. Beloch, Julius, *Die Bevölkerung der griechisch-römischen Welt,* Leipzig, 1886, see esp. 245 n., 258.

675. Mommsen, Theodor, *The Provinces of the Roman Empire from Caesar to Diocletian,* translated by William P. Dickson, New York, 1887, II, 184 f., 208–213. (Theodor Mommsen, *The History of Rome.*)

676.* Amitaï, L. K., *Romains et Juifs. Étude critique sur les rapports publics et privés qui ont existé entre les Romains et les Juifs jusqu'à la prise de Jérusalem par Titus,* Paris, 1894, pp. vi, 136.

677. Seeck, O., "Alabarches," in Pauly-Wissowa, *Real-Encyclopädie der classischen Altertumswissenschaft,* I, 1894, 1271.

678. Reinach, Théodore, *Textes d'auteurs grecs et romains relatifs au Judaïsme réunis, traduits et annotés,* Paris, 1895, pp. xxii, 375. (Publications de la société des études juives, *Fontes rerum judaicarum,* I.)
†Reviewed by Hugo Willrich, *Berliner philologische Wochenschrift,* XV (1895), 987–989; and †by Leopold Cohn, *Monatsschrift für Geschichte und Wissenschaft des Judenthums,* XLI (1897), 285–288.

679.* Bertholet, Alfred, *Die Stellung der Israeliten und der Juden zu den Fremden,* Freiburg i. B. and Leipzig, 1896; see 274–291.

680.* Kaerst, Julius, *Studien zur Entwickelung und theoretischen Begründung der Monarchie im Altertum,* München and Leipzig, 1898, pp. 109. (*Historische Bibliothek,* VI.)

681.† Willrich, Hugo, *Judaica,* Göttingen, 1900, 127–130. (*Forschungen zur hellenistisch-jüdischen Geschichte und Litteratur.*)

682. Schürer, Emil, "Alexandria, Egypt—Ancient," *The Jewish Encyclopedia,* New York and London, I, 1901, 361–366.

683. Wendland, Paul, "Alexandrian Philosophy," *The Jewish Encyclopedia,* New York and London, I, 1901, 368–371.

684. Harnack, Adolf, "Das Judentum, seine Verbreitung und Entschränkung," *Die Mission und Ausbreitung des Christentums in den ersten drei Jahrhunderten,* Leipzig, 1902, 1–12.
Second edition, Leipzig, 1905; third edition, *ibid.,* 1915. English translation (of the second edition): *The Mission and Expansion of Christianity in the First Three Centuries,* by James Moffatt, London and New York, 1908, I, 1–18.

685.† Dobschütz, Ernst von, "Jews and Antisemites in Ancient Alexandria," *The American Journal of Theology,* VIII (1904), 728–755.

686. Stähelin, Felix, *Der Antisemitismus des Altertums in seiner Entstehung und Entwicklung,* Basel, 1905, pp. 54.

687. Wilcken, Ulrich, "Zum Alexandrinischen Antisemitismus," *Abhandlungen der philologisch-historischen Klasse der Königlich Sächsischen Gesellschaft der Wissenschaften,* XXVII (1909), 783–839.
*Republished, Leipzig, 1909, with same pagination.

688. Juster, Jean, *Examen critique des sources relatives à la condition juridique des Juifs dans l'empire romain,* Thèse (Paris), Paris, 1911, pp. viii, 140.

689. Juster, Jean, *Les droits politiques des Juifs dans l'empire romain,* Thèse (Paris), Paris, 1912, pp. xiii, 104.

690. Motzo, Bacchisio, "La condizione giuridica dei Giudei di Allessandria sotto i Lagidi e i Romani," *Atti della R. Accademia delle Scienze di Torino,* XLVIII (1912–1913), 577–598.

*Reprinted, Turin, 1913, pp. 22.
Reviewed by Otto Stählin, *Berliner philologische Wochenschrift,* XXXVI (1916), 935.

691. Motzo, Bacchisio, "Il κατὰ Ἰουδαίων di Apione," *Atti della R. Accademia delle Scienze di Torino,* XLVIII (1912–1913), 459–468.
Reprinted, Turin, 1913, pp. 10. (From *Bollettino delle pubblicazioni italiane . . . 1913,* Firenze, 1914, no. 4908.)
Reviewed by Otto Stählin, *Berliner philologische Wochenschrift,* XXXVI (1916), 934.

692.* Juster, Jean, *Les Juifs dans l'empire romain: leur condition juridique, économique et sociale,* Paris, 1914, 2 vols., xviii, 510, viii, 338.

693.* Askowith, Dora, *The Toleration of the Jews Under Julius Caesar and Augustus,* Diss. (Columbia), New York, 1915, pp. xiv, 235.

694. Klaussner, J., *Historia Yisreelit* (Jewish History), Odessa and Jerusalem, 1915–25, 4 vols.

695.* Radin, Max, *The Jews among the Greeks and Romans,* Philadelphia, 1915, pp. 421.

696. Weber, W., "Eine Gerichtsverhandlung vor Kaiser Traian," *Hermes,* L (1915), 47–92.

697. Krauss, Samuel, *Synagogale Altertümer,* Berlin and Wien, 1922, pp. viii, 470.

698.† Engers, Maurits, "Die staatsrechtliche Stellung der alexandrinischen Juden," *Klio,* XVIII (1922–1923), 79–90.

699. Loewe, Herbert, "The Petrie-Hirschfeld Papyri," *The Journal of Theological Studies,* XXIV (1922–1923), 126–141.

700. Modona, Aldo Neppi, "Antichissimi papiri ebraici rinvenuti recentemente a Ossirinco," "Ancora sui papiri ebraici di Ossirinco Petrie-Hirschfeld," *Aegyptus,* IV (1923), 31–37, 125–131.

701. Bell, H[arold] Idris, *Jews and Christians in Egypt: The Jewish Troubles in Alexandria and the Athanasian Controversy,* [London], 1924, pp. 140.

702. Fuchs, Leo, *Die Juden Aegyptens in ptolemäischer und römischer Zeit,* Wien, 1924, pp. 156.

703. Bell, H[arold] I[dris], *Juden und Griechen im römischen Alexandreia,* Leipzig, 1926, pp. 52. (Wilhelm Schubart, *Beihefte zum Alten Orient,* IX.)
Reviewed in no. 537, LXXIII (1929), 430.

704. Engers, M[aurits], "Πολίτευμα," *Mnemosyne,* N.S. LIV (1926), 154–161.

705.* Forster, E. M., "Philo's Little Trip," *Pharos and Pharillon,* 3rd edit., Richmond (Surrey), 1926, 32–36.

706. Zielinski, Thaddée, "L'empereur Claude et l'idée de la domination mon-

diale des Juifs," *Revue de l'Université de Bruxelles*, XXXII (1926–1927), 128–148.

707. La Piana, George, "Foreign Groups in Rome during the First Centuries of the Empire," *The Harvard Theological Review*, XX (1927), 183–403.

708.* Margolis, Max L., and Marx, Alexander, *A History of the Jewish People*, Philadelphia, 1927, 287–296.

709.* Hopkins, Clark, "The Date and Trial of Isidorus and Lampo before Claudius, B.G.U. II, 511, and P. Cair. 10448," *Yale Classical Studies*, New Haven, I (1928), 169–177.

710. Jacob, B., "Antisemitismus." I. "Im Altertum," *Encyclopaedia Judaica*, Berlin, II, [1928], 957–972.

711. Laqueur, [R.], "Manethon," in Pauly-Wissowa-Kroll, *Real-Encyclopädie der classischen Altertumswissenschaft*, XIV, i, 1928, 1060–1101.

712. Leon, H. J., "The Jewish Catacombs and Inscriptions of Rome: An Account of their Discovery and Subsequent History," *Hebrew Union College Annual*, Cincinnati, V (1928), 299–314.

713. Heinemann, Isaak, "Ursprung und Wesen des Antisemitismus im Altertum," *Festgabe zum zehnjährigen Bestehen der Akademie für die Wissenschaft des Judentums*, Berlin, [1929], 76–91.

714. Leon, Harry Joshua, "New Material about the Jews of Ancient Rome," *The Jewish Quarterly Review*, N.S. XX (1929–1930), 301–312.

715. Dessau, Hermann, *Geschichte der römischen Kaiserzeit*, Berlin, II, ii, 1930, 667–676, 706–831.

716. Frey, Jean-Baptiste, "Les Communautés juives à Rome aux premiers temps de l'Église," *Recherches de Science Religieuse*, XX (1930), 269–297; XXI (1931), 129–168.

717. Friedmann, Kalman, "Le fonti per la storia degli Ebrei di Cirenaica nell' antichità," *Miscellanea di studi ebraici in memoria H. P. Chajes*, Florence, 1930, 39–55.

718.† Momigliano, Arnaldo, "Aspetti dell'antisemitismo alessandrino in due opere di Filone," *La rassegna mensile di Israel*, V (1930), 275–286.

719. Tscherikover, A. [Victor], *Ha-Yehudim ve-ha-Yevanim ba-tekufah ha-hellenistit* (Jews and Greeks in the Hellenistic Period), [Tel-Aviv, 1930], pp. 416.

720. Zmigryder-Konopka, Zdzisław, "Les Romains et la circoncision des Juifs," *Eos*, XXXIII (1930–1931), 334–350.

721. Frey, J[ean]-B[aptiste], "Le judaïsme à Rome aux premiers temps de l'Église," *Biblica*, XII (1931), 129–156.

722. Heinemann, I[saak], "Antisemitismus," in Pauly-Wissowa-Kroll, *Real-*

Encyclopädie der classischen Altertumswissenschaft, Suppl. vol. V, 1931, 3–43.

723. Ostersetzer, J., "On the Legal Status of the Alexandrian Jews in the Roman Period" (Hebrew), *Sepher ha-Yobel li-kebod Dr. Mordecai Zeeb Braude,* Warsaw, 1931, 75–122. (From no. 800.)

724.* Fink, Walther, *Der Einfluss der jüdischen Religion auf die griechisch-römische,* Diss. (Bonn), Bonn, 1932, pp. 117.

725. Janne, H., "Un passage controversé de la lettre de Claude aux Alexandrins," *Revue archéologique,* 5th S. XXXV (1932), 268–281.

726. Lewy, Hans, "Hekataios von Abdera περὶ 'Ιουδαίων," *Zeitschrift für die neutestamentliche Wissenschaft,* XXXI (1932), 117–132.

727.* Sachs, Hanns, *Bubi Caligula,* 2nd edit., Wien, 1932, pp. 150.

728. Segrè, A., "Note sullo *Status Civitatis* degli ebrei nell' Egitto tolemaico e imperiale," *Bulletin de la Société Royale d'Archéologie d'Alexandrie,* N.S., VIII (1933), 143–182.

729. Silberschlag, E., "The Earliest Record of Jews in Asia Minor," *Journal of Biblical Literature,* LII (1933), 66–77.

730. Friedmann, Kalman, "Condizioni e cultura degli Ebrei di Cirenaica nell' antichità," *Gironale della Società Asiatica Italiana,* N.S., II, iv (1934), 323–334.

731.* Harmon, Austin M., "Egyptian Property-Returns," *Yale Classical Studies,* New Haven and London, IV (1934), 133–230; see esp. 143 n. and 144 n.

732. Lepape, A., "Tiberius Iulius Alexander, Préfet d'Alexandrie et d'Egypte," *Bulletin de la Société Royale d'Archéologie d'Alexandrie,* no. 29 (N.S. VIII, 3) (1934), 331–341.

733. Stein, Edmund Menahem, "Pseudo-Hecateus, His Time, and the Bearing of His Book on the Jews and Their Country" (Hebrew), *Siyyon,* VI (1934), 1–11.

734. Frey, Jean-Baptiste, *Corpus inscriptionum Iudaicarum: Recueil des inscriptions juives qui vont du IIIe siècle avant Jésus-Christ au VIIe siècle de notre ère,* Vol. I., Europe, Città del Vaticano, 1936, pp. cxliv, 687. (*Sussidi allo studio delle antichità cristiane, pubblicati per cura del Pontificio Istituto di Archeologia Cristiana,* I.)
Frey's bibliography is valuable for his own earlier publications on Jewish epigraphy (largely subsumed in this volume), and for the field in general.
Reviewed in no. 798.

735. Wenger, Leopold, *Nationales, griechisches und römisches Recht in Aegypten,* Milan, 1936.

Reprint from the *Atti del IV Congresso Internazionale di Papirologia* (Firenzo, Aprile-Maggio, 1935), 159–181.

736. Lewy, Hans, "Aethiopier und Juden in der antiken Literatur," *Monatsschrift für Geschichte und Wissenschaft des Judentums,* LXXXI (1937), 65–71.

737. Marmorstein, A., "The Synagogue of Claudius Tiberius Polycharmus in Stobi," *The Jewish Quarterly Review,* N.S. XXVII (1937), 373–384.

VI. GENERAL STUDIES ON HELLENIS-TIC JUDAISM

738. Guerike, Henric. Ernest. Ferd., *De schola quae Alexandriae floruit, cate-chetica commentatio historica et theologica,* Halle, 1824–5, parts 1 and 2, pp. 119; viii, 456.

739. Scheffer, Guilielmus, *Quaestionum Philonianarum. Particula I, sive de ingenio moribusque Judaeorum per Ptolemaeorum saecula. Particula II, De usu Philonis in interpretatione Novi Testamenti,* Marburg, 1829, 1831, pp. 52, 136.

740. Gruppe, O[tto] F[r.], *Ueber die Fragmente des Archytas und der äl-teren Pythagoreer, Eine Preisschrift,* Berlin, 1840, pp. x, 161.
    Cf. Zeller (no. 921), III, ii, 1903, 123, n. 5, who rejects Gruppe's theory here set forth that these fragments are of Hellenistic Jewish origin.

741. Kirschbaum, Eli 'ës. Sina, *Der jüd. Alexandrinismus, eine Erfindung christlicher Lehrer, oder Beiträge zur Kritik jüd. Geschichte u[nd] Literatur,* (published in separate parts), Leipzig, 1841–42. (From no. 528.)

742. Herzfeld, L., "Von den ägyptischen Juden," *Geschichte des Volkes Jis-rael von der Zerstörung des ersten Tempels bis zur Einsetzung des Makkabäers Schimon zum hohen Preister und Fürster,* Braunschweig, 1847, III, 436–579.
    Abbreviated in smaller edition with same title, Leipzig, 1870, 452–510.

743. Lutterbeck, Joh. Ant. Bernh., *Die neutestamentlichen Lehrbegriffe oder Untersuchungen über das Zeitalter der Religionswende, die Vorstufen des Christenthums und die erste Gestaltung desselben,* Mainz, 1852, I: "Der essenische Lehrbegriff," 270–322; "Der jüdisch-hellenistische Lehrbegriff," 392–417.

744.* Biet, F. Joseph, *Essai historique et critique sur l'école juive d'Alexan-drie,* Paris, 1854, pp. viii, 343.

745.* Nicolas, Michel, *Des doctrines religieuses des Juifs pendant les deux siècles antérieurs à l'ère chrétienne,* Paris, 1860, pp. viii, 404.

746. Geiger, Abraham, *Das Judenthum und seine Geschichte,* Breslau, I, 1864, 74–87.
    Translated by Maurice Mayer, *Judaism and its History,* New York, 1865; see 140–168.

747. Schultz, H., "Die jüdische Religionsphilosophie bis zur Zerstörung Jeru-salems," Gelzers *Protestantische Monatsblätter,* XXIV (1864), Heft 4. (From no. 539.)

748. Holtzmann, Heinr[ich], "Die Diaspora und das alexandrinische Judenthum," *Judenthum und Christenthum im Zeitalter der apokryphischen
und neutestamentlichen Literatur*, Leipzig, 1867, 33–89. (Georg Weber
and Heinr. Holtzmann, *Geschichte des Volkes Israel und der Entstehung des Christenthums*, II.)

749.† Lipsius, "Alexandrinische Religionsphilosophie," in Daniel Schenkel,
*Bibel-Lexikon: Realwörterbuch zum Handgebrauch für Geistliche
und Gemeindeglieder*, Leipzig, I, 1869, 85–99.

750. Freudenthal, J., *Alexander Polyhistor und die von ihm erhaltenen Reste
judäischer und samaritanischer Geschichtswerke*, Breslau, 1875, pp.
238. (*Hellenistische Studien*, Heft 1, 2.)
Reviewed by Langen, *Theologisches Literaturblatt*, Bonn, X (1875),
298–299.

751. Siegfried, Carl, "Der jüdische Hellenismus: Ein Rückblick auf seine
geschichtliche Entwickelung mit Beziehung auf die neuesten Forschungen innerhalb seines Gebietes," *Zeitschrift für wissenschaftliche
Theologie*, XVIII (1875), 465–489.

752.† [Graetz, H.], "Der angebliche judäische Peripatetiker Aristobulos und
seine Schriften," *Monatsschrift für Geschichte und Wissenschaft des
Judenthums*, XXVII (1878), 49–60, 97–109.

753. Jellinek, Ad., "Babylon, Alexandrien und Palästina," in no. 490, 65–71.

754. Joël, M., *Blicke in die Religionsgeschichte zu Anfang des zweiten christlichen Jahrhunderts*, Breslau, 1880, 1883, 2 vols., pp. vii, 177; x, 190.

755.† Ziegler, "Über die Entstehung der alexandrinischen Philosophie," *Ver-
handlungen der sechsunddreissigsten Versammlung deutscher Philo-
logen und Schulmänner in Karlsruhe, . . . 1882*, Leipzig, 1883, 136–
145.

756.† Hild, J.-A., "Les Juifs à Rome devant l'opinion et dans la littérature,"
Revue des études juives, VIII (1884), 1–37; XI (1885), 18–59, 161–194.

757. Karpeles, Gustav, *Geschichte der jüdischen Literatur*, Berlin, 1886, I,
206–262; 2nd edit., Berlin, 1909, 196–201.

758. Siegfried, C[arl], "Bedeutung und Schicksal des Hellenismus in dem
Leben des jüdischen Volkes," *Jahrbücher für protestantische Theologie*, XII (1886), 228–253.

759.* Bois, Henri, *Essai sur les origines de la philosophie judéo-alexandrine*,
thèse (Montauban), Toulouse, 1890, pp. 414.

760.* Ryle, Herbert Edward, and James, Montague Rhodes, Ψαλμοὶ Σολο-
μῶντος. *Psalms of the Pharisees, commonly called The Psalms of Solomon. The text newly revised from all the MSS. Edited, with introduction, English translation, notes*, Cambridge (England), 1891, pp. xciv,
176.

761.† Neel, J.-E., "Le philonisme avant Philon," *Revue de théologie et de philosophie*, XXV (1892), 417–433.

762.* Friedländer, M[oriz], *Das Judenthum in der vorchristlichen griechischen Welt. Ein Beitrag zur Entstehungsgeschichte des Christenthums*, Wien and Leipzig, 1897, pp. 74.

763.* Friedländer, M[oriz], *Der vorchristliche jüdische Gnosticismus*, Göttingen, 1898, pp. x, 123.

764. Ludwich, Arthurus, *De Philonis carmine graeco-iudaico*, Königsberg, 1900, pp. 8.
Reviewed by Paul Wendland, *Berliner philologische Wochenschrift*, XX (1900), 1575–1576.

765.† Deissmann, Adolf, "Die Hellenisierung des semitischen Monotheismus," *Neue Jahrbücher für das klassische Altertum, Geschichte und Deutsche Literatur*, XI (1903), 161–177.

766.* Friedländer, Moriz, *Die religiösen Bewegungen innerhalb des Judentums im Zeitalter Jesu*, Berlin, 1905, pp. xxx, 380.

767. Hirsch, S. A., "The Temple of Onias," *Jews' College Jubilee Volume*, London, 1906, 39–80.

768. Wendland, Paul, *Die hellenistisch-römische Kultur in ihren Beziehungen zu Judentum und Christentum;* 1st edit. 1907; 2nd and 3rd edits., Tübingen, 1912, 192–211. (*Handbuch zum Neuen Testament*, I, ii.)

769.* Friedländer, Moriz, *Synagoge und Kirche in ihren Anfängen*, Berlin, 1908, pp. xxii, 247.

770.* Krüger, Paul, *Hellenismus und Judentum im neutestamentlichen Zeitalter*, Leipzig, 1908, pp. 47.

771.* Stearns, Wallace Nelson, *Fragments from Graeco-Jewish Writers collected and edited with brief introductions and notes*, Chicago, 1908, pp. ix, 126.

772.* Petrie, W. M. Flinders, *Personal Religion in Egypt before Christianity*, London and New York, 1909, pp. ix, 174. (*Harper's Library of Living Thought.*)

773.* Focke, Friedrich, *Die Entstehung der Weisheit Salomos. Ein Beitrag zur Geschichte des jüdischen Hellenismus*, Göttingen, 1913, pp. 132. (*Forschungen zur Religion und Literatur des Alten und Neuen Testaments*, N.F. 5.)

774. Motzo, Bacchisio, "Aristea," *Atti della Reale Accademia delle Scienze di Torino*, L (1914–1915), 202–225, 547–570.
*Republished, Turin, 1915.

775. Nairne, A[lexander], *The Alexandrine Gospel (Sirach, Wisdom, Philo, the Epistle to the Hebrews)*, London and New York, 1917, pp. 126. (*Liverpool Diocesan Board of Divinity Publications*, XVII.)

776.* Bentwich, Norman, *Hellenism,* Philadelphia, 1919, pp. 386. (*Movements in Judaism.*)

777. Geffcken, Johannes, *Der Ausgang des griechisch-römischen Heidentums,* Heidelberg, 1920, pp. 346. (Wilhelm Streitberg, *Religionswissenschaftliche Bibliothek,* VI.) Nachtrag by Geffcken, Heidelberg, 1929, 347–365.
† Reviewed by I. Heinemann, *Monatsschrift für Geschichte und Wissenschaft des Judentums,* LXVII (1923), 281.

778.* Stählin, Otto, "Die hellenistisch-jüdische Litteratur," in Wilhelm von Christ, *Geschichte der griechischen Litteratur,* 6th edit. by Wilhelm Schmid, München, II, 1920, 535–656. (Iwan von Müller, *Handbuch der klassischen Altertums-Wissenschaft,* VII, i.)
For Philo see 625–655.

779. Gressmann, Hugo, "Hellenistisches oder rabbinisches Judentum?" *Theologische Blätter,* [N.F.] II (1923), 144–6.

780.† Lichtenstein, Hans, "Zur Geschichte der Juden in Alexandreia," *Monatsschrift für Geschichte und Wissenschaft des Judentums,* LXIX (1925), 357–361.

781.* Bentwich, Norman, *Josephus,* Philadelphia, 1926, pp. 266.

782.† Bousset, Wilhelm. *Die Religion des Judentums im späthellenistischen Zeitalter,* 3rd edit. by Hugo Gressmann, Tübingen, 1926, 432–468, and *passim* (see Index). (Hans Lietzmann, *Handbuch zum Neuen Testament,* 21.)

783.* Fairweather, William, *The Background of the Gospels; or, Judaism in the Period between the Old and New Testaments. The Twentieth Series of the Cunningham Lectures,* 4th edit., Edinburgh, 1926, pp. xxiv, 456.

784. Bergmann, Juda, "Das Judentum in der hellenistisch-römischen Zeit," in *Entwicklungsstufen der jüdischen Religion,* Giessen, 1927, 27–42. (*Vorträge des Institutum Judaicum an der Universität Berlin,* I, 1925–26.)

785.* Bevan, Edwyn R., "Hellenistic Judaism," in Edwyn R. Bevan and Charles Singer, *The Legacy of Israel,* Oxford, 1927, 42–67.

786.* Gressmann, Hugo, "Jewish Life in Ancient Rome," *Jewish Studies in Memory of Israel Abrahams by the Faculty and Visiting Teachers of the Jewish Institute of Religion,* published under the auspices of the Alexander Kohut Memorial Foundation, New York, 1927, 170–191.

787. Tarn, W. W., "Hellenism and the Jews," *Hellenistic Civilisation,* London, 1927, 166–192.

788.* Vogelstein, Hermann, "Einige Probleme der jüdischen Geschichte der Zeit des zweiten Tempels," *Jewish Studies in Memory of Israel Abra-*

hams by the Faculty and Visiting Teachers of the Jewish Institute of Religion, published under the auspices of the Alexander Kohut Memorial Foundation, New York, 1927, 416–425.

789.* Tracy, Sterling, "III Maccabees and Pseudo-Aristeas, A Study," *Yale Classical Studies*, New Haven, I (1928), 239–252.

790. Lewy, H[ans], "Hellenismus," *Encyclopaedia Judaica*, Berlin, VII, [1931], 1141–1149.

791.† Momigliano, Arnaldo, "Intorno al *Contro Apione*," *Rivista di filologia e di istruzione classica*, N.S. IX, or LIX (1931), 485–503.

792. Zoller, I., "Il significato delle pitture nelle catacombe giudaiche a Roma," *Studi e materiali di storia delle religioni*, VII (N.S. IV) (1931), 144–152. (*Pubblicati della Scuola di Studi Storico-Religiosi della R. Università di Roma.*)

793. Wieneke, Joseph, *Ezechielis Iudaei poetae Alexandrini fabulae quae inscribitur* Ἐξαγωγή *fragmenta recensuit atque enarravit*, Diss. (Münster), Münster, 1931, pp. xii, 135.

†Reviewed by I. Heinemann, *Monatsschrift für Geschichte und Wissenschaft des Judentums*, LXXVI (1932), 269.

794.* Angus, S., *The Environment of Early Christianity*, New York, 1932; see Index.

795.* Heinemann, I[saak], *Die griechische Weltanschauungslehre bei Juden und Römern*, Berlin, 1932, pp. 48. (*Morgenreihe*, 10.)

Reprinted from *Der Morgen*, VII, 407–422, 488–503, and VIII, 42–54.

796. Bonsirven, J., *Les idées juives au temps de Notre-Seigneur*, Paris, 1934, pp. 220.

Reviewed by E. Dhorme, *Revue critique d'histoire et de littérature*, N.S. CI (1934), 105 f.; and in *The Jewish Quarterly Review*, N.S. XXVI (1935–1936), 411.

797. Meecham, Henry G., *The Letter of Aristeas: A Linguistic Study with Special Reference to the Greek Bible*, Manchester, 1935, pp. xxi, 355.

798.* Goodenough, Erwin R[amsdell], "Archeology and Jewish History," *Journal of Biblical Literature*, LV (1936), 211–220.

798a. Jean, Charles-F., *Le milieu biblique avant Jésus-Christ*. III, *Les idées religieuses et morales*, Paris, 1936, 595–616.

Reviewed by W. F. Albright in *Journal of Biblical Literature*, LVI (1937), 417 f.

799.* Shroyer, Montgomery J., "Alexandrian Jewish Literalists," *Journal of Biblical Literature*, LV (1936), 261–284.

*Reprinted with same pagination.

799a. Zucker, Hans, *Studien zur jüdischen Selbstverwaltung im Altertum*, Berlin, 1936, pp. 200.

800.* Baron, Salo Wittmayer, *A Social and Religious History of the Jews,* New York, 1937, 3 vols.; see I, 128–224 and Index in vol. III *s.v.* "Philo."

801. Goodenough, Erwin R[amsdell], "New Light on Hellenistic Judaism," *Journal of Bible and Religion,* V (1937), 18–28. *Reprinted, pp. 12.

802. Goodenough, Erwin R[amsdell], "Symbolism in Hellenistic Jewish Art: The Problem of Method," *Journal of Biblical Literature,* LVI (1937), 103–114.

See also nos. 570, 593 (§33), 668–672, 679, 1340 (pp. 353–402).

VII. STUDIES ON PHILO'S WRITINGS

803.† Dähne, August Ferdinand, "Einige Bemerkungen über die Schriften des Juden Philo, angeknüpft an eine Untersuchung über deren ursprüngliche Anordung," *Theologische Studien und Kritiken,* VI (1833), 984–1040.

804. Grossmann, Chr[istian] Gottl[ob] Orthob. [Leberecht], *De Philonis Iudaei operum continua serie et ordine chronologico comment.,* Leipzig, 1841, 1842, pp. 28, 31.
†Translated by Julius Fürst: "Dr. Grossmann's Abhandlung über die Reihenfolge und die chronologische Ordnung der Schriften des Juden Philo," *Literaturblatt des Orients,* II (1841), 795–800, 807–810; III (1842), 11–13, 29–32, 45–48, 108–110, 125–126, 157–160, 166–176, 183–186.

805.* [Mai, Angelo], *Patrum nova bibliotheca,* Rome, 1853, VI, ii, 67 f.

806. Christ, Wilhelm, *Geschichte der griechischen Litteratur,* München, 1889, pp. viii, 663. (Iwan von Müller, *Handbuch der klassischen Altertums-Wissenschaft,* VII.)
Sixth edition by Wilhelm Schmid, München, II, 1, 1920, 625 f., and Index in II, ii, 1924.

807.† Massebieau, M. L., "Le classement des oeuvres de Philon," *Bibliothèque de l'École des Hautes Études . . . Sciences religieuses,* Paris, I (1889), 1–91.
Reviewed by C. Siegfried, *Deutsche Litteraturzeitung,* XI (1890), 977–979.

808.† Cohn, Leopold, "Einteilung und Chronologie der Schriften Philos," *Philologus,* Supplbd. VII, iii (1899), 387–435.
Published separately, Leipzig, 1899, pp. 51.
Reviewed by J. R. Asmus, *Wochenschrift für klassische Philologie,* XVI (1899), 1336–1341; by M. F., *Literarisches Centralblatt für Deutschland,* [L] (1899), 1262 f.; by C. Siegfried, *Deutsche Litteraturzeitung,* XX (1899), 1708–1710; and by Otto Stählin, *Berliner philologische Wochenschrift,* XX (1900), 486–490.

809.† Hart, J. H. A., "Philo of Alexandria," *The Jewish Quarterly Review,* XVII (1904–1905), 78–122, 726–746; XVIII (1905–1906), 330–346; XX (1907–1908), 294–329.

810. Massebieau, L. and Bréhier, É[mile], "Essai sur la chronologie de la vie et des oeuvres de Philon," *Revue de l'histoire des religions,* LIII (1906), 25–64, 164–185, 267–289. (*Annales du Musée Guimet.*)
*Reprinted, Paris, 1906, pp. 84.

811.* Lawlor, Hugh Jackson, *Eusebiana: Essays on the Ecclesiastical History of Eusebius Bishop of Caesarea,* Oxford, 1912, 138–145.

812.* Adler, Maximilian, *Studien zu Philon von Alexandreia,* Breslau, 1929, pp. 102.

†Reviewed by I. Heinemann, *Monatsschrift für Geschichte und Wissenschaft des Judentums,* LXXIII (1929), 437–439; †by Paul Heinisch, *Theologische Revue,* XXIX (1930), 238; by A. Puech, *Revue de philologie, de littérature et d'histoire anciennes,* IV (III. S.) (1930), 413–414; †by Otto Stählin, *Philologische Wochenschrift,* L (1930), 867–871; †by H. Windisch, *Theologische Literaturzeitung,* LV (1930), 509–510; by Willy Theiler, *Gnomon,* VII (1931), 39–43; by Hans Leisegang, *Theologisches Literaturblatt,* LIII (1932), 1–3; and *by Marcus in no. 543, pp. 470–471.

813.† Priessnig, Anton, "Die literarische Form der Patriarchenbiographien des Philon von Alexandrien," *Monatsschrift für Geschichte und Wissenschaft des Judentums,* LXXIII (1929), 143–155.

*Reviewed by Marcus in no. 543, p. 473 f.

814.* Goodenough, Erwin R[amsdell], "Philo's Exposition of the Law and his De vita Mosis," *The Harvard Theological Review,* XXVI (1933), 109–125.

*Reviewed by Marcus in no. 543, p. 485 f.

815.* Braun, Martin, *Griechischer Roman und hellenistische Geschichtschreibung,* Frankfurt am Main, 1934, *passim.* (Walter F. Otto, *Frankfurter Studien zur Religion und Kultur der Antike,* VI.)

816. Adler, Maximilian, "Das philonische Fragment De deo," *Monatsschrift für Geschichte und Wissenschaft des Judentums,* LXXX (1936), 163–170.

See also nos. 778, 1429.

VIII. STUDIES ON INDIVIDUAL TREATISES OF PHILO

817.* Possevinus, Antonius, *Apparatus ad omnium gentium historiam. Expenduntur historici graeci, latini, et alii. Quonam modo per seriem temporum legendi, & ad vsum adhibendi. Quinam veraces, aut supposititii, vel mendaces, vel labe aliqua, aut haeresibus aspersi,* Venetiis, 1597, fol. 142v.

818. Gottleber, Ioannes Christoph., *Animadversiones historico-criticae ad Legationem Philonis,* Five programs, Meissen, 1773-75.

819.* Ausfeld, Ricardus, *De libro* περὶ τοῦ πάντα σπουδαῖον εἶναι ἐλεύθερον *qui inter Philonis Alexandrini opera fertur,* Diss. (Göttingen), Göttingen, 1887, pp. 58.
   Reviewed by Johannes Dräseke, *Wochenschrift für klassische Philologie,* IV (1887), 1606-1610; by A. Harnack, *Theologische Literaturzeitung,* XII (1887), 493-495; and in *Literarisches Centralblatt für Deutschland,* [XXXIX] (1888), 1258-1259.

820.† Conybeare, Fred. C., "The Lost Works of Philo," *The Academy,* XXXVIII (1890), 32.

821. Wendland, Paul, *Philos Schrift über die Vorsehung. Ein Beitrag zur Geschichte der nacharistotelischen Philosophie,* Berlin, 1892, pp. vii, 120.
   Reviewed by F. Čáda, *Listy filologické,* XIX (1892), 395-397; by Fr., *Literarisches Centralblatt für Deutschland,* [XLIV] (1893), 68-69; by Lucien Herr, *Revue critique d'histoire et de littérature,* XXVII, i (N.S. XXV) (1893), 259, 262-263; by Karl Praechter, *Berliner philologische Wochenschrift,* XIII (1893), 615-618, 650-654; and by Siegfried Reiter, *Zeitschrift für die österreichischen Gymnasien,* XLIV (1893), 108-109.

822.* Krell, Emil, *Philo,* περὶ τοῦ πάντα σπουδαῖον εἶναι ἐλεύθερον, *die Echtheitsfrage,* Programm, Augsburg, 1896, pp. 38.

823. Motzo, Bacchisio, "Le Ὑποθετικά di Filone," *Atti della R[eale] Accademia delle Scienze di Torino,* XLVII (1911-1912), 556-573.
   *Republished, Turin, 1912, pp. 20.
   Reviewed by Otto Stählin, *Berliner philologische Wochenschrift,* XXXVI (1916), 933-934.

824.* Tappe, Georgius, *De Philonis libro qui inscribitur* Ἀλέξανδρος ἢ περὶ τοῦ λόγον ἔχειν τὰ ἄλογα ζῷα: *Quaestiones selectae,* Diss. (Göttingen), Göttingen, 1912, pp. 80.

239

825.* Reiter, Siegfried, "'Ἀρετή und der Titel von Philos 'Legatio,'" Ἐπι-τύμβιον, *Heinrich Swoboda dargebracht,* Reichenberg, 1927, 228–237.

826. Krokiewicz, Adam, "De duobus Philonis libris Romae scriptis," *Eos,* XXXIII (1930–1931), 395–410.

827.† Marcus, Ralph, "The Armenian Translation of Philo's *Quaestiones in Genesim et Exodum,*" *Journal of Biblical Literature,* XLIX (1930), 61–64.

827a. Leisegang, Hans, "Philons Schrift über die Ewigkeit der Welt," *Philologus: Zeitschrift für das klassische Altertum,* XCII (1937), 156–176.

See also nos. 1099, 1218, 1228, 1266, 1279, 1285, 1290, 1291, 1304, 1312, 1597–1603.

IX. STUDIES ON TEXT AND LEXI-COGRAPHY

828.* Augustinus Eugubinus (Steuchus), *Recognitio Veteris Testamenti ad hebraicam veritatem, collata etiam editione Septuaginta interprete cum ipsa veritate hebraica, nostraq̇: translatione, Cum expositione Hebraeorum ac Graecorum, qui passim toto opere citantur. Vbi quantum fieri potest, monstrantur loci, qui in editione latina, & graeca discrepant a codicibus hebraeorum,* Venetiis in Aedibus Aldi & Andreae Soceri, 1529, 212 leaves, 4to; see 5r, 21v, 102v, 103r, 104r and v, 105v, 106r, 107v, 111r and v, 114v, 144r.

829. Loesnerus, Christophorus Fridericus, *Lectionum Philonianarum Specimen,* Leipzig, [1758], pp. 32.

830.† Creuzer, Fr[iedrich], "Zur Kritik der Schriften des Juden Philo," *Theologische Studien und Kritiken,* V (1832), 3-43.
Reprinted in his *Deutsche Schriften, neue und verbesserte,* Leipzig and Darmstadt, 1847, III, ii, 407-446.

831.* Müller, J. G., *Ueber die Texteskritik der Schriften des Juden Philo,* Basel, 1839, pp. 23.

832. Cobet, C[arolus] G[abriel], *Variae lectiones quibus continentur observationes criticae in scriptores graecos,* 2nd edit., Lugduni Batavorum (Leyden), 1873, 129 f.

833.* Holwerda, J. H., "Annotatio critica in Philonem Judaeum," *Verslagen en Mededeelingen der Koninklijke Akademie van Wetenschappen. Afdeeling Letterkunde,* II, iii (1873), 271-288.

834.† Condos (Κόντος), Constantinos S., "Συμμικτὰ κριτικά," *Bulletin de correspondance hellénique,* I (1877), 67, 77-78 (notes on *Virt.,* 67; *Legat.,* 343); II (1878), 237-239 (note on *Mundo,* 9).

835.† Condos (Κόντος), Constantinos S., "Κριτικὰ καὶ γραμματικά §8" (note to *Conf.,* 185), 'Αθηναίον, VII (1878), 366-369.

836.* Holwerda, J. H., "Annotatio critica in Philonis Judaei librum de posteritate Caini," *Verslagen en Mededeelingen der Koninklijke Akademie van Wetenschappen, Afdeeling Letterkunde,* III, i (1884), 274-286.

837. Hanssen, Fridericus, "Emendationes Philoneae," (note to *Opif.,* §§ 80, 158, 170), *The American Journal of Philology,* IX (1888), 463.

838. Massebieau, L., "Encore un mot sur la vie contemplative," *Revue de l'histoire des religions,* XVII (1888), 230-232. (*Annales de Musée Guimet.*)

839.† Wendland, Paul, "Philo's Schrift περὶ τοῦ πάντα σπουδαῖον εἶναι ἐλεύθερον," *Archiv für Geschichte der Philosophie*, I (1888), 509–517.

840. Conybeare, Frederick Cornwallis, *Specimen lectionum armeniacarum, or a Review of the Fragments of Philo Judaeus*, as newly edited by James Rendel Harris, privately printed, Oxford, 1889, pp. 15. (From no. 536.)

841.* Hatch, Edwin, *Essays in Biblical Greek*, Oxford, 1889, pp. x, 293; see for Philo's use of διαθήκη, 48; παράκλητος, πίστις, 82–88; "Psychological terms in Philo," 109–130; "Early Quotations from the Septuagint," 131–202.

842.† Cohn, Leopold, "Zur indirekten Ueberlieferung Philo's und der älteren Kirchenväter," *Jahrbücher für protestantische Theologie*, XVIII (1892), 475–492 (pp. 490–492 are a Nachtrag by P. Wendland).
Reviewed by P. Wendland, *Byzantinische Zeitschrift*, I (1892), 604–609.

843. Conybeare, Fred. C., "Note on the Philonean Reading of two Passages in the Timaeus, 38 B and 28 B," *The Journal of Philology*, XXI (1893), 71–72.

844.* Cohn, Leopold, *Diassorinos und Turnebus. Ein Beitrag zur Textgeschichte der Philonischen Schriften*, Breslau, 1896, pp. 15.
Reprinted from *Satura Viadrina. Festschrift zum fünfundzwanzigjährigen Bestehen des philologischen Vereins zu Breslau*, Breslau, 1896, 110–121.

845. Cohn, Leopold, "Kritisch-exegetische beitraege zu Philo," *Hermes*, XXXI (1896), 107–148.
*Republished, Berlin, 1896, same pagination.

846.† Conybeare, Fred. C., "Emendations of Philo de Sacrificantibus," *The Classical Review*, X (1896), 281–284.

847.† Wendland, P[aul], "Philo und Clemens Alexandrinus," *Hermes*, XXXI (1896), 435–456.
Reviewed by F. C. Conybeare, *The Jewish Quarterly Review*, IX (1896–1897), 151–155.

848.† Wendland, Paul, "Kritische und exegetische Bemerkungen zu Philo," *Rheinisches Museum für Philologie*, N.F. LII (1897), 465–504; N.F. LIII (1898), 1–36.

849.† Wendland, Paul, "Zu Philos Schrift *de posteritate Caini*: (Nebst Bemerkungen zur Rekonstruktion der Septuaginta)," *Philologus*, LVII or N.F. XI (1898), 248–288.

850. Weyman, Carl, "Varia," *Rheinisches Museum für Philologie*, N.F. LIII (1898), 316.

851.† Drexler, W., "Zu Philo de posteritate Caini §161," *Philologus*, LVIII or N.F. XII (1899), 316–318.

852.* Cohn, Leopold, and Wendland, Paul, "Zur neuen Philo-Ausgabe," *Philologus,* LIX or N.F. XIII (1900), 521–536.

853.† Nestle, Eb., "Zur neuen Philo-Ausgabe," *Philologus,* LIX or N.F. XIII (1900), 256–271; LX or N.F. XIV (1901), 271–276.

854.† Radermacher, L., "Varia," *Rheinisches Museum für Philologie,* LV (1900); see 150.
A note on the reading of *Ebr.,* 22.

855.† Nestle, Eb., "Zu Philo, de somniis, II, 44," *Philologus,* LXI or N.F. XV (1902), 311–312.

856.† Cohn, Leopold, "Beitraege zur Textgeschichte und Kritik der philonischen Schriften," *Hermes,* XXXVIII (1903), 498–545.
*Reprinted, Berlin, 1903, with same pagination.

857. Nestle, Eb., "Ein falsches Bibelzitat der neuen Philo-Ausgabe," *Philologus,* LXIII or N.F. XVII (1904), 477–478.

858. Cohn, L[eopold], "Ein Philo-Palimpsest (Vat. gr. 316)," *Sitzungsberichte der Königlich Preussischen Akademie der Wissenschaften,* I (1905), 36–52.

859.† Cohn, Leopold, "Neue Beiträge zur Textgeschichte und Kritik der philonischen Schriften," *Hermes,* XLIII (1908), 177–219.

860.† Grégoire, Henri, "Zur Textkritik Philons," *Hermes,* XLIV (1909), 318–320.

861.† Bréhier, Émile, "Philon d'Alexandrie, De specialibus legibus, I, §82 Cohn," *Revue de philologie de littérature et d'histoire anciennes,* N.S. XXXIV (1910), 235–237.

862. Motzo, Bacchisio, "Per il testo del 'Quod omnis probus liber' di Filone," *Atti della R. Accademia delle Scienze di Torino,* XLVII (1911–1912), 173–178.
*Reprinted, Turin, 1912, pp. 8.
Reviewed by Otto Stählin, *Berliner philologische Wochenschrift,* XXXVI (1916), 933.

863.† Shorey, Paul, "Emendation of Philo De praemiis et poenis I (II, p. 408 M; 5, p. 336 Cohn)," *Classical Philology,* VII (1912), 248.

864.† Mercati, Giovanni, "Appunti dal palinsesto Vaticano di Filone," *Revue biblique,* N.S. XII (1915), 541–555.

865.† Cohn, Leopold, "Kritische Bemerkungen zu Philo," *Hermes,* LI (1916), 161–188.

866.† Brinkmann, August, "Lückenbüsser," *Rheinisches Museum für Philologie,* LXXII (1917–1918), 319–320.

867.† Wilamowitz-Moellendorff, U. v[on], "Lesefrüchte," *Hermes,* LIV (1919); see 72–74.

868. Woodhead, W. D., "Philo Judaeus De Somniis i. 8," *Classical Philology,* XV (1920), 392.

869.† Adler, Maximilian, "Bemerkungen zu Philos Schrift περὶ μέθης," *Wiener Studien,* XLIII (1922–1923), 92–96; XLIV (1924–1925), 220–223; XLV (1926–1927), 117–120, 245–248.
*Reviewed by Marcus in no. 543, p. 464.

870.† Harris, [James] Rendel, "An Archeological Error in the Text of Philo Judaeus," *The Classical Review,* XXXVIII (1924), 61–63.
*Reviewed by Marcus in no. 543, p. 464.

871.* Adler, Maximilian, "Zu Philo Alexandrinus," Ἐπιτύμβιον *Heinrich Swaboda dargebracht,* Reichenberg, 1927, 15–17.
Critical notes to *Ebr.,* §4; *Jos.,* §34; *LA,* iii, §24.

872. Waddell, W. G., "On the Oxyrhynchus Papyrus of Philo (P. Oxy. IX, 1173; XI, 1356)," *Études de papyrologie,* I (1932), 1–6.

873. Kittel, Gerhard, *Theologisches Wörterbuch zum Neuen Testament,* Stuttgart, 1933—(in progress).
Philo is constantly used, so this is one of the best aids to Philonic Greek.

874.† Marcus, Ralph, "An Armenian-Greek Index to Philo's *Quaestiones* and *De vita contemplativa,*" *Journal of the American Oriental Society,* LIII (1933), 251–282.

See also nos. 812, 894, 897.

X. PHILO'S LITERARY STYLE

875.* Steinhart, Carolus Henricus Augustus, *Quaestionum de dialectica Plotini ratione fasciculus primus,* program, Numburgus, 1829, 18.

876. Bernays, [Jacob], "Über die Herstellung des Zusammenhanges in der unter Philo's Namen gehenden Schrift περὶ ἀφθαρσίας κόσμου durch Blätterversetzung," *Monatsberichte der Königlichen Preuss. Akademie der Wissenschaften zu Berlin, aus dem Jahre 1863,* Berlin, 1864, 34–40.
   *Reprinted in Usener, H., *Gesammelte Abhandlungen von Jacob Bernays,* Berlin, 1885, I, 283–290.

877.* Jessen, Julius, *De elocutione Philonis Alexandrini,* Hamburg, 1889, pp. 12. (*Philologorum nestori Hermanno Sauppe,* 1–12.)

878.* Unna, Isak, *Über den Gebrauch der Absichtssätze bei Philo von Alexandrien,* Diss. (Würzburg), Frankfurt a. M., 1895, pp. 51.

879.* Reik, Karl, *Der Optativ bei Polybius und Philo von Alexandria,* Leipzig, 1907, pp. xii, 197.
   Reviewed by Mayser, *Korrespondenz-Blatt für die Höheren Schulen Württembergs,* XIV (1907), 483–485; by Albert Thumb, *Deutsche Literaturzeitung,* XXVIII (1907), 2201–2203; by Ph. Weber, *Neue philologische Rundschau,* 1907, 608–614; by Helbing, *Wochenschrift für klassische Philologie,* XXV (1908), 820–822; by H. Kallenberg, *Berliner philologische Wochenschrift,* XXVIII (1908), 1203–1206; by E. M., *Literarisches Zentralblatt für Deutschland,* LIX (1908), 1638 f.; by My., *Revue critique d'histoire et de littérature,* XLII, i (N.S. LXV) (1908), 347 f.; by Fr. Stolz, *Zeitschrift für die österreichischen Gymnasien,* LIX (1908), 23 f.; and by J. Vendryes, *Revue des études grecques,* XXII (1909), 196 f.

880. Wilamowitz-Moellendorff, Ulrich von, "Die griechische Literatur des Altertums," *Die Kultur der Gegenwart,* I, viii, 3rd edit., Berlin and Leipzig, 1912; see 231 f.

881. Tschuschke, Alexander, *De πρίν particulae apud scriptores aetatis Augusteae prosaicos usu,* Diss. (Breslau), Trebnitz, 1913, 25–31.

882.* De Groot, A[lbert] W[illem], *A Handbook of Antique Prose-rhythm. I. History of Greek prose-metre: Demosthenes, Plato, Philo, Plutarch and others; bibliography, curves, index,* Groningen, 1919, pp. xi, 228; see especially 54–58, 60, 111–117, 130, 137, 196, 222, and tables.

See also nos. 813, 932.

XI. PHILO'S TESTIMONY TO THE SEPTUAGINT

883. Possevino, A[ntonio], *Apparatus sacer ad scriptores Veteris et Novi Testamenti*, Coloniae Agrippinae, 1608, II, 281–286. (From no. 626 and B.M.)

884. Hodius, Humfredus, *De Bibliorum textibus originalibus, versionibus graecis & latina vulgata libri IV*, Oxford, 1705, 195–198.

885. Werner, D. G., *De Philone Judaeo teste integritatis scriptorum Mosaïcorum*, 1743, fol. (From no. 535.)

886. Horneman, Claudius Frees, *Specimina I, II, III, Exercitationum criticarum in versionem LXX interpretum ex Philone*, Göttingen, 1773–79.

887.* Frankel, Z[ach], *Historisch-kritische Studien zu der Septuaginta*, I, i, Leipzig, 1841; see xv, xvi, 5, 34, 39, 45–47, 52–55, 58 n., 65, 67, 70, 77, 99 f., 123 n., 124, 175, 179, 185, 186 n., 217, 251, 254 f.

888.† Siegfried, Carl, "Philonische Studien," *Archiv für wissenschaftliche Erforschung des Alten Testamentes*, II (1872), 143–163.

889.† Siegfried, Carl, "Philo und der überlieferte Text der LXX," *Zeitschrift für wissenschaftliche Theologie*, XVI (1873), 217–238, 411–428, 522–540.

890. Pick, B., "Philo's Canon of the Old Testament and his Mode of Quoting the Alexandrian Version," *Journal of the Society of Biblical Literature and Exegesis*, [IV] (1884), 126–143.

891.† Conybeare, Fred. C., "Upon Philo's Text of the Septuagint," *The Expositor*, 4. S. IV (1891), 456–466.

892.* Ryle, Herbert Edward, *The Canon of the Old Testament: An Essay on the Gradual Growth and Formation of the Hebrew Canon of Scripture*, London and New York, 1892, 91, 148–150, 169 f.

893.† Conybeare, F[rederick] C[ornwallis], "On the Philonean Text of the Septuagint," *The Jewish Quarterly Review*, V (1892–1893), 246–280; VIII (1895–1896), 88–122.

894.* Ryle, Herbert Edward, *Philo and Holy Scripture; or The Quotations of Philo from the books of the Old Testament, with introduction and notes*, London and New York, 1895, pp. xlviii, 312.
   †Reviewed by [Paul] Wendland, *Berliner philologische Wochenschrift*, XV (1895), 1281–1285; and by John Gibb, *The Critical Review*, VI (1896), 41–43.

895. Swete, Henry Barclay, *Introduction to the Old Testament in Greek*, Cambridge, 1900, 372–380.

896. Gesenius, William, *A Hebrew and English Lexicon of the Old Testament with an appendix containing the Biblical Aramaic,* translated by Edward Robinson, edited by Francis Brown, S. R. Driver and Charles A. Briggs, Boston, New York and Chicago, 1906, pp. xix, 1127.

897.* Schröder, Augustus, *De Philonis Alexandrini Vetere Testamento,* Diss. (Gryphia), Gryphia, 1907, pp. 50.

898. Heinisch, Paul, *Griechische Philosophie und Altes Testament,* Münster in Westf., I. *Die palästinensischen Bücher,* 1913, pp. 79; II. *Septuaginta und Buch der Weisheit,* 1914, pp. 39. (*Biblische Zeitfragen,* VI, vi, vii; VII, iii.)

899. Dodd, C. H., *The Bible and the Greeks,* London, [1935], pp. 264. Reviewed by Arthur Darby Nock, *American Journal of Philology,* LVII (1937), 483-485.

See also nos. 828, 849, 935.

XII. PHILO'S USE OF ALLEGORY

900. Horneman, Claudius Frees, *Observationes ad illustrationem doctrinae de canone Veteris Testamenti ex Philone,* Diss., Havnia (Copenhagen), [1775], pp. 67.

901. Planck, Henricus, *Commentatio de principiis et caussis interpretationis Philonianae allegoricae,* Diss., Göttingen, [1806], pp. iv, 72.

902.* Frankel, Z[ach], *Ueber den Einfluss der palästinischen Exegese auf die alexandrinische Hermeneutik,* Leipzig, 1851, pp. x, 354.

903.* Siegfried, Carl [Gustav Adolf], *Die hebräischen Worterklärungen des Philo und die Spuren ihrer Einwirkung auf die Kirchenväter,* Magdeburg, 1863, pp. 37.

904. Lightfoot, J. B., "The Faith of Abraham," "Philo's Allegory of Hagar and Sarah," *St. Paul's Epistle to the Galatians,* London, 1865. Frequently republished. See the editions of London, 1880 and 1921, 158–164, 197–200. (*The Epistles of St. Paul,* II, 3.)

905. Schmiedl, A., "Zur Geschichte der allegorischen Schriftauslegung," *Monatsschrift für Geschichte und Wissenschaft des Judenthums,* XIV (1865); see 298 f.

906.* Siegfried, Carl [Gustav Adolf], *Philo von Alexandria als Ausleger des alten Testaments,* Jena, 1875, pp. vi, 418.
Reviewed in Wilhelm Hauck's *Theologischer Jahresbericht,* X (1875), 417–419; †by F. (Frankel ?), *Monatsschrift für Geschichte und Wissenschaft des Judenthums,* XXIV (1875), 229–240; by Langen, *Theologisches Literaturblatt,* Bonn, X (1875), 296–298; by D. O., *Literarisches Centralblatt für Deutschland,* [XXVI] (1875), 731–733; by Eb. Schrader, *Jenaer Literaturzeitung,* II (1875), 290.

907.* Ginzberg, Louis, "Allegorical Interpretation," *The Jewish Encyclopedia,* New York, I, 1901, 403–411.

908. Lauterbach, Jacob Z., "The Ancient Jewish Allegorists in Talmud and Midrash," *The Jewish Quarterly Review,* N.S. I (1910–1911), 291–333, 503–531.

909.† Treitel, L[eopold], "Ursprung, Begriff und Umfang der allegorischen Schrifterklärung," *Monatsschrift für Geschichte und Wissenschaft des Judentums,* LV (1911), 543 f.
Reprinted in no. 643, pp. 114–122.

910.† Stein, Edmund, *Die allegorische Exegese des Philo aus Alexandreia,* Giessen, 1929, pp. 61. (*Beihefte zur Zeitschrift für die alttestamentliche Wissenschaft,* 51.)
Reviewed by I. Heinemann, *Monatsschrift für Geschichte und Wis-*

senschaft des Judentums, LXXIII (1929), 431–434; †in *The Expository Times*, XLI (1929–1930), 278 f.; by A[bel], *Revue biblique*, XXXIX (1930), 142 f.; by Joseph Bonsirven, *Recherches de science religieuse*, XX (1930), 336–368; †by Shirley Jackson Case, *The Journal of Religion*, X (1930), 414 f.; †by Paul Heinisch, *Theologische Revue*, XXIX (1930), 111 f.; †by Hans Leisegang, *Theologisches Literaturblatt*, LI (1930), 19–21; †by Otto Michel, *Theologische Literaturzeitung*, LV (1930), 55 f.; by G. A. van den Bergh van Eysinga, *Nieuw theologisch Tijdschrift*, XIX (1930), 79 f.; †by M. Dibelius, *Orientalistische Literaturzeitung*, XXXIV (1931), 1035–1038; and *by Marcus in no. 543, p. 469.

911.* Stein, Edmund, *Philo und der Midrasch: Philos Schilderung der Gestalten des Pentateuch verglichen mit der des Midrasch*, Giessen, 1931, pp. 52. (*Beihefte zur Zeitschrift für die Alttestamentliche Wissenschaft*, LVII.)

*Reviewed by John E. McFadyen, *The Expository Times*, XLIII (1931–1932), 377 f.; †by I. Heinemann, *Deutsche Literaturzeitung*, LIII (3.F. III) (1932), 635 f.; †by the same, *Monatsschrift für Geschichte und Wissenschaft des Judentums*, LXXVI (1932), 266–267; by G. A. van den Bergh van Eysinga, *Nieuw theologisch Tijdschrift*, XXI (1932), 367 f.; by Mordecai M. Kaplan, *The Jewish Quarterly Review*, N.S. XXIII (1932–1933), 285–291; and *by Marcus in no. 543, p. 476 f.

912. Stein, Edmund, "De Celso Platonico Philonis Alexandrini imitatore," *Eos*, XXXIV (1932–1933), 205–216.

913.* Stein, Edmund, *Alttestamentliche Bibelkritik in der späthellenistischen Literatur*, Lwów, 1935, pp. 48. Reprinted from *"Collectanea Theologica" Societatis Theologorum Polonorum*, XVI (1935).

914. Heinemann, Isaak, *Altjüdische Allegoristik*, Breslau, 1936; see Index.

See also nos. 1145, 1489.

XIII. THE RELATION OF PHILO'S IDEAS TO GREEK PHILOSOPHY[1]

915.*Agrippa, Henry Cornelius, *The Vanity of Arts and Sciences,* London, 1676, pp. [8], 10, 368.
(Probably the third English edition of a translation of Agrippa. The first was Englished by Ja[mes] San[ford], and was printed in 1569, the second in 1575.) On p. 132 Philo the Jew is cited in support of one of the theories of Pythagoras.

916. Fabricius, M. Joh. Albertus, *Exercitatio de Platonismo Philonis Judaei,* Leipzig, [1693], pp. [12].
*Reprinted in B. Jo. Albertus Fabricius, *Opusculorum historico-critico-literariorum, sylloge quae sparsim viderant lucem,* Hamburg, 1738, 147–160.
The first paper in the later volume is made up of a series of notes of 100 suspected plagiarisms, fictitious authors, and works known only by title and probably non-existent; Philo's *De Mundo* is discussed in this connection on p. 68 n.

917.* Suidas, *Lexicon, graece & latine. Textum graecum cum manuscriptis codicibus collatum a quamplurimis mendis purgavit, notisque perpetuis illustravit: versionem latinam Aemilii Porti innumeris in locis correxit; indicesque auctorum et rerum adjecit Ludolphus Kusterus,* Cambridge (England), 1705, 3 vols.; see III, 613.

918. Wesseling, Peter, *Epistola . . . ad virum celeberrimum H. Venemam de Aquilae in scriptis Philonis Jud. fragmentis et Platonis epistola XIII. &c.,* Trajecti ad Rhenum (Utrecht a. R.), 1748, pp. 51.

919.† Pelagius [Joseph Priestley?], "Of the Platonism of Philo," J. Priestley, *The Theological Repository* (Birmingham), IV (1784), 408–420.

920.† Jahnius, Albertus, "Plagiarium Herennium personatum cum expilato Philone Iudaeo comparat," *Archiv für Philologie und Paedagogik* (Supplementband to *Neue Jahrbücher für Philologie und Paedagogik*), X (1844), 165–176.

1. There is no certain trace of Philo in any ancient pagan document. Geffcken (no. 956a, pp. 88 and 277 n. 3) says that Heliodorus, *Aethiopica,* IX, 9 (edit. of Immanuel Bekker, Leipzig, 1855), contains a quotation from Philo. Heliodorus: θεοπλαστοῦσι τὸν Νεῖλον Αἰγύπτιοι, καὶ κρειττόνων τὸν μέγιστον ἄγουσιν, ἀντίμιμον οὐρανοῦ τὸν ποταμὸν σεμνηγοροῦντες. Philo, *Mos.,* ii, 195: θεοπλαστοῦσι τῷ λόγῳ τὸν Νεῖλον Αἰγύπτιοι ὡς ἀντίμιμον οὐρανοῦ γεγονότα καὶ περὶ τῆς χώρας σεμνηγοροῦσιν. The two statements are certainly very similar, and the whole passage in Heliodorus is clearly from a mystic source. But Philo also drew from mystic Pythagorean material so heavily that A. D. Nock, *Conversion; the Old and the New in Religion from Alexander the Great to Augustine of Hippo,* Oxford, 1933, seems more correct in his note (p. 286) where he suggests a common source for the two, than in the text (p. 29) where he states that the Heliodorus passage is from Philo.

921. Zeller, Eduard, *Die Philosophie der Griechen. Eine Untersuchung über Charakter, Gang und Hauptmomente ihrer Entwicklung*, III, ii, Tübingen, 1852, 559–665; *ib.*, Leipzig, 1868, 208–367; *ib.*, Leipzig, 1881, 242–418; *ib.*, Leipzig, 1903, 261–467.

922. Biet, F. Joseph, *Quid in interpretatione Scripturae sacrae allegorica Philo Judaeus a graecis philosophis sumpserit*, Diss. (Paris), Sancti-Clodoaldi, 1854, pp. 95.

923.† Joël, M., "Ueber einige geschichtliche Beziehungen des philonischen Systems," *Monatsschrift für Geschichte und Wissenschaft des Judenthums*, XII (1863), 19–31.

*Reprinted in his *Beiträge zur Geschichte der Philosophie*, Breslau, 1876, I, appendix, 53–67.

924. Cook, Keningale, "A Ray from the Sphere of Plato," *The University Magazine*, V (1880), 288.

925.* Arnim, Hans von, *Quellenstudien zu Philo von Alexandria*, Berlin, 1888, pp. 142. (*Philologische Untersuchungen*, XI.)

Reviewed by C. Bigg, *The Classical Review*, II (1888), 320–321; in *Literarisches Centralblatt für Deutschland*, [XL] (1889), 44–45; by Lucien Herr, *Revue critique d'histoire et de littérature*, XXIII, i (N.S. XXVII) (1889), 322–325; †by D. A. Hilgenfeld, *Wochenschrift für klassische Philologie*, VI (1889), 116–118; and by P. Wendland, *Deutsche Litteraturzeitung*, XI (1890), 742–744.

926.† Hense, Otto, "Bion bei Philon," *Rheinisches Museum für Philologie*, XLVII (1892), 219–240.

927. Schmekel, A[ugust], *Die Philosophie der mittleren Stoa in ihrem geschichtlichen Zusammenhange dargestellt*, Berlin, 1892, 409–423, 430–432.

928.* Wendland, Paul, *Die philosophischen Quellen des Philo von Alexandria in seiner Schrift über die Vorsehung*, Programm no. 59, Berlin, 1892, pp. 27.

929. Höhne, E., *Die Berührungspunkte zwischen Moses u[nd] Plato: das ist zwischen Altem Testamente u[nd] platon[ischer] Philosophie, zum Teil nach Philo* (Expanded Lecture), Leipzig, 1893, pp. 39. (From Kayser's *Büch. Lex.*)

930.† Norden, Eduard, "Über den Streit des Theophrast und Zeno bei Philo περὶ ἀφθαρσίας κόσμου," in "Beiträge zur Geschichte der griechischen Philosophie," *Jahrbücher für classische Philologie*, Supplbd. XIX (1893), 440–452. (Supplement to *Neue Jahrbücher für Philologie und Paedagogik*.)

931.* Elter, Anton, *De gnomologiorum graecorum historia atque origine commentatio*, a series of programs, VIII, VIIII, Bonn, 1895, 1896.

932. Wendland, P[aul], "Philo und die kynisch-stoische Diatribe," in Paul

Wendland and Otto Kern, *Beiträge zur Geschichte der griechischen Philosophie und Religion,* Berlin, 1895, 1–75.

†Reviewed by Karl Praechter, *Berliner philologische Wochenschrift,* XVI (1896), 867–873, 901–905; and by F. C. Conybeare, *The Jewish Quarterly Review,* IX (1897), 151.

933.† Wendland, Paul, "Eine doxographische Quelle Philo's," *Sitzungsberichte der Königlich Preussischen Akademie der Wissenschaften zu Berlin,* 1897, pp. ii, 1074–1079.

934. Horovitz, Jakob, *Das platonische* Νοητὸν Ζῷον *und der philonische* Κόσμος Νοητός, Diss. (Marburg), Marburg, 1900, xi, 103. See no. 935.

935.* Horovitz, Jakob, *Untersuchungen über Philons und Platons Lehre von der Weltschöpfung,* Marburg, 1900, pp. xiii, 127.

Identical with no. 934, but with four supplementary essays: I. "Der Einfluss des Timäus auf δυνάμεις und λόγος." II. "Wie verwendet Philon Gen. I, 2a in seiner Beschreibung der Idealwelt?—Septuaginta und Ideenlehre." III. "Einflüsse Philons auf 'Timäus Locrus.'" IV. "Die von unseren Septuagintahand Schriften abweichende Lesart Philons in Gen. II, 15 und ihre Entstehung."

Reviewed in *Literarisches Centralblatt für Deutschland,* LII (1901), 1132 f.; by H. v. Arnim, *Deutsche Litteraturzeitung,* XXII (1901), 2069 f.; †by Julien Weill, *Revue des études juives,* XLII (1901), 283–286; by P. Wendland, *Berliner philologische Wochenschrift,* XXI (1901), 387–390; and by G. Heinrici, *Theologische Literaturzeitung,* XXVIII (1903), 82–84.

936.* Praechter, Karl, *Hierokles der Stoiker,* Leipzig, 1901, pp. viii, 159.

937.* Borghorst, Gerhardus, *De Anatolii fontibus,* Diss. (Berlin), Berlin, 1904, 4–11.

938.* Bohnenblust, Gottfried, *Beiträge zum Topos* περὶ φιλίας, Diss. (Bern), Berlin, 1905; see Index.

939.† Barth, Paul, "Die stoische Theodizee bei Philo," *Philosophische Abhandlungen. Max Heinze zum 70. Geburtstage gewidmet von Freunden und Schülern,* Berlin, 1906, 14–33.

940.* Falter, Gustav, *Beiträge zur Geschichte der Idee. Teil I: Philon und Plotin,* Giessen, 1906, pp. 37–102. (Hermann Cohen and Paul Natorp, *Philosophische Arbeiten,* I, ii.)

Reviewed by H. E. Müller, *Berliner philologische Wochenschrift,* XXVI (1906), 1633–1638; by Adolf Dyroff, *Deutsche Literaturzeitung,* XXVIII (1907), 1175–1177; and by My., *Revue critique d'histoire et de littérature,* XLI, i (N.S. LXIII) (1907), 422.

941.* Guyot, Henri, *Les réminiscences de Philon le Juif chez Plotin. Étude critique,* Thèse (Paris), Paris, 1906, pp. 92.

942.* Apelt, Mathilda, *De rationibus quibusdam quae Philoni Alexandrino cum Posidonio intercedunt*, Diss. (Jena), Leipzig, 1907.
Reprinted with the same pagination from *Commentationes philologae Ienenses*, VIII, i (1907), 89–141. (*Ediderunt seminarii philologorum Ienensis professores*.)
Reviewed by Max Pohlenz, *Berliner philologische Wochenschrift*, XXIX (1909), 935–940.

943.* Barth, Paul, "Die Nachwirkung in der jüdischen Philosophie des Altertums," *Die Stoa*, 2nd edit., revised and enlarged, Stuttgart, 1908; see Index. (Richard Falckenberg, *Frommanns Klassiker der Philosophie*, XVI.)

944.* Bonhöffer, Adolf, *Epiktet und das Neue Testament*, Giessen, 1911; see 37, 62 n., 184–188, 191 n., 220. (Richard Wünsch and Ludwig Deubner, *Religionsgeschichtliche Versuche und Vorarbeiten*, X.)

945. Leisegang, Hans, *Die Raumtheorie im späteren Platonismus, insbesondere bei Philon und den Neuplatonikern*, Diss. (Strassburg), Weida i. Th., 1911, pp. 93.

946.† Bergmann, "Die stoische Philosophie und die jüdische Frömmigkeit," *Judaica, Festschrift zu Hermann Cohens siebzigstem Geburtstage*, Berlin, 1912, 145–166.

947.† Leisegang, Hans, "Die Begriffe der Zeit und Ewigkeit bei Philon," *Die Begriffe der Zeit und Ewigkeit im späteren Platonismus*, Münster i. W., 1913, 10–14. (*Beiträge zur Geschichte der Philosophie des Mittelalters*, XIII, 4.)

948. Bentwich, Norman, "From Philo to Plotinus," *The Jewish Quarterly Review*, N.S. IV (1913–1914), 1–21.

949.* Gronau, Karl, *Poseidonios und die jüdisch-christliche Genesisexegese*, Leipzig and Berlin, 1914, pp. viii, 313; see Index.

950. Kroll, Josef, *Die Lehren des Hermes Trismegistos*, Münster i. W., 1914, pp. xii, 441; see Index. (Clemens Baeumker, *Beiträge zur Geschichte der Philosophie des Mittelalters. Texte und Untersuchungen*, XII, 2–4.)
*Second edition, 1928.

951.* Lorenz, Siegfried, *De progressu notionis* φιλανθρωπίας, Diss. (Leipzig), Leipzig, 1914; see 47.

952.* Bousset, Wilhelm, *Jüdisch-christlicher Schulbetrieb in Alexandria und Rom. Literarische Untersuchungen zu Philo und Clemens von Alexandria, Justin und Irenäus*, Göttingen, 1915, pp. viii, 319.
†Reviewed by Max Radin, *The Jewish Quarterly Review*, N.S. IX (1918–1919), 245–248; and †by I. Heinemann, *Monatsschrift für Geschichte und Wissenschaft des Judentums*, LXVII (1923), 284–287.

953. Galbiatius, Iohannes, *De fontibus: M. Tullii Ciceronis librorum qui manserunt de re publica et de legibus quaestiones,* Milan, 1916, 183–187, 297–301, 475 n.

954.* Inge, William Ralph, *The Philosophy of Plotinus; the Gifford Lectures at St. Andrews, 1917–1918,* London and New York, 1918, 2 vols.; see the 3rd edit., London, 1929, I, 97–99, 149 f.; II, 14, 56 f., 111, 155.

955.* Billings, Thomas Henry, *The Platonism of Philo Judaeus,* Diss. (Chicago), Chicago, 1919, pp. 103.
    Reviewed by T. Leslie Shear, *The Classical Weekly,* XIII (1919–1920), 126; †by Roger Miller Jones, *Classical Philology,* XVII (1922), 179–184; by D. Roy Mathews, *Journal of the Society of Oriental Research,* VI (1922), 96 f.

956.† Cumont, Franz, "Lucrèce et le symbolisme pythagoricien des enfers," *Revue de philologie, de littérature et d'histoire anciennes,* N.S. XLIV (1920), 229–240.

956a. Geffcken, Johannes, *Der Ausgang des griechisch-römischen Heidentums,* Heidelberg, 1920; see Index. (*Religionswissenschaftliche Bibliothek,* VI.)

957.* Heinemann, I[saak], *Poseidonios' metaphysische Schriften,* Breslau, 1921, 1928, 2 vols.; see Index (vol. II).

958. Leisegang, Hans, *Hellenistische Philosophie von Aristoteles bis Plotin,* Breslau, 1923; see Index. (*Jedermanns Bücherei.*)
    †Reviewed by I. Heinemann, *Monatsschrift für Geschichte und Wissenschaft des Judentums,* LXVII (1923), 280 f.

959.* Nestle, Wilhelm, *Die Nachsokratiker. Deutsch in Auswahl mit Einleitungen,* Jena, 1923, I, 122–127; II, 293–307. (*Die griechischen Philosophen,* III, IV.)
    †Reviewed by I. Heinemann, *Monatsschrift für Geschichte und Wissenschaft des Judentums,* LXVII (1923), 280.

960.* Heinemann, Isaak, *Die Lehre von der Zweckbestimmung des Menschen im griechisch-römischen Altertum und im jüdischen Mittelalter,* Breslau, 1926, 19, 31, 39 n., 42 n., 88, 95, 98.
    †Reviewed by Julius Guttmann, *Monatsschrift für Geschichte und Wissenschaft des Judentums,* LXX (1926), 422–424.

961.† Jones, Roger Miller, "The Ideas as Thoughts of God," *Classical Philology,* XXI (1926), 317–326.

962.† Jones, Roger Miller, "Posidonius and the Flight of the Mind through the Universe," *Classical Philology,* XXI (1926), 97–113.

963.† Pohlenz, Max, "Stoa und Semitismus," *Neue Jahrbücher für Wissenschaft und Jugendbildung,* II (1926), 257–269.

964.* Reinhardt, Karl, "Philo und Boëthos," *Kosmos und Sympathie. Neue Untersuchungen über Poseidonios,* München, 1926, 20–25 and *passim.*

965.* Gomperz, Heinrich, *Die Lebensauffassung der griechischen Philosophen und das Ideal der inneren Freiheit. Zwölf gemeinverständliche Vorlesungen mit Anhang: Zum Verständnis der Mystiker,* Jena, 1927, 38, 291–294, 344.

966.* Turowski, Edmund, *Die Widerspiegelung des stoischen Systems bei Philon von Alexandreia,* Diss. (Königsberg), Borna, Leipzig, 1927, pp. v, 59.
*Reviewed by Marcus in no. 543, p. 467.

967.† Nebel, Gerhard, *Plotins Kategorien der intelligiblen Welt,* Tübingen, 1929, 26–33. (Ernst Hoffmann and Heinrich Rickert, *Heidelberger Abhandlungen zur Philosophie und ihrer Geschichte,* 18.)

968. Peterson, Erik, *"Zur Bedeutungsgeschichte von παρρησία,"* in Wilhelm Koepp, *Reinhold-Seeberg Festschrift,* Leipzig, 1929, I, 283–297.
*Reprinted, Leipzig, 1929, pp. 15.

969. Theiler, Willy, *Die Vorbereitung des Neuplatonismus,* Berlin, 1930, pp. viii, 166. (*Problemata, Forschungen zur klassischen Philologie,* Heft I.)

969a. Baudry, J., *Le problème de l'origine et de l'éternité du monde dans la philosophie de Platon à l'ère chrétienne,* Thèse (Paris), Paris, 1931; see Index.

970.* Goodenough, Erwin R[amsdell], "A Neo-Pythagorean Source in Philo Judaeus," *Yale Classical Studies,* New Haven, III (1932), 115–164.

971.* Witt, R. E., "Ύπόστασις," *Amicitiae Corolla. . . . Essays Presented to James Rendel Harris,* edited by H. G. Wood, London, 1933, 319–343.

972. Hoffmann, Ernst, *Platonismus und Mystik im Altertum,* Heidelberg, 1935, 56–58, 131. (*Sitzungsberichte der Heidelberger Akademie der Wissenschaften, Philosophisch-historische Klasse,* 1934–1935, 2.)

973.* Steur, K., *Poimandres en Philo. Een vergelijking van Poimandres §12–§32 met Philo's uitleg van Genesis I, 26–27 en II, 7,* Purmerend, 1935, pp. xvi, 214. (From following review.)
Reviewed by J. de Ghellinck, *Nouvelle revue théologique,* LXIII (1936), 555 f.

974.* Willms, Hans, Είκών: *eine begriffsgeschichtliche Untersuchung zum Platonismus. I. Teil: Philon von Alexandreia, mit einer Einleitung über Platon und die Zwischenzeit,* Munster i. W., 1935, pp. vii, 121.
Reviewed by D. T., *The Journal of Hellenic Studies,* LVI (1936), 263.

975. Boyancé, Pierre, *Le culte des muses chez les philosophes grecs: Études d'histoire et de psychologie religieuses,* Paris, 1937; see Index. (*Bibliothèque des Écoles Françaises d'Athènes et de Rome,* CXLI.)

See also nos. 571, 603, 621, 740, 819, 821, 830, 1042, 1053, 1054, 1066, 1084, 1096, 1099, 1110a, 1118, 1142a, 1157, 1164, 1170, 1477, 1500, 1501.

XIV. PHILO'S RELATION TO JEWISH TRADITIONS

976. Flavius Josephus, *Antiquitates Ioudaicae,* XVIII, viii, 1–3. The best edition of the text is by Benedictus Niese, *Flavii Josephi Opera,* Berlin, 1887, 1885–95; see IV, 186–189. *See also the Loeb edition by H. St. J. Thackeray and Ralph Marcus, London and New York, (Cambridge), 1926—.

977. Luther, Mart[in], "Vorrhede auff die Weisheit Salomonis," *Apocrypha. Das sind Bücher: so nicht der heiligen Schrifft gleich gehalten: und doch nutzlich und gut zu lesen sind,* Wittemberg, 1534, [Hans Lufft], folio XIr.

978. Rossi, Azariah ben Moses dei (Bonaiuto), *Séfer Mě'or 'ēnayīm,* [Mantua, 1573, 74].
    Republished Wien, 1829, and *(edited by David Cassell) Wilna, I, 1863, 152, 162, 166, 168, 176.

979. Strigel, Victorin[us], *Sirach Sapientia, interprete Victorino Strigelio,* Lips[iae], 1575 [1570?], 277. (From no. 992, and B.M.)

980. Rainoldus, Johannes, *Censura librorum apocryphorum Veteris Testamenti,* etc., Oppenheim, I, 1611, 174–191.

981. Castabadius, Joh., *Liber singularis de libro Sapientiae,* Bredae, 1648. (From no. 992.)

982. Calovius, Abraham, *Biblia Testam. Veteris et Novi illustrata, in quibus simul annotata Hugonis Grotii exhibentur,* [Dresdae & Lipsiae, 1719], III, 33. (From no. 992 and U.C.)

983.* Buddeus, Io. Franciscus, *Introductio ad historiam philosophiae Ebraeorum. Accedit dissertatio de Haeresi Valentiniana,* Glaucha-Halensis, 1720; see 30, 38 f., 76–80, 96 f., 215–217, 621 n.

984. Grube, Joannes Christophorus, *Dissertationem . . . de auctore libri Sapientiae Philone potius Alexandrino quam Seniore publicae ventilationi subjiciunt,* Regiomonti, [1739]. (From B.M.)

985. Gerhardus, Ioannes, *Loci theologici cum pro adstruenda veritate tum pro destruenda quorumvis contradicentium falsitate,* edited by Io. Fridericus Cotta, Tübingen, II, 1763, 159–164.

986. Grossmann, Chr[istian] Gottlob Leber[echt], *De philosophia Sadducaeorum commentatio,* Leipzig, I and II, 1836; III and IV, 1838.

987. Moses ben Maimon, *Dalalat al Haiirin, Zurechtweisung der Verirrten,* translated into German by Simon Scheyer, III, Frankfurt am Main, 1838, Hebrew and German text on opposite pages; see 314 and 392.

988. Grossmann, Christian Gottlob Leber[echt], *De Pharisaismo Iudaeorum Alexandrino commentatio,* Leipzig, I, [1846], pp. 18; II, [1847], pp. 30; III, [1850], *De disciplina Ascetica,* pp. 40.

989.* Joël, D. H., מדרש הזוהר (*Midrash ha-Zohar*): *Die Religionsphilosophie des Sohar und ihr Verhältniss zur allgemeinen jüdischen Theologie. Zugleich eine kritische Beleuchtung der Franck'schen "Kabbala,"* Leipzig, 1849, pp. xxii, 394; see esp. 349–374.
*Reprinted, Berlin, 1923.

990. Grossmann, Christian Gottlob Leber[echt], *De collegio Pharisaeorum commentatio,* Program, Leipzig, 1851, pp. 32.

991. Krochmal, Nachmann [Kohen], *More Neboche ha-seman, sive Director errantium nostrae aetatis, Opus ad illustrandas Juddeorum antiquitates et leges, philosophiamque,* completed and published posthumously by L[eopold] Zunz, Leopoli (Lemberg), 1851 (added title page in Hebrew); 2nd edit., 1863.
Published also in the collected edition of his works: *Nachman Krochmals Werke,* edited by S. Rawidowicz, Berlin-Charlottenberg, c. 1924 (added title page in Hebrew). (In S. Wininger, *Grosse Jüdische National-Biographie,* III, [1928], 541, and *Jüdisches Lexikon,* III, [1927], 911, the Hebrew title is transliterated *More něwuche hasman* or *hasěman,* but in Zunz's edition as above.)

992. Grimm, Carl Ludwig Wilibald, *Kurzgefasstes exegetisches Handbuch zu den Apokryphen des Alten Testamentes:* VI, *Das Buch der Weisheit,* Leipzig, 1860, 21–24 and *passim.*

993.† Brüll, Nehemias, "Was Philo dem Judenthume war," *Illustrirte Monatshefte für die gesammten Interessen des Judenthums,* I (1865), 149–152.

994. Maybaum, Siegmund, *Die Anthropomorphien und Anthropopathien bei Onkelos und den spätern Targumim mit besonderer Berücksichtigung der Ausdrücke Memra, Jᵉkara und Schechintha,* Breslau, 1870, pp. 66.

995. Weiss, I. H., *Zur Geschichte der jüdischen Tradition* (Hebrew), Wien, I, [1871], 213–222, (added title page in Hebrew).

996. Treitel, L., "Die Bedeutung der jüdischen Feste nach Philo," *Das Jüdische Literaturblatt* (*Literarische Beilage zur Israelitische Wochenschrift,* III [1872]), I (1872), 74–75, 82–83.
Reprinted in no. 643, pp. 1–5.

997.† [Graetz, H.], "Das Korbfest der Erstlinge bei Philo," *Monatsschrift für Geschichte und Wissenschaft des Judenthums,* XXVI (1877), 433–442.

998. Hamburger, J[acob], "Hellenisten," "Philo der Philosoph," *Real-Ency-*

clopädie für Bibel und Talmud, Strelitz, 2nd edit., II, 1883, 374–380, 904–908.

999.* Perez, Francesco, *Sopra Filone Alessandrino e il suo libro detto La Sapienza di Salomone, saggio storico-critico, seguito da una versione poetica del libro stesso e da una appendice,* Palermo, 1883, pp. 200.
†Reviewed by G. Jaré, *Mosè antologia israelitica,* VII (1884), 76–78, 111–114, 180–184; and by C. Siegfried, *Berliner philologische Wochenschrift,* IV (1884), 426.

1000.* Weisse, Samson, *Philo von Alexandrien und Moses Maimonides. Ein vergleichender Versuch,* Diss. (Halle), Halle a. S., 1884, pp. 31.

1001.† Derenbourg, J., "Gloses d'abou Zakariya Ben Bilam sur Isaïe," *Revue des études juives,* XVII (1888), 172–180.

1002.† Epstein, A., "Le Livre des Jubilés, Philon et le Midrasch Tadsché," *Revue des études juives,* XXI (1890), 80–97, XXII (1891), 1–25.

1003.* Graetz, H., *History of the Jews,* Philadelphia, 1891–1898, 6 vols.; see II, 144–145, 176, 184–187, 191, 194, 209–215, 373; III, 162; IV, 614; V, 684.

1004. Winter, J[acob], and Wünsche, Aug., *Die jüdische Litteratur seit Abschluss des Kanons. Eine prosaische und poetische Anthologie mit biographischen und litterargeschichtlichen Einleitungen; I, Geschichte der jüdisch-hellenistischen und talmudischen Litteratur. Zugleich eine Anthologie für Schule und Haus,* Trier (slip pasted over, Berlin), 1894, 18–28.

1005.* Karppe, S., "Philon et le Zohar, deux expressions analogues de l'allégorisme," *Étude sur les origines et la nature du Zohar, précédée d'une étude sur l'histoire de la Kabbale,* Paris, 1901, 527–581.

1006.* Kohler, Kaufmann, "Moses," *The Jewish Encyclopedia,* New York and London, IX, 1905, 44–57.

1007.* Lauterbach, Jacob Zallel, "Philo Judaeus—His Relation to the Halakah," *ibid.,* X, 1905, 15–18.

1008.† Poznanski, Samuel, "Philon dans l'ancienne littérature judéo-arabe," *Revue des études juives,* L (1905), 10–31.

1009.* Neumark, David, *Geschichte der jüdischen Philosophie des Mittelalters,* Berlin, 1907, 1910, 2 vols.; see II, 391–473 and *passim.*

1010. Ginzberg, Louis, *The Legends of the Jews,* (translated from the German manuscript by Henrietta Szold and Paul Radin), Philadelphia, 1909–1938.
The amazingly learned notes in volumes V and VI, with their comparison of Philo and other Jewish traditions, are our most important source for a study of Philo's relation to Judaism in general. See the Index volume.

1011.† Treitel, Leopold, "Agada bei Philo," *Monatsschrift für Geschichte und Wissenschaft des Judentums,* LIII (1909), 28–45, 159–173, 286–291. Reprinted in no. 643, pp. 85–113.

1012.† Hart, J. H. A., "Philo and the Catholic Judaism of the First Century," *The Journal of Theological Studies,* XI (1909–1910), 25–42.

1013.† Horowitz, J[acob], "Entwicklung des alexandrinischen Judentums unter dem Einflusse Philos," *Judaica. Festschrift zu Hermann Cohens siebzigstem Geburtstage,* Berlin, 1912, 535–567.

1014. Aptowitzer, V., *Kain und Abel in der Agada, den Apokryphen, der hellenistischen, christlichen und muhammedanischen Literatur,* Wien and Leipzig, 1922, pp. 184. (*Veröffentlichungen der Alexander Kohut Memorial Foundation,* I.)
†Reviewed by Bernhard Heller, *Monatsschrift für Geschichte und Wissenschaft des Judentums,* LXX (1926), 476–479.

1015. Aptowitzer, V., "Zur Erklärung einiger merkwürdiger Agadoth über die Schöpfung des Menschen," *Festskrift: anledning af Professor David Simonsens 70-aarige födselsdag,* Copenhagen, 1923, 112–118.

1016.* Ginsburg, Christian D., *The Kabbalah: Its Doctrines, Development, and Literature,* London, 1925, 88 n., 113 n.

1017. Halévy, M. A., *Moïse dans l'histoire et dans la légende,* Paris, 1927, 70–72. (P.-L. Couchoud, *Judaïsme,* VI.)
†Reviewed by Bernard Heller in *Monatsschrift für Geschichte und Wissenschaft des Judentums,* LII (1928), 631–633.

1018.* Moore, George Foot, *Judaism in the First Centuries of the Christian Era, The Age of the Tannaim,* Cambridge (Massachusetts), 1927–1930, 3 vols. (I and II, 3rd impression, 1932); see I, 211–214 and II, Indices I and II.

1019. Büchler, A., *Studies in Sin and Atonement in the Rabbinic Literature of the First Century,* London, 1928, 384–393, 398, 401–404. (*Jews' College Publications,* 11.)

1020. Treitel, Leop[old], "Zur Entwicklungsgeschichte der Predigt in Synagoge und Kirche als des Beitrags, den das Judentum für allgemeine Kultur gestiftet hat," *Festschrift zum 75 jährigen Bestehen des jüdisch-theologischen Seminars fraenckelscher Stiftung,* Berlin, 1929, II, 373–376.

1021. Guttmann, Julius, *Die Philosophie des Judentums,* München, 1933, pp. 412. (*Geschichte der Philosophie in Einzeldarstellungen,* I, 3.)
†Reviewed by Hermann Vogelstein, *Theologische Literaturzeitung,* LXI (1936), 379–383.

1022. Heinemann, I[saak], "Moses," in Pauly-Wissowa-Kroll, *Real-Encyclopedia für klassische Altertumswissenschaft,* XVI, i, 1933, 359–375.

1023.† Finkelstein, Louis, "Is Philo Mentioned in Rabbinic Literature?" *Journal of Biblical Literature,* LIII (1934), 142–149.
*Reviewed by Marcus in no. 543, p. 488.

1024. Kaminka, A., "Die mystischen Ideen des R. Simon ben Johai," *Hebrew Union College Annual,* Cincinnati, X (1935), 149–168.

1025. Knox, Wilfred Lawrence, "Abraham and the Quest for God," *Harvard Theological Review,* XXVIII (1935), 55–60.

1026.* Minkin, Jacob S., *The Romance of Hassidism,* New York, 1935, 12–15.

1027.* Levine, Israel, "Philo and Maimonides," *Faithful Rebels: A Study in Jewish Speculative Thought,* London, 1936, 43–56; see also 123, 136.

1028.* Macdonald, Duncan Black, *The Hebrew Philosophical Genius: A Vindication,* Princeton, 1936; see Index.

See also nos. 902, 905, 908, 909, 1081, 1091, 1092, 1161, 1171, 1172, 1181, 1184, 1185.

XV. THE DOCTRINE OF GOD

1029.* Alix, Peter, *The Judgment of the Ancient Jewish Church Against the Unitarians, in The Controversy upon the Holy Trinity, and the Divinity of our Blessed Saviour,* London, 1699, pp. xxii, 476; see esp. 75–83, 120–131, 145–155, 186–205, etc.

1030.† Paulides, Panagiotes, "Ἡ περὶ θεοῦ διδασκαλία κατὰ Φίλωνα τὸν Ἰουδαῖον," Ἀθήναιον, I (1872), 191–207, 328–353.

1031.* Guyot, Henri, *L'Infinité divine depuis Philon le Juif jusqu'à Plotin. Avec une introduction sur le même sujet dans la philosophie grecque avant Philon le Juif,* Paris, 1906, pp. xii, 260.

1032. Baudissin, Wolf Wilhelm Grafen, *Kyrios als Gottesname im Judentum und seine Stelle in der Religionsgeschichte,* Giessen, 1929, 4 vols.; see Index in IV.
†Reviewed by Alfred Bertholet in *Theologische Literaturzeitung,* LVII (1932), 52–57.

1033. Marcus, Ralph, *Divine Names and Attributes in Hellenistic Jewish Literature,* off-print from *Proceedings of the American Academy for Jewish Research, 1931–32,* [Philadelphia, 1932], 43–120.
A valuable Index Verborum.

1034. Marmorstein, A., "Philo and the Names of God," *The Jewish Quarterly Review,* N.S. XXII (1931–1932), 295–306.

1035.† Mondolfo, Rodolfo, "L'infinità divina da Filone ai Neoplatonici e i suoi precedenti," *Atene e Roma,* 3. S. I (1933), 192–200.
Republished in Mondolfo's, *L'infinito nel pensiero dei Greci,* Firenze, 1934, 393–409; and see Index. (*Studi filosofici diretti da G. Gentile,* N.S. X.)

See also nos. 939, 1117.

XVI. THE DOCTRINES OF LOGOS, SOPHIA, SPIRIT, AND OTHER INTERMEDIARIES

1036. Waeyen, J. van der, "Dissertatio de λογω adversus J. Clericum," published with Stephen Rittangle's *Libra Veritatis, et de Paschate tractatus,* Frankfort a. M., 1698. (From no. 528 and B.M.)

1037. Kidder, Rich., "The Testimony of Philo the Jew concerning the Holy Trinity, and the λόγος considered," *Demonstration of the Messias,* London, 1700, p. III c. 5 u. 6. (From no. 528.)

1038. Nye, Stephen, "An Account of the Opinions and Books of Philo Judaeus, more especially, concerning the λόγος or Word," *Doctrine of the Holy Trinity,* London, 1701, 58–98. (From no. 528.)

1039.* Witsius, Hermannus, *Miscellaneorum sacrorum libri, editio nova,* Ludduni Batavorum (Leyden), 1736, 2 vols., II, 72–74, 77–79.

1040. Carpzov, Iohannes Benedictus, *De λόγῳ Philonis, non Iohanneo adversus Thomam. Mangey,* Helmstadt, 1749, pp. 44.
Reprinted in no. 1368.

1041.* Bryant, Jacob, *The Sentiments of Philo Judeus concerning the λόγος, or Word of God; together with large extracts from his writings, compared with the Scriptures, on many other particular and essential doctrines of the Christian religion,* Cambridge, 1797.

1042.* Grossmann, Christian Gottlob Leberecht, *Quaestiones Philoneae,* I. "De theologiae Philonis fontibus et auctoritate," II. "De λόγῳ Philonis," Leipzig, 1829, pp. 65, 70.

1043. Dorner, I[saac] A[ugust], *Entwicklungsgeschichte der Lehre von der Person Christi von den ältesten Zeiten bis auf die neuesten dargestellt,* Stuttgart, 1839.
Second edition, Stuttgart, [1845] 1851–54, 2 parts in 3 vols. English translation by William Lindsay Alexander, *History of the Development of the Doctrine of the Person of Christ,* Edinburgh, [1861–63], 5 vols. See, in the English translation, I, i, 19–41, 327–343. (*Clarke's Foreign Theological Library,* III, xi.)

1044. Baur, Ferdinand Christian, *Die christliche Lehre von der Dreieinigkeit und Menschwerdung Gottes in ihrer geschichtlichen Entwicklung,* Tübingen, I, 1841, 59–78, 92–102.

1045.† Semisch, Carl, *Justin der Märtyrer,* Breslau, II, 1842, 267–274. English translation by J. E. Ryland, *Justin Martyr: His Life, Writings, and Opinions,* Edinburgh, II, 1843, 165–207, esp. 170–180.

1046.* Keferstein, Friedrich, *Philo's Lehre von den göttlichen Mittelwesen. Zugleich eine kurze Darstellung der Grundzüge des philonischen Systems*, Leipzig, 1846, pp. vii, 256.

1047.* Bucher, Jordan, *Philonische Studien. Versuch, die Frage nach der persönlichen Hypostase in den philonischen Schriften auftretenden Logos auf historisch-pragmatischem Wege zu lösen. Zugleich eine gedrängte Darlegung des philonischen Systems*, Tübingen, 1848, pp. xii, 44.

1048.† Lutterbeck, Joh. Ant. Bernh., "Der philonische Lehrbegriff," *Die Neutestamentlichen Lehrbegriffe, oder Untersuchungen über das Zeitalter der Religionswende, die Vorstufen des Christenthums und die erste Gestaltung desselben*, Mainz, 1852, I, 418–446; see also Index in II.

1049.* Gaillard, Jean-Jacques, *Essai sur l'origine de la théorie du Logos et sur les rapports de la doctrine de Jean avec celle de Philon*, Thèse (Strasbourg), Strasbourg, 1864, pp. 35.

1050. Liddon, Henry Parry, *The Divinity of our Lord and Saviour Jesus Christ*, The Bampton Lectures for 1866, London, Oxford, and Cambridge, 1867, 95–108. Frequently republished.

1051.* Treitel, Leopold, *De Philonis Judaei sermone*, Diss. (Vratislavia), Vratislaviae (Breslau), 1870, pp. 29.

1052. Buschmann, [Joseph], *Eine exegetische Studie über den Logos des Philo*. Progr. d. Stiftsschule, 4, Aachen, 1872, pp. 26. (From no. 532.)

1053.* Heinze, Max, *Die Lehre vom Logos in der griechischen Philosophie*, Oldenburg, 1872, 204–297.

1054.† Rippner, "Ueber die Ursprünge des philonischen Logos," *Monatsschrift für Geschichte und Wissenschaft des Judenthums*, XXI (1872), 289–305.

1055.* Buschmann, Joseph, *Die Persönlichkeit des philonischen Λόγος. Eine exegetische Studie über Philo's Λόγος unter Zugrundlegung seiner eigenen Schriften*, Aachen, 1873, pp. 65.

1056.* Anet, Kennedy, *La notion du Logos dans la philosophie grecque, dans Saint Jean & dans les pères apologètes grecs*, Thèse, Liége, 1874, pp. 84.

1057. Lake, J[ohn] W., *Plato, Philo, and Paul; or, The Pagan Conception of a "Divine Logos" shewn to have been the basis of the Christian dogma of the Deity of Christ*, London, [1874], pp. 76. (*Thomas Scott's publications*.) Translated into Italian, *Platone, Filone et Paolo*, Milan, 1876, pp. 80. (From no. 531, vol. VIII [1877], 136.)

1058.* Soulier, Henry, *La doctrine du Logos chez Philon d'Alexandrie*, Diss. (Leipzig), Turin, 1876, pp. viii, 165.
Reviewed by Carlo Passaglia, *Rivista di filologia e d'istruzione classica*,

IV (1876), 614–664; by M.H., *Literarisches Centralblatt für Deutschland*, [XXVIII] (1877), 455 f.

1059.* Réville, Jean, *Le Logos d'après Philon d'Alexandrie*, Thèse (Geneva), Geneva, 1877, pp. 94.

1060. Καλεγορᾶς, Ν., "Περὶ λόγου, διδασκαλίου Φίλωνος τοῦ Ἰουδαίου," Σωτηρ, Ἔτος α', φυλλ. γ', pp. 33–48.

1061. Klasen, Frz., *Die alttestamentliche Weisheit und der Logos der jüdisch-alexandrinischen Philosophie auf historischer Grundlage in Vergleich gesetzt. Beitrag zur Christologie*, Freiburg i. Br., 1878, pp. vi, 87. (From Heinsius, *Bücher Lexikon*.)

1062. Harnoch, Agathon, *De Philonis Judaei λόγῳ inquisitio*, Regiomonti, (Königsberg), 1879, pp. 38.

1063. Hillen, W., *Die alttestamentliche Chochma, der platonisch-philonische Logos, und das chinesische Tao*, program, Coesfeld, 1882. (From no. 539.)

1064.* Swainson, Charles Anthony, "Logos, the Word," in William Smith and Henry Wace, *A Dictionary of Christian Biography, Literature, Sects and Doctrines*, London, III, 1882, 735–737.

1065. Aall, Anathon, *Der Logos. Geschichte seiner Entwickelung in der griechischen Philosophie und der christlichen Litteratur*, Leipzig, 1896, 1899, I, 184–231, and Index in II.

1066. Heinze, M., "Emanatismus," in Albert Hauck, *Realencyklopädie für protestantische Theologie und Kirche*, Leipzig, V, 1898, 329–336, esp. 331 f.

1067. Mills, Lawrence, "Was Vohu Manah Philo's Logos?" *The Imperial and Asiatic Quarterly Review*, 3. S. IX (1900), 351 f.

1068. Mills, Lawrence [H.], "The Avesta not Philonian," *The Imperial and Asiatic Quarterly Review*, 3. S. XI (1901), 124–127.

1069.† Mills, Lawrence [H.], "Philo's δυνάμεις and the Amesha Spenta," *The Journal of the Royal Asiatic Society of Great Britain and Ireland*, 1901, 553–568.

1070.* Reitzenstein, R[ichard], *Zwei religionsgeschichtliche Fragen nach ungedruckten griechischen Texten der Strassburger Bibliothek*, Strassburg, 1901; see 12, 53 n., 75 n., 84, 100, 102.

1071. Kirn, O., "Logos," in Albert Hauck, *Realencyklopädie für protestantische Theologie und Kirche*, Leipzig, XI, 1902, 599–605.

1072. Kohler, Kaufmann, "Memra," *The Jewish Encyclopedia*, New York, VIII, 1904, 464 f.

1073. Giambelli, Carlo, "Dell' opera pseudo-Aristotelica intitolata: *Theologia sive mystica philosophia*. Saggio critico sulla coltura filosofica e letteraria del Risorgimento, preceduto da brevi cenni sopra Filone Ales-

sandrino," *Rendiconti della Reale Accademia dei Lincei, Classe di scienze morali, storiche e filologiche,* XV (1906), 243–277.
*Reprinted, Rome, 1906, pp. 39.

1074.* Mills, Lawrence Heyworth, "The Philonian Lógos," *Zaraθuštra, Philo, the Achaemenids and Israel,* Chicago, 1906, I, 136–208.

1075. Krebs, Engelbert, *Der Logos als Heiland im ersten Jahrhundert. Ein religions- und dogmengeschichtlicher Beitrag zur Erlösungslehre. Mit einem Anhang: Poimandres und Johannes. Kritisches referat über Reitzensteins religionsgeschichtliche Logosstudien,* Freiburg i. B., 1910; see Index.

1076.* Lebreton, J., "The Logos," *The Catholic Encyclopedia,* New York, IX, [1910], 328–331.

1077.* Salmon, Stewart Dingwall Fordyce, and Greive, Alexander James, "Logos," *The Encyclopaedia Britannica,* 11th edit., XVI, 1911, 919–921.

1078.† Cohn, Leopold, "Zur Lehre vom Logos bei Philo," *Judaica, Festschrift zu Hermann Cohens siebzigstem Geburtstage,* Berlin, 1912, 303–331.
Reviewed by Nathan Porges, *Deutsche Literaturzeitung,* XXXVII (1916), 1542.

1079.† Treitel, L[eopold], "Die alexandrinische Lehre von den Mittelwesen oder göttlichen Kräften, insbesondere bei Philo, geprüft auf die Frage, ob und welchen Einfluss sie auf das Mutterland Palästina gehabt," *Judaica. Festschrift zu Hermann Cohens siebzigstem Geburtstage,* Berlin, 1912, 177–184.
Reprinted in no. 643, pp. 123–130.

1080.* Watson, John, *The Interpretation of Religious Experience. The Gifford Lectures delivered in the University of Glasgow in the Years 1910–12,* Glasgow, 1912, 2 vols., I, 27, 51–54.

1081. Schencke, Wilhelm, *Die Chokma (Sophia) in der jüdischen Hypostasenspekulation: Ein Beitrag zur Geschichte der religiösen Ideen im Zeitalter des Hellenismus,* Kristiania, 1913, 50–73, esp. 67–69. (*Videnskapsselskapets Skrifter. II. Hist.-Filos. Klasse,* 1912, 6.)

1082. Andres, Friedrich, *Die Engellehre der griechischen Apologeten des zweiten Jahrhunderts und ihr Verhältnis zur griechisch-römischen Dämonologie,* Paderborn, 1914, 163–5. (A. Ehrhard and J. P. Kirsch, *Forschungen zur christlichen Literatur- und Dogmengeschichte,* XII, 3.)

1083.† Kellermann, Benzion, "Licht und Logos bei Philo," in his edit. of *Die Kämpfe Gottes von Lewi ben Gerson,* Berlin, 1916, II, 307–336.

(*Schriften der Lehranstalt für die Wissenschaft des Judentums,* V, 1–3.)

1084.* Leisegang, Hans, *Der heilige Geist. Das Wesen und Werden der mystischintuitiven Erkenntnis in der Philosophie und Religion der Griechen,* Leipzig and Berlin, 1919, pp. 267.

1085.† Heinemann, I[saak], "Die Lehre vom Heiligen Geist in Judentum und in den Evangelien," *Monatsschrift für Geschichte und Wissenschaft des Judentums,* LXVI (1922), 169–180, 268–279; LXVII (1923), 26–35.

1086.* Leisegang, Hans, *Pneuma Hagion: Der Ursprung des Geistbegriffs der synoptischen Evangelien aus der griechischen Mystik,* Leipzig, 1922, pp. 150. (*Veröffentlichungen des Forschungsinstituts für vergleichende Religionsgeschichte an der Universität Leipzig,* 4.)

1087.† Lagrange, M.-J., "Le Logos de Philon," *Revue biblique,* XXXII (1923), 321–371.

1088.† Leisegang, [Hans], "Logos," in Pauly-Wissowa-Kroll, *Real-Encyclopädie der classischen Altertumswissenschaft,* XIII, i, 1926, 1035–1081.

1089.† Leisegang, [Hans], "Sophia," in Pauly-Wissowa-Kroll-Mittelhaus, *Real-Encyclopädie der classischen Altertumswissenschaft,* III A, i, 1927, 1019–1039.

1090.† Hoyle, R. Birch, "Spirit in the Writings and Experience of Philo," *The Biblical Review,* XIII (1928), 351–369.
*Reviewed by Marcus in no. 543, p. 468.

1091. Bieler, Majer, *Der göttliche Wille (Logosbegriff) bei Gabirol,* Diss. (Würzburg), 1932 (imprint 1933), pp. 89.
Reviewed by I. Heinemann, *Monatsschrift für Geschichte und Wissenschaft des Judentums,* LXXVI (1932), 493.

1092. Box, G. H., "The Idea of Intermediation in Jewish Theology: A note on Memra and Shekinah," *The Jewish Quarterly Review,* N.S. XXIII (1932–1933), 103–119.

1093.* Jackson, F. J. Foakes, *The History of the Christian Church from the Earliest Times to A.D. 461,* New York and London, 1933, 156–161.

See also nos. 944, 1103, 1377–1397, 1399, 1483.

XVII. MAN

1094. Bengel, Ernestus Theoph. de, "Dissertatio historico-theologica, quid doctrina de animorum immortalitate religioni Christianae debeat, ex caussae natura et ex rebus factis monstrans," *Opuscula Academica,* edited by M. Jo. Godofr. Pressel, Hamburg, 1834, 45–272; see esp. 203–214.

1095. Schreitet, "Sur l'immortalité," *Analecta de Keil et Tschirner,* t.I (H.2) et t.III (H.2). (From no. 626.)

1096. Freudenthal, Max, *Die Erkenntnislehre Philos von Alexandria,* Diss. (Greifswald), Berlin, 1891, pp. 78, with bibliographical foot-notes. *Reprinted, Berlin, 1891.
   Reviewed by Johannes Dräseke, *Wochenschrift für klassische Philologie,* VIII (1891), 1361–1365; by R. Ausfeld, *Neue philologische Rundschau,* 1892, 298–301; †by P[aul] Wendland, *Berliner philologische Wochenschrift,* XII (1892), 751 f.; by Whlrb., *Literarisches Centralblatt für Deutschland,* [XLIII] (1892), 4; and by Ch. Wirth, *Blätter für das Gymnasial-Schulwesen herausgegeben vom Bayer. Gymnasiallehrervereine,* XXIX (1893), 25 f.

1097. Cremer, "Fleisch," in Albert Hauck, *Realencyklopädie für protestantische Theologie und Kirche,* Leipzig, VI, 1899, 98–105, esp. 100 f.

1098. Cremer, "Inspiration," in Albert Hauck, *Realencyklopädie für protestantische Theologie und Kirche,* Leipzig, IX, 1901, 183–203, esp. 186 f.

1099.† Dickerman, Sherwood Owen, "Some Stock Illustrations of Animal Intelligence in Greek Psychology," *Transactions and Proceedings of the American Philological Association,* XLII (1911), 123–130.

1100.† Colson, F. H., "Philo on Education," *The Journal of Theological Studies,* XVIII (1916–1917), 151–162.

1101.† Heinemann, I[saak], "Philons Lehre vom Heiligen Geist und der intuitiven Erkenntnis," *Monatsschrift für Geschichte und Wissenschaft des Judentums,* LXIV (1920), 8–29, 101–122.

1102.† Mühl, Max, "Ἄνθρωπος ἡμερώτατον ζῷον," *Philologische Wochenschrift,* XLIV (1924), 405.

1103. Stegmann, Basil Augustine, *Christ, the "Man from Heaven": A Study of 1 Cor. 15, 45–47 in the Light of the Anthropology of Philo Judaeus,* Diss. (Catholic University), Washington, 1927, pp. xvi, 104; bibliography xi–xiv. (*The Catholic University of America New Testament Studies,* VI.)

1104.* Mühl, Max, *Die antike Menschheitsidee in ihrer geschichtlichen Ent-*

wicklung, Leipzig, 1928; see 90–93, 101. (Otto Immisch, *Das Erbe der alten Schriften über Wesen und Wirkung der Antike,* II, xiv.)

1105.* Gross, Josef, *Philons von Alexandreia Anschauungen über die Natur des Menschen,* Diss. (Tübingen), Tübingen, 1930, pp. 90.
Reviewed in *Literarisches Zentralblatt für Deutschland,* LXXXII (1931), 684; and *by Marcus in no. 543, p. 474.

1106.* Kuhlmann, Gerhardt, *Theologia naturalis bei Philon und bei Paulus: eine Studie zur Grundlegung der paulinischen Anthropologie,* Gütersloh, 1930, pp. 145. (Otto Schmitz, *Neutestamentliche Forschungen,* I, 7.)
*Reviewed by W. Foerster, *Theologisches Literaturblatt,* LII (1931), 402–403; †by Ernst Jacob, *Monatsschrift für Geschichte und Wissenschaft des Judentums,* LXXV (1931), 333–334; and †by H. Windisch, *Theologische Literaturzeitung,* LVII (1932), 9–12.

1107.† Puech, Henri-Charles, "Μορμωτός. A propos de Lycophron, de Rab et de Philon d'Alexandrie," *Revue des études grecques,* XLVI (1933), 311–333.

1108.* Schmidt, Helmut, *Die Anthropologie Philons von Alexandreia,* Diss. (Leipzig), Würzburg, 1933, pp. vii, 179.
Republished as monograph, Würzburg, 1933.
*Reviewed by Marcus in no. 543, pp. 486–487.

1109. Juhnke, Johannes, *Das Persönlichkeitsideal in der Stoa im Lichte der paulinischen Erlösungslehre,* Greifswald, 1934, pp. 92. (*Greifswalder Theologische Forschungen,* 5.)
Reviewed by G. Breithaupt, *Theologische Literaturzeitung,* LXI (1936), 466–467.

1110.* Knuth, Werner, *Der Begriff der Sünde bei Philon von Alexandria,* Diss. (Jena), Würzburg, 1934, pp. vi, 85.
*Republished as monograph, Würzburg, 1934.

1110a. Husner, Fritz, *Leib und Seele in der Sprache Senecas,* Leipzig, 1924; see Index. (*Philologus,* Supplementband, XVII, iii.)

See also nos. 1084, 1086, 1148.

XVIII. MYSTERY, MYSTICISM, SALVATION, FAITH, AND RELIGIOUS EXPERIENCE

1111. Thalemann, Christian Guil., *Tractatus de nube super Arca Foederis . . . Accesit commentatio de auctoritate Philonis et Iosephi in historia rituum sacrorum,* Lipsiae, 1771, 125–172.

1112. Grossman, Chr[istian] Gottlob Lebr[echt], *De Judaeorum disciplina arcani,* [Leipzig], [1833–1834], parts I and II, pp. 28, 44.

1113.* Schlatter, A[dolf], *Der Glaube im Neuen Testament. Eine Untersuchung zur neutestamentlichen Theologie,* Leiden, 1885; see esp. 84–105, 545–552.

Fourth edition, Stuttgart, 1927, 60–80, 575–581.

1114.† Ziegert, Paul, "Über die Ansätze zu einer Mysterienlehre aufgebaut auf den antiken Mysterien bei Philo Judäus," *Theologische Studien und Kritiken,* LXVII (1894), 706–732.

1115.† Hort, F. J. A. and Murray, J. O. F., "Εὐχαριστία—Εὐχαριστεῖν," *The Journal of Theological Studies,* III (1901–1902), 594–598.

1116.* Reitzenstein, R[ichard], *Poimandres: Studien zur griechisch-ägyptischen und frühchristlichen Literatur,* Leipzig, 1904; see Indices.

1117.† Carman, Augustine S., "Philo's Doctrine of the Divine Father and the Virgin Mother," *The American Journal of Theology,* IX (1905), 491–518.

1118. Pelli, Amedeo, "Filone e i padri della Chiesa," "Filone Plotino e i Neoplatonici," "Il misticismo e l'estasi di Filone," *Studi su Filone Giudeo,* Bologna, 1906, pp. 59.

1119.* Windisch, Hans, *Die Frömmigkeit Philos und ihre Bedeutung für das Christentum,* Leipzig, 1909, pp. iv, 140.

1120. Reitzenstein, Richard, *Die hellenistischen Mysterienreligionen,* Leipzig and Berlin, 1910; see Index.

Second edition, *ibid.,* 1920; third edition, *ibid.,* 1927.

1121.† Schermann, Theodor, "Εὐχαριστία und Εὐχαριστεῖν in ihrem Bedeutungswandel bis 200 n. Chr.," *Philologus,* LXIX (N.F. XXIII) (1910), 375–410.

1122. Wetter, Gillis Pison, Φῶς. *Eine Untersuchung über hellenistische Frömmigkeit, zugleich ein Beitrag zum Verständnis des Manichäismus,* Upsala and Leipzig, [1915]; see the Index, p. 186. (*Skrifter utgifna af kungl. humanistiska Vetenskaps-Samfundet,* XVII, 1.)

1123. Casel, Odo, *De philosophorum graecorum silentio mystico*, Giessen, 1919, 72–86. (Ludolf Malten and Otto Weinreich, *Religionsgeschichtliche Versuche und Vorarbeiten*, XVI, 2.)

1124.* Kennedy, H[arry] A[ngus] A[lexander], *Philo's Contribution to Religion*, London, 1919, pp. xi, 245.
Reviewed by H. Windisch, *Theologische Literaturzeitung*, XLV (1920), 197–198.

1125.* Williger, Eduard, *Hagios. Untersuchungen zur Terminologie des Heiligen in den hellenisch-hellenistischen Religionen*, Giessen, 1922, 102–108. (Albrecht Dieterich and Richard Wünsch, *Religionsgeschichtliche Versuche und Vorarbeiten*, XIX, 1.)
† Reviewed by I. Heinemann, *Monatsschrift für Geschichte und Wissenschaft des Judentums*, LXVII (1923), 279 f.

1126.* Peterson, Erik, "Der Gottesfreund: Beiträge zur Geschichte eines religiösen Terminus," *Zeitschrift für Kirchengeschichte*, XLII (N.F. V) (1923), 161–202; see esp. 172, 178–182, 187, 191.

1127.† Cerfaux, Lucien, "Influence des Mystères sur le Judaisme alexandrin avant Philon," *Le Muséon: Revue d'études orientales*, XXXVII (1924), 29–88.
†Reviewed by L[agrange], *Revue biblique*, XXXIV (1925), 150–152; and *by Marcus in no. 543, p. 463 f.

1128.* Horodetske, S. A., "Philo and the Jewish Mystery" (Hebrew), *Debir*, II (1924), 165–175.

1129.* Angus, S., *The Mystery-Religions and Christianity. A Study in the Religious Background of Early Christianity*, New York, 1925, pp. xvi, 359; see Index.

1130.† Heinemann, I[saak], "Der Begriff des Übermenschen in der jüdischen Religionsphilosophie," *Der Morgen*, I (1925); see 5–9.
*Reviewed by Marcus in no. 543, pp. 466.

1131.† Heinemann, I[saak], "Messianismus und Mysterienreligion," *Monatsschrift für Geschichte und Wissenschaft des Judentums*, LXIX (1925), 337–355.

1132.* Moore, George Foot, *Metempsychosis*, Cambridge (Massachusetts) and London, 1925; see 49 f., 82 n. (*Ingersoll Lectures on Immortality*, 1914.)

1133.* Reitzenstein, Richard, "Griechische Lehren," part I of R. Reitzenstein and H. H. Schaeder, *Studien zum antiken Synkretismus aus Iran und Griechenland*, Leipzig and Berlin, 1926; see 8, 10, 23–26, 30–32. (Fritz Saxl, *Studien der Bibliothek Warburg*, VII.)

1134.* Baeck, Leo, "Ursprung und Anfänge der jüdischen Mystik," *Entwicklungsstufen der jüdischen Religion*, Giessen, 1927, 91–103. (*Vorträge des Institutum Judaicum an der Universität Berlin*, I.)

1135.* Kraeling, Carl H., *Anthropos and Son of Man. A Study in the Religious Syncretism of the Hellenistic Orient*, New York, 1927; see 51 n., 77–79, 117, 176 f.
*Reviewed by Marcus in no. 543, p. 468.

1136.† Hogg, James Edward, " 'A Virgin-Birth in Philo' (Exod. 2:21)," *The American Journal of Semitic Languages and Literatures*, XLIV (1927–1928), 206 f.

1137.* Angus, S., *The Religious Quests of the Graeco-Roman World. A Study in the Historical Background of Early Christianity*, New York, 1929; see Index.

1138.* Lewy, Hans, *Sobria Ebrietas. Untersuchungen zur Geschichte der antiken Mystik*, Giessen, 1929, pp. 174. (Hans Lietzmann, *Beihefte zur Zeitschrift für die neutestamentliche Wissenschaft und die Kunde der älteren Kirche*, 9.)
†Reviewed by I. Heinemann, *Monatsschrift für Geschichte und Wissenschaft des Judentums*, LXXIII (1929), 434–437; †by A. D. Nock, *The Journal of Theological Studies*, XXXI (1929–1930), 308–310; †by Shirley Jackson Case, *The Journal of Religion*, X (1930), 415; †by J. Coppens, *Revue d'histoire ecclésiastique*, XXVI (1930), 670–672; †by Jules Lebreton, "Saint Cyprien et Origène," *Recherches de science religieuse*, XX (1930), 160–162; †by Georges Vajda, *Revue des études juives*, XC (1931), 109–112; †by K. H. E. de Jong, *Museum. Maandblad voor Philologie en Geschiedenis*, XLI (1933–1934), 160 f.; and *by Marcus in no. 543, p. 469.

1139.* Reitzenstein, R[ichard], "Philos Lehre von der Wiedergeburt," *Die Vorgeschichte der christlichen Taufe*, Leipzig and Berlin, 1929, 103–126.
Reviewed by Hans Heinrich Schaeder, *Gnomon*, V (1929), 353–370; and *by Marcus in no. 543, pp. 472 f.

1140. Reitzenstein, R[ichard], "Zwei Arten religionsgeschichtlicher Forschung," *Archiv für Religionswissenschaft*, XXVII (1929); see 252–277.

1141.* Willoughby, Harold R., "The Mysticism of Philo," *Pagan Regeneration: A Study of Mystery Initiations in the Graeco-Roman World*, Chicago, 1929, 225–262.
*Reviewed by Marcus in no. 543, p. 472.

1142.* Reitzenstein, R[ichard], "Heilige Handlung," *Vorträge, 1928–1929, über die Vorstellungen von der Himmelsreise der Seele*, Leipzig and Berlin, 1930, 21–41. (Fitz Saxl, *Vorträge der Bibliothek Warburg*, [VIII].)

1142a. Amann, Julius, *Die Zeusrede des Ailios Aristides*, Stuttgart, 1931; see Index. (*Tübinger Beiträge zur Altertumswissenschaft*, XII.)

1143. Boughton, J. S., "Conscience and the Logos in Philo," *The Lutheran Church Quarterly*, IV (1931), 121–133.

1144.* Pascher, Joseph, ἡ βασιλικὴ ὁδός. *Der Königsweg zu Wiedergeburt und Vergottung bei Philon von Alexandreia*, Paderborn, 1931, pp. 280. (*Studien zur Geschichte und Kultur des Altertums*, XVII, 3, 4.)
Reviewed by G. A. van den Bergh van Eysinga, *Nieuw theologisch Tijdschrift*, XXI (1932), 368–370; by W. Wilbrand, *Theologische Revue*, XXXI (1932), 444–449; *by Jules Lebreton, *Recherches de science religieuse*, XXIII (1933), 334–337; by H. Rahner, *Zeitschrift für katholische Theologie*, LVII (1933), 103–109; by Herbert Preisker, *Theologische Literaturzeitung*, LIX (1934), 177 f.; and *by Marcus in no. 543, p. 475 f.

1145.† Wenschkewitz, Hans, "Philo von Alexandria," *Die Spiritualisierung der Kultusbegriffe Tempel, Priester und Opfer im Neuen Testament*, Leipzig, 1932, 67–87. (Gottfried Polster, Ἄγγελος, *Archiv für neutestamentliche Zeitgeschichte und Kulturkunde, Beiheft* 4.)
*Reviewed by Marcus in no. 543, p. 482.

1146.* Goodenough, Erwin R[amsdell], *By Light, Light: The Mystic Gospel of Hellenistic Judaism*, New Haven and London, 1935, pp. xv, 436.
†Reviewed in *The Times Literary Supplement*, London, XXXIV, Oct. 24, 1935, p. 675; †by B. S. E[aston], *The Living Church*, XCII (1935), 812; †by W. E. G[arrison], *The Christian Century*, LII (1935), 856; †by E. F. Scott, *Church History*, IV (1935), 228 f.; †by Shirley Jackson Case, *The Journal of Religion*, XV (1935), 484 f.; in *Jewish Examiner*, XIII (1935), no. 25, p. 4; †by E. F. Scott, *The American Historical Review*, XLI (1935–1936), 321 f.; †by Abram Simon, *The Catholic Historical Review*, XXI (1935–1936), 451–453; †by Boaz Cohen, *Journal of the American Oriental Society*, LVI (1936), 500–505; by M.-J. Lagrange, *Revue biblique*, XLV (1936), 265–269; by K. Lake, *Journal of Biblical Literature*, LV (1936), 90–93; †by J. Leipoldt, *Theologische Literaturzeitung*, LXI (1936), 175 f.; †by Ralph Marcus, *American Journal of Philology*, LVII (1936), 203–205; †by Harold R. Willoughby, *Anglican Theological Review*, XVIII (1936), 36–38; by Arthur Darby Nock, *Gnomon*, XIII (1937), 156–165; by G. C. Richards, *The Journal of Theological Studies*, XXXVIII (1937), 414–416; by S. Belkin, *The Jewish Quarterly Review*, N.S. XXVIII (1937–1938), 279–282; and by *H. P. Kingdon, *The Journal of Egyptian Archeology*, XXIII (1937), 139 f.

1147.* Peisker, Martin, *Der Glaubensbegriff bei Philon, hauptsächlich dargestellt an Moses und Abraham*, Diss. (Breslau), Aue i. Sa., 1936, pp. 35.

1148. Sevenster, Jan Nicolaas, *Het verlossingsbegrip bij Philo vergeleken met de verlossingsgedachten van de synoptische evangeliën*, Assen, 1936, pp. 190. (*Van Gorcum's Theologische Bibliotheek*, IV.)

†Reviewed by G. A. van den Bergh van Eysinga, *Nieuw theologisch Tijdschrift*, XXV (1936), 274–276.

1149. Goodenough, Erwin Ramsdell, "Literal Mystery in Hellenistic Judaism," *Quantulacumque: Studies Presented to Kirsopp Lake by Pupils, Colleagues and Friends,* edited by Robert P. Casey, Silva Lake, and Agnes K. Lake, London, [1937], 227–241.

See also nos. 962, 972, 1084, 1085, 1086, 1101, 1110, 1198, 1200, 1203, 1295.

XIX. ETHICS

1150.† [Frankel, Zach.], "Zur Ethik des jüdisch-alexandrinischen Philosophen Philo," *Monatsschrift für Geschichte und Wissenschaft des Judenthums*, XVI (1867), 241–252, 281–297.

1151.† Wolff, M., "Die philonische Ethik in ihren wesentlichsten Punkten zusammengestellt," *Philosophische Monatshefte*, XV (1879), 333–350.

1152.* Tiktin, Salomon, *Die Lehre von den Tugenden und Pflichten bei Philo von Alexandrien*, Diss. (Bern), Breslau, 1895, pp. 59.

1153. Clarke, John C[aldwell] C[alhoun], "The Exposition of the Bible by Philo, the Alexandrian Jew," *Man and his Divine Father*, Chicago, 1900, 143–183.

1154.† Lumbroso, Giacomo, "Lettere al Signor Professore Breccia," *Bulletin de la Société Archéologique d'Alexandrie*, N.S. IV (1918), 72 f.

1155. Bolkestein, H., *Een geval van sociaal-ethisch syncretisme*, Amsterdam, 1931, pp. 52. (*Mededeelingen der koninklijke Akademie van Wetenschappen [te Amsterdam]*, *Afdeeling Letterkunde*, 72, Serie B., 1.)
†Reviewed by H[ans] Windisch, *Theologische Literaturzeitung*, LVII (1932), 194–196.

1156.* Geiger, Franz, *Philon von Alexandreia als sozialer Denker*, Stuttgart, 1932, pp. xi, 118. (*Tübinger Beiträge zur Altertumswissenschaft*, XIV.)
†Reviewed by "p. b.," *Ricerche religiose*, IX (1933), 471–472; †by [I.] Heinemann, *Monatsschrift für Geschichte und Wissenschaft des Judentums*, LXXVII (1933), 233; †by Jules Lebreton, *Recherches de science religieuse*, XXIII (1933), 337–338; by Arnaldo Momigliano, *Rivista di filologia e d'istruzione classica*, LXI (N.S. XI) (1933), 94–98; by Franz Schehl, *Deutsche Literaturzeitung*, LIV (3. F. 4) (1933), 57–62; by Paul Shorey, *Classical Philology*, XXVIII (1933), 146–148; and *by Marcus in no. 543, p. 483 f.

1157.* Schäfer, Maximilian, *Ein frühmittelstoisches System der Ethik bei Cicero. Untersuchung von Ciceros drittem Buche "de finibus bonorum et malorum" nach Aufbau und Zugehörigkeit auf Grund griechischer Quellen zur stoischen Ethik*, München, 1934; see 25, 66, 72, 239, 282.

XX. LAW AND POLITICAL THEORY

1158.* Seldenus, Ioannes, *De iure naturali & gentium, iuxta disciplinam ebraeorum, libri septem*, Londinum, Richardus Bishopius, 1640; see 27–30 and *passim*.

1159.† Delaunay, Ferdinand, "Note sur le système politique de Philon," *Académie des Sciences Morales et Politiques, Compte-Rendu*, XCIX (1873), 305–313.

1160.† Bernays, [Jacob], "Philon's Hypothetika und die Verwünschungen des Buzyges in Athen," *Monatsberichte der Königlich Preussischen Akademie der Wissenschaften zu Berlin, aus dem Jahre, 1876*, 1877, 589–609.
Reprinted in H. Usener, *Gesammelte Abhandlungen von Jacob Bernays*, Berlin, 1885, I, 262–282.

1161.* Ritter, Bernhard, *Philo und die Halacha. Eine vergleichende Studie unter steter Berücksichtigung des Josephus*, Leipzig, 1879, pp. x, 139. Reviewed in *The Academy*, XVI (1879), 174; by C. Siegfried, *Jenaer Literaturzeitung*, VI (1879), 478 f.; and by H. Str., *Literarisches Centralblatt für Deutschland*, [XXX] (1879), 1554.

1162.* Pantasopulos, Elias Ar., *Die Lehre vom natürlichen und positiven Rechte bei Philo Judaeus*, München, 1893, pp. 28.

1163. Nicole, Jules, "Avillius Flaccus préfet d'Egypte et Philon d'Alexandrie d'après un papyrus inédit," *Revue de philologie, de littérature et d'histoire anciennes*, N.S. XXII (1898), 18–27.

1164.† Hirzel, Rudolf, " ᾿Αγραφος νόμος," *Abhandlungen der philologisch-historischen Classe der Königlich Sächsischen Gesellschaft der Wissenschaften*, XX, i (1900), pp. 98.

1165.* Weyl, Heinrich, *Die jüdischen Strafgesetze bei Flavius Josephus in ihrem Verhältnis zu Schrift und Halacha*, Diss. (Bern), Berlin, 1900, pp. 162.

1166.* Hirzel, Rudolf, *Der Eid: Ein Beitrag zu seiner Geschichte*, Leipzig, 1902; see 6, 11 n., 15, 16 n., 18 n., 27 n., 56, 88 n., 89 n., 109 n., 110 n., 123 n., 124 n., 130 n.

1167.† Treitel, L[eopold], "Der Nomos, insonderheit Sabbat und Feste, in philonischer Beleuchtung, an der Hand von Philos Schrift De Septenario," *Monatsschrift für Geschichte und Wissenschaft des Judenthums*, XLVII (1903), 214–231, 317–321, 399–417, 490–514.
Reprinted in no. 643.

1168.† Hart, J. H. A., "Corban," *The Jewish Quarterly Review*, XIX (1906–1907), 615–650.

1169. Hirzel, Rudolf, *Themis, Dike und Verwandtes,* Leipzig, 1907; see 124 n., 224 n., 227 n., 228 n., 376 n., 380 n., 388 n., 396.

1170.† Heinemann, J[saak], "Philos Lehre vom Eid. Eine quellenkritische Untersuchung," *Judaica. Festschrift zu Hermann Cohens siebzigstem Geburtstage,* Berlin, 1912, 109–118.

1171.* Revel, Bernard, *The Karaite Halakah and its Relation to Sadducean, Samaritan and Philonian Halakah,* Part I, Thesis (Dropsie College), Philadelphia, 1913, pp. 88.

1172. Revel, Bernard, "The Penalty of Perjury in Philo and Maimonides" (Hebrew), *Horeb,* 1913.

1173.† Mann, Jacob, "Oaths and Vows in the Synoptic Gospels," *The American Journal of Theology,* XXI (1917), 260–274.

1174.† Aptowitzer, V., "Observations on the Criminal Law of the Jews," *The Jewish Quarterly Review,* N.S. XV (1924–1925), 55–118.

1175.† Aptowitzer, V., "The Rewarding and Punishing of Animals and Inanimate Objects," *Hebrew Union College Annual,* Cincinnati, III (1926); see 125–130.

1176.* Goodenough, Erwin Ramsdell, "Philo and Public Life," *The Journal of Egyptian Archaeology,* XII (1926), 77–79.
†Reviewed by H. I. Bell, *The Journal of Egyptian Archaeology,* XIII (1927), 109; and *by Marcus in no. 543, p. 446 f.

1177.† Leisegang, Hans, "Der Ursprung der Lehre Augustins von der Civitas Dei," *Archiv für Kulturgeschichte,* XVI (1926), 127–158.

1178.† Heinemann, I[saak], "Die Lehre vom ungeschriebenen Gesetz im jüdischen Schrifttum," *Hebrew Union College Annual,* Cincinnati, IV (1927), 149–171, esp. 152–159.
*Reviewed by Marcus in no. 543, p. 467.

1179. Revel, B[ernard], "Philonian Halakah," *The Jewish Forum,* XI (1928), 120–122.

1180.* Goodenough, Erwin Ramsdell, *The Jurisprudence of the Jewish Courts in Egypt: Legal Administration by the Jews under the early Roman Empire as Described by Philo Judaeus,* New Haven and London, 1929, pp. vii, 268.
†Reviewed in *The Times Literary Supplement,* London, XXIX (April 3, 1930), 296; †by I. Heinemann, *Monatsschrift für Geschichte und Wissenschaft des Judentums,* LXXIV (1930), 363–369; by the same, *Deutsche Literaturzeitung,* LI (III. Folge, I) (1930), 1127–1131; †by Nic. Hohlwein, *Bulletin Bibliographique et Pédagogique du Musée Belge,* XXXIV (1930), 9 f.; †by J. G. M[ilne], *The Journal of Hellenic Studies,* L (1930), 353; †by Max Radin, *Yale Law Journal,* XXXIX (1930), 1222–1225 (†cf. Goodenough's answer, *ibid.,* XL

[1930], 146–149); by Max Radin, *Classical Philology*, XXV (1930), 294–297; †by William Renwick Riddell, *American Bar Association Journal*, XVI (1930), 812 f.; †by N. Bentwich, "Philo as Jurist," *The Jewish Quarterly Review*, N.S. XXI (1931), 151–157; †by Paul Collart, *Revue de philologie de littérature et d'histoire anciennes*, 3. S. V (1931), 147 f.; †by S. Krauss, *Orientalistische Literaturzeitung*, XXXIV (1931), 451–453; *by S. Levy, *The Jewish Chronicle, The Organ of British Jewery*, XC, *Supplement*, no. 130 (October, 1931), p. vi; †by M. San Nicolò, *The Journal of Egyptian Archaeology*, XVIII (1932), 116–118; †by F. de Zulueta, *The Journal of Egyptian Archaeology*, XVIII (1932), 94 f.; †by F. Heichelheim, *Gnomon*, X (1934), 108 f.; and *by Marcus in no. 543, p. 47 f.

1181. Gulak, A., "Deed of Betrothal and Oral Stipulations in Talmudic Law" (Hebrew), *Tarbiz*, III (1931–1932), 361–376.

1182.* Lietzmann, Hans, "Der Sinn des Aposteldekretes und seine Textwandlung," in H. G. Wood, *Amicitiae Corolla, A Volume of Essays Presented to James Rendel Harris*, London, 1933; see 205–207.

1183.* Tracy, Sterling, *Philo Judaeus and the Roman Principate*, Williamsport (Pennsylvania), 1933, pp. 55.
†Reviewed by Henri Henne, *Revue des études anciennes*, XXXVI (1934), 542–545; and *by Marcus in no. 543, p. 487 f.

1184.† Allon, G., "Studies in Philonian Halacha" (Hebrew), *Tarbiz*, V (1933–1934), 28–36, 241–246; VI (1934–1935), 30–37, 452–459.

1185.* Belkin, Samuel, *The Alexandrian Halakah in Apologetic Literature of the First Century C.E.*, Philadelphia, [1936], pp. 70.
*Reviewed by E. R. G[oodenough], *Journal of Biblical Literature*, LV (1936), 319–320.

1186. Langstadt, Erich, "Zu Philos Begriff der Demokratie," in Bruno Schindler, *Occident and Orient . . . [Moses] Gaster Anniversary Volume*, London, [1936], 349–364.

1186a. Belkin, Samuel, *Philo and the Oral Law*, Cambridge (Mass.), pp. 340. (*Harvard Semitic Series*.) To be published in 1938.

See also nos. 659, 665, 666, 735, 1156, 1482.

XXI. APOLOGETICS

1187.* Friedländer, Moriz, *Geschichte der jüdischen Apologetik als Vorge-schichte des Christenthums,* Zürich, 1903, pp. xv, 499.
1188.† Krüger, Paul, *Philo und Josephus als Apologeten des Judentums,* Leipzig, 1906, pp. 82.

XXII. THE MESSIAH

1189.† Frankel, [Z.], "Alexandrinische Messiashoffnungen," *Monatsschrift für Geschichte und Wissenschaft des Judenthums,* VIII (1859), 241–261, 285–308, 321–330.

1190.* Müller, J. G., *Die messianischen Erwartungen des Juden Philo,* Program, Basel, 1870, pp. 25.

1191. Kroll, Josef, "Poseidonios und Vergils vierte Ekloge," *Hermes,* L (1915), see 139–141.

1192. Grégoire, F., "Le Messie chez Philon d'Alexandrie," *Ephemerides theologiae lovanienses,* 1935. (From no. 800.)

See also no. 1131.

XXIII. MAGIC, ALCHEMY, AND NUMBER

1193.* Brown[e], [Sir] Thomas, *Pseudodoxia Epidemica: or, Enquiries into very many Received Tenents, and commonly Presumed Truths . . . The Fifth Edition. With Marginal Observations, and a Table Alphabetical. Whereunto are now added Two Discourses, The one of Urn-Burial, or Sepulchrall Urns, lately found in Norfolk. The other of the Garden of Cyrus, or Network Plantations of the Antients*, London, for the Assigns of Edward Dod, 1669, quarto; see 242–244, 316, 319 f., 366 (misnumbered after p. 322 for 14 pages).
*In the collected edition by Geoffrey Keynes, London, III, 1928, 54–56, 163, 167, 192, 262; V, 1931, 8.

1194.† Carvallo, J., "Paragraphes du livre de la création de Philon relatifs aux propriétés des nombres," *Revue des études juives*, VI (1882–1883), 273–278.

1195. Treitel, L[eopold], *Zu Ph[ilons] Zahlenspekulation (de opif. m.* 15, 47 p. 15, 9 ff. C.). (From no. 539, p. 182*.)

1196.* Lippmann, Edmund O. von, *Entstehung und Ausbreitung der Alchemie*, Berlin, 1919, 1931, 2 vols.; see I, 156; II, 161, and Indices.

1197. Robbins, Frank Egleston, "Posidonius and the Sources of Pythagorean Arithmology," *Classical Philology*, XV (1920), 309–322.

1198.* Thorndike, Lynn, *A History of Magic and Experimental Science*, London and New York, 1923–34, 4 vols., I, 348–359 and Indices to all volumes.

1199.† Robbins, Frank Egleston, "Arithmetic in Philo Judaeus," *Classical Philology*, XXVI (1931), 345–361.

1200.* Staehle, Karl, *Die Zahlenmystik bei Philon von Alexandreia*, Leipzig and Berlin, 1931, pp. vi, 92.
Reviewed by Willy Theiler, *Deutsche Literaturzeitung*, LIV (3. F., IV) (1933), 1304 f.; †by K. H. E. de Jong, *Museum. Maandblad voor Philologie en Geschiedenis*, XLI (1933–1934), 159 f.; †by A[ristide] C[alderini], *Aegyptus*, XIV (1934), 112; and *by Marcus in no. 543, p. 475.

XXIV. PHILO'S RELATION TO GNOSTICISM

1201. Michaelis, Ioannes Davidis, "Dissertatio de indiciis gnosticae philoso-phiae tempore LXX interpretum et Philonis Iudaei," *Syntagma Commentationum*, Goettingen, part II, 1767, 249–276.
1202. Tittmann, C. C., *Tractatus de vestigiis gnosticorum in Novo Testamento frustra quaesitis*, Leipzig, 1773; see esp. 39–53.
1203. Horn, Joh[ann], *Ueber die biblische Gnosis; pragmatische Darstellung der Religionsphilosophie des Orientes zur Erklärung der Heiligen Schrift*, Hannover, 1805, 39, 61–63, 321 f., 357, 362 f., 366–389, 402, 419.
1204. Baur, Ferdinand Christian, *Die christliche Gnosis oder die christliche Religions-Philosophie in ihrer geschichtlichen Entwiklung*, Tübingen, 1835, 12–15, 37–42.
1205.* Hilgenfeld, Adolf, *Die Ketzergeschichte des Urchristenthums*, Leipzig, 1884; see 87–89, 92, 98, 101 f., 105–118, 128, 193 n., 236 n.
1206.† Buonaiuti, Ernesto, "Una reminiscenza filoniana nello gnostico Valentino," *Bollettino di Filologia Classica*, XXV (1918–1919), 27–29.
1207. Steffes, J. P., *Das Wesen des Gnostizismus und sein Verhältnis zum katholischen Dogma: Eine dogmengeschichtliche Untersuchung*, Paderborn, 1922; see Index. (*Forschungen zur christlichen Literatur- und Dogmengeschichte*, XIV, iv.)
1208. Leisegang, Hans, *Die Gnosis*, Leipzig, [1924]; see Indices. (*Kröners Taschenausgabe*, 52.)
1209. Jonas, Hans, *Der Begriff der Gnosis*, (*Teildruck*), Diss. (Marburg), Marburg, 1930, 36–40.

See also nos. 763, 766, 769, 1135.

XXV. ESSENES AND THERAPEUTAE

1210.* Theuet, André, *Cosmographie de Levant,* Lyon, Ian de Tournes et Guil. Gazeau, 1554; see 165 f.

1211.* Godwin, Thomas, "De Essenis," *Mose & Aaron, seu civiles & ecclesiastici ritus antiquorum Hebraeorum, tam quos illi nulli genti debent, quàm quos iidem ab Ethnicis, & hi ad Hebraeis per* κακοζηλίαν *asciverunt,* London, 1625; see the 4th edit., Ultrajecti (Utrecht), 1698, 113–130.

1212. Gale, Theoph., *The Court of the Gentiles,* Oxford, II, 1671, 146–156.

1213. Willemerus, M. Joh. Helvicus, *Dissertatio philologica de* אסיא *Essenis, Judaeorum ascetis,* Moeno-Francof. (Frankfort a. M.), 1680, pp. 56.

1214. Bruno, Th. [Thomas Browne], "Dissertatio de Therapeutis Philonis adversus H. Valesium," in Paul Colomesius, *S. Clementis Epistolae duae ad Corinthios,* London, 1687, 171–209; republished 1694. (From no. 528 and B.M.)

Robert Watt, *Bibliotheca Britannica,* Edinburgh and London, 1824, lists as a distinct item: *Dissertatio de Therapeutis Philonis adversus Hen. Valesium,* Lond., 1687.

1215. Serarius, Nicolaus, "Trihaeresium, seu de celeberrimis tribus, apud Judaeos, Pharisaeorum, Sadducaeorum, et Essenorum Sectis," in Jacobus Triglandius, *Trium scriptorum illustrium de tribus Judaeorum sectis syntagma,* Delphis, 1703, Part I; see 105–198.

1216. Scaligerus, Josephus, "Elenchus Trihaeresii Nicolai Serarii," in *ibid.,* Part I, 421–496.

1217. Serarius, Nicolaus, "Minerval Josepho Scaligero et Johanni Drusio depensum," in *ibid.,* Part II, 122–180.

1218.* Montfaucon, Bernard de [and Bouhier, J.], *Lettres pour et contre sur la fameuse question, si les Solitaires, appellez Thérapeutes, dont a parlé Philon le Juif, étoient Chrétiens,* Paris, 1712, pp. [x], 381.

1219. Prideaux, Humphrey, *The Old and New Testament Connected in the History of the Jews and Neighboring Nations,* London, 1716–1718, 2 vols. Many times republished and translated. See the 13th edition, Glasgow, 1763, II, iii, 363–386.

1220. Carpzov, Ioh. Gottlob, "De Essenis," *Apparatus historico criticus antiquitatum sacri codicis et gentis Hebraeae,* Frankfort and Leipzig, 1748, 215–240.

1221. Jennings, David, *Jewish Antiquities,* London, 1766, I, 463–472.

1222. Adams, H., *History of the Jews from the Destruction of Jerusalem,* Boston, 1813, I, 60–62. (From no. 1269.)

1223. Bellermann, Joh. Joach., *Geschichtliche Nachrichten aus dem Alter-thume über Essäer und Therapeuten,* Berlin, 1821, pp. viii, 180.

1224. Beer, P., *Geschichte, Lehren und Meinungen aller religiösen Sekten der Juden,* Brünn, 1822, I, 68 ff. (From nos. 1227 and 1269.)

1225. Credner, "Über Essäer und Ebioniten und einen theilweisen Zusam-menhang derselben," in Winer's *Zeitsch. für wissenschaftl. Theol.,* Bd. I, Heft 2 (1827), 211–264, Heft 3 (1829), 277–328. (From no. 593.)

1226. Grossmann, Christ[ian] Gottlob Leberecht, *De Ascetis Judaeorum veterum ex Philone,* Altenburg, [1833], pp. 26.

1227. [Raphall, Morris J.], "The Sect of the Essenes," *The Hebrew Review,* III (1836), 123–127, 138–141, 156–157.
A discussion of the section on the Essenes in no. 1224.

1228. Schoell, Joh. Ludov., *De vitae contemplativae in Gentilismo et in Ju-daica Religione quae extant vestigiis, addita quaestione de causis ejus-dem vivendi formae a Christianis susceptae,* Diss. (Strassburg), Argen-torati (Strassburg), 1838, pp. 41.

1229. [De Quincy, Thomas], "On the Essenes," *Blackwood's Edinburgh Magazine,* CCXCI (1840), 105–116, 453–473, 639–649.
Reprinted in his collected works, frequently republished; see the edi-tion, Edinburgh, IX, 1862, 253–300.

1230. Dähne, "Essäer," in J. S. Ersch and J. G. Gruber, *Allgemeine Ency-klopädie der Wissenschaften und Künste,* Leipzig, I, xxxviii, 1843, 173–192.

1231. Beard, J. R., "Essenes," in John Kitto, *Cyclopaedia of Biblical Litera-ture,* New York, 1845–46, I, 657–661.

1232. Frankel, [Z.], "Die Essäer," *Zeitschrift für die religiösen Interessen des Judenthums,* III (1846), 441–461.

1233. De Quincey, Thomas, "Secret Societies," *Tait's Magazine,* [2. S.] XIV (1847); see 661–670.
Reprinted in his collected works with a supplement concerning the Essenes; see the edition, Edinburgh, VI, 1863, 271–310.

1234. Hall, Wm., "The Essenes, Morally and Historically Considered," *The Biblical Repository and Classical Review,* 3rd Series III (1847), 162–173.

1235. Böttger, *Über den Orden der Essäer,* Dresden, 1849. (From no. 1277.)

1236. Frankel, [Z.], "Die Essäer nach talmudischen Quellen," *Monatsschrift für Geschichte und Wissenschaft des Judenthums,* II (1853), 30–40, 61–73.

1237. Ritschl, Albrecht, "Ueber die Essener," *Theologische Jahrbücher*, XIV (1855), 315–356.

1238. Uhlhorn, G., "Essener," in [J. J.] Herzog, *Real-Encyklopädie für protestantische Theologie und Kirche*, 1st edit., IV, Stuttgart and Hamburg, 1855, 174–177; 2nd edit., Leipzig, IV, 1879, 341–344; 3rd edit. edited by Albert Hauck, Leipzig, V, 1898, 524–527.

1239. Mangold, Wilhelm, *Die Irrlehrer der Pastoralbriefe*, Marburg, 1856, 32–134.

1240. Edersheim, Alfred, *History of the Jewish Nation*, Edinburgh, 1856; see esp. 456–460.

1241. Hilgenfeld, A[dolph], *Die jüdische Apokalyptik in ihrer geschichtlichen Entwickelung*, Jena, 1857, 243–286.

1242. Ritschl, Albrecht, *Entstehung der altkatholischen Kirche*, 2nd edit., Bonn, 1857, 179–203.

1243. Hilgenfeld, A[dolph], "Das Urchristenthum und seine neuesten Bearbeitungen von Lechler und Ritschl," §2. "Der Essäismus und das Judenchristenthum," *Zeitschrift für wissenschaftliche Theologie*, I (1858), 116–140.

1244. Hilgenfeld, A[dolph], "Die jüdische Apokalyptik und die neuesten Forschungen," §4. "Die essäischen Vereine," *Zeitschrift für wissenschaftliche Theologie*, III (1860), 358–362.

1245. Westcott, Brooke Foss, "Essenes," in William Smith, *Dictionary of the Bible*, Boston, I, 1860, 581–583.
    Reprinted with a supplement by Ezra Abbot in the edition revised by H. B. Hackett and Ezra Abbot, Boston, I, 1880, 771–774.

1246. Ginsburg, Christian D., "Essenes or Essaens," in John Kitto, *A Cyclopaedia of Biblical Literature*, Edinburgh, 1862; see the 3rd edit., edited by William Lindsay Alexander, Philadelphia, 1865, 827–830.

1247. Löwy, Jacob Ezechiel, "Essäer, Essener" (Text in Hebrew), *Kritisch-talmudisches Lexicon*, Wien, I, 1863, 268–287 (added title in Hebrew).

1248. Ginsburg, Christian D., *The Essenes: Their History and Doctrines*, London, 1864, pp. 82.
    Reprinted from *The Transactions of the Literary and Philosophical Society of Liverpool*.

1249. Benamozegh, Elia, *Storia degli Esseni*, Firenze, 1865, pp. iv, 552.

1250.* Harnischmacher, *De Essenorum apud Iudaeos societate*, Program, Bonn, 1866, 1–26.

1251. Derenbourg, J[oseph], *Essai sur l'histoire et la géographie de la Palestine, d'après les Thalmuds et les autres sources rabbiniques*, Paris, 1867, 166–175, 460–462.

1252. Hilgenfeld, A[dolph], "Der Essäismus und Jesus," *Zeitschrift für wissenschaftliche Theologie*, X (1867), 97–111.

1253. Wise, an article on the Essenes reported in *The Israelite*, Nov. 1, 1867, by Pick (no. 1269).

1254. Clemens, Guilelm., *De Essenorum moribus et institutis*, Diss., Königsberg, 1868, pp. 32. (From Heinsius, *Bücher-Lexikon*.)

1255. Hilgenfeld, A[dolph], "Noch ein Wort über den Essäismus," *Zeitschrift für wissenschaftliche Theologie*, XI (1868), 343–352.

1256. Tideman, Bruno, *Het Essenisme*, Leiden, 1868, pp. 115.

1257. Clemens, Wilh[elm], "Die Quellen für die Geschichte der Essener," *Zeitschrift für wissenschaftliche Theologie*, XII (1869), 328–352.

1258. Clemens, W[ilhelm], *Die Therapeuten*, Pr[ogram], Königsb[erg], 1869. (From no. 539, p. 180*.)

1259. Lauer, *Die Essäer und ihr Verhältniss zur Synagoge und Kirche*, Wien, 1869.
   Reprinted from *Oesterreich. Vierteljahrschr. für kathol. Theol.*, Jahrg. VII, Heft 4. (From no. 593.)

1260. Lipsius, "Essäer oder Essener," in Daniel Schenkel, *Bibel-Lexikon: Realwörterbuch zum Handgebrauch*, Leipzig, 1869, II, 181–192.

1261.† Delaunay, Ferdinand, "Introduction au livre de Philon d'Alexandrie ayant pour titre: De la vie contemplative," *Revue Archéologique*, N.S. XXII (1870–1871), 268–282.

1262. Clemens, Wilhelm, "Die essenischen Gemeinden," *Zeitschrift für wissenschaftliche Theologie*, XIV (1871), 418–431.

1263. [Geiger, Abraham], "Die jüdischen Sibyllinen und der Essenismus," *Jüdische Zeitschrift für Wissenschaft und Leben*, IX (1871), 30–56.

1264. Hilgenfeld, A[dolph], "Die jüdischen Sibyllen und der Essenismus," *Zeitschrift für wissenschaftliche Theologie*, XIV (1871), 30–59.

1265. Tideman, B[runo], "Esseners en Therapeuten," *Theologisch Tijdschrift*, V (1871), 177–188.

1266.† Delaunay, Ferdinand, "Sur l'authenticité de livre de Philon d'Alexandrie qui a pour titre: De la vie contemplative," *Revue archéologique*, N.S. XXVI (1873), 12–22.
   Reviewed in *Comptes rendus de la Société Française de Numismatique et d'Archéologie*, VI (1875), 21 f.

1267.* Delaunay, Ferdinand, *Moines et sibylles dans l'antiquité judéo-grecque*, 2nd edit., Paris, 1874, pp. xix, 403.

1268. Tideman, B[runo], "De apocalypse van Henoch en het Essenisme," *Theologisch Tijdschrift*, IX (1875), 260–296.

1269. Pick, B., "Die englische Literatur über die Essäer," *Zeitschrift für die gesammte lutherische Theologie und Kirche*, XXXIX (1878), 397–399.

1270.* Lucius, P[aul] E[rnst], *Die Therapeuten und ihre Stellung in der Geschichte der Askese. Eine kritische Untersuchung der Schrift: De vita contemplativa*, Strassburg, 1879 (1880), pp. 210.
†Reviewed by Ernest Renan, *Journal des Savants*, 1892, 83–93.

1271. Bestmann, H[ugo] J[ohannes], *Geschichte der christlichen Sitte*, I, *Die sittlichen Stadien in ihrer geschichtlichen Entwicklung*, Nördlingen, 1880, 308–318.

1272.* Ginsburg, Christian D., "Essenes," in William Smith and Henry Wace, *A Dictionary of Christian Biography, Literature, Sects and Doctrines*, London, II, 1880, 198–208.

1273.† Hilgenfeld, A[dolph], "Philo und die Therapeuten," *Zeitschrift für wissenschaftliche Theologie*, XXIII (1880), 423–440.
†Translated by Alfred G. Langley, "Philo and the Therapeutae," *The Baptist Quarterly Review*, IV (1882), 36–56.

1274. Lucius, P[aul] E[rnst], *Der Essenismus in seinem Verhaeltniss zum Judenthum*, Strassburg, 1881, pp. 131.
Reviewed by Ernest Renan, *Journal des Savants*, 1892, 83–93.

1275.† Hilgenfeld, A[dolph], "Die Essäer," *Zeitschrift für wissenschaftliche Theologie*, XXV (1882), 257–292.

1276. Klöpper, Albert, *Der Brief an die Colosser*, Berlin, 1882, 76–96.

1277. Lightfoot, J. B., *Saint Paul's Epistles to the Colossians and to Philemon*, 6th edit., London, 1882, 347–419.

1278. Hamburger, J[acob], "Essäer," *Real-Encyclopädie für Bibel und Talmud*, Strelitz, 2nd edit., II, 1883, 172–178.

1279.† Massebieau, L., "Le traité de la vie contemplative et la question des Thérapeutes," *Revue de l'histoire des religions*, XVI (1887), 170–198, 284–319.
†Reviewed by J. Derenbourg (from reprint, Paris, 1888, pp. 65), *Revue des études juives*, XVI (1888), 151–153; and †by R. Ohle, *Theologische Literaturzeitung*, XIII (1888), 493–499.

1280. Ohle, R., "Die Essäer des Philo. Ein Beitrag zur Kirchengeschichte," *Jahrbücher für protestantische Theologie*, XIII (1887), 298–344, 376–394.
*Reprinted, Altenburg, pp. 70.
Reviewed by A. Harnack, *Theologische Literaturzeitung*, XII (1887), 493–495.

1281. Ohle, R., "Die Essener. Eine kritische Untersuchung der Angaben des Josephus," *Jahrbücher für protestantische Theologie*, XIV (1888), 221–274, 366–387.

1282. Ohle, R., *Die pseudophilonischen Essäer und die Therapeuten*, Berlin, 1888, pp. 78. (*Beiträge zur Kirchengeschichte*, I.)

1283.† Ohle, R., "Ueber die Essäer in Quod omnis probus liber, Ein Nachtrag," *Jahrbücher für protestantische Theologie*, XIV (1888), 314–320.

1284. Wendland, Paul, "Die Essäer bei Philo," in *ibid.*, 100–105.

1285.* Fayot, Georges, *Étude sur les Thérapeutes et le traité de la vie contemplative*, Thèse (Montauban), Genève, 1889, pp. 114.

1286. [Anonymous], "Essenes," in John M'Clintock and James Strong, *Cyclopaedia of Biblical, Theological, and Ecclesiastical Literature*, New York, 1891, III, 301–305.

1287. B. P., "Therapeutae," in *ibid.*, X, 336–342.

1288.* Weinstein, N. I., *Beiträge zur Geschichte der Essäer*, Wien, 1892, pp. 92.

1289. Siegfried, C., "Ueber die dem Philo von Alexandrien zugeschriebene Schrift 'vom beschaulichen Leben,'" *Protestantische Kirchenzeitung für das evangelische Deutschland*, XLIII (1896), 972–982.

1290.† Stahl, J. M., "Zu Philons Schrift vom beschaulichen Leben," *Rheinisches Museum für Philologie*, LI (1896), 157–160.

1291.* Wendland, Paul, *Die Therapeuten und die philonische Schrift vom beschaulichen Leben. Ein Beitrag zur Geschichte des hellenistischen Judentums*, Leipzig, 1896.
Reprint from *Jahrbücher für classische Philologie*, Supplbd. XXII (1896), 693–770, with the same pagination.
Reviewed by Alfred W. Benn, *The Academy*, L (1896), 174; by Leopold Cohn, *Wochenschrift für klassische Philologie*, XIII (1896), 1025–1031; by W. F., *Historische Zeitschrift*, LXXVII or N.F. XLI (1896), 163; by G. Kr., *Literarisches Centralblatt für Deutschland* [XLVII] (1896), 828 f.; by Ch. Lécrivain, *Revue historique*, LXII (1896), 117 f.; †by Karl Praechter, *Berliner philologische Wochenschrift*, XVI (1896), 1125–1134; by T[héodore] R[einach], *Revue des études grecques*, IX (1896), 356 f.; by E. Schürer, *Theologische Literaturzeitung*, XXI (1896), 313–316; by C. Siegfried, *Deutsche Litteraturzeitung*, XVII (1896), 740–742; by C. W., *Historisches Jahrbuch*, XVII (1896), 413 f.; by F. C. Conybeare, *The Jewish Quarterly Review*, IX (1896–1897), 151–155; by A. H., *Zeitschrift für wissenschaftliche Theologie*, XL (1897), 154–158; by A. C. Headlam, *The English Historical Review*, XII (1897), 325–330; by P. L[ejay], *Revue critique d'histoire et de littérature*, XXXI, i (N.S. XLIII) (1897), 489–491; by L. Lévy, *Univers Israélite*, LII, 760–764; and by L. Pautigny, *Bulletin critique*, XVIII (2. S. III) (1897), 23 f.

1292. Bartlet, Vernon, "*De Vita Contemplativa*, 483, 46 f.," *The Classical Review*, XII (1898), 104–106.

1293.* Conybeare, Fred. C., "Essenes," in James Hastings, *A Dictionary of the Bible,* New York and Edinburgh, I, 1898, 767–772.

1294. Regeffe, A., *La secte des esséniens: essai critique sur son organisation, sa doctrine, son origine,* Thèse (Lyon), Lyon, 1898, pp. 104. (From U.C.)

1295. Zeller, E[duard], "Zur Vorgeschichte des Christenthums. Essener und Orphiker," *Zeitschrift für wissenschaftliche Theologie,* XLII (N.F. VII) (1899), 195–269.

1296. Jülicher, G. A., "Essenes," in T. K. Cheyne and J. Sutherland Black, *Encyclopaedia Biblica,* II, New York and London, 1901, 1396–1400.

1297.* Kohler, Kaufmann, "Essenes," *The Jewish Encyclopedia,* New York and London, V, 1903, 224–232.

1298. Ermoni, V., "L'Essénisme," *Revue des questions historiques,* LXXIX (N.S. XXXV) (1906), 5–27.

1299.* Kohler, Kaufmann, "Therapeutae," *The Jewish Encyclopedia,* New York and London, XII, 1906, 138 f.

1300. Harnack, A[dolf], "Therapeuten," in Albert Hauck, *Realencyklopädie für protestantische Theologie und Kirche,* Leipzig, XIX, 1907, 677–680.

1301.* Graham, E. P., "Essenes," *The Catholic Encyclopedia,* New York, [c. 1909], V, 546 f.

1302. Uhlhorn, G., "Essenes," *The New Schaff-Herzog Encyclopedia of Religious Knowledge,* New York and London, IV, [1909], 179 f.

1303.* Kirkup, Thomas, and Stock, St George, "Essenes," *The Encyclopaedia Britannica,* 11th edit., IX, 1910, 779–781.

1304. Motzo, Bacchisio, "Un' opera perduta di Filone (περὶ βίου πρακτικοῦ ἢ Ἐσσαίων)," *Atti della R. Accademia delle Scienze di Torino,* XLVI (1910–1911), 860–880.
  *Reprinted, Turin, 1911, pp. 23.
  Reviewed by Otto Stählin, *Berliner philologische Wochenschrift,* XXXVI (1916), 932 f.

1305. Harnack, Adolf, "Therapeutae," *The New Schaff-Herzog Encyclopedia of Religious Knowledge,* New York and London, XI, [1911], 410 f.

1306.* Stock, St George, "Therapeutae," *The Encyclopaedia Britannica,* 11th edit., XXVI, 1911, 793.

1307. Moffatt, James, "Essenes," in James Hastings, *Encyclopaedia of Religion and Ethics,* New York and Edinburgh, V, 1912, 396–401.

1308. Bugge, Chr., "Zum Essäerproblem," *Zeitschrift für die neutestamentliche Wissenschaft,* XIV (1913), 145–174.

1309. Mosbech, Holger, *Essaeismen, et bidrag til senjödedommens religionshistorie,* Köbenhavn, 1916; see esp. 2–14.

1310. Niven, William Dickie, "Essenes," in James Hastings, *Dictionary of the Apostolic Church*, New York and Edinburgh, 1916, I, 367–369.

1311. Abrahams, Israel, "Philo on the 'Contemplative Life,'" *Bypaths in Hebraic Bookland*, Philadelphia, 1920, 24–31.

1312. Boll, Franz, *Vita Contemplativa. Festrede zum zehnjährigen Stiftungsfeste der Heidelberger Akademie der Wissenschaften*, Heidelberg, 1920, pp. 34. (*Sitzungsberichte der Heidelberger Akademie der Wissenschaften, Stiftung Heinrich Lanz, Philosophisch-historische Klasse*, 1920, Abh. 8.)
†Reviewed by I. Heinemann, *Monatsschrift für Geschichte und Wissenschaft des Judentums*, LXVII (1923), 280.

1313. Moffatt, James, "Therapeutae," in James Hastings, *Encyclopaedia of Religion and Ethics*, New York and Edinburgh, II, 1922, 315–319.

1314. Weber, Max, *Gesammelte Aufsätze zur Religionssoziologie. III. Das antike Judentum*, Tübingen, 1923, 423–430.

1315. Bauer, "Essener," in Pauly-Wissowa-Kroll, *Real-Encyclopädie der classischen Altertumswissenschaft*, Supplbd. IV, 1924, 386–430; with excellent bibliography.

1316. Perles, Felix, "The Hebrew Names of the Essenes and Therapeutae," *The Jewish Quarterly Review*, XVII (1926–1927), 405 f.

1317. Cumont, Franz, "Esséniens et Pythagoriciens, d'après un passage de Josèphe," *Académie des Inscriptions & Belles-Lettres: Comptes rendus des séances de l'année*, 1930, 99–112.

1318. [Escande, Alfred], "Esséniens," in Alexandre Westphal, *Dictionnaire encyclopédique de la Bible*, Paris, 1932, 373 f.

1319. Modi, Jivanji Jamshedji, "Who were the Persian Magi, who Influenced the Jewish Sect of the Essenes?" *Festschrift Moriz Winternitz*, Leipzig, 1933, 209–211.

1320. Heinemann, I[saak], "Die Sektenfrömmigkeit der Therapeuten," *Monatsschrift für Geschichte und Wissenschaft des Judentums*, LXXVIII (1934), 104–117.

1321.† Heinemann, I[saak], "Therapeutai," in Pauly-Kroll-Mittelhaus, *Real-Encyclopädie der classischen Altertumswissenschaft*, V A, 1934, 2321–2346.

1322. Marchel, L., "Esséniens," in Louis Pirot, *Dictionnaire de la Bible . . . Supplément*, Paris, II, 1934, 1109–1132.

See also nos. 569 (II, 299–356), 570 (I, 439–497), 589, 591 (pp. 132–146), 593 (§30), 619, 743, 921 (III, ii, 298–384), 995 (pp. 120 ff.), 1003 (3rd edit., III, 99 ff., and 657–663).

XXVI. THE RELATION OF PHILONIC AND NEW TESTAMENT IDEAS

1324.† Albertus, Joannes, "Annotationum philologicarum in Novum Testamentum, ex Philone Judaeo collectarum, Specimen," *Museum historico-philologico-theologicum,* Bremae, 1728, I, i, 104–126.

1325.* Loesnerus, Christophorus Frider., *Observationes ad Novum Testamentum e Philone Alexandrino,* Leipzig, 1777, pp. 508, [28].

1326. Kühnius, Adamus Fridericus, *Spicilegium Christophori Friderici Loesneri observationum ad Novum Testamentum e Philone Alexandrino,* Pfoertenae (Porta?), 1785, pp. 172.

1327. Grinfield, Edu. Gul., *Scholia hellenistica in Novum Testamentum Philone et Josepho patribus apostolicis aliisq[ue] ecclesiae antiquae scriptoribus necnon libris apocryphis maxime depromta,* London, 1848, 2 vols., pp. xii, 944 (paged continuously).

1328.* Keerl, Philipp Friedrich, "Philo im Neuen Testament," *Die Apokryphenfrage mit Berücksichtigung der darauf bezüglichen Schriften Dr. Stier's und Dr. Hengstenberg's aufs Neue beleuchtet,* Leipzig, 1855, 287–348.

1329.* Bauer, Bruno, *Philo, Strauss und Renan und das Urchristenthum,* Berlin, 1874, pp. 155.
Reviewed by W. Weiffenbach, *Jenaer Literaturzeitung,* I, (1874), 305 f.

1330. Holtzmann, Heinrich Julius, *Lehrbuch der neutestamentlichen Theologie,* Freiburg and Leipzig, 1897, 2 vols. See the 2nd edit. revised and edited by A. Jülicher and W. Bauer, Tübingen, 1911, I, 110–169; II, 329–335, 409–421. (*Sammlung theologischer Lehrbücher.*)

1331. Holtzmann, Oscar, *Leben Jesu,* Tübingen und Leipzig, 1901; see Index.

1332. Adeney, Walter F., "The Relation of New Testament Theology to Jewish Alexandrian Thought," *The Biblical World,* XXVI (1905), 41–54.

1333. Pfleiderer, O., "Philon von Alexandrien," *Vorbereitung des Christentums in der griechischen Philosophie. 1.–10. Tausend,* Tübingen, 1906, 60–66. (Fr. Michael Schiele, *Religionsgeschichtliche Volksbücher,* III, 1.)

1334. Lietzmann, Hans, *Handbuch zum Neuen Testament,* Tübingen, 1907—.
Most of the writers who have contributed to this series were well read in Philo, and their commentaries on the various books of the New

Testament are filled with valuable discussion of Philonic parallels. A few are singled out for special mention.

1335. Watson, John, *The Philosophical Basis of Religion, A Series of Lectures,* Glasgow, 1907; see esp. 190–247.

1336.* Conybeare, Fred[erick] Cornwallis, *Myth, Magic, and Morals. A Study of Christian Origins,* Boston, 1910; see 40, 69, 142, 150, 154, 156–159, 162, 166–168, 198–200, 211, 226, 231, 271, 280, 331, 353, 355.

1337. Bouillon, Léon, *L'église apostolique et les Juifs philosophes jusqu'à Philon,* Orthez, I, 1913, 381–390, 404–429; II, 1914, 66–68, 79–84, 126–133, 145–164.

1338. Heinrici, C. F. Georg, *Die Hermes-Mystik und das Neue Testament,* edited by Ernst von Dobschütz, Leipzig, 1918; see Index. (*Arbeiten zur Religionsgeschichte des Urchristentums,* I, i.)

1339. Jackson, F. J. Foakes, and Lake, Kirsopp, *The Beginnings of Christianity,* London, 1920–1933, 5 vols.; see Indices.

1340.* Meyer, Eduard, *Ursprung und Anfänge des Christentums,* Stuttgart and Berlin, 1921–1923, 3 vols.; see esp. I, 35, 202–205; II, 279 n., 346–402, 430; III, 461 f., 541–544.

1341. Weinel, H., *Biblische Theologie des Neuen Testaments,* Tübingen, 1921; see Index. (*Grundriss der theologischen Wissenschaften,* III, ii.)

1342.* Barton, George A., "Some Influences of Apollos in the New Testament, I," *Journal of Biblical Literature,* XLIII (1924), 207–223.

1343.† Harris, J. Rendel, "The Influence of Philo upon the New Testament," *The Expository Times,* XXXVII (1925–1926), 565 f.

1344.* Barton, George A., *Studies in New Testament Christianity,* Philadelphia, 1928, pp. ix, 150; see Index.

1345.* Worcester, Elwood, "Philo Judaeus," *Studies in the Birth of the Lord,* New York and London, 1932, 156–166; see also 55 f., 59, 167 f., 281–288.

1346. Dodd, Charles Harold, "Hellenism and Christianity," in *Independence, Convergence, and Borrowing in Institutions, Thought, and Art,* Cambridge (Massachusetts), 1937, 109–131. (*Harvard Tercentenary Publications,* Harvard Tercentenary Conference of Arts and Sciences, August 31–September 12, 1936.) *Reprinted, *Harvard Divinity School Bulletin,* April 24, 1937, 24–44. (*Official Register of Harvard University,* XXXIV, 16.)

1347.* Lake, Kirsopp and Silva, *An Introduction to the New Testament,* New York and London, 1937, 15, 53, 59, 72 n., 152, 161 f., 223 f.

See also nos. 589, 739, 775, 873, 1041, 1043, 1044, 1048, 1050, 1056, 1057, 1061, 1065, 1071, 1075, 1085, 1086, 1094, 1103, 1109, 1113, 1115, 1119, 1124, 1168, 1204, 1240, 1244, 1252.

XXVII. PHILO AND PAUL

1348.* Carpzovius, Ioh[annes] Bened[ictus], *Stricturae theologicae et criticae in epistolam S. Paulli ad Romanos. Adspersi subinde sunt flores ex Philone Alexandrino*, 2nd edit., Helmstadt, 1758, pp. viii, 376.

1349.* Jowett, Benjamin, "St. Paul and Philo," *The Epistles of St. Paul to the Thessalonians, Galatians, Romans, with critical notes and dissertations*, London, 1859, I, 448–514; see also II, *passim*.
*Third edition, by Lewis Campbell, London, 1894, I, 382–434, and II, 65, 87, 111.

1350. Todd, J. F., *The Apostle Paul and the Christian Church at Philippi . . . with an introduction illustrating the doctrine and character of the Apostle Paul by contrast with his contemporaries, with special reference to the Alexandrian Philo*, Cambridge, 1864. (From B.M.)

1351.* Vollmer, Hans, *Die alttestamentlichen Citate bei Paulus textkritisch und biblisch-theologisch gewürdigt nebst einem Anhang ueber das Verhältnis des Apostels zu Philo*, Freiburg i. B. and Leipzig, 1895, pp. viii, 103.

1352. Abbott, T. K., *A Critical and Exegetical Commentary on the Epistles to the Ephesians and to the Colossians*, New York, 1897; see Index. (*The International Critical Commentary.*)
*Republished, 1905.

1353. Robertson, Archibald, and Plummer, Alfred, *A Critical and Exegetical Commentary on the First Epistle of St Paul to the Corinthians*, New York, 1911; see Index. (*The International Critical Commentary.*)

1354. Johnston, Charles, "Paul and Philo," *The Constructive Quarterly*, I (1913), 810–825.

1355. Plummer, Alfred, *A Critical and Exegetical Commentary on the Second Epistle of St. Paul to the Corinthians*, New York, 1915; see Index. (*The International Critical Commentary.*)

1356.* Hatch, William Henry Paine, *The Pauline Idea of Faith in its Relation to Jewish and Hellenistic Religion*, Cambridge (Massachusetts) and London, 1917; see 46 f., 79–81, 83. (*Harvard Theological Studies*, II.)

1357.* Leitzmann, Hans, *Die Briefe des Apostels Paulus. I. Einführung in die Textgeschichte der Paulusbriefe: an die Römer*, 2nd edit., Tübingen, 1919; see 20, 30–35, 38 f., 54, 59, 71–73, 93, 102 f., 106, 109, 113, 127 f. (*Handbuch zum Neuen Testament*, III, i.)

1358. Burton, Ernest De Witt, *A Critical and Exegetical Commentary on the*

Epistle to the Galatians, New York, 1920; see Index. (*The International Critical Commentary.*)

1359. Toussaint, C., *L'Hellénisme et L'Apôtre Paul,* Paris, 1921; see esp. 220–225.

1360. Vitti, A., "Christus-Adam: De Paulino hoc conceptu interpretando eiusque ab extraneis fontibus independentia vindicanda," *Biblica,* VII (1926), 121–145; see esp. "Theoria Philonis," 140–144.

1361. Porter, Frank Chamberlin, *The Mind of Christ in Paul: Light from Paul on Present Problems of Christian Thinking,* New York and London, 1930, pp. xiii, 323.

1362.* Scott, E. F., *The Epistles of Paul to the Colossians, to Philemon and to the Ephesians,* New York, 1930, 21.

1363. Windisch, Hans, *Die katholischen Briefe,* 2nd edit., Tübingen, 1930, *passim.* (Hans Lietzmann, *Handbuch zum Neuen Testament,* XV.)

1364.† Andrews, Mary E., "Paul, Philo, and the Intellectuals," *Journal of Biblical Literature,* LIII (1934), 150–166.
*Reviewed by Marcus in no. 543, p. 488.

1365. Lagrange, M.-J., "Les origines du dogme paulinien de la divinité du Christ," *Revue biblique,* XLV (1936), 5–33.

1366. Oepke, Albrecht, *Der Brief des Paulus an die Galater,* Leipzig, 1937; see Index. (*Theologischer Handkommentar zum Neuen Testament,* IX.)

1367. Wikenhauser, Alfred, *Die Kirche als der mystische Leib Christi nach dem Apostel Paulus,* Münster i. W., [1937]; see Index.

See also nos. 1103, 1106.

XXVIII. PHILO AND THE LETTER TO THE HEBREWS

1368. Carpzovius, Joh[annes] Bened[ictus], *Sacrae exercitationes in S. Paulli epistolam ad Hebraeos ex Philone Alexandrino. Praefixa sunt Philoniana prolegomena, in quibus de non adeo contemnenda Philonis eruditione hebraica, de conuenientia stili Philonis cum illo D. Paulli in epistola ad Hebraeos, et de aliis nonnullis varii argumenti, exponitur,* Helmstadt, 1750, pp. clxiiii, 664, [17].

1369. Cabantous, Jules, *Philon et l'Épître aux Hebreux, ou Essai sur les rapports de la christologie de l'Épître aux Hébreux avec la philosophie judéo-alexandrine,* Thèse (Montauban), Montauban, 1895, pp. 77.

1370. Zahn, Th., "Hebräerbrief," in Albert Hauck, *Realencyklopädie für protestantische Theologie und Kirche,* Leipzig, VII, 1899, 492–506, esp. 500–501.

1371. Windisch, Hans, *Der Hebräerbrief,* Tübingen, 1913. ([Hans Lietzmann], *Handbuch zum Neuen Testament,* IV, iii.)

1372.* Scott, E[rnest] F., *The Epistle to the Hebrews: Its doctrine and significance,* Edinburgh, 1923, pp. vii, 216; see Index.

1373. Moffatt, James, *A Critical and Exegetical Commentary on the Epistle to the Hebrews,* New York, 1924; see Index. (*The International Critical Commentary.*)

1374. Wenschkewitz, Hans, *Die Spiritualisierung der Kultusbegriffe Tempel, Priester und Opfer im Neuen Testament,* Leipzig, 1932, 145–149. (Gottfried Polster, Ἄγγελος, *Archiv für neutestamentliche Zeitgeschichte und Kulturkunde,* Beiheft 4.)

1375. Burch, V[acher], *The Epistle to the Hebrews. Its Source and Message,* London, 1936, pp. 148. (From the following review.)
Reviewed by R. V. G. Tasker, *The Journal of Theological Studies,* XXXVIII (1937), 184–186.

XXIX. PHILO AND THE JOHANNINE
WRITINGS

1376.* Ballenstedt, Heinrich Christian, *Philo und Johannes oder fortgesetzte Anwendung des Philo zur Interpretation der Johanneischen Schriften, mit besonderer Hinsicht auf die Frage: Ob Johannes der Verfasser der ihm zugeschriebenen Schriften seyn könne?* Göttingen, 1812, pp. 148.

1377.† Lücke, Friedrich, *Commentar über das Evangelium des Johannes,* 3rd edit., Bonn, I, 1840, 290–294, 630–650.

1378.† [Niedner, Christian Wilhelm], "De subsistentiâ τῷ θείῳ λόγῳ apud *Philonem* Judaeum et *Joannem* Apostolum tributâ," *Zeitschrift für die historische Theologie,* XIX (N.F. XIII) (1849), 337–381.

1379. Tholuck, A[ugust], *Commentar zum Evangelium Johannis,* 7th edit., Gotha, 1857, 65 ff.
   English translation by Charles P. Krauth, New York and Boston, 1867, 57 ff.

1380.† [Reubelt, John A.], "The Logos of Philo Judaeus and that of St. John," *Methodist Quarterly Review,* XL (4th S. X) (1858), 110–129.

1381.† Delitzch, Fr[anz], "Johannes und Philo," *Zeitschrift für die gesammte lutherische Theologie und Kirche,* XXIV (1863), 219–229.
   †Translated, "The Logos in John and Philo," *The American Presbyterian and Theological Review,* II (1864), 506–515; name misspelled Deletzsch.

1382. De Wette, W[ilhelm] M[artin] L[eberecht], *Kurze Erklärung des Evangeliums und der Briefe Johannis,* 5th edit. by Bruno Brückner, Leipzig, 1863, 5–10. (W. M. L. de Wette, *Kurzgefasstes exegetisches Handbuch zum Neuen Testament,* I, iii.)

1383. Cremer, Hermann, "Λόγος," *Biblico-Theological Lexicon of New Testament Greek,* translated from the German by D. W. Simon and William Urwick, Edinburgh, 1872, 399–407.

1384. Pahud, Constantin, *Le Logos de Philon et les rapports avec la doctrine chrétienne,* Diss. (Lausanne), Lausanne, 1874, pp. 84. (From the following review.)
   Reviewed in *Theologischer Jahresbericht,* X (1875), 72 f.

1385. Weiss, Bernhard, *Das Johannes-Evangelium,* rev. edit., Göttingen, 1880; see the 9th edit., Göttingen, 1902, 34–42. (Heinr[ich] Aug. Wilh. Meyer, *Kristisch-exegetischer Kommentar über das Neue Testament,* II.)

1386.* Réville, Jean, *La doctrine du Logos dans le quatrième évangile et dans les oeuvres de Philon*, Paris, 1881, pp. 181.

1387. Westcott, B[rooke] F[oss], *The Gospel according to St. John: The Authorised Version with Introduction and Notes*, London, 1882, xvi–xviii.
(Reprinted from *The Speaker's Commentary*.) 2nd edit., London, 1908, I, xxxiv–xxxix.

1388. Weiss, Bernhard, "Die Fleischwerdung des Logos," *Lehrbuch der Biblischen Theologie des Neuen Testaments*, 4th edit., Berlin, 1884, 616–624.

1389. Muretov, *Filosofia Filona Alexandriiskago v otnoshenii k ucheniu Ioanna Bogoslova o Logose*, 1885.

1390. Schanz, Paul, *Commentar über das Evangelium des heil. Johannes*, Tübingen, 1885, pp. iv, 599. (From Heinsius, *Bücher-Lexikon*.)

1391. Holtzmann, H. J., *Evangelium, Briefe und Offenbarung des Johannes*, Freiburg, 1891, 6–8, 32–36. (H. J. Holtzmann and others, *Hand-Commentar zum Neuen Testament*, IV.)

1392. Ball, W. E., "St. John and Philo Judaeus," *The Contemporary Review*, LXXIII (1898), 219–234.
*Reprinted in *St. Paul and the Roman Law*, Edinburgh, 1901, 95–133.

1393.* Purves, G. T., "Logos," in James Hastings, *A Dictionary of the Bible*, etc., New York and Edinburgh, III, 1900, 132–136.

1394. Grill, Julius, *Untersuchungen über die Entstehung des vierten Evangeliums*, Tübingen and Leipzig, I, 1902, pp. xii, 408; II, 1923, pp. vii, 443.

1395. Loisy, Alfred, *Le Quatrième Évangile*, Paris, 1903; see Index.
Second edit., Paris, 1921, 88–94.

1396.† Sachsse, Eugen, "Die Logoslehre bei Philo und bei Johannes," *Neue kirchliche Zeitschrift*, XV (1904), 747–767.

1397.* D'Alma, Jean, *Philon d'Alexandrie et le Quatrième Évangile*, Paris, 1910, pp. viii, 117.
†Reviewed by P. Dhorme, *Revue biblique*, N.S. VIII (1911), 305–306; and by Alfred Loisy, *Revue critique d'histoire et de littérature*, XLV, i, or N.S. LXXI (1911), 404–405.

1398. Wendt, Hans Hinrich, "Das Verhältnis des Prologs zum Philonismus," *Die Schichten im vierten Evangelium*, Göttingen, 1911, 98–103.

1399. Bauer, Walter, *Johannes*, Tübingen, 1912, 5–8 and *passim*. (*Handbuch zum Neuen Testament*, II, ii.)

1400.* Smith, Bertram Tom Dean, "The Johannine Theology," in F. J. Foakes-Jackson, *The Parting of the Roads. Studies in the Development of Judaism and Early Christianity, by members of Jesus College, Cambridge*, London, 1912, 239–282.

1401.* Thompson, J. M., "Symbolism in the Fourth Gospel," in *Society of Historical Theology, Abstract of Proceedings for the Year 1913–1914,* Oxford, [1914], 24–29.

1402. Wetter, Gillis P:son, *"Der Sohn Gottes:" Eine Untersuchung über den Charakter und die Tendenz des Johannes-Evangeliums,* Göttingen, 1916; see Index. (Wilhelm Bousset and Hermann Gunkel, *Forschungen zur Religion und Literatur des Alten und Neuen Testaments,* Neue Folge, 9.)

1403. Johnston, Charles, "The Logos in the Fourth Gospel," *The Constructive Quarterly,* VI (1918), 347–362.

1404. Büchsel, Friedrich, *Johannes und der hellenistische Synkretismus,* Gütersloh, 1928, pp. 114. (A. Schlatter and W. Lütgert, *Beiträge zur Förderung christlicher Theologie,* 2. Reihe, 16.)

1405.* Bernard, J. H., *A Critical and Exegetical Commentary on the Gospel according to St. John,* edited by A. H. McNeile, New York, 1929, I, cxxxviii–cxli. (*The International Critical Commentary.*)

1406. Odeberg, Hugo, *The Fourth Gospel: Interpreted in its relation to contemporaneous religious currents in Palestine and the Hellenistic-Oriental world:* Part I, *The Discourses of John* 1_{19}–12, Uppsala Och Stockholm, [1929], pp. 336.

1407.* Scott, E[rnest] F., *The Fourth Gospel: Its purpose and theology,* Edinburgh, 2nd edit., 1930, pp. ix, 379; see Index and 13, 21, 54–64, 146–160, 195.

1408.* Bacon, Benjamin W., *The Gospel of the Hellenists,* edited [posthumously] by Carl H. Kraeling, New York, [1933]; see 130 f., 158 f., 163 f., 238, 310, 315, 321 f., 327, 353, 375, 392.

1409. Hadidian, Yervant H., "Philonism in the Fourth Gospel," *The Macdonald Presentation Volume,* Princeton, 1933, 211–222.

1410.* Sikes, Walter W., *The Theology of Philo and of John. An Introduction to the Religious Ideas of Philo Judaeus and their Relationship to the Johannine Literature,* 1934, pp. 113.

S.T.M. diss., not published; typewritten copy at Union Theological Seminary, New York.

See also no. 1064.

XXX. PHILO IN LATER CHRISTIAN TRADITION

(In the following, *PG* = J.-P. Migne, *Patrologiae Cursus Completus* . . .
Series Graeca; PL = *ibid., Series Latina; GCS* = *Die griechischen christ-*
lichen Schriftsteller der ersten drei Jahrhunderte, Leipzig; *CSEL* = *Corpus*
Scriptorum Ecclesiasticorum Latinorum, Vienna.)

1411. Clemens Romanus: see J. B. Lightfoot, *The Apostolic Fathers,* London, I, ii, 1890, 44 f., 98, 130, 164, 183, 214.

1412. Barnabas: see Hans Windisch, *Die Apostolischen Väter,* III: *Der Bar-*
nabasbrief, Tübingen, 1920, *passim.* (Hans Lietzmann, *Handbuch*
zum Neuen Testament, Ergänzungs Band.)

1413. Aristides: see the Introduction and notes *passim* in *J. Geffcken, *Zwei*
griechische Apologeten, Leipzig and Berlin, 1907, 3–96.

1414. Justinus Martyr: see Geffcken, *ibid.,* 103 n., and nos. 1488, 1489, 1491,
1497.

1415. Tatianus: see Geffcken, *ibid.,* 112 f.

1416. Athenagoras: see the note by Ioann. Carol. Theod. Otto, *Corpus apolo-*
getarum christianorum saeculi secundi, Jena, VII, 1857, 3; also the
notes by Geffcken, *op. cit.,* 155–238.

1417. Theophilus Antiochenus: see the notes by Otto, *op. cit.,* VIII, 1861, 52,
77, 92, 101, 108, 232.

1418. Clemens Alexandrinus: refers to Philo in *Stromata,* I, 31, 1; 72, 4; 141,
3; 153, 2; II, 100, 3 (Stählin's edition). Every editor has pointed out
Philonic parallels throughout Clement. The matter is best approached
through the notes of Otto Stählin, *Clemens Alexandrinus,* Leipzig,
1905–36, 4 vols. (*GCS*); see the Index, IV, 47–49, 189.

1419. Irenaeus: see Renatus Massuetus, "Dissertationes praeviae in Irenaei
Libros," *PG,* VII, 40D, 49D. See also the notes by *Adolphus Stieren,
Sancti Irenaei Episcopi Lugdunensis quae supersunt omnia, II, i, Leip-
zig and London, 1848, 69, 76, 248, 378, 617, 662, 745, 800, 807; II, ii,
Leipzig, 1853, 884, 913, 915, 959, 961, 962; and by W. Wigan Harvey,
Sancti Irenaei Episcopi Lugdunensis libros quinque adversus haereses,
Cambridge, 1857, I, 266, 288.

1420. Origenes: see the indices to the volumes of his work in *GCS:* II, 430
(for I and II, edited by Paul Koetschau, 1899); III, 316 (edited by
Erich Klostermann, 1901); IV, 594 (edited by Erwin Preuschen, 1903).
See also notes by Delarue, *PG,* XIII, 1857, 1260A; XIV, 1857, 171D.

1421. (Justinus Martyr): *Cohortatio ad Graecos,* chs. 9, 10, 13: see also the notes by Prudentus Maranus, *PG,* VI, 267D; and by Io. Car. Th. eques. de Otto, *Corpus apologetarum christianorum saeculi secundi,* 3rd edit., Jena, III, 1879, 57, 74, 102–104.

De resurrectione: see the notes by Otto, *op. cit.,* 213, 246.

Acta Martyrii Justini et Sociorum: see the note by Otto, *ibid.,* 271.

1422. Eusebius Pamphilus: *Historia ecclesiae,* II, iv, v, xvii, xviii; VI, xiii, 7; VII, xxxii, 16 (edition of Eduard Schwartz, *Eusebius Werke,* II, i, ii, Leipzig, 1903, 1908, *GCS*).[1] The most useful notes to these passages

1. Eusebius' list of Philo's writings according to Schwartz's text of the *H. E.*: 1. Τὰ κατὰ Γαῖον Ἰουδαίοις συμβάντα πέντε βιβλίοις (II, v, 1); 2. Ἡ πρεσβεία (II, v, 6); 3. Περὶ ἀρετῶν (II, vi, 3; xviii, 8); 4. Περὶ βίου θεωρητικοῦ ἢ ἱκετῶν (II, xvii, 3; xviii, 7); 5. Νόμων ἱερῶν ἀλληγορίαι (II, xviii, 1); 6. Τὰ ἐν Γενέσει καὶ τὰ ἐν Ἐξαγωγῇ ζητήματα καὶ λύσεις (II, xviii, 1) (in II, xviii, 5 E. says he knows 5 books of the *QE*); 7. Περὶ γεωργίας δύο (II, xviii, 2); 8. Περὶ μέθης τοσαῦτα (II, xviii, 2); 9. Περὶ ὧν νήψας ὁ νοῦς εὔχεται καὶ καταρᾶται (II, xviii, 2); 10. Περὶ συγχύσεως τῶν διαλέκτων (II, xviii, 2); 11. Περὶ φυγῆς καὶ εὑρέσως (II, xviii, 2); 12. Περὶ τῆς πρὸς τὰ παιδεύματα συνόδου (II, xviii, 2); 13. Περὶ τοῦ τίς ὁ τῶν θείων ἐστὶ κληρονόμος, ἢ περὶ τῆς εἰς τὰ ἴσα καὶ ἐναντία τομῆς (II, xviii, 2); 14. Περὶ τῶν τριῶν ἀρετῶν ἃς σὺν ἄλλαις ἀνέγραψεν Μωυσῆς (II, xviii, 2); 15. Περὶ τῶν μετονομαζομένων καὶ ὧν ἕνεκα μετονομάζονται (II, xviii, 3); 16. Περὶ διαθηκῶν α' β' (II, xviii, 4); 17. Περὶ ἀποικίας (II, xviii, 4); 18. [Περὶ] βίου σοφοῦ τοῦ κατὰ δικαιοσύνην τελειωθέντος ἢ νόμων ἀγράφων (II, xviii, 4) (Schwartz notes that the omission of this περὶ makes this and the foregoing erroneously a single work. I have supplied the περὶ); 19. Περὶ γιγάντων, ἢ περὶ τοῦ μὴ τρέπεσθαι τὸ θεῖον (II, xviii, 4); 20. Περὶ τοῦ κατὰ Μωυσέα θεοπέμπτους εἶναι τοὺς ὀνείρους α' β' γ' δ' ε' (II, xviii, 4); 21. Περὶ τῆς σκηνῆς (II, xviii, 5); 22. Περὶ τῶν δέκα λογίων (II, xviii, 5); 23. Περὶ τῶν ἀναφερομένων ἐν εἴδει νόμων εἰς τὰ συντείνοντα κεφάλαια τῶν δέκα λόγων α' β' γ' δ' (II, xviii, 5); 24. Περὶ τῶν εἰς τὰς ἱερουργίας ζώων καὶ τίνα τὰ τῶν θυσίων (II, xviii, 5); 25. Περὶ τῶν προκειμένων ἐν τῷ νόμῳ τοῖς μὲν ἀγαθοῖς ἄθλων, τοῖς δὲ πονηροῖς ἐπιτιμίων καὶ ἀρῶν (II, xviii, 5); 26. Περὶ προνοίας (II, xviii, 6); 27. Περὶ Ἰουδαίων (II, xviii, 6); 28. ὁ Πολιτικός (II, xviii, 6); 29. Ἀλέξανδρος, ἢ περὶ τοῦ λόγον ἔχειν τὰ ἄλογα ζῷα (II, xviii, 6); 30. Περὶ τοῦ δοῦλον εἶναι πάντα φαῦλον (II, xviii, 6); 31. Περὶ τοῦ πάντα σπουδαῖον ἐλεύθερον εἶναι (II, xviii, 6); 32. Τῶν ἐν νόμῳ καὶ προφήταις Ἑβραϊκῶν ὀνομάτων αἱ ἑρμηνεῖαι (II, xviii, 7).

These titles in the translation of Rufinus, text of Theodor Mommsen, published in the same volumes of *GCS,* read: 1. *Temporibus Gai quanta Iudaeis acciderunt mala, quinque voluminibus;* 2. *De sua legatione;* 3. *De virtutibus;* 4. *De vita theoretica vel supplicum;* 5. *Sacrae legis explanatio figuralis;* 6. *Quaestiones et absolutiones de Genesi et Exodo;* 7. *De agricultura duo;* 8. *De temulentia duo;* 9. *Pro quibus mens debet ovare deum;* 10. *De confusione linguarum;* 11. *De natura et inventione;* 12. *De his, quae congregari debeant ad erudiendum;* 13. *Quis sit qui heres sit divinorum, quae sit aequalium et inaequalium divisio;* 14. *De tribus virtutibus, quas descripsit cum ceteris Moyses;* 15. *De his, quorum in scripturis nomina commutata sunt et quibus ex causis commutata sunt;* 16. *De testamentis primum et secundum;* 17. *De captivitate;* 18. *De vita sapientis eius qui secundum iustitiam perfectam et leges naturales consummatus est;* 19. *De gigantibus;* 19a. *De eo quod inconvertibile sit quod divinum est;* 20. *De Moysi vita;* 20a. *Libros quinque de eo, quod a deo sint somnia;* 21. *De tabernaculo;* 22. *De decem verbis legis;* 23. *De his, quae inferuntur sub specie decalogi;* 24. *De animalibus, quae sacrificiis deputata sunt, et quae sunt species sacrificiorum* (possibly this second clause was understood as a separate title); 25. *Quae sunt proposita in lege bonis praemia et malis maledicta;* 26. *De providentia;* 27. *De Iudaeis apologeticus liber, hoc est de vita urbana* (the second phrase was a separate title, no. 28, in Greek); 29. *Ad Alexandrum dicentem rationem habere muta animalia;* 30. *De eo quod servus sit omnis qui peccat;* 31. *De eo quod liber sit omnis qui bonis studiis operam praebet;* 32. *Interpretationes nominum hebraeicorum quae sunt in lege et phophetis.*

are by *Arthur Cushman McGiffert, *The Church History of Eusebius,*
New York, Oxford, and London, 1890. (Henry Wace and Philip
Schaff, *A Select Library of Nicene and Post-Nicene Fathers of the
Christian Church,* Second Series, I.) See also the Loeb Classical Li-
brary edition, *Eusebius. The Ecclesiastical History,* London and New
York, I by Kirsopp Lake, 1926; II by J. E. L. Oulton and H. J. Lawlor,
1932.

Praeparatio evangelica, VII, xii, 14–xiii, 7 (322d–323d); xvii, 4–
xviii, 12 (331a–333b); xx, 9–xxi, 5 (336b–337a); VIII, v, 11–vii, 21
(355b–361b); x, 19–xiv, 73 (378c–400a); XI, xiv, 10–xv, 7 (533a–534a);
xxiii, 12–xxiv, 12 (546d–548c); XIII, xviii, 12–17 (704b–705b): see the
notes to these passages by Franciscus Vigerus (and others) in *PG,*
XXI, 1857; and by *E. H. Gifford, *Eusebii Pamphili evangelicae
praeparationis Libri XV,* Oxford, 1903, 4 vols. in 5.

Chronicon: see Rudolf Helm, *Eusebius Werke,* VII: *Die Chronik des
Hieronymus,* i, Leipzig, 1913, 177e (*GCS*).

See also no. 1496.

1423. Epiphanius: *Panarion,* Proem., II, 3, 1; 29, 5: in Karl Holl, *Epiphanius,*
1915, I, 171, 326 (*GCS*). See also the notes in Dionysius Petavius Aure-
lianensis, *S. P. N. Epiphanii Constantiae . . . opera omnia,* Paris,
1622, II, ii, 22, 23, 25, 53, 54, 159, 169, 335, 378, 380, 461.

1424. *Constitutiones Apostolicae:* see the notes by J. B. Cotelerius in *PG,* I,
1857, 561C, 565D, 672D, 682D, 688C, 728C, 732D, 746C, 855D, 919D–
920D, 934C, 985D, 986C, 1028D, 1226D, 1382D, 1385D. See also nos.
1146, 1493.

1425. Basilius Magnus: *Epistolae,* II, cxc, 3; *PG,* XXXII, 1857, 700C.

1426. Eusebius Hieronymus: *Epistola,* XXII, xxxv, 8; LXX, 5, 3: edition of
Isidorus Hilberg, *CSEL,* LIV, 1910, 200, 704. *Adversus Jovinianum,*
II, 14: *PL,* XXIII, 1845, 303B. *De viris illustribus,* viii, xi: Ernest
Cushing Richardson, *Hieronymus liber de viris inlustribus, Genna-
dius liber de viris inlustribus,* Leipzig, 1896, 14 f. (*Texte und Unter-
suchungen zur Geschichte der altchristlichen Literatur,* XIV, i, a).[2]
De nominibus hebraicis, Praefatio: *PL,* XXIII, 1845, 771–772. *Libri*

---

2. In this edition the titles of Philo's works are listed as follows: 1. *De confusione linguarum
liber unus;* 2. *De natura et inventione liber unus;* 3. *De his quae sensu precamur et detestamur
liber unus;* 4. *De eruditione liber unus;* 5. *De herede divinarum rerum liber unus;* 6. *De divisione aequalium et contrariorum liber unus;* 7. *De tribus virtutibus liber unus;* 8. *Quare quorundam in scripturis mutata sint nomina liber unus;* 9. *De pactis libri duo;* 10. *De vita sapientis
liber unus;* 11. *De gigantibus liber unus;* 12. *Quod somnia mittantur a Deo libri quinque;* 13.
Quaestionum et solutionum in Exodum libri quinque; 14. *De tabernaculo et decalogo libri quattuor;* 15. *De victimis et repromissionibus sive maledictis;* 16. *De providentia;* 17. *De Iudaeis;* 18.
De conversatione vitae; 19. *De Alexandro et quod propriam rationem muta habeant;* 20. *Quod
omnis insipiens servus sit;* 21. *De apostolicis viris* quem et inscripsit Περὶ βίου θεωρητικοῦ
ἱκετῶν; 22. *De agricultura duo;* 23. *De ebrietate duo.*

nominum hebraicorum pars quaedam ex operibus Philonis Judaei collecta: PL, XXIII, 1845, 1281–1290. *Praefatio in libros Salomonis: PL,* XXVIII, 1846, 1242A, 1243A. *Praefatio in librum Job: PL,* XXVIII, 1846, 1082A.[3]

1427. Ambrosius: *Epistolae:* see the notes of Frische and Naurry, *PL,* XVI, 1845, 912 ff., 1047 f., 1051, 1084 f., 1089 f., 1136, 1140, 1142 ff., 1228.

On various treatises see the notes by Carolus Schenkl, *CSEL,* XXXII, *i and ii, 1896 and 1897.

Only a relatively small part of the works of Ambrose have been published to date in the *CSEL*. There is no doubt that as the modern edition of his works continues much more use of Philo will appear. See also nos. 1481, 1482, 1503, 1505, 1560.

1428. [Ambrosius]: *Apologia David altera:* see the edition of Carolus Schenkl, *CSEL,* XXXII, ii, 1897, 383, 11.

Expositio evangelii secundum Lucan: edition of Carolus Schenkl, continued by Henricus Schenkl, *CSEL,* XXXII, iv, 1902, 300, 14.

1429. Sophronius: the reputed author of the Greek translation of Jerome's *De viris inlustribus:* the text was first published by Erasmus, says Wentzel, in 1516, from a manuscript which then disappeared (a statement we have been unable to verify). As a result many scholars thought the work a forgery of Erasmus himself, until the manuscript was rediscovered in 1895. From the manuscript a new edition was published: Oscar von Gebhardt, *Hieronymus de viris inlustribus in griechischer Übersetzung (Der sogenannte Sophronius)*, Leipzig, 1896 (*Texte und Untersuchungen zur Geschichte der altchristlichen Literatur,* XIV, i, b). The importance of Sophronius' translation is that it was the basis for the list of works of Philo in both Photius and Suidas. See Georg Wentzel, *Die griechische Übersetzung der Viri inlustres des Hieronymus,* Leipzig, 1895 (*Texte und Untersuchungen zur Geschichte der altchristlichen Literatur,* XIII, iii); for Philo see pages 28 f., 47–49.[4]

---

3. Mr. Goodhart has in his collection a very interesting Bible manuscript in which this passage appears. Written in an Italian hand about 1270, it was collated, according to a notation in the manuscript, in 1832 by Aloisi Ungarelli for the librarian of the Vatican, Cardinal Luigi Lambruschini. Ungarelli points out in his notes the differences from other early texts.

4. The works of Philo in Gebhardt's text, page 14 f., are: περὶ συγχύσεως γλωσσῶν λόγος εἷς; περὶ φύσεως καὶ εὑρήματος; περὶ ὧν κατὰ νοῦν εὐχόμεθα καὶ ἀπομαρτυρόμεθα λόγος εἷς; περὶ παιδεύσεως λόγος εἷς; περὶ κληρονόμου τῶν θείων πραγμάτων εἷς; περὶ μερισμοῦ ἴσων καὶ ἐναντίων λόγος εἷς; περὶ τριῶν δυνάμεως λόγος εἷς; περὶ τῶν ἐναλλαγεισῶν γραφῶν παρά τινων λόγος εἷς; περὶ συνθηκῶν λόγοι δύο; περὶ βίου φιλοσοφικοῦ λόγος εἷς; περὶ γιγάντων λόγος εἷς; περὶ τοῦ τοὺς ὀνείρους παρὰ θεοῦ πέμπεσθαι λόγοι πέντε; ζητημάτων καὶ ἑρμηνευμάτων τῆς Ἐξόδου λόγοι πέντε; περὶ τῆς σκηνῆς καὶ δεκαλόγου λόγοι τέσσαρες; περὶ θυσίων; περὶ ὑποσχέσεων ἤτοι καταρῶν; περὶ προνοίας; περὶ Ἰουδαίων; περὶ διαγωγῆς βίου; περὶ Ἀλεξάνδρου καὶ ὅτι

1430. (Johannes Chrysostomus): *In Pascha,* VII, 2: *PG,* LIX, 1859, 748.

1431. Aurelius Prudentius: see the note by Faustinus Arevalus, *PL,* LIX, 1862, 843D.

1432. Aurelius Augustinus: *Contra Faustum,* XII, 39: *edition of Josephus Zycha, *CSEL,* XXV, vi, 1, 1891, 365–366. See also nos. 1494, 1498.

1433. Isidorus Pelusiota: *Epistolae,* II, cxliii; III, xix, lxxxi: *PG,* LXXVIII, 1860, 585B, 745A, 788C.

1434. Paulus Orosius: *Historiae adversum paganos:* edition of Carolus Zangemeister, *CSEL,* V, 1882, VII, v, 6, 7.

1435. Dracontius: see the note to *Carmen de Deo,* III, line 290, by Faustinus Arevalus, *PL,* LX, 1862, 865D.

1436. Hermias Sozomen: *Historia ecclesiastica,* I, xii: *PG,* LXVII, 1859, 893–896.

1437. Valerianus: see the introductory essay by Theophilus Raynaudus, *PL,* LII, 1864, 767C.

1438. Gennadius Massiliensis: see the notes to *de dogmatibus ecclesiasticis,* XII, XXI, LIX, by Elmenhorst, *PL,* LVIII, 1862, 1019D, 1023B, 1035D.

1439. Vigilius Tapsensis: see the note to *de Trinitate,* VI, by Petrus Chif-fletius, *PL,* 1863, LXII, 535A.

1440. Aurelius Cassiodorus: says in *de institutione divinarum litterarum* that Jerome was right in ascribing *Wisdom of Solomon* to Philo: *PL,* LXX, 1865, 1117B.

1441. Dionysius Areopagita: see nos. 1486, 1573.

1442. Anastasius Sinaita: *Viae dux adversus Acephalos,* XIV: *PG,* LXXXIX, 1860, 244D, 248B.

1443. Dionysius Exiguus: see the notes to *Codex canonum ecclesiae universae* by Christophorus Justellus, *PL,* LXVII, 1865, 108D, 114A.

1444. Maximus Confessor: *S. Maximi Confessoris graecorum theologi eximiique philosophi opera, Opera & studio* R. P. Francisci Combefis, Paris, 1675; see II, 530, 548, 554, 556, 559, 561, 567 f., 574, 584, 588 f., 599, 603, 610, 612, 615, 620, 623, 633, 635, 642, 646, 658, 660 f., 670, 674, 681, 685 f.

1445. *Chronicon Paschale: PG,* XCII, 1860, 560B.

1446. Ioannes Damascenus: *Iacobus Billius, *Sancti Ioannis Damasceni opera, multo quam vnquam antehac auctiora, magnáque ex parte nunc de integro conuersa,* Paris, Guillelmus Chaudiere, 1577; see folios 2v, 3v, 5v, 7r, 11v, 17r and v, 19v, 22v, 23v, 24v, 26v, 28r, 29v, 30v, 31r, 32r, 37r, 38r, 40v, 41r and v, 51v, 52r and v, 56r and v, 68v, 76r, 83r, 87r,

---

ἴδιον λογισμὸν ἔχει τὰ ἄλογα; ὅτι πᾶς ἄφρων δοῦλός ἐστι; περὶ διαγωγῆς τῶν ἡμετέρω
. . . ἀποστόλων ὃν ἐπέγραψε περὶ βίου θεωρητικοῦ ἱκετῶν; περὶ γεωργίας λόγοι δύο;
περὶ μέθης δυο.

88r, 95r, 97r, 99v, 100r, 101r, 117v, 124v, 127r, 135r and v, 141v, 148v, 153r, 155r and v, 157r.

1447. Photius: *Bibliotheca,* ciii, cv, cclxxix: Immanuel Bekker, *Photii Bibliotheca,* Berlin, I, 1824, 86a, lines 30–41; see also 529b, lines 25–29.[5]

1448. Ephraemius Chronographus: *Caesares,* Caius: *PG,* CXLIII, 1865, 13, 3.

1449.* King Alfred: *King Alfred's Orosius,* edited by Henry Sweet, London, I, 1883, 259. (Early English Text Society.)
The first reference to Philo in the English language. This translated into modern English: *King Alfred's Books,* by G. F. Browne, London, 1920, 122. See also no. 378.

1450. Leo Diaconus: Carolus Benedictus Hasius discusses several words for comparison between Philo and Leo in *PG,* CXVII, 1864: δορυφόρος, 717C; γνωσιμαχία, 859C; κακοπραγία, 901D.

1451. Suidas: see Ada Adler, *Suidae Lexicon,* Leipzig, IV, 1935, 737 f.,[6] *s.v.* "Philo, Judaeus." (*Lexicographi Graeci . . . Volumen I.*) See also no. 1575. No attempt is made to list the numerous editions of Suidas.

1452. Petrus Damianus: *Apologeticus monachorum adversus canonicos: PL,* CXLV, 1867, 511D.

1453. Joel Chronographus: *Compendiaria: PG,* CXXXIX, 1865, 248C.

1454. Petrus Abaelardus: *Epistolae,* VII: *PL,* CLXXVIII, 1855, 233D–235A.
The first edition of the Letters was *Petri Abaelardi, filosofi et theologi, abbatis ruyensis, et Heloisae coniugis eius, primae Paracletensis Abbatissae, opera, nunc primum edita ex MMS. codd. V. illust. Francisci Amboesii,* Paris, 1616, bound in 2 vols., 4to.

1455. Ekkehardus: *Chronicon Wirziburgense: PL,* CLIV, 1853, 462A; *Monumenta germaniae historica, Scriptores,* VI, edidit Georgius Heinricus Pertz, Hannover, 1844, 17, line 57.

---

5. The works of Philo as listed in this edition are: νόμων ἱερῶν ἀλληγορίαι; περὶ βίου πολιτικοῦ; τῶν παρὰ Ἰουδαίοις φιλοσοφησάντων τήν τε θεωρητικὴν καὶ τὴν πρακτικὴν φιλοσοφίαν βίοι; Γάϊος ψεγόμενος; Φλάκκος ἢ Φλάκκων ψεγόμενος.

6. The works of Philo according to Adler's text are: 1. Περὶ συγχύσεως γλωσσῶν βιβλίον α'; 2. Περὶ φύσεως καὶ εὑρήματος α'; 3. Περὶ ὧν κατὰ νοῦν τις εὔχεται α'; 4. Περὶ παιδεύσεως α'; 5. Περὶ κληρονόμου τῶν θείων πραγμάτων α'; 6. Περὶ μερισμοῦ ἴσων καὶ ἐναντίων α'; 7. Περὶ τῶν τριῶν δυνάμεων; 8. Περὶ ἐναλλαγεισῶν γραφῶν παρά τινων; 9. Περὶ συνθηκῶν λόγοι β'; 10. Περὶ βίου φιλοσόφου; 11. Περὶ Γιγάντων α'; 12. Περὶ ὀνείρων ε'; 13. Περὶ ζητημάτων καὶ ἑρμηνευμάτων τῆς Ἐξόδου ε'; 14. Περὶ τῆς σκηνῆς καὶ δεκαλόγου δ'; 15. Περὶ θυσίων; 16. Περὶ ὑποσχέσεων ἤτοι καταρῶν; 17. Περὶ προνοίας; 18. Περὶ Ἰουδαίων α'; 19. Περὶ ἀγωγῆς βίου; 20. Περὶ Ἀλεξάνδρου; 21. Περὶ τοῦ ὅτι ἴδιον λογισμὸν ἔχει τὰ ἄλογα; 22. Περὶ τοῦ πᾶς ἄφρων δοῦλός ἐστι; 23. Περὶ τῆς διαγωγῆς τῶν Χριστιανῶν; 24. Περὶ βίου θεωρητικοῦ; 25. Περὶ ἱκετῶν; 26. Περὶ γεωργίας λόγοι β'; 27. Περὶ μέθης β'; 28. Περὶ τοῦ Μωσέως βίου; 29. Εἰς τὰ χερουβίμ, τουτέστι τὴν φλογίνην ῥομφαίαν; 30. Εἰς τὴν πεντάτευχον Μωϋσέως καὶ εἰς αὐτὸν τὸν Μωϋσῆν, λόγοι ε'. (Perhaps the second of these should be read as a distinct title.)

1456. Joannes Zonaras, *Annales,* VI, 10: *PG,* CXXXIV, 1864, 488A.

1457. Michael Glyca, *Annales,* III, IV: *PG,* CLVIII, 1866, 444A, 525D.
The second passage seems a confusion of some ecclesiastical writer with Philo.

1458. Bacon, Roger: see *The Opus Majus of Roger Bacon: A Translation,* by Robert Belle Burke, Philadelphia, 1928, II, 810. A reference to Philo as the author of Ecclesiasticus and the Wisdom of Solomon.

1459. Bonaventura: see no. 1528.

1460. Nicephorus Callistus: *Ecclesiastica historia,* II, 9, 15, 18: *PG,* CXLV, 1865, 780A, 792D, 795D–801D.

1461. Antoninus, St.: see no. 1545.

1462. Jacobus Philippus Bergomensis: see nos. 1542, 1557.

1463. Donatus Bossius: see no. 1558.

1464. Sabellicus, Marcus Antonius: see no. 1540.

1465. Alliaco, Petrus de: see no. 1552.

1466. Picus Mirandulus, Johannes: see no. 1553.

1467. Schedel, Hartmann: see nos. 1561, 1562, 1579.

1468. Reuchlin, Johann: see no. 1563.

1469. Tritheim, Johann: see no. 1564.

1470. Augustinus Eugubinus (Steuchus): see no. 828.

1471. [Servetus, Michael], *Christianismi restitutio,* [Lugduni?] (Lyons), 1553; see 102, 104, 118, 131, 139, 201, 202, 204, 223, 225, 240, 285, 692, 713, 728, 733.
From reprint [Nuremberg, 1790], believed to be an exact copy.

1472. Hoeschel, Dav., Philonis loca emendata. Zu Joh. Damascenus „Homilia et acrostichis" Μώσης θεοῦ πρόσωπον ἐν Θαβωρ ἴδε: Aug. Vind., 1588, 8vo, 95–104. (From no. 528.)

1473.* [Camden, William], *Remaines Concerning Brittaine: But especially England, and the Inhabitants thereof . . . The fourth Impression, reuiewed, corrected, and increased,* London, 1629; see 45, 47, 63 f., 72 f., 278.

1474. Grotius, Hugo, "De veritate religionis Christianae," *Opera theologica,* III, London, 1679; see 86 f.
Translated by Symon Patrick, *The Truth of Christian Religion: In Six Books. Written in Latin . . . and Now Translated into English, with the Addition of a Seventh Book Against the present Roman Church,* 3rd edit., London, 1689; see 22, 105, 1065.

1475.* Kircherus, Athanasius, *Turris Babel, sive Archontologia qua primo priscorum post diluvium hominum vita, mores rerumque gestarum magnitudo, secundo turris fabrica civitatumque exstructio, confusio linguarum, & inde gentium transmigrationis, cum principalium inde*

enatorum idiomatum historia, multiplici eruditione describuntur &
explicantur, Amsterdam, 1679; see 22–24, 35, 123, 217.

1476.* Fabricius, Io[annes] Albertus, *Bibliographia Antiquaria sive Intro-*
ductio in notitiam scriptorum qui antiquitates hebraicas, graecas, ro-
manas et christianas scriptis illustrarunt. Editio tertia ex mscpto B.
auctoris insigniter locupletata et recentissimorum scriptorum recen-
sione aucta studio et opera Paulli Schaffshavsen, Hamburg, 1760; see
1 f., 258, 262, 309 n., 398, 405, 439, 531, 733, 824, 825, 902.

1477. Morgan, Caesar, *An Investigation of the Trinity of Plato and of Philo*
Judaeus, and of the effects, which an attachment to their writings had
upon the principles and reasonings of the fathers of the Christian
Church, London, 1795, pp. [19], 180; *edited by H. A. Holden, Cambridge (England) and London, 1853, pp. xiv, 166.

1478. Jones, John, *Ecclesiastical Researches; or, Philo and Josephus proved to*
be historians and apologists of Christ, of his followers, and of the Gos-
pel, London, 1812, pp. xxx, 564.

1479.* Neander, Augustus, *Lectures on the History of Christian Dogmas,*
ed. by J. L. Jacobi and translated from the German by J. E. Ryland,
London, 1872, 2 vols.; see I, 38–40, 90, 96 f., 106, 117, 134 f., 166, 177,
194.

1480. Kuenen, A[braham], *National Religions and Universal Religions,*
New York, 1882, 203–221. (The Hibbert Lectures, 1882.)

1481. Förster, Th., *Ambrosius, Bischof von Mailand,* Halle a. S., 1884, 102–
112.

1482.† Ihm, Max, "Philon und Ambrosius," *Neue Jahrbücher für Philologie*
und Paedagogik, (Jahrbücher für classische Philologie), CXLI (1890),
282–288.

1483. Dienstfertig, Meyer, *Die Prophetologie in der Religionsphilosophie des*
ersten nachchristlichen Jahrhunderts, unter besonderer Beachtung der
Verschiedenheit in den Auffassungen des Philon von Alexandrien und
des Flavius Josephus, Diss. (Erlangen), Breslau, 1892, pp. 33.

1484. Harnack, Adolf, *Geschichte der altchristlichen Litteratur bis Eusebius,*
Leipzig, I, 1893, 858–861.

1485.* Krumbacher, Karl, *Geschichte der byzantinischen Litteratur von Jus-*
tinian bis zum Ende des oströmischen Reiches (527–1453), München,
1897; see 126 n., 127 n., 130, 215, 431 n., 552, 696.

1486. Koch, Hugo, *Pseudo-Dionysius Areopagita in seinen Beziehungen*
zum Neuplatonismus und Mysterienwesen, Mainz, 1900; see Index.
(A. Ehrhard and J. P. Kirsch, *Forschungen zur Christlichen Littera-*
tur- und Dogmengeschichte, I, 2 and 3.)

1487.† Karppe, S., "Philon et la Patristique," *Essais de critique et d'histoire de philosophie,* Paris, 1902, 1–33. (*Bibliothèque de philosophie contemporaine.*)

1488. Feder, Alfred Leonhard, *Justins des Märtyrers Lehre von Jesus Christus, dem Messias und dem menschgewordenen Sohne Gottes,* Freiburg im Breisgau, 1906; see Index.

1489.* Heinisch, Paul, *Der Einfluss Philos auf die älteste christliche Exegese (Barnabas, Justin, und Clemens von Alexandria). Ein Beitrag zur Geschichte der allegorisch-mystischen Schriftauslegung im christlichen Altertum,* Münster i. W., 1908, pp. 296. (J. Nikel, *Alttestamentliche Abhandlungen,* 1, 2.)

An extension of the author's *dissertation (Breslau), Münster i. W., 1907, pp. 64, which included §§ 1–6, 3.

Reviewed by J. Geffcken, *Deutsche Literaturzeitung,* XXIX (1908), 1492 f.; by Ed. König, *Literarisches Zentralblatt für Deutschland,* LIX (1908), 835; and †by Leopold Cohn, *Monatsschrift für Geschichte und Wissenschaft des Judentums,* LIII (1909), 244–251.

1490.* Mead, G. R. S., "Philo von Alexandrien und die hellenistische Theologie," *Vierteljahrsschrift für Bibelkunde,* III (1908), 183–226.

1491. Pfättisch, Ioannes Maria, *Der Einfluss Platos auf die Theologie Justins des Märtyrers,* Paderborn, 1910, 55–57. (A. Ehrhard and J. P. Kirsch, *Forschungen zur Christlichen Literatur- und Dogmengeschichte,* X, i.)

1492. Glawe, Walther, *Die Hellenisierung des Christentums in der Geschichte der Theologie von Luther bis auf die Gegenwart,* Berlin, 1912; see Index. (N. Bonwetsch and R. Seeberg, *Neue Studien zur Geschichte der Theologie und der Kirche,* XV.)

1493. Bousset, W[ilhelm], "Eine jüdische Gebetssammlung im siebenten Buch der apostolischen Konstitutionen," *Nachrichten von der Königlichen Gesellschaft der Wissenschaften zu Göttingen. Philologisch-historische Klasse, aus dem Jahre 1915,* Berlin, 1916, 435–489.

1494. Rüting, W., *Untersuchungen über Augustins Quaestiones und Locutiones in Heptateuchum,* Paderborn, 1916; see Index. (A. Ehrhard and J. P. Kirsch, *Forschungen zur Christlichen Literatur- und Dogmengeschichte,* XIII, 3 and 4.)

1495. Bousset, Wilhelm, *Kyrios Christos: Geschichte des Christusglaubens von den Anfängen des Christentums bis Irenaeus,* 2nd edit., Göttingen, 1921; see Indices.

1496. Doergens, Heinrich, *Eusebius von Cäsarea als Darsteller der griechischen Religion: Eine Studie zur Geschichte der altchristlichen Apologetik,* Paderborn, 1922; see Index. (A. Ehrhard and J. P. Kirsch, *Forschungen zur Christlichen Literatur- und Dogmengeschichte,* XIV, iii.)

1497.* Goodenough, Erwin R[amsdell], *The Theology of Justin Martyr,* Jena, 1923, pp. 320.

Reviewed by Gustav Krüger, *Theologische Blätter,* [N.F.] II (1923), 255–256; †by H. A. van Bakel, *Nieuw Theologisch Tijdschrift,* XII (1923), 212–214; †*The Expository Times,* XXXV (1923–1924), 20–21; †by M.-D. Chenu, *Revue des sciences philosophiques et théologiques,* XIII (1924), 236–237; and †by H. Windisch, *Theologische Literaturzeitung,* XLIX (1924), 39–40.

1498.* Fuchs, Harald, *Augustin und der antike Friedensgedanke, Untersuchungen zum neunzehnten Buch der Civitas Dei,* Berlin, 1926; see 33 n., 105 n., 124 f., 174 n., 180–182. (Werner Jaeger, *Neue philologische Untersuchungen,* III.)

1499.* Gore, Charles, *The Reconstruction of Belief: Belief in God. Belief in Christ. The Holy Spirit and the Church,* new edit., New York, 1926; see Index.

1500.* Lebreton, Jules, *Histoire du dogme de la Trinité des origines au Concile de Nicée,* Paris, see I, 8th edit., 1927, 178–251 and Indices; II, 3rd edit., 1928, Indices. (*Bibliothèque de théologie historique.*)

1501.† Techert, Marguerite, "La notion de la Sagesse dans les trois premiers siècles de notre ère," *Archiv für Philosophie und Sociologie,* Abt. I, *Archiv für Geschichte der Philosophie und Soziologie,* XXXIX (N.F. XXXII) (1929), 1–27.

1502.* McGiffert, Arthur Cushman, *A History of Christian Thought,* New York and London, 1932, 1933, 2 vols.; I, 22, 184, 195 f., 203–205; II, 55.

1503. Huhn, J., *Ursprung und Wesen des Bösen und der Sünde nach der Lehre des Kirchenvaters Ambrosius,* Paderborn, 1933; see Index. (A. Ehrhard and J. P. Kirsch, *Forschungen zur christlichen Literatur- und Dogmengeschichte,* XVII, 5.)

1504.* Means, Stewart, *Faith: An Historical Study,* with an introduction by Erwin R. Goodenough, New York, 1933; see 10, 32–37, 45, 56, 94 f.

1505.* Dudden, F[rederick] Homes, *The Life and Times of St. Ambrose,* Oxford, 1935, 2 vols.; see Index I in vol. II.

1506.* Wulf, Maurice de, *History of Mediaeval Philosophy,* translated by Ernest C. Messenger, 3rd English edit., based on 6th French edit., London, [1935], 77, 89, 304.

1507. Hitchcock, F. R. Montgomery, "Loofs' Theory of Theophilus of Antioch as a Source of Irenaeus," *The Journal of Theological Studies,* XXXVIII (1937), 130–139, 255–266.

See also nos. 842, 847, 903, 906, 1080, 1118, 1177.

XXXI. MENTION OF PHILO IN PRINTED BOOKS OF THE FIFTEENTH CENTURY

1508.* Hieronymus, *Epistolae,* [Rome, Sixtus Riessinger, ca. 1467], 2 vols., folio. Probably the first edition, preceded by Aristeas, "De lxx interpretibus," translated by Mathias Palmerius. Hain *8550. See I, folio 91vA; II, folios 124rB, 127rB, 147vA, 241rB.[1]

1509.* Hieronymus, *Epistolae,* edited by Joannes Andreae, Bishop of Aleria, Rome, Conradus [Sweynheym] & Arnoldus [Pannartz], 13 December 1468, 2 vols., folio. First dated edition. Hain 8551. See I, folio 49r; II, folios 81v, 148r, 280v, 281r.[2]

1510.* Bessarion, [Joannes], *Aduersus calumniatore Platonis,* Rome, Conradus Sweynheym & Arnaldus Pannartz, [before 13 September, 1469], folio. First edition. Hain *3004. See folios 4v, 46r, 64r.

1511.* Eusebius Pamphilus [Caesariensis], *De euangelica praeparatione,* translated by [Georgius Trapezuntius], Ueneta, Nicolaus Ienson, 1470, folio. First edition. Hain *6699. See VII, v, vii, viii; VIII, ii, iiii, v; XI, x, xi, xii.

1512.* Hieronymus, *Epistolae,* Moguntina (Mainz), Peter Schoeffer, 1470, large folio. Hain *8554. See folios [130]vA, [172]rA, [224]rA, [225]vA and B, [294]vA.

---

1. The works of Philo as they appear listed in this edition are: *De confusione linguarum, liber unus; De natura et inventione, liber unus; De iis que sensu precamur et detestamur, liber unus; De eruditionibus, liber unus; De herede divinarum rerum, liber unus; De divisione equalium et contrariorum, liber unus; De tribus virtutibus, liber unus; Quare quorundam in scripturis immutata sunt nomina, liber unus; De pactis, libros duos; De vita sapientum, liber unus; De gigantibus, liber unus; Quod somnia mittantur a deo, libros quinque; Questionum in Exodo, libros quinque; De tabernaculo et decalogo, libros quattuor; De victimis et repromissionibus sive maledictis; De providentia; De iudeis; De conversatione vitae; De Alexandro et quod propriam rationem muta animalia habere dicat; De vita nostrorum, idest de apostolicis viris; De agricultura; De ebrietate, libros duos.*

2. The works of Philo as they appear listed in this edition are: *De confusione linguarum, liber unus; De natura et inventione bestiarum repentium, volatilium, et piscium, libri tres; De iis que sensu precamur et testamur, liber unus; De eruditione, liber unus; De herede divinarum rerum, liber unus; De divisione equalium et contrariorum, liber unus; De tribus virtutibus, liber unus; Quare quorundam in scripturis mutata sunt nomina, liber unus; De pactis, libri duo; De vita sapientis, liber unus; De gigantibus, liber unus; Quod somnia mittantur a deo, libri quinque; Questionum et solutionum in exodo, libri quinque; De tabernaculo et catalogo, libri quattuor; De victimis et repromissionibus sive maledictis; De providentia; De iudeis; De conversatione vite; De Alexandro dicente quod propriam rationem multa animalia habeant; Quod omnis insipiens servus sit; De vita nostrorum, idest de apostolicis vitis, hoc est de vita contemplativa; De agricultura duo; De ebrietate duo.*

1513.* Josephus, Flavius, *De antiquitate judaica, De bello judaico,* Augusta (Augsburg), Johann Schussler, 28 June–23 August, 1470, 2 parts in 1, folio. First dated Latin edition. Hain *9451. See folio [182].

1514.* Lactantius, [Lucius Coelius] Firmianus, *Opera,* edited by Iohannes Andreae, Bishop of Aleria, Rome, Conradus Suueynheym and Arnoldus Pannartz, 1470, folio. Hain 9808. See book I, iiii.

1515.* Tacitus, [Publius] Cornelius, *Opera,* [Venice, Vindelinus de] Spira, [ca. 1470], folio. First edition. Hain *15218. Although containing no reference to Philo himself, it mentions various members of his family as follows: folio 51r (Tiberius Alexander); 68v (Tiberius Alexander); 86r (Bernice); 100r (Tiberius Alexander); 101r (Tiberius Alexander); 101v (Bernice).

1516.* Orosius, Paulus, *Historiographi disciplis sancti Augustini (Historiae),* Augusta (Augsburg), Iohannes Schussler, 1471, folio. First edition. Hain *12101. See Book VII, iiii.

1517.* Cassiodorus, Magnus Aurelius, *Ecclesiastica et tripertite historice ex Socrate, Sozomeno, et Theodorico,* Augusta (Augsburg), Johann Schussler, 5 February 1472, folio. First edition. Hain *4573. See the History of Sozomen, folio 12.

1518.* Lactantius, L[ucius] Coelius Firmianus, *Opera,* [Venice], Vindelinus [de Spira], 1472, folio. Hain *9810. See book I, iiii.

1519.* Voragine, Jacobus [de], *Legenda aurea sanctorum. Alias lombartica hystoria,* [Basel, Michael Wenssler, not after 1474], folio. Copinger 6399. In the account of St. Mark, Philo is given as the authority for the statement that St. Mark went to Alexandria at the behest of St. Peter. See folio 72v (sig. h₄v).

1520.* Eusebius [Pamphilus Caesariensis], *Chronicon,* with the continuations of Hieronymus Prosper and Matthaeus Palmerius [Florentinus], [Milan], Philippus Lauanius, [ca. 1475], quarto. Hain 6716. See A.D. 35, 40, 41.

1521.* Orosius, Paulus, *Historiarum initium ad Aurelium Augustinum (Historiae),* edited by Aeneas Vulpes and Laurentius Brixiensis, [Vicenza], Hermannus [Liechtenstein] de Colonia, [ca. 1475], folio. Hain *12099. See folio [81]r and v (Book VII, 3rd folio r and v).

1522.* Orosius, Paulus, *Historiarum initium ad Aurelium Augustinum,* edited by Aeneas [Vulpes], [Vicenza], Leonardus [Achates] de Basilea, [ca. 1475], folio. Hain *12300 (12100). See sig. l₆r.

1523.* Tacitus, [Publius] Cornelius, *Opera,* edited by Franciscus Puteolanus, [Milan, Antonius Zarotus, ca. 1475], folio. Hain 15219. See (for mention of members of Philo's family) sigs. k₈v, n₁v, p₁r, p₂r and v.

1524.* Eusebius [Pamphilus] Caesariensis, *Historia ecclesiastica,* translated by Ruffinus, Rome, Iohannes Philippus de Lignamine, 15 May, 1476, folio. Hain *6710. See Book II, chs. v, vi, xvii, xviii, xix; VI, xiii; VII, xxx.[3]

1525.* Hieronymus, *Epistolae,* [edited by Theodorus Lelius], Venetiis, Antonius Bartolomei Miscomini, 22 January, 1476, 2 vols., folio. Hain *8556. See I, sig. c₉rB; II, f₅vA, f₆vB, f₇rA and B, g₇r, m₁vB.[4]

1526.* Mareschinus, Joannes, *Mamotrectus super totam Bibliam,* Venetijs, Franciscus [Renner] de Hailbrun, 1476, quarto. Hain-Copinger 10557. See sig. g₈. First printed, 1470.

1527.* [Riccobaldus Ferrariensis], *Cronica summorum pontificum imperatorumque,* Rome, Iohannes Schurener de Bopardia, 10 February, 1476, folio. Second edition. Hain 10858. See folio [13]r (in the account of Gaius Augustus).

1528.* Bonaventura, St., *Super secundum sentiarum scriptum Petri Lombardi,* Taruisii (Treviso), Hermanus Lichtenstein, 1477, folio. First edition. Hain *3539. See sigs. B₅vB, C₃vB, C₆vA, C₇vB, D₂rA, F₇rB, F₁₀vA and B, G₂vA and B, G₃vA, G₅vA, G₁₀vA, c₃rA, c₄rA, c₇vB-c₈rA, d₄vA, d₁₀rA, r₁rA and *passim.*

1529.* Rolewinck, Werner, *Fasciculus temporum omnes antiquorum,* Spiren (Speier), Petrus Drach, [24 November], 1477, folio. Hain *6921. See folios XXVIv and XXVIIr.

1530.* Cassiodorus, Magnus Aurelius, *Ecclesiastice tripertite historie,* [Cologne, Conrad Winters, before 6 May 1478], folio. Second edition. Hain *4571. See folio [9]v (Chapter XI).

1531.* Eusebius [Pamphilus] Caesariensis, *Historia ecclesiastica,* translated by Rufinus, Mantua, Ioannes Schallus, [not before 15 July] 1479, folio. Hain *6711. See II, v, xvi, xvii, xviii; VI, xi (x); VII, xxviii.[5]

---

3. The works of Philo as listed in this edition are: *Sacrae legis explanatio figuralis; Questiones et absolutiones de Genesi et Exodo; De agricultura duo; De temulentia duo; Pro quibus mens debet orare deum; De confusione linguarum; De natura et inventione; De his que congregari debeant ad erudiendum; Que sit qui heres sit divinarum; Que sit equalium et inequalium divisio; De tribus virtutibus; De his quorum in scripturis nomina commutata sunt; De captivitate; De vita sapientis eius qui secundum iusticiam perfectam et leges naturales consumatus est; De gigantibus; De eo quod inconvertibile sit quod divinum sit; De moysi vite libros. v; De eo quod a deo sint somnia; In Exodum questionum et absolutionum libri quinque; De tabernaculo; De decem verbis legis; De his que inferunt sub specie Decalogi; De animalibus que sacrificiis deputata sunt; Que sunt species sacrificorum; Que sunt proposita in lege bonis premia et malis maledicta; De providentia; De iudeis apologeticus liber, hoc est de vita urbana; Ad Alexandrum dicentem rationem habere muta animalia; De eo quod servus sit omnis qui peccat; De eo qui liber sit omnis qui bonis studiis operam prebet; De vita theorica vel supplicium; Interpretationes nominum Hebraicorum que sunt in lege et prophetis; De impietate atque impuritate gaii quamplurima.. que per ironiam de virtutibus attitulavit.*

4. The works of Philo as here listed are identical with those in no. 1508, except: *De natura et inventione bestiarum repentium volatilium et piscium libri tres;* and *Quare quorundam in scripturis mutata sunt nomina liber unus.*

5. The works of Philo as listed in this edition are: *Sacrae legis explanatio figuralis; Quaestiones et absolutiones de genesi et exodi; De agricultura duo; De temulentia duo; Pro quibus mens debet orare deum; De confusione linguarum; De natura et inventione; De his que con-*

1532.* Platina, [Bartholomaeus (Sacchi) de], *Vitae pontificum ad Sixtum IIII, Pontificem maximum,* [Venice], Iohannes de Colonia and Iohannes Mathen, [11] June, 1479, folio. First edition. Hain *13045. See sigs. a₆v and a₈v.

1533.* Eusebius Pamphilus [Caesariensis], *De evangelica praeparatione,* translated by Georgius Trapezuntius, edited by Hieronymus Bononius, Taruisii (Treviso), Michael Manzolinus, 12 January 1480, folio. Hain *6702. See sigs. g₅r, g₆r, h₁r and v, h₁₁r, h₅r, i₁r, i₁vv, m₂v.

1534.* Hieronymus (St. Jerome), *Liber de viris illustribus. Accedunt Gennadii, Isidori et aliorum de scriptoribus ecclesiasticis,* [Cologne, Bartholomaeus de Unkel, ca. 1480], quarto. Hain *8582. See sigs. a₁₁₁r, b₁₁r and b₁₁₁r–b₁₁₁₁r.

1535.* Iuuenalis, [Decimus] Iunius, *Satyre,* in the Italian translation of Georgius Summaripa, Tarvisii (Treviso), Michaelis Manzolinus, 1480, folio. Hain 9720. The reference to Tiberius Alexander is quite changed (see sig. A_vv line 230), but the one to Queen Bernice follows the Latin closely; see sig. D₁₁v, lines 275, 278, 282.

1536.* Josephus, Flavius, *De bello Iudaico. De antiquitate Iudaeorum contra Appionem,* [in the translation of Rufinus Aquiliensis], edited by Ludouicus Cendrata, Verona, Petrus Maufer, 25 December 1480. Hain *9452. See first leaf of introduction.

1537.* [Rolewinck, Werner], *Fasciculus temporum,* translated into Dutch, Vtrecht, Jan Veldenar, 1480, folio. First edition in Dutch. Hain 6946. See folios lxxviiir and lxxixr.

1538.* Origenes, *Contra Celsum et in fidei christianae defensionem,* Romae, Georgius Herolt de Bamberga, January, 1481, folio and quarto. First edition, first issue. Hain *12078. See I, folio [10]r and IV, folio [125]v.

1539.* Rolewinck, Werner, *Fasciculus temporum,* [Cologne, Ludwig von Renchen, ca. 1481], folio. Hain *6914. See sig. d₆r and v.

1540.* Sabellicus, M[arcus] Antonius, *De vetustate Aquileiensis patrie,* with various tracts in verse, [Venice, Antonius de Avignon, ca. 1482], quarto. First edition. Hain *14058. See sig. a₁v and sig. c₂v.

---

gregari debeant ad erudiendum; Quis sit qui heres sit divinorum; Que sit equalium et inequalium divisio; De tribus virtutibus; Item de his quorum in scripturis nomina commutata sunt; De captivitate; De vita sapientis ejus que secundum iusticiam perfectum et reges naturales consumatus est; De gigantibus; De eo quod inconvertibile sit quod divinum est; De moysi vita libri. v; De eo quod a deo sint somnia; In exodum questionum et absolutionum libri v; De tabernaculo; De decem verbis legis; De his que inferunt sub specie decalogi; De animalibus que sacrificiis deputata sunt; Que sunt species sacrificorum; Que sunt proposita in lege bonis premia et malis maledicta; De providentia; De iudeis, apologeticus liber, hoc est de vita urbana; Ad Alexandrum dicentem rationem habere muta animalia; De eo quod servus sit omnis qui peccat; De eo quod liber sit omnis qui bonis studiis operam prebet; De vita theorica vel supplicium; Interpretationes nominum hebraicorum que sunt in lege et prophetis; De impietate atque impuritate Gaii quamplurima que per hyroniam de virtutibus articulavit.

1541.* Voragine, Iacobus de, *Legenda aurea,* Colonia (Cologne), [Ulrich Zef], 19 May, 1482, folio. Copinger 6428. See folio LXXVIvA. (See no. 1519.)

1542.* Bergomensis, Jacobus Philippus, *Supplementum chronicarum,* Ciuitate Uenetiarum (Venice), Bernardinus Benalius, 23 August 1483, folio. First edition. Hain *2805. On sig. A6v is an account of Philo and a list of his works, stated by the author to be taken from Hieronymus. On sig. A8r is an account of the embassy to Gaius, taken from Josephus.

1543.* Eusebius [Pamphilus] Caesariensis, *Chronicon,* with the continuations of Prosper and Matthaeus Palmerius, [edited by J. L. Santritter], Venetiis, Erhardus Ratdolt Augustensis, [13] September, 1483, quarto. Hain *6717. See folio l₄r and v.

1544.* Orosius, Paulus, *Historiae initium ad Aurelium Augustinum,* edited by Aeneas Vulpes, Venetii, Octauianus Scotus, [30 July], 1483, folio. Hain *12102. See sig. l₁r.

1545.* Antoninus, St., *Chronicon* or *Opus historiale,* Nuremberg, Anton Koberger, 31 July, 1484, 3 vols., folio. First edition. Hain *1159. See folios CLXv and CLXIr.

1546.* Platina, [Bartholomaeus (Sacchi) de], *Vitae pontificum ad Sixtum IIII, pontificem maximum,* [Treviso (or Venice)], Ioannes Vercelensis, 10 February, 1485, folio. Hain *13048. See a₁₁₁₁v and a₅r.

1547.* [Rolewinck, Werner], *Fasciculus temporum,* Venetiis, Erhardus Ratdolt Augustensis, [8] September 1485, folio. Fifth edition. Hain *6935. See folios 26v and 27r.

1548.* Voragine, Iacobus de, *Legenda sanctorum,* Argentinus (Strassburg), [by the printer of the 1483 Jordanus de Quedlinburg], 4 May, 1485, folio. Copinger 6443. See sig. k₄rA. (See no. 1519.)

1549.* Josephus, Flavius, *Opera,* in the translation of Rufinus Aquileiensis, edited by Hieronimus Squarzaficus, Veneciis, Joannes [Rubeus] Vercelensis, 23 October 1486, 2 vols. in 1, folio. Hain *9454. See sig. u₁₁₁₁.

1550.* Iuuenalis, [Decimus] Iunius, *Satyrae,* with the commentary of Domitius Calderinus, Venetiis, Bartolameus de Zanis, 3 October 1487, folio. Hain *9699. The Satyres of Juvenal merit a place in the bibliography of Philo on account of a passage in Satyre I, lines 129–132, which later commentators have explained using Philo to authenticate their statements. The reference is to the *aegyptius atque arabarches* on sig. a₅r in which present day commentators see a reference to Tiberius Alexander, son of Alexander the Alabarch, Philo's brother. Satyre VI, sig. d₁₁₁₁r and v, lines 155–159, contains a reference to Queen Bernice who was married to Marcus, the oldest son of Alexander Alabarch, and who was hence a niece by marriage of Philo Judaeus. The comments of Domitius Calderinus, sig. d₁₁₁₁v, are particularly interesting.

1551.* Hieronymus, *Epistolae,* Basilea, Nicolaus Kesler, 8 August 1489, 2 vols. in 1, folio. Hain *8559. See I, folio XXXVIIIvB; II, folios LXVIIIrA, LXIXrB, LXIXvA and B, LXXXIIrB, CXXXIXvA.

1552.* Alliaco, Petrus de, *Concordantia astronomie cum theologia,* edited by Joannes Angelus, Auguste (Augsburg), Erhard Ratdolt, [2] January, 1490, quarto. First edition. Hain *834. In ch. 40 of the Second Part (sig. d₁v) there is a reference to the writings of Philo in connection with the setting up of statues to Caius Caligula in the Jewish synagogues.

1553.* Picus Mirandulus, Iohannes, *Heptaplus de septiformi sex dierum geneseos enarratione,* [Florence, Bartolommeo de Libri, ca. 1490], folio. First edition. Hain *13001. On a₂v Philo is coupled with Lucas, and on a₄r, he is mentioned among the Greek interpreters.

1554.* Voragine, Iacobus de, *Legenda aurea sanctorum,* [Lyons, ca. 1490], folio. Copinger 6400. See sig. i₋ᵥ₁₁₁vA. (See no. 1519.)

1555.* Voragine, Iacobus de, *Lombardica hystorica* (*Legenda aurea*), Basilee, [Michael Wenssler], 1490, folio. Copinger 6455. See folio LXVIIIr, B. (See no. 1519.)

1556.* Iuuenalis, Decius Iunius, *Satyrae,* with the commentaries of Domitius Calderinus and Georgius Valla, Venetiis, Theodorus de regazonibus, 16 June, 1491, folio. Hain 9704. See sigs. c₁₁₁₁r and v, i₁₁₁v and i₁₁₁₁r.

1557.* Bergomensis, Jacobus Philippus, *Supplemento de cronicha de tuto el mondo vulgare,* (*Supplementum chronicarum*), [translated into Italian by Francescus C.], Venetia, Bernardinus Rizus de Nouara, 8 October, 1491, folio. Second edition. Hain 2812. The account of Philo is on folio 124r and v. There is no list of his works, as in the Latin edition, the translator explaining that to enumerate his works is not necessary. The account of Philo's embassy is on folio 126r.

1558.* Bossius, Donatus, *Chronica Bossiana,* Mediolani, Antonius Zarotus, [1] March 1492, folio. First edition. Hain *3667. See sig. d₆r.

1559.* Cassiodorus, Magnus Aurelius, *Hystorie ecclesiastice* (*tripartita*) *ex Socrate, Sozomeno, et Theodorico,* [Paris], Georges Wolff [at the Soleil d'Or, 1492(?)]. Third edition. Hain *4570. See sigs. a₆vB and aᵥ₁₁rA.

1560.* Ambrosius, *Opera,* Basilee, Ioannes de Amerbach, 1492, 3 vols., folio. First edition. Hain *896. See nos. 1427, 1482.

1561.* [Schedel, Hartmann], *Liber cronicarum,* Nuremberg, Anthonius Koberger, 12 July 1493, folio. First edition. Hain *14508. There are two accounts of Philo, one on folio LXXXVr, the second on folio

XCVIIr; both of these accounts are accompanied by woodcuts of Philo. See Plate VIII.

1562.* [Schedel, Hartmann], *Das buch der Croniken und geschichten,* translated by Georgius Alt, Nůrmburg, Anthon Koberger, 25 December 1493, folio. Hain *14510. There are two accounts of Philo each accompanied by woodcuts which are different from those used in the Latin edition. The first is on folio LXXXVr, the second on folio XCVIIr.

1563.* Reuchlin, Ioannis, *De verbo mirifico,* Basilaea, Iohannes Amerbachius, ca. 1494, folio. Hain *13880. See c_6r.

1564.* Tritheim, Johann, *Liber de scriptoribus ecclesiasticis,* Basileae, Iohannes de Amerbach, [after 28 August] 1494. Hain *15613. The account of Philo Judaeus is on folio 3r, and is a digest of the account by Jerome. But the list of works by Philo which follows differs from that of Jerome on so many points that it suggests that Tritheim may have had a Philo manuscript now lost.[6]

1565.* Juuenalis, [Decimus Junius], *Satyrae,* with the commentaries of Domitius Calderinus and Georgius Valla, Lugdunus (Lyons), Johannes de Vingle, 18 May 1495, quarto. Hain 9708. See folios XXIr, LXVIIv, and LXVIIIr.

1566.* Philelfus, [Johannes] Marius, *Epistolare,* Basileae, Ioannes de Amerbach, 1495, quarto. Hain *12979. See s_7r.

1567.* Hieronymus, *Epistolae* [with other tracts], in urbe Venetiarum, Joannes Rubeus Vercellensis, 7 January, 12 July, 1496, 2 parts in one, folio. Hain *8563. See folios 31v, 220r, 221v, 232r, 280r.

1568.* Hieronymus, *Epistole,* [Venice, Pincius, ca. 1496(?)], folio. Hain *8564. See folios 31vA, 220rB, 221vA and B, 232rB, 280rA.

1569.* Iuuenalis, Decius Iunius, *Satyrae,* with the comments of Domitius Calderus, Georgius Merula, and Georgius Valla, Venetia, Symonis Biuilaqua Papiensis, [1496?], folio. Hain *9712. See bb_{vi}v, cc_ir, kk_{iii}r and v.

1570.* Voragine, Jacobus de, *Lombardica historia* (*Legenda aurea*), Argentinus (Strassburg), [printer of the 1483 Jordanus de Quedlinburg, ca. 12 May], 1496, folio. Copinger 6467.[7] See sig. k_2vB. (See no. 1519.)

---

6. Tritheim's list reads: *De vita sapientis, liber unus; De conversatione vitae, li. i; De confusione linguarum, li. i; De natura quadrupedum, li. iii; De his quae sensu testamur, li. i; De eruditione, li. i; De haerede divinarum rerum, li. i; De tribus virtutibus, li. i; De natura et inventione, li. i; De pactis, li. i; De generatione successu, li. i; De mutatione nominum, li. i; De gigantibus, li. i; In quinque libros Moysi, li. v; De somniis, li. i; De tabernaculo, li. iiii; De vita contemplativa, li. i; De agricultura, li. ii; De ebrietate, li. ii; De victimis et repromissionibus, li. i; De providentia, li. i; De iudeis, li. i; De Alexandro, li. i; De ratione animalium, li. i; Quod omnis insipiens servus sit, li. i; alia quoque multa scripsisse legitur: quae ad noticiam meam non venerunt.*

7. It is interesting to note that in the Jenson, Italian edition of Voragine's Golden Legend, as well as in all the editions printed in English by Caxton, Wynken de Worde, and Pynson, the reference to Philo is omitted.

PHILO

From the Nuremberg Chronicle.

See Bibliography, no. 1561

1571.* Eusebius Pamphilus [Caesarensis], *De euangelica praeparatione,* translated by Georgius Trapezuntius, Venetiis, Bernardinus Benalius, [31 May] 1497, folio. Hain *6706. See sigs. g$_v$r, g$_{vi}$r, h$_1$r, h$_{ii}$r, h$_v$r and v, h$_{viii}$v, i$_{vi}$r, l$_v$v, l$_{vi}$r.

A reprint of no. 1533 with generally the same contents.

1572.* Iuuenalis, [Decimus] Iunius, *Satyrae,* with commentaries of Antonius Mancinellus, Domitius Calderinus, and Georgius Valla, Nurnberge, Antonius Koberger, 6 December, 1497, folio. Hain *9711. The reference to Tiberius Alexander in Sat. I is to be found on folios XVr and v and XVIr, and the reference to Queen Bernice on folio LXXIIr and v. Valla's comments on the Bernice passages are to be found on folio LXXIIIr and are most detailed and interesting.

1573.* Dionysius Areopagita, *Opera,* Parhisi(orum) (Paris), Ioannes Higmanus and Wolfgangus Hopylius, February 6, 1498, folio. First edition. Hain *6233. See sigs. A$_{iii}$v, A$_{iv}$v, and folios 59v, 60r, 81v, 82r.

1574.* Josephus, [Flavius], *De antiquitatibus ac de bello judaico,* translated by Ruffinus Aguiligiensus, edited by Hyeronimus Squarzaficus, Venetiis, Albertinus Vercellensis, 23 October, 1499, folio. Hain *9455. See folio CLIIIv.

1575.* Suidas, Λεξικόν, (*Lexicon graecum*), edited by Demetrius Chalcondyles, Mediolanus, Ioannes Bissolus & Benedictus Mangius, 15 November 1499, folio. First edition. Hain *15135. See folio GG$_{iii}$v.[8]

1576.* Eusebius Pamphilus Caesariensis, *Ecclesiastica hystoria diui Eusebii et Ecclesiastica historia gentis Anglorum venerabilis Bede,* Argentinen (Strassburg), Georg Husner, 14 March 1500, folio. Hain *6714. See sigs. b$_3$rA and B, b$_5$vA–b$_6$vB, h$_3$vA, k$_5$rB.

1577.* Orosius, Paulus, *Viri doctissimi historiae initium ad Aurelium Augustinum,* Venetii, Bernardinus Veneti de Vitalibus, 12 October, 1500, folio. Hain 12104. See sig. l$_{iiii}$r.

1578.* Eusebius Pamphilus [Caesariensis], *De euangelica praeparatione,* translated by Georgius Trapezuntius, Venetiis, [Bartolomaeus de Zanis], 10 November, 1500, folio. Hain *6707. See folios 31r and v, 32r, 36r and v, 48v, 49r, 50v, 51r.

8. In this edition the works of Philo are listed as follows: περὶ τῆς συγκύσεως γλωσσῶν βιβλίον α'; περὶ φύσεως καὶ εὑρήματος α'; περὶ ὧν κατὰ νοῦν τις εὔχεται α'; περὶ παιδεύσεως ἕν; περὶ κληρονόμου τῶν θείων πραγμάτων α'; περὶ μερισμοῦ ἴσων καὶ ἐναντίων α'; περὶ τῶν τριῶν δυνάμεως; περὶ ἐναλλαγεισῶν γραφῶν παρά τινων; περὶ συνθηκῶν λόγους β'; περὶ βίου φιλοσόφου; περὶ γιγάντων α'; περὶ ὀνείρων ε'; περὶ ζητημάτων καὶ ἑρμηνευμάτων τῆς Ἐξόδου ε'; περὶ τῆς Σκηνῆς, καὶ Δεκαλόγου δ'; περὶ θυσιῶν; περὶ ὑποσχέσεων, ἤτοι καταρῶν; περὶ προνοίας; περὶ Ἰουδαίων α'; περὶ ἀγωγῆς βίου; περὶ Ἀλεξάνδρου καὶ περὶ τοῦ ἴδιον λογισμὸν ἔχειν τὰ ἄλογα; περὶ τοῦ, πᾶς ἄφρων δοῦλός ἐστι; περὶ τῆς διαγωγῆς τῶν Χριστιανῶν; περὶ βίου θεωρητικοῦ; περὶ ἱκετῶν; περὶ γεωργίας λόγους β'; περὶ μέθης β'; περὶ τοῦ Μωσέως βίου; εἰς τὰ χερουβίμ· τουτέστι, τὴν φλογίνην ῥομφαίαν; εἰς τὴν πεντάτευχον Μωϋσέως, καὶ εἰς αὐτὸν Μωυσῆν λόγους ε'.

1579.* [Schedel, Hartmann,] *Das bůch Der Croniken vnnd geschichten mit figuren vnnd pildnussen von Anbeginn der welt biss auff dise Vnsere Zeÿt,* translated by Georgius Alt, Auspurg (Augsburg), Hannsen Schŏnsperger, 1500, folio. Hain *14512. The two accounts of Philo occur on folios xciiirB–xciiivA and cviirB–cviivA respectively, each being accompanied by a woodcut portrait.

See also no. 387.

XXXII. MISCELLANEOUS REFERENCE TO PHILO

1580.* Platina, [Bartholomaeus (Sacchi) de], *De vitis maxi. ponti. historia periocunda,* Venetiis, Gulielmus de Fontaneto de Monteferrato, 15 December, 1518, small folio.
Annotated and corrected by Paulus Manutius, son and successor of Aldus. See folios iiiiv and vir.

1580a.* [Rivers, A.], *The Sad Condition of a Distracted Kingdome, Expressed in a Fable of Philo the Jew,* London, 1645, pp. [iv], 31.
A political tract in verse based upon a legend in *De plantatione Noemi* (*sic*) (§§127–129).

1580b. M[ilton], J[ohn], *The Doctrine and Discipline of Divorce: Restor'd to the good of both Sexes,* 2nd edition, revised and enlarged, London, 1644, 36. See Chilton Latham Powell and Frank Allen Patterson, *The Works of John Milton,* New York, III, ii, 1931, 435.

1580c. M[ilton], J[ohn], *Tetrachordon: Expositions upon the foure chief places in Scripture, which treat of Marriage, or nullities in Marriage,* London, 1645, 45. See Chilton Latham Powell, *The Works of John Milton,* New York, IV, 1931, 146.

1580d. Milton, Ioannes, *Pro populo anglicano defensio,* London, 1650, 19. See the translation by Samuel Lee Wolff in the edition of Clinton W. Keyes, *The Works of John Milton,* New York, VII, 1932, 79.

1581.* Evelyn, J[ohn], *An Essay on the First Book of T. Lucretius Carus, De rerum natura, Interpreted and Made English Verse,* London, 1656.
The first edition of any part of Lucretius in the English language. The "Animadversions," p. 183, mention Philo among others as teaching the corruptibility of the world.

1582.* Evelyn, John, *Sculptura; or, The History and Art of Chalcography, and Engraving in Copper: with an ample Enumeration of the most renowned Masters and their Works,* 2nd edit., London, 1755; see 14, 28.

1583.* [Judd, Sylvester], *Philo: An Evangeliad,* Boston, 1850, pp. 244.
Except for the use of the name of Philo, references to Biblical history and slight references to some of his teachings, this volume is only interesting as it is clearly modeled on no. 1580a. It is a poem (similar in form to the *Sad Condition* in opposition to the war of the United States with Mexico and enlisting sympathy against the institution of slavery.

1584. Dietrich, Rudolf, "Tace, sed memento!" *Philologische Wochenschrift,* XLVI (1926), 399–400.

1585.* France, Anatole, *La rôtisserie de la Reine Pédauque,* Paris, 1926, 118.

1586.* Feuchtwanger, Lion, *Die Söhne,* Amsterdam, 1935; translated by Willa and Edwin Muir, *The Jew of Rome,* New York, 1936, 312, 339, 343 f., 371.

XXXIII. PSEUDO-PHILONIC WRITINGS

A. THE FORGERY OF GIOVANNI NANNI

Under the pseudonym "Joannes Annius da Viterbo," Nanni published a famous book of forgeries, of which the fourteenth was a small treatise to which he gave the name "Philonis brevarium de temporibus"; he embellished it with an elaborate "commentary" by the forger. First published in Rome, 1498, and reprinted in Venice the same year, it was many times reprinted during the next century or more. The whole series of forgeries was widely discussed for two hundred years before the last attempt to defend it collapsed. The best account of the work and of those who have discussed it is by Ginguiné in *Biographie universelle, ancienne et moderne,* Paris, II, 1811, 223–226. We have made no attempt to include the literature of this controversy, and list only such items as are in Mr. Goodhart's collection, or ones we have encountered in other bibliographies of Philo.

1587.* Annius, Joannes, *Commentaria super opera diuersorum auctorum de antiquitatibus loquentium,* Rome, Eucharius Silber, 10 July, 3 August 1498, sigs. G₁₁r–H₁ᵥ₁₁₁r. Hain *1130. With Nanni's "commentary."

1588.* [Pausanius Historicus], *Auctores Vetustissimi,* [Venice], Bernardinus Venetus [de Vitalibus], 1498, quarto. Hain 12527. See sigs. c₃v–d₂v. Text only without the "commentary."

1589. *Berosus babylonicus. De his que praecesserunt inundationem terrarum . . . Philo in brevario temporum,* [edited by G. Tory], [Paris], G. de Marnef., [1510]. (From B.M.)
Reprint of no. 1588.

1590.* *Berosus babylonicus. De his quae praecesserunt inundationem terrarum,* [Strassburg, 1511?], 8vo, sigs. f₁₁r–f₁₁₁₁r. Reprint of no. 1588.

1591.* Annius, Joannes, *Antiquitatum variarum volumina, XVII. A venerando . . . Io. Annio hoc serie declarata,* [Paris], Jadocus Badius & Joannes Paruus, 1512, folios XCIIII–CIIII. (In the colophon: "opera Ascensiana.") Reprint of no. 1587.
Reprinted, 1515. (From B.M.)

1592.* Modonese, Pietro Lauro, *I cinque libri de le antichita de Beroso, sacerdote caldeo. Con lo commento di Giovanni Annio di Viterbo . . . Tradotti hora pur in Italiano,* Venetia, Baldissera Constantini, 1550, folios 221v–242v. Italian translation of no. 1587.

1593.* *Berosi sacerdotis chaldaici, Antiquitatum Italiae ac totius orbis libri quinque, Commentarijs Ioannis Annij Viterbensis . . . adiecto nunc*

primum indice locupletissimo . . . Aeditio vltima, caeteris longe casti-
gatior, Antverpiae, Ioan. Steelsius, 1552, 247–290. Reprint of no. 1587.
Another edition, 1554, I. (From B.M.)

1594. As. de' Rossi, ס' הָעְתִּים, *Das Buch Philon's von den Zeiten, aus der
lat. Version in's Hebräische übersetzt. In dessen im 5. Theile, genannt*
יְמֵי עוֹלָם, *aufgenommen:* Mantua, 1574, 4; Berlin, 1794, 8; Wien,
1829, 8. (From no. 528.)

1595.* Sansovino, M. Francesco, *Le antichità di Beroso caldeo sacerdote, et
d'altri scrittori, cosi hebrei, come greci et latini, che trattano delle
stesse materie. Tradotte, dichiarate, & con diuerse vtili, & necessarie
annotationi, illustrate,* Vinegia, Altabellus Salicatus, 1583, 105r–106v.

1596.* *Berosi sacerdotis chaldaici antiquitatum libri quinque, cumm com-
mentariis Ioannis Annii Viterbensis,* Wittenberg, 1612, folios 223r–
245r. (A reprint of no. 1587.)

B. DISCUSSION OF THE *DE AETERNITE MUNDI* (*AET.*)

1597.* Zeller, E[douard], "Der Streit Theophrasts gegen Zeno über die
Ewigkeit der Welt," *Hermes,* XI (1876), 422–429.
Reprinted in Otto Leuze, *Eduard Zellers kleine Schriften,* Berlin, I,
1910, 166–174.

1598.* Buecheler, Franciscus, "Philonea," *Rheinisches Museum für Philologie,* N.F. XXXII (1877), 433–444.

1599.† Zeller, E[douard], "Der pseudophilonische Bericht über Theophrast,"
Hermes, XV (1880), 137–146.
Reprinted in Otto Leuze, *Eduard Zellers kleine Schriften,* Berlin, I,
1910, 215–225, with two critical letters (225–227) by Jacob Bernays.

1600.* Bernays, J[acob], "Über die unter Philon's Werken stehende Schrift
über die Unzerstörbarkeit des Weltalls," *Abhandlungen der Königlichen Akademie der Wissenschaften zu Berlin, aus dem Jahre 1882,*
Berlin, 1883, *Philosophisch-historische Klasse,* Abh. III, pp. 82.
*Republished, Berlin, 1883.

C. THE *BIBLICAL ANTIQUITIES* (*ANTIQ.*)

1601.* Cohn, Leopold, "An Apocryphal Work Ascribed to Philo of Alexandria," *The Jewish Quarterly Review,* X (1897–1898), 277–332.

1602.† James, [M. R.], "Transmission of an Old Text (Pseudo-Philo *Antiquitatum biblicarum liber*)," *Proceedings of the Cambridge Philological Society,* C–CII (1915), London and Edinburgh, 1916, 9–10.
Reprinted from *Cambridge University Reporter,* 1 June, 1915.

1603. Cohn, Leopold, "Pseudo-Philo und Jerachmeel," *Festschrift zum sieb-zigsten Geburtstage Jakob Guttmanns,* Leipzig, 1915, 173–185. (*Schriften herausgegeben von der Gesellschaft zur Förderung der Wissenschaft des Judentums.*)

INDEX I

INDEX TO *PHILO'S POLITICS*

Numbers refer to pages.

INDEX II

INDEX TO THE BIBLIOGRAPHY OF MANUSCRIPTS

The numbers in italics refer to numbers of the Bibliography.

INDEX III

INDEX TO THE BIBLIOGRAPHY

Numbers refer to items in the Bibliography.

335